I0576875

DISCARD

EXPLORING THE NEW TESTAMENT

Volume 1

A Guide to the Gospels and Acts

After studying theology in Cambridge and Manchester Universities, David Wenham taught in central India for some years. On his return he was Director of the Tyndale House Gospels Research project, moving from that to the staff of Wycliffe Hall in the University of Oxford. He is the author of books on the parables of Jesus, and most recently has focused his studies on the relationship of Jesus and Paul, with his *Paul, Follower of Jesus or Founder of Christianity?* (Eerdmans 1995). He is also involved in parochial ministry in a group of villages north of Oxford. He is married to Clare, and they have two grown-up sons.

Steve Walton has been Lecturer in Greek and New Testament Studies at London Bible College since 1999, having previously taught New Testament at St John's College, Nottingham and Bedford College. He is a member of a number of scholarly societies, and chairs the Acts seminar of the British New Testament Conference.

His recently published *Leadership and Lifestyle* (Cambridge University Press, 2000) is a major study of Paul's Miletus speech and I Thessalonians. His other published books and articles include *A Call to Live: Vocation for Everyone* (SPCK/Triangle, 1994).

Steve is an ordained Anglican minister and has worked in parish ministry in Merseyside, and with the Church Pastoral Aid Society as their Vocation and Ministry Adviser, as well as in academic teaching posts. He referees volleyball at international level, and lives in Hertfordshire with his wife, Ali, who is also ordained.

NEW
TESTAMENT

Exploring the
New Testament

A Guide to
the Gospels & Acts

DAVID WENHAM & STEVE WALTON

Volume
One

InterVarsity Press
Downers Grove, Illinois

InterVarsity Press
P.O. Box 1400, Downers Grove, IL 60515-1426
World Wide Web: www.ivpress.com
E-mail: mail@ivpress.com

©2001 by David Wenham and Steve Walton

Published in the United States of America by InterVarsity Press, Downers Grove, Illinois, with permission from the Society for Promoting Christian Knowledge, London, England.

All rights reserved. No part of this book may be reproduced in any form without written permission from InterVarsity Press.

InterVarsity Press® is the book-publishing division of InterVarsity Christian Fellowship/USA®, a student movement active on campus at hundreds of universities, colleges and schools of nursing in the United States of America, and a member movement of the International Fellowship of Evangelical Students. For information about local and regional activities, write Public Relations Dept., InterVarsity Christian Fellowship/ USA, 6400 Schroeder Rd., P.O. Box 7895, Madison, WI 53707-7895.

Scripture quotations, unless otherwise noted, are from the New Revised Standard Version of the Bible, *copyright 1989 by the Division of Christian Education of the National Council of the Churches of Christ in the USA. Used by permission. All rights reserved.*

ISBN 0-8308-2557-6

Printed in Great Britain

Library of Congress Cataloging-in-Publication Data

Wenham, David.
  Exploring the New Testament / David Wenham & Steve Walton.
    p. cm.
  Includes bibliographical references.
  Contents: v. 1. A guide to the Gospels & Acts.
  ISBN 0-8308-2555-X (cloth: alk. paper)
    1. Bible. N.T. Gospels—Criticism, interpretation, etc. 2. Bible. N.T. Acts—Criticism,
interpretation, etc. I. Walton, Steve, Dr. II. Title.
  BS2548 .W46 2001
  225.6'1—dc21

                                                                                    2001024403

P	25	24	23	22	21	20	19	18	17	16	15	14	13	12	11	10	9	8	7	6	5	4	3	2	1
Y	25	24	23	22	21	20	19	18	17	16	15	14	13	12	11	10	09	08	07	06	05				

Contents

THE GOSPELS AND ACTS

C. UNDERSTANDING JESUS

D. GETTING INTO THE FOUR GOSPELS

HOW TO USE THIS BOOK

This book has been a number of years in the making, and stems from our desire to provide a book which can provide the basis of an introductory course on the NT Gospels and Acts for first- or second-year students in a university, theological college or seminary; a companion volume will follow on the NT Letters and the book of Revelation. Typically, we have in mind a one-term or one-semester course which is a mixture of lecture input and seminar-based discussion, and both of us have taught such courses in Pune (India), Oxford, Bedford, Nottingham and London. This section aims to help you, whether a teacher or a student, to get the most from our book.

OUR AIMS AND OBJECTIVES

We are particularly concerned to get students reading and engaging with the Gospels and Acts for themselves, rather than simply learning at second hand what these books say or merely absorbing a lot of interesting theories about them. So in our chapters we have endeavoured to provide enough references to the Gospels and Acts, and other pertinent ancient literature, so that students can read the texts alongside our discussion. We have also built into each

chapter three sorts of further study for students to pursue, many of which we have used ourselves in the classroom.

What do you think? boxes provide questions and issues that we estimate will take 30-60 minutes for a typical student, and might then be used as the basis of a brief class discussion, perhaps in small groups if the class is too large to discuss all together.

Digging deeper boxes offer a piece of research which will take 2-3 hours of private study, and which could form the basis of a one-hour seminar class led by the teacher or by some of the students. Having two or three students lead such a discussion, in our experience, enables the student leaders to engage with the topic at greater depth, since they must set the agenda for the seminar, and also enables students to debate views with each other in a way that facilitates learning. Sometimes we have suggested how a seminar hour might be structured to handle the topic.

Essay topics at the end of each chapter or section provide ideas on topics to research at more depth, which are to be presented in written form. They are intended to be about

2,500-3,000 words in length, although a number could be longer (or a little shorter) if the course being taught required that. Some are identified as 'Introductory', and are intended for first-year students, and some as 'Intermediate', which are intended for second years.

In each case, there are too many for a student to do all of them, and the teacher will need to select those which best fit the particular aims and objectives of the course being taught, or to guide students in their choice of which to pursue. And we hope that our suggestions will stimulate teachers to add their own good ideas!

Further reading lists at the end of each chapter or section provide a basis for the research on the essay topics, as well as for further study in greater depth on particular issues within each section of the book, and we have chosen books which are generally available in European and North American college and university libraries. Within each chapter we have referred to books by the 'author and date' system (e.g. Wright 1996), and full publication details can be found in the 'Further reading' sections. Where a book has a British and an American edition, we have endeavoured to provide place of publication and publisher for both editions.

Because many students studying the Gospels and Acts are Christians, as we ourselves are, and will therefore want to ask about the relevance of their studies to living as Christians today, we have provided occasional sections called **Some issues for today** which sketch some of our thoughts in the light of our studies. These are designed to be jumping-off points and models to encourage students (and teachers) to make their own connections between then and now.

STRUCTURE OF THE BOOK

The book falls into five sections: first, we set out the key contexts, historical and religious, within which the lives of Jesus and the early churches need to be seen. Here, we focus on the Jewish contexts; the companion volume on the NT Letters and Revelation will set the Graeco-Roman context, which is more relevant to those NT books.

Second, we outline methods of study used in approaching the Gospels, including the question of the kind of literature that they are, their origins and how to interpret the Gospels today.

Third, we focus on the main figure of the Gospels, Jesus himself. After surveying scholarly study of Jesus over the last 150 years or so and highlighting key issues, we outline what can be known of the life of Jesus from historical study, and then look at the major points of his teaching and his aims.

Fourth, we study each of the Gospels in turn, beginning with Mark. We start here because Mark is the shortest and is usually held to be the first; this allows our chapters on Matthew and Luke to focus on the distinctive contributions of these Gospels. The chapter on John is rather longer because John 'stands apart' from the others in his style and presentation of Jesus. Each chapter looks at the contents, structure, major themes and emphases of each Gospel, with a brief consideration of who wrote each book and when.

Finally, we study Acts, the continuation of the story into the life of the earliest Christians, again considering its contents, organization, major themes and emphases, as well as discussing modern debates about Acts, including its authorship and date.

A **glossary** at the end provides references to the main places in our book where key technical terms and words are introduced and explained, particularly in boxes within the chapters.

WHO WROTE WHAT?

We have planned this book together (and also with Stephen Travis and Howard Marshall, who are writing the companion volume on the NT Letters and Revelation), and both of us have read and commented on the other's drafts of chapters and sections. So while we share responsibility for the whole book, the following chapters/sections were the particular responsibility of each of us:

David Wenham: chs 1, 'A note on the apocryphal Gospels' (part of 3), 5 (except pp. 81–100), 6, 7, 10 and 12.
Steve Walton: chs 2, 3 (except for 'A note on the apocryphal Gospels'), 4, 'Tools for interpreting the Gospels' and 'An approach to exegesis of the Gospels' (part of 5), 8, 9, 11 and 13.

ACKNOWLEDGEMENTS

Both of us are very grateful to our students over the years, who have experienced much of this material at first hand, and whose feed- back has led to it being better than it might have been. We have also valued our collaboration with Stephen Travis (in whose mind the two-volume project came to birth) and Howard Marshall, as well as the fine help of Robin Keeley, Ruth McCurry and Mary Matthews of SPCK.

David Wenham would like to acknowledge the help of his colleague at Wycliffe Hall, Dr Jeremy Duff, and the constant support of his wife, Clare.

Steve Walton has valued the opportunity to teach alongside (and sometimes with) colleagues in Nottingham and London who have contributed to his thinking, particularly Stephen Travis, Colin Hart, Max Turner and Conrad Gempf: a number of their ideas are likely to have influenced my chapters. Prof. James Edwards of Whitmore College, Spokane, WA kindly commented on a draft of ch. 9, and the Rev. Rob Bewley of the University of Cambridge on a draft of ch. 8. Last, but by no means least, I cannot overstate the importance of the love, support and encouragement of Ali, my wife, without whom this book would never have come to birth.

ABBREVIATIONS

Generally, we have used the abbreviations in Patrick H. Alexander, John F. Kutsko, James D. Ernest, Shirley A. Decker-Kucke and David L. Petersen, eds, *The SBL Handbook of Style*, Peabody, MA: Hendrickson, 1999, ch. 8. We list below the main abbreviations used.

AJT	*American Journal of Theology*
Ag. Ap.	Josephus, *Against Apion*
Ant.	Josephus, *Antiquities*
DJG	J. B. Green, S. McKnight, and I. H. Marshall (eds.), *Dictionary of Jesus and the Gospels*. Leicester/ Downers Grove: IVP, 1992.
Hist. eccl.	Eusebius, *Ecclesiastical History*
JW	Josephus, *Jewish War*
LCL	Loeb Classical Library
Life	Josephus, *The Life of Flavius Josephus*
LXX	Septuagint
NIV	New International Version
NRSV	New Revised Standard Version
RSV	Revised Standard Version
ZNW	*Zeitschrift für die neutestamen-thiche Wissenschaft*

A NOTE ON JOSEPHUS REFERENCES

The works of Josephus have two widely used reference systems, one found in Whiston's translation (dividing his works into books, chapters and verses) and the other found in the Loeb Classical Library edition (dividing his works simply into books and verses). We have normally used the Loeb edition for our quotations, but we have given both types of reference when we have referred to Josephus, so that you should be able to find the reference whichever edition you use.

Section A

SETTING
THE SCENE

Chapter 1

THE HISTORICAL CONTEXT OF JESUS AND THE NEW TESTAMENT

This chapter:

- describes the historical sources that we can draw on;
- outlines the history of the 'intertestamental period' (i.e. the period between the OT and NT) until the Roman takeover of Palestine in 63 BC, and then to the fall of Jerusalem in AD 70, drawing attention to particular significant events;
- does the same for the Roman period until the fall of Jerusalem in AD 70;
- highlights some of the key ingredients in Jesus' context.

FROM THE PERSIAN PERIOD TO THE JEWISH WAR

Stained-glass windows are often beautiful, and express a deep piety. But the picture of Jesus and the early Christians which they portray is usually as remote from historical reality as it is from the contemporary reality of the modern observer or worshipper.

To understand the NT we need to transport ourselves into the world of first-century Palestine, and to see Jesus in his historical, social and religious context. In that context he becomes a credible flesh-and-blood person, not a romantic religious icon.

SOURCES OF INFORMATION

How do we know about Jesus' context? What sources of information have we?

OLD AND NEW TESTAMENTS

The Old and New Testaments are hugely informative – the NT directly since it comprises writings of the earliest Christian movement, and the OT indirectly, since it was the basis of the Jews' understanding of themselves, their history and their religion.

JEWISH SOURCES

There is a substantial body of Jewish literature deriving from the so-called 'Second Temple' period (approximately 538 BC to AD 70). Solomon's temple was the first, the 'second' was that built in the period of Ezra and Nehemiah, as described in the OT, and then restored by Herod the Great. Historically, most important are:

The books of Maccabees
These four books were written over a period of years (from about 100 BC onwards) by a number of different authors, and describe the period when the 'Maccabees' were Israel's leading family, i.e. from 167 BC. The first book is the most valuable historically,

and describes, from a very pro-Jewish, pro-Maccabean viewpoint, the catastrophic events that took place in and after 167 BC (notably the setting up of the 'abomination of desolation') and the heroic Jewish response to these events. (See further below.)

The writings of Josephus

Josephus, who lived from AD 37 to about AD 100, is easily our most important source of information about the times of Jesus. He was a well-educated Jew who lived in Palestine until the Jewish War of AD 66-70. In the war he was a commander on the Jewish side, but then went over to the Romans, and thereafter lived in Rome. He wrote various books (partly to explain and defend himself), most notably a history of the *Jewish War*, and then also a history of the Jewish people, the *Antiquities*. Both are invaluable sources of information about Palestine in the NT period.

Exactly what he said about Jesus himself is uncertain, since his writings were preserved for us by Christian scribes who seem to have 'Christianized' his account of Jesus – in order, no doubt, to improve its accuracy, from their point of view.

The changes made by the scribes were probably minor, but the result is that we cannot be certain what exactly Josephus wrote about Jesus. However, this does not seriously diminish the enormous value of Josephus' description of the NT period.

The Dead Sea Scrolls

Probably the most famous archaeological discovery of the twentieth century was the finding of scrolls in caves by the Dead Sea in 1947. The story of their discovery (by a shepherd boy looking for a lost sheep and throwing stones – which then fell into the caves that had been undisturbed since the first century), and then of their dissemination and publication is an intriguing one. The scrolls were found in 11 caves, some well-preserved, some very fragmentary; they include copies of OT books, commentaries on OT books (called 'pesharim' by scholars, from a Hebrew word 'pesher' meaning interpretation), and other documents relating to the community whose library they were. These documents include books of hymns/psalms, instructions for the community's life (e.g. on what to do if someone falls asleep in one of the community assemblies!), books on the future and on the hidden purposes of God.

What do you think?
JOSEPHUS ON JESUS

Antiquities 18:63-64 (=18.3.3) reads: 'About this time there lived Jesus, a wise man, if indeed one ought to call him a man. For he was one who wrought surprising feats and was a teacher of such people as accept the truth gladly. He won over many Jews and many of the Greeks. He was the Messiah. When Pilate, upon hearing him accused by men of the highest standing amongst us, had condemned him to be crucified, those who had in the first place come to love him did not give up their affection for him. On the third day he appeared to them restored to life, for the other prophets of God had prophesied these and countless other marvelous things about him. And the tribe of the Christians, so called after him, has still to this day not disappeared.'

What do you think might be original Josephus, and what is more likely Christian scribe?

SOME IMPORTANT DEAD SEA SCROLLS

The scrolls are identified with a number relating to the cave they were found in, e.g. 4Q means cave 4 at Qumran, and then a letter or number identifying the scroll in question. Thus 4QpHab means the pesher (or commentary) on the OT book of Habakkuk found in cave 4 at Qumran.

Other important scrolls include:
1QS – the Community Rule, from cave 1, which gives instructions for the life of the Qumran community;
1QH – the Hymn Scroll, a community hymnbook;
1QM – the War Scroll, instructions for the future war of the 'sons of light' versus the 'sons of darkness'.

The books are not histories, but are still of considerable interest to the historian (a) because of some historical allusions, (b) because they emanate from a first-century Palestinian Jewish group (most usually identified with the 'Essenes'), and (c) because it is possible that the early Christian movement had something to do with this group – John the Baptist is sometimes thought to have been at Qumran.

Other Jewish sources
Other Jewish sources that throw some light on the NT period include:

● the so-called Apocrypha – books not in the Hebrew Bible, but in the Greek translation of the OT, the Septuagint (commonly referred to as the LXX) and in the Roman Catholic OT. In the Apocrypha are the books of Maccabees (see above), and others such as Ecclesiasticus or the Wisdom of Ben Sira (written about 180 BC) and the Wisdom of Solomon (first century BC).
● the Pseudepigrapha – other writings such as 1 Enoch, some of them ascribed to sages

of the past, including various 'apocalyptic' writings, containing heavenly visions of various sorts.
● the writings of the Jewish philosopher and politician Philo who came from Alexandria in Egypt and lived in the first century AD.
● the sayings of the Rabbis, recorded in the Mishnah (compiled about AD 200) and Talmud (about AD 400).
● the Targums, being Aramaic translations and paraphrases of the OT, which were probably current orally in the NT period but which were written down much later.

GREEK AND ROMAN HISTORIANS
Palestine at the time of Jesus was part of the Roman empire, and for centuries before had

---

JOHN THE BAPTIST AND THE QUMRAN COMMUNITY

The Qumran community was a priest-led community. Luke tells us that John the Baptist was son of a priest (Luke 1–2).
● Qumran was in the desert near where the river Jordan enters the Dead Sea. Luke tells us that John 'was in the desert' until the start of his ministry when he baptized in the river Jordan (Luke 1:80).
● The Qumran community saw themselves as fulfilling prophecy, including Isa 40:3, on preparing the Lord's way in the desert (1QS 8:14). The NT applies this text to John (e.g. Mark 1:3).
● The Qumran community was a pious protest movement against the religious hierarchy, who emphasized ritual washing and also the work of the 'spirit of holiness' (1QS 3). John called people out, denounced false religion and baptized people, speaking of a future baptism with the 'Holy Spirit'.
● The Qumran community were conscious of living in the last days and were looking forward to the coming of one or more Messiah. John announced the coming of God's kingdom and of one greater than he.

---

been directly or indirectly controlled by the big empires that dominated what we would call the Mediterranean and the Middle East. For this reason the writings of the Greek and Roman historians (notably Polybius c.200–120 BC, Diodorus c.90–30 BC, Tacitus c.AD 56–120 and Suetonius c.AD 75–150) are important, even if they say little (or nothing) about the Christian movement itself. Tacitus refers to the Christian movement when he discusses the great fire of Rome in AD 64, which the Roman emperor Nero blamed on the Christians (*Ann* XV.38–44). Suetonius has a reference to the Jewish community in Rome being expelled from the city by the emperor Claudius, because they had been 'rioting at the instigation of Chrestus' (*Claudius* 25.4); this is plausibly taken to refer to troubles within the Jewish community over the activities of enthusiastic followers of Jesus *Christus* in the capital city.

BEFORE THE ROMANS

The OT story ends in the Persian period, with the Jews returning from exile in Babylon (modern Iraq) to Palestine, their promised land. The return to their home-land (with all its historical and religious significance) was very important for the Jewish people. But it was far from being a straightforward return to former glory.

- Relatively few did actually return. Many remained in Babylonia; others had dispersed to other countries such as Egypt.
- The rebuilding was slow and, when eventually the temple in Jerusalem was rebuilt, it was a shadow of its former self. The wealth of Solomon was not available for the rebuilding, and there was opposition from other people in the area.
- The returning Jews were still subject to the Persians and did not have a substantial

---

KEY ROMAN HISTORIANS

Tacitus
AD 56–120 approx., an influential Roman, who wrote two major works on Roman history: the Annales, 18 volumes covering the period of AD 14–68, and the Historiae, covering the period AD 69–96. He describes the Christians as 'a deadly sect' (*Ann* XV.44.2–8).

Suetonius
AD 75–150 approx., wrote 'The Lives of Twelve Emperors', starting with Caesar and ending with Domitian, i.e. the second half of the first century BC and most of the first century AD.

---

army with which to defend themselves, so were vulnerable to opposition from others and to the whims of their Persian masters (see the books of Ezra and Nehemiah).

Some of the local opposition came from people in the neighbouring region of Samaria, who seem to have been a hotch-potch of nationalities and religions. Although they professed some sort of allegiance to the God of Israel, the Jews were suspicious of their motives and hostile towards their offers of collaboration (Ezra 4). They regarded them as half-pagans at best. This cold-shouldering of the Samaritans is presumably one of the factors that led the Samaritans to build their own temple on Mount Gerizim, probably sometime in the fourth century BC. Inevitably this alternative temple in the promised land infuriated the Jews, and, although a lot happened between these events and the NT period, this is one of the roots of the Jew-Samaritan tensions that are evident in the NT.

The Persian period is important not just because it brought Jews back to Palestine, but also because it was a time when the Jews were struggling to maintain their own religious and social identity in a context of political powerlessness and economic weakness. For the pious it was important to maintain the traditional law of Moses, to keep themselves pure (from people like the Samaritans) and to uphold the sanctity of the temple (from people like the Samaritans!). Not that everyone felt this way. The temptation was to give up and to assimilate into the surrounding culture, and there is evidence that a significant number of Jews went a long way in that direction. Even among those who didn't, there may have been more assimilation of ideas than they would have liked to admit. Thus the greater prominence of angels and demons in the NT by comparison with the OT may have something to do with Persian religious influence.

THE GREEKS

Philip, king of Macedonia in northern Greece, formed a united kingdom of Greece. He was succeeded by his son Alexander in 336 BC, who had been educated in part by the famous philosopher Aristotle. He proceeded to conquer the known world in a brilliant campaign that took him across the Persian empire to Egypt in the south and India in the east. He created probably the largest empire the world had ever known within about ten years, only to die prematurely in 323 BC.

Although his empire did not last, his vision of spreading Greek culture was remarkably realized. He founded Greek cities, such as Alexandria in Egypt, and in the time of Jesus Greek was the international language of the day (rather like English is today). Ordinary people across the Roman empire, including in Palestine, could speak it. In the NT period there were synagogues where the worship was in Greek, and one of the early tensions in the Christian community was between Aramaic-speaking Christians and Greek-speakers. But Greek was generally a positive thing for the early Christians, facilitating mission across the Roman empire.

A power struggle followed Alexander's death, and his huge empire was divided – Palestine was first ruled by the Ptolemies of Egypt. There was a lot of traffic between Palestine and Egypt, with many Jews settling there, so that the great city of Alexandria had a large Jewish minority. But then control of Palestine passed to the Seleucids, whose capital was in Syrian Antioch.

The Ptolemies, like the Persians, had followed a rather lenient, hands-off approach towards the Jews, allowing them religious freedom and considerable autonomy. But this policy began to give way under the Seleucids, who were themselves under some pressure from the Romans who had imposed punitive reparations on them after a military defeat.

THE MACCABEES VERSUS THE SELEUCID EMPIRE

Things came to a head with the Seleucid ruler, Antiochus 4, who ruled from 175 to 163 BC, and who took the name 'Epiphanes'. The name means something like 'manifestation', and represented a claim to be a divine manifestation. He was motivated by enthusiasm for hellenizing the world (i.e. spreading Greek culture and religion), and by the need to raise funds. This led him to interfere in the religious affairs of the Jews, notably over the appointment of the high priest in Jerusalem. The high priesthood was the highest and

BC	RULING EMPIRE	EFFECTS IN JUDEA	WRITINGS ETC.
600	597-539 BABYLON 538 – PERSIA	597 Jerusalem taken by Nebuchadnezzar II. 587 Jerusalem destroyed. People go into exile.	
500	PERSIA	539 Cyrus of Persia conquers Babylon in Jerusalem. 538 Return of exiles to Jerusalem, rebuilding of temple begun 516 Temple completed.	450 approx – Ezra and Nehemiah
400	PERSIA 332 – GREECE 332 Alexander conquers, builds cities. 323 Death of Alexander Greek empire divided. 323 – EGYPT Ptolemies rule.	323 Judea is in the area under Ptolemy rule.	Spread of Greek thought and language.
300		High priests rule in Jerusalem on behalf of the Ptolemies.	
200	SYRIA 198 Seleucids take over Palestine from Ptolemies. 190 Romans inflict major defeat on Seleucids and impose reparations. Antiochus IV 'Epiphanes' enthroned (ruled 175-163).	Seleucid empire in control in place of the Ptolemies. High priest in Jerusalem favours Antiochus Epiphanes, but in 167 Antiochus desecrates the temple and builds an altar to Zeus Olympus (desolating sacrilege). 166 Death of Mattathias; Judas Maccabeus becomes leader of revolt. 164 Judas cleanses temple; battles with Syria. **Hasmonean dynasty** 167 Onwards Maccabees dominant in Israel. 160 Death of Judas. 160-52 Jonathan leader of forces; becomes high priest in 152. 143 Jonathan killed, succeeded by brother Simon. 134 Hyrcanus I succeeds. 128 Jews destroy Samaritan temple on Mount Gerizim. 104 Aristobulus I; 103 Alexander Janneus (his brother); 76 Alexandra (wife), 67 Hyrcanus II and Aristobulus (sons). Hasmoneans ruled until 63 BC.	Previous century and this century Septuagint translation of OT into Greek. 200-120 BC Polybius, Roman historian. 159 approx – Essene Teacher of Righteousness. Development of Pharisees and Essenes.
100	63 – ROME 63 Jerusalem taken by Pompey.	High priests rule under the Romans. Civil wars break out in the Roman world.	100 BC onwards – Four books of Maccabees written.

Date		The Herods / The Caesars	
44	44 Julius Caesar murdered in Rome.	**The Herods** 55 Antipater (father of Herod the Great) given title procurator of Judea. 40 Herod son of Antipater declared king of Judea in Rome; he appoints his supporters as high priests. 37-4 Herod the Great rules. 19 Herod starts rebuilding temple (consecrated 9 BC). 4 Death of Herod; kingdom divided: (1) Herod Antipas rules Galilee and Perea until AD 38; marries Herodias. (2) Herod Archelaus rules Judea, Samaria, Idumea (deposed in AD 6). (3) Philip rules Northern Palestine until AD 34.	Also Ecclesiasticus, The Wisdom of Ben Sira (c. 180 BC) and Wisdom of Solomon. 90-30 Diodorus, Roman historian. 4 BC approx date of Jesus' birth.
AD 1	**The Caesars** 14 Augustus (emperor) dies. 14-37 Tiberius. 37-41 Gaius. 41-54 Claudius. 49 Jews expelled from Rome by Claudius. 54 Jews return to Rome. 54-68 Nero. Fire of Rome; persecution of Christians. 68-69 Year of four emperors: Galba, Otho, Vitellius, Vespasian. 69-79 Vespasian. 79-81 Titus. 81-96 Domitian. 96-98 Nerva.	AD 6 Judea and Samaria become a Roman province ruled by Roman prefects. Census riots. 18 Caiaphas becomes high priest. 26-37 Pontius Pilate is Roman procurator. 39 Roman governor Gaius orders statue of himself set up in Jerusalem temple. 40 Herod Agrippa becomes king in the north, 41 also king in the south, after assassination of Gaius. 44 Famine; death of Herod Agrippa. 52 Roman governor Cumanus removed from office for poor handling of Jews and Samaritans. Felix succeeds. 59-62 Festus Governor. 63 Temple completed. 66-70 Jewish war. 70 Titus takes Jerusalem. 74 Capture of Masada – last stronghold of the Jews	c. 31-33 Crucifixion of Jesus; c. 1-4 years after: Conversion of Saul. 37-100 Life of Josephus. 41 Agrippa executes James the brother of John. Late 40s-late 50s Paul's missionary journeys. 49-51 Paul in Corinth. Jewish philosopher and diplomat Philo lived in this century. Tacitus (56-120) and Suetonius (75-150) Roman historians. 62 James Brother of Jesus killed by high priest Annas II.
100	98-117 Trajan. 117-138 Hadrian. 138-161 Antoninus Pius. 161-180 Marcus Aurelius. 180-192 Commodus.	115-117 Jewish revolts in Egypt, Cyrene, Cyprus. 132 Hadrian makes anti-semitic laws – temple of Jupiter in Jerusalem. 133-5 Rebellion of Simeon Bar Kochba.	Pliny governor of Bithynia. 110-115 Letters of Ignatius. Justin Martyr (d. 165). Polycarp (d. 156). Irenaeus, Bishop of Lyon 180s-190s. Tertullian c.160-220.
200			Mishnah (Sayings of the Rabbis) compiled.

most sacred position that a Jew could hold, and Antiochus twice intervened to put in men who would support him financially and support his hellenizing. His first appointment, Jason, built a gymnasium near the temple in Jerusalem, where Greek games could be held – something very alien to Jewish culture – and his second, Menelaus, was not even from the proper high priestly family.

Such meddling by the arrogant superpower was resented, and sparked off a series of events, which eventually led to Antiochus attacking Jerusalem, killing many of his opponents and looting the temple. He went on to attempt forcibly to impose Hellenistic culture and religion on the city. He prohibited the observance of the Jewish law, including the circumcision of baby boys, and, most offensively of all, rededicated the temple to Olympian Zeus, erecting a pagan altar. This 'desolating sacrilege' remained in place from 167 until 164 BC.

His attempts to annihilate Judaism failed, thanks to the heroic resistance of the people, led and inspired by one particular priestly family, the Hasmoneans. Mattathias refused to offer a pagan sacrifice in his village of Modein, and then called people to flee to the mountains: 'Let everyone who is zealous for the law and supports the covenant come out with me!' (1 Macc. 2:27). A courageous guerilla campaign ensued, under the leader-ship of his sons. The first and most famous of these was Judas (whose nickname Maccabeus – 'hammer' – became attached to the whole family of the 'Maccabees'). He led a series of daring attacks on the Seleucid forces, which resulted eventually in their tactical withdrawal and to the rededication of the temple by the Jews in 164 BC, some-thing that has been celebrated by Jews ever

since in the Feast of Dedication ('Hanukkah' in Hebrew; referred to in John 10:22).

It is hard to over-emphasize the importance of these events for the NT. The actions of Antiochus came to epitomize for the Jews the ultimate disaster, and in the centuries that followed there was continual anxiety about the possible repetition of the horrific events. This fear is reflected in Jesus' use of the idea of 'the desolating sacrilege' when referring to future disaster coming on Jerusalem in Mark 13:14, and in Paul's references to 'the man of lawlessness' setting himself up in the temple in 2 Thess. 2. The actions of the Maccabees and those with them became the epitome of religious courage and faithfulness in the face of powerful paganism. Their zeal was the inspiration of numerous freedom fighters and so-called 'zealots' in Jesus' lifetime.

THE HASMONEAN DYNASTY

The victory of Judas was famous, but not the end of the story, and in the years that followed there were many ups and downs, with the Seleucids continuing to exert a con-trolling influence on affairs in Jerusalem to a greater or lesser extent. Judas himself was killed, as were his brothers Jonathan and Simon who succeeded him in turn. But a family dynasty had been established, and the Hasmonean family continued to rule until 63 BC, when Judea became a part of the Roman empire.

The Hasmonean period was up and down in all sorts of ways. Politically and militarily there were successes, as when Simon achieved freedom from Seleucid taxation for Judea, and also when Hyrcanus 1 (son of Simon) conquered Samaria, Idumea and part of Galilee, forcing their residents to accept Judaism and circumcision. Josephus

What do you think?
THE DESOLATING SACRILEGE

I Macc. 1:41-61:

> Then the king wrote to his whole kingdom that all should be one people, and that all should give up their particular customs. All the Gentiles accepted the command of the king. Many even from Israel gladly adopted his religion; they sacrificed to idols and profaned the Sabbath. And the king sent letters by messengers to Jerusalem and the cities of Judah; he directed them to follow customs strange to the land, to forbid burnt offerings and sacrifices and drink offerings in the sanctuary, to profane Sabbaths and festivals, to defile the sanctuary and the priests, to build altars and sacred precincts and shrines for idols, to sacrifice swine and other unclean animals, and to leave their sons uncircumcised. They were to make themselves abominable by everything unclean and profane, so that they would forget the law and change all the ordinances. He added: 'And whoever does not obey the command of the king shall die.'
>
> In such words he wrote to his whole kingdom. He appointed inspectors over all the people and commanded the towns of Judah to offer sacrifice, town by town. Many of the people, every one who forsook the law, joined them, and they did evil in the land; they drove Israel into hiding in every place of refuge they had.
>
> Now on the fifteenth day of Chislev, in the one hundred forty-fifth year, they erected a desolating sacrilege on the altar of burnt offering. They also built altars in the surrounding towns of Judah, and offered incense at the doors of the houses and in the streets. The books of the law which they found they tore to pieces and burned with fire ... On the twenty-fifth day of the month they offered sacrifice on the altar which was on the top of the altar of burnt offering. According to the decree, they put to death the women who had their children circumcized, and their families and those who circumcized them; and they hung the infants from their mothers' necks.
>
> But many in Israel stood firm and were resolved in their hearts not to eat unclean food. They chose to die rather than to be defiled by food or to profane the holy covenant; and they did die. Very great wrath came upon Israel.

What was offensive in the actions of Antiochus? What differing attitudes were evident among the Jews? Why?

describes the attack on Samaria as a prolonged and brutal affair, which included the destruction of the Samaritans' temple in 128 BC. It is easy to see how this would have left deep wounds in the mind of the Samaritans in the time of Jesus. There were also moments of humiliation, notably in 63 BC when a family feud led to an invitation to the Romans, under the leadership of Pompey, to intervene.

Theologically it was also a period of ups and downs. In the original successful campaign against the Seleucids, Judas and his brothers were enthusiastically supported by pious Jews, including the so-called hasidim (pious ones), who may well have been the forerunners of later movements such as the Pharisees and the Essenes. But relations became very strained later, when the Hasmoneans took increasing powers to

11

KEY DATES

From the OT to the Roman takeover
BC

538 Release of Jews from exile under Cyrus the Persian.

336 Alexander the Great becomes king of Macedonia in northern Greece.

323 Death of Alexander leads to the division of his great empire: Ptolemy founds the Ptolemaic empire in Egypt with capital Alexandria.

312 Seleucus founds Seleucid empire with capital Antioch in Syria.

198 Palestine, which until now was part of the Ptolemaic empire, is taken over by the Seleucids after battle at Paneion.

190 Seleucid king, Antiochus 3, is seriously defeated by Romans at Lydia and forced to make large payments to Rome.

167 Antiochus 4 sets up pagan altar, 'the desolating sacrilege', in Jerusalem temple and tries to eradicate Jewish religion.

164 Temple rededicated after successful campaign by Judas Maccabeus, from the Hasmonean family.

160 Judas killed, and his brother Jonathan takes over.

152 Jonathan accepts position of high priest, though not himself from Zadokite high-priestly family.

143 Jonathan killed and succeeded by his brother Simon, who soon achieves freedom from taxation for Judea.

134 Simon assassinated; succeeded by his son Hyrcanus 1.

128 Hyrcanus's forces destroy Samaritan temple on Mount Gerizim.

104 Aristobulus 1 succeeds his father Hyrcanus; conquers Galilee.

103 Aristobulus dies suddenly, and is succeeded by his brother Alexander Janneus, who greatly expands territory, and takes title king of Judea.

76 Alexander dies, and is succeeded by his wife Alexandra, who favours the Pharisees (whom her husband had oppressed).

63 Pompey and the Romans take over Jerusalem.

themselves. Thus Jonathan (who succeeded Judas) allowed himself to be regarded as high priest, and Aristobulus a generation later took the title of 'king'. This establishment of a high-priestly and royal dynasty was unacceptable to strictly pious Jews – the Hasmoneans were not from the high priestly line nor from the family of David. Things reached rock bottom with Alexander Janneus (brother and successor of Aristobulus), who ruled from 103 to 76 BC. He was militarily successful, but more interested in power than piety, and he came into violent conflict with the Pharisees, among others. Josephus says that he crucified hundreds of Pharisees and killed in all over 50,000 of his opponents. The situation was redeemed to some extent by Alexander's wife, Alexandra, who succeeded him on his death, and favoured the Pharisees, but the relief was temporary, since it was the squabbling of her sons, Hyrcanus 2 and Aristobulus, that led to the Roman intervention and the end of the Hasmonean dynasty.

HASMONEAN LEADERS OF JUDEA
167–63 BC

167	Mattathias
166	Judas (son)
160	Jonathan (brother)
143	Simon (brother)
134	Hyrcanus 1 (son)
104	Aristobulus 1 (son)
103	Alexander Janneus (brother)
76	Alexandra (wife)
67	Hyrcanus 2 and Aristobulus 2 (sons)

(Relationship to predecessor in brackets)

THE ROMANS

The republic of Rome had been growing increasingly powerful in the Mediterranean world for two centuries, and the first century BC saw its formidable armies under their powerful leaders (the most famous being Pompey, Julius Caesar, Anthony and Octavian, later called Augustus when he was emperor), taking over what had once been Alexander the Great's empire – from Turkey, into Syria and to Egypt.

In 63 BC Pompey entered Jerusalem, including the Holy of Holies (the central shrine in the Jerusalem temple). This caused offence, but Pompey had no anti-Jewish agenda, and the immediate impact of the arrival of Rome was not huge, since Hyrcanus 2 – one of Alexandra's squabbling sons – was given authority to rule in Jerusalem under the Romans.

The impact was, however, considerable as time went on, since the Romans were now the power to reckon with, and everyone with aspirations to positions of political power and influence (which included the high priests) had to look to Rome.

THE HEROD FAMILY

The famous family to come to prominence under the Romans was that of Antipater, father of the man known to us as Herod the Great. Antipater was a cunning politician (apparently from an Idumean or Edomite family, the Idumeans having been conquered and forced to accept Judaism in the heyday of the Hasmoneans). He had supported Hyrcanus in his quarrel with his brother, and soon managed to ingratiate himself with the Romans, notably by giving military aid to the Roman leader Julius Caesar, when he was in a dangerous situation in Egypt. He was rewarded by being made governor of Judea and later by the granting of particular privileges in the Roman empire to the Jews (e.g. they were exempted from regular military service, and were allowed to meet for worship).

Neither Antipater nor Julius Caesar lasted long, both being assassinated. But Antipater's younger son, Herod, in the face of considerable opposition, established himself in the favour of the Romans, and with their help fought his way into Jerusalem and into power. His ruthless campaign ended in 37 BC with a three-month siege of Jerusalem. From then on until his death in 4 BC, he was supreme in Jerusalem, king of all Judea, Samaria and Galilee.

Two characteristics are notable about Herod's rule: first, his insecurity – political, to start with, and psychological. Having fought his way into power, he faced continuing opposition and uncertainty for the early years of his reign. He successfully played off different Roman leaders against each other, and ruthlessly put down internal opposition to his rule. Members of his own family, including his father-in-law and his wife Mariamme (of whom he was very fond, but who had Hasmonean blood in her), fell foul of his suspicions and were killed. In due course he became firmly established in power; but he continued to be nervous, and in the latter years of his life he was obsessed about possible threats to his position. Three of his own sons were executed, including his favourite Antipater, just days before Herod's own death. Herod's Palestine was a police state, living in fear. As for Herod's family, the emperor Augustus may not actually have said, 'It is better to be Herod's pig than his son', but he might appropriately have done so (Macrobius, *Saturnalia* II iv 11). The account in Matthew's Gospel of Herod's murderous reaction to the announcement of the birth of a 'king of the Jews' (Matt. 2:2) is entirely in character.

A second more positive characteristic of Herod's reign was his achievement as a builder. He built fortresses, palaces, temples and theatres. For example, by the Dead Sea there was Machaerus on the East coast, where John the Baptist was imprisoned and finally executed, and Masada, the magnificent hill-top fortress complex on the west side of the Dead Sea, where the Jews would so heroically resist the Romans in the war of AD 66–70. Herod built the port of Caesarea on the Mediterranean, providing a massive artificial harbour on a coast where there is hardly any natural harbour. This became the key entry/exit point to the country, through which almost everyone would have passed (including the apostle Paul following his arrest, Acts 23:33). Herod did great building work in Samaria, but most famous of all was his work in the Jerusalem area, where he built a whole variety of buildings, including a palace for himself, a theatre, an amphitheatre and a hippodrome, where crowds would come to watch sports and shows.

It was, however, his work on the Jerusalem temple that was most striking and is most important for NT studies. This was started around 19 BC. The work on the main part of the temple took about ten years to complete, but the whole work went on until AD 63 – just a few years before it was to be destroyed by the Romans in AD 70. Nehemiah's temple was a modest affair, not in good repair when Herod came to power. He, however, transformed it into one of the wonders of the ancient world, employing a huge workforce – Josephus speaks of 18,000

being unemployed when the work finally stopped in AD 63. He extended the temple area so as to cover twice the area of the original temple built by Solomon (Herod's temple was about 500 yards long, 325 yards wide); the central shrine was surrounded by courtyards, colonnades and other surrounding buildings, built and decorated magnificently, with gold and silver and ornamental gateways (see pp. 32–3).

The importance of the temple for a study of the NT is clear. The Jews had very mixed feelings about Herod: he was ruthless, and he taxed them heavily, as he needed to, to pay for his building work and his own lavish lifestyle. He was seen as an outsider (as an Idumean) and not as a proper Jew. Culturally he was more Greek than Jewish, as his building programme showed (it included building temples to the Roman imperial family), in the use of Greek as the court language and in his own lifestyle. However, despite everything, the temple, which he did so much for, was something that inspired admiration and devotion.

Herod died in 4 BC, and in his will left his domain to the three of his sons in whom he still had confidence – he bequeathed Judea and Samaria (including the title 'king of Judea') to Archelaus; Galilee and Perea to Antipas; and parts of Northern Transjordan and Gaulinitis (the area of the Golan Heights) to Philip. All three sons headed off to Rome, to gain Roman support; Antipas pressed his claim over against that of Archelaus. A delegation of Jews also went asking that none of the Herodians be appointed king. However, the Roman emperor Augustus eventually confirmed the will, except that he declined to give Archelaus the title of 'king'.

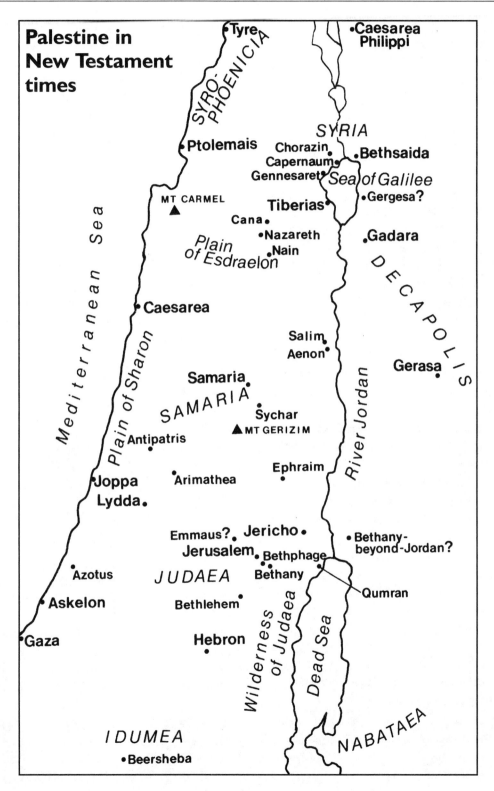

Palestine in New Testament times

Tyre

Caesarea Philippi

SYRO-PHOENICIA

SYRIA

Ptolemais

Chorazin
Capernaum
Gennesaret
Bethsaida
Sea of Galilee
Gergesa?

MT CARMEL

Cana
Tiberias

Nazareth
Nain
Gadara

Plain of Esdraelon

Mediterranean Sea

DECAPOLIS

Caesarea

Salim
Aenon
Gerasa

Plain of Sharon

Samaria

SAMARIA

Sychar
MT GERIZIM

River Jordan

Antipatris

Ephraim

Joppa
Arimathea

Lydda

Emmaus?
Jericho
Bethany-beyond-Jordan?

Jerusalem
Bethphage

Azotus

JUDAEA
Bethany

Qumran

Askelon

Bethlehem

Wilderness of Judaea

Dead Sea

Gaza

Hebron

IDUMEA

NABATAEA

Beersheba

What do you think?
HEROD ANTIPAS' EXECUTION OF JOHN THE BAPTIST

Compare the account in Mark 6:14-29 with that of Josephus Ant. 18:116-119 (=18.5.2):

> To some of the Jews the destruction of Herod's army seemed to be divine vengeance, and certainly a just vengeance, for his treatment of John, surnamed the Baptist. For Herod had put him to death, though he was a good man and had exhorted the Jews to lead righteous lives, to practise justice towards their fellows and piety towards God, and so doing to join in baptism. In his view this was a necessary preliminary if baptism was to be acceptable to God. They must not employ it to gain pardon for whatever sins they committed, but as a consecration of the body implying that the soul was already thoroughly cleansed by right behaviour. When others too joined the crowds about him, because they were aroused to the highest degree by his sermons, Herod became alarmed. Eloquence that had so great an effect on mankind might lead to some form of sedition, for it looked as if they would be guided by John in everything that they did. Herod decided therefore that it would be much better to strike first and be rid of him before his work led to an uprising, than to wait for an upheaval, get involved in a difficult situation and see his mistake. Though John, because of Herod's suspicions, was brought to Machaerus, the stronghold that we have previously mentioned, and there put to death, yet the verdict of the Jews was that the destruction visited upon Herod's army was a vindication of John, since God saw fit to inflict such a blow on Herod.

How do the accounts of Mark and Josephus differ? To what extent do they contradict or complement each other?

During the gap between the death of Herod and the establishment of his sons, there were various anti-Roman risings in Jerusalem, in Judea (led by a shepherd Athronges) and in Galilee (led by a man called Judas, who took over the Galilean town of Sepphoris). This revolt led the Roman governor of Syria to march into Palestine with his legions: he destroyed Sepphoris, a new town near Nazareth, and had 2,000 Jews in Jerusalem put to death by crucifixion.

Of the Herod sons, the two who are of most interest from a NT point of view are:

a **Archelaus** His brutality and his interference in temple affairs (e.g. in deposing two high priests) made him a hated man and, in response to delegations from Judea and Samaria, he was removed from office by the Romans in AD 6 (Matt. 2:22). Direct Roman rule was then being imposed.

b **Herod Antipas** He was a much more able ruler, who ruled in Galilee until AD 39. He followed his father as a builder, for example building a magnificent city, Tiberias, on the west shore of Lake Galilee. He was more sensitive to Jewish feelings and scruples than others in his family, though he upset the pious Jews by divorcing his wife and marrying Herodias, who had been married to a brother of his. He was denounced among others by John the Baptist, a popular prophet. Herod arrested John, and in due course executed him, at the instigation of Herodias.

Herodias eventually proved the downfall of her husband, when she, with her usual ambition, persuaded Antipas to ask the Romans for the honour and title of king.

HEROD FAMILY: A SELECTIVE FAMILY TREE

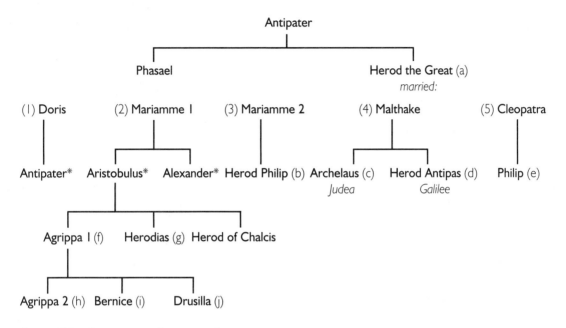

Some NT references to these people

(a) Matt. 2; (b) Matt.14:3; (c) Matt. 2:22; (d) Matt.14:1f.; Luke 23:7f.; (e) Luke 3:1; (f) Acts 12; (g) Matt.14:3f. – Herodias was wife of Herod Philip (b), then of Herod Antipas (d), and had a daughter Salome; (h) Acts 25, 26; (i) Acts 25:13f.; (j) Acts 24:24.

* executed by Herod the Great

The Romans suspected his ambitions, and he was rewarded with being deposed from office and sent to exile in France.

Although Jesus' ministry was mostly in Antipas's Galilean territory, the Gospels only describe them meeting once, in Jerusalem after Jesus had been arrested (Luke 23:6-12). Herod had heard plenty about Jesus (e.g. Mark 6:14), but it may be that Jesus deliberately kept out of the way of the man who killed his friend and mentor John the Baptist (cf. Luke 13:31-33). Jesus is never described as visiting the big Greek towns of Sepphoris and Tiberias where Herod's influence and rule will have been strongest.

Jesus, then, was in Antipas's territory when ministering in Galilee, though villages to the north like Bethsaida and Caesarea Philippi were in Philip's territory. But when he visited Jerusalem he left Antipas's jurisdiction.

Judea and Samaria had been under the direct rule of the Romans, in the form of a Roman governor (a 'prefect' or 'procurator'), since the time of Archelaus. Although Archelaus had been much disliked, direct rule was not universally welcomed by the Jews, since it represented the extending of pagan rule over their land. In fact, when it was first introduced in AD 6, there was a major rebellion against a census conducted, for taxation purposes, by Quirinius, the Roman governor of Syria. The census was resented both for financial and theological reasons. The rebellion was led by a Judas from Galilee, but was swiftly crushed.

We need not delay to comment on the first three governors of Judea. The fourth was Valerius Gratus, who ruled from AD 15 to 26 and who seems to have been less conciliatory to the Jews than his predecessors. He kept deposing the high priest, until finally lighting on Joseph Caiaphas, who was high priest from AD 18 to 36.

CAIAPHAS'S TOMB

In 1990 the tomb of a wealthy family was found near Jerusalem, and it appears to be the tomb of the high-priestly family of Caiaphas, referred to in the Gospels. It contained ossuaries (stone boxes for the bones of the deceased), one of which is inscribed with the high priest's full name:

JOSEPH BAR CAIPHA.

PONTIUS PILATE

Easily the most famous Roman governor was Pontius Pilate, who was appointed in AD 26. He may have been a protégé of Sejanus, a very powerful figure in the Roman imperial court with anti-Jewish tendencies. Certainly he managed to offend the Jews soon after taking office. For example, breaking with earlier precedent, he ordered the Roman troops who were stationed in Jerusalem to carry their military standards into the city; the Jews were infuriated at what they saw as pagan images entering the holy city. The popular protests eventually forced Pilate to withdraw the order.

What do you think?
PILATE AND THE STANDARDS

Text of Josephus *JW* 2:169–77 (= 2.9.2–3):

Pilate being sent by Tiberius as procurator in Judea, introduced into Jerusalem by night and under cover, the effigies of Caesar which are called standards. This proceeding, when day broke, aroused immense excitement among the Jews; those on the spot were in consternation, considering their laws to have been trampled under foot, as those laws permit no image to be erected in the city; while the indignation of the townspeople stirred the country-folk, who flocked together in crowds. Hastening after Pilate to Caesarea, the Jews implored him to remove the standards from Jerusalem and to uphold the laws of their ancestors. When Pilate refused, they fell prostrate around his house and for five whole days and nights remained motionless in that position.

On the ensuing day Pilate took his seat on his tribunal in the great stadium and summoning the multitude, with the apparent intention of answering them, gave the arranged signal to his armed soldiers to surround the Jews. Finding themselves in a ring of troops, three deep, the Jews were struck dumb at this unexpected sight. Pilate, after threatening to cut them down, if they refused to admit Caesar's images, signalled to the soldiers to draw their swords. Thereupon the Jews, as by concerted action, flung themselves in a body on the ground, extended their necks, and exclaimed that they were ready rather to die than to transgress the law. Overcome with astonishment at such intense religious zeal, Pilate gave order for the immediate removal of the standards from Jerusalem.

What do we learn from this passage about the Jewish context in which Pilate was governor? How does Pilate come over as a person?

In a rather similar incident Pilate upset people by trying to have some golden shields inscribed with his name and that of the emperor erected in Herod's palace in Jerusalem. This time the Jews protested to the Roman emperor himself, who told Pilate to move them to Caesarea. Pilate also caused offence by raiding the temple treasury to help pay for an aqueduct into the city. This secular (even if admirable) use of sacred funds again led to protests and violence.

Pilate's dealings with Jesus and the Jewish authorities, at the time of Jesus' arrest, must be seen in the context of (a) Pilate's previous record of poor relations with the Jews, which will have made his position vulnerable in all sorts of ways (e.g. to the threat of being denounced to Rome); and (b) the general

---

LEADERS/RULERS OF JUDEA IN THE ROMAN PERIOD

BC

55	Antipater (HF)
40	Herod the Great (HF)
4	Archelaus (HF)

AD

6	Coponius (gov)
9	Marcus Ambivius (gov)
12	Annius Rufus (gov)
15	Valerius Gratus (gov)
26	Pontius Pilate (gov)
37	Marullus (gov)
41	Herod Agrippa I (HF)
44	Fadus (gov)
46	Tiberius Alexander (gov)
48	Cumanus (gov)
52	Felix (gov)
59	Festus (gov)
62	Albinus (gov)
64/65	Florus (gov)

(HF = Herod family;
gov = Roman governor)

ROMAN LEADERS/EMPERORS

BC

c.60	Pompey, Julius Caesar, Crassus
49	Julius Caesar
44	Antony and Octavian (later Augustus)
31	Augustus (first emperor)

AD

14	Tiberius
37	Gaius Caligula
41	Claudius
54	Nero
68	Galba,
69	Otho, Vitellius, Vespasian

---

resentment in Palestine against foreign rule, a resentment that burst into flame from time to time. The Gospels refer to 'an insurrection' at the time of Jesus, and to 'bandits (or robbers)' being crucified with Jesus, who could have been nationalist freedom fighters (Luke 23:25).

Pilate's governorship came to an end suddenly, following his mishandling of a religious uprising in Samaria. A self-styled prophet, perhaps Messiah, had attracted a crowd to Mount Gerizim. Pilate sent in his troops, who inflicted heavy bloodshed. The result was a strong protest to the senior Roman governor of the area – based in Syria – who ordered Pilate back to Rome. Pilate's failure to manage the religious affairs of his subjects wisely was finally his downfall.

AFTER PILATE

Pilate's immediate successor, Marullus (AD 37-41), presided over a crisis of the first order in AD 39, when the megalomaniac Roman emperor, Gaius Caligula, took offence at the Jews and ordered his statue to be set up in the Jerusalem temple itself. This looked like being another 'desolating sacrilege'. The

Jews were in uproar, and furious efforts were made to stop the order being carried out (including by Agrippa, one of the Herod family, who was a friend of Gaius). The thing that decisively saved the day was the death in Rome of Gaius by assassination.

Marullus was succeeded by Agrippa, the last of the Herods to have power in Jerusalem. He ruled from AD 41 to 44, and was popular with the Jews, living rather piously and also, according to the NT, taking action against the unpopular Christians (Acts 12:1-2).

The following period of rule by Roman governors was turbulent. Fadus (AD 44-46) put down and beheaded a prophet called Theudas, who promised to lead people dry-foot through the Jordan to conquer the promised land. Tiberius Alexander (AD 46-48) crucified two sons of Judas the Galilean, presumably for nationalist violence. His governorship was marked by a particularly severe period of famine. Cumanus (AD 48-52) presided over various troubles, including an incident in Jerusalem when a soldier offended Jewish sensitivities, leading to a disturbance in which, according to Josephus, 20,000 people were killed. There were also major tensions between Jews and Samaritans. The governorship of Felix (AD 52-60) saw more unrest in Palestine, with groups of revolutionaries or 'zealots' (such as the 'sicarii' who specialized in assassination) and religious prophets (including a Jew from Egypt) being active and gaining support. Felix was ruthless in response (Tacitus, *Hist.* 5:9). He was followed in

---

KEY DATES IN THE ROMAN PERIOD

BC

63 Judea becomes part of Roman empire.

55 Antipater (father of Herod the Great) given title 'procurator of Judea'.

44 Julius Caesar murdered in Rome; Antipater murdered a year later.

37 Herod the Great captures Jerusalem, having previously been named king of Judea by the Romans.

19 Renovation of Jerusalem temple begun.

4 Approximate date of Jesus' birth. Herod dies, to be succeeded by Archelaus in Judea and Samaria (until AD 6), Antipas in Galilee and Perea (until AD 39), Philip in area north of Galilee (until AD 33).

AD

6 Judea and Samaria put under direct Roman rule. Quirinius governor of Syria conducts census, provoking revolt led by Judas the Galilean.

26 Pontius Pilate governor of Judea until AD 36.

31 Approximate date of Jesus' crucifixion and resurrection

39 Roman emperor Gaius orders a statue of himself to be set up in Jerusalem temple.

41 Gaius assassinated. Herod Agrippa 1 appointed king of Judea, until his sudden death in AD 44.

49 Claudius, emperor, banishes Jews from Rome for rioting at the instigation of 'Chrestus'. Many people killed in Jerusalem, due to incident involving Roman soldier.

52 Cumanus governor of Judea removed from office for poor handling of Jews and Samaritans. Succeeded by Felix, who has difficulties with Jewish nationalists including 'sicarii'.

59 Festus governor.

62 Festus dies. High priest Annas 2 has James, brother of Jesus, killed, before arrival of new governor Albinus.

64 The great fire in Rome, and persecution of Christians. Florus governor of Judea.

66 Jewish revolt begins in Jerusalem.

70 Jerusalem finally overrun after siege and bitter resistance.

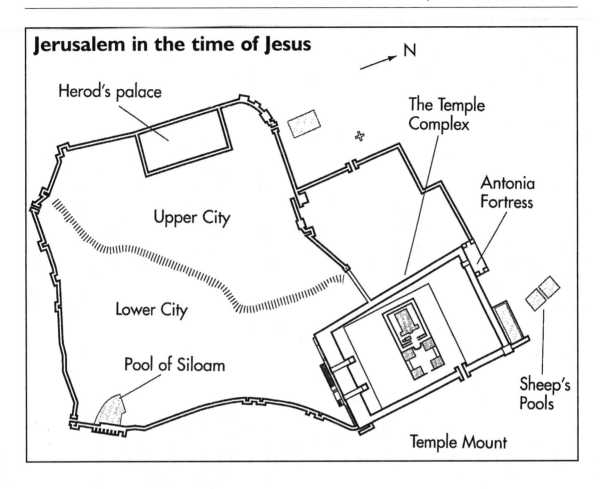

Jerusalem in the time of Jesus

N

Herod's palace

The Temple Complex

Antonia Fortress

Upper City

Lower City

Pool of Siloam

Sheep's Pools

Temple Mount

office by Festus (AD 59-62), Albinus (AD 62-64/5) and Florus (AD 64/5-66), whose brutal and rapacious rule triggered rebellion, and the Jewish war. The Jews fought fiercely and hoped for a Maccabean-style deliverance; but it did not come, and the infighting between different groups in Jerusalem did nothing to help. In AD 70 Jerusalem was captured, the temple destroyed and burned down.

JESUS' CONTEXT

The brief sketch that we have presented of the history has brought out various of the ingredients which made up Jesus' world: **Living under a pagan superpower** From the time of the OT right through and into NT times, the Jews of Palestine had been living under the shadow of a powerful pagan superpower. In the NT era Rome was militarily powerful, culturally vibrant, rich and pagan. Although the Romans did not seek to suppress Judaism, still the culture and way of life of the master race infiltrated Palestine, and many of the rich and influential people, notably the Herods, were into the Graeco-Roman way of life. The architecture, the entertainment and other aspects of the foreign rulers were attractive to many. Some of the Jews, for example the high-priestly families and the tax collectors, were doing very well under the Romans, and had a vested interest in the survival of the status quo.

Rich and poor People had been dispossessed to make room for the friends of the governing class, and the gap between rich and poor was wide. Taxation hit most people, often very hard – there were individual taxes, taxes on goods, as well as the traditional temple tax. Tax collectors were unscrupulous and unpopular. Debt was a major problem.

A new desolating sacrilege There was also the fear of what might happen in the future, and of a new 'desolating sacrilege'. The great fear was that the Romans might become much less benign, and defile things that Jews felt sacred. From time to time things did happen to enflame people's anxieties. Whereas some of the Roman officials were shrewd and sensitive, some were provocative and even violent. Society was generally violent in a way that some of us can hardly imagine: crucifixions and massacres of people who opposed or offended the masters were commonplace.

Maintaining the traditions In face of the foreign imperialist, some people became lax about their old religious loyalties. Thus at the time of Antiochus Epiphanes a significant number of Jews were willing to go along with his introduction of Hellenistic culture. There was plenty of glamour and attraction in the Graeco-Roman culture and way of life. But many were spurred on to greater loyalty: in the absence of political freedom, the traditions of Judaism became all the more important as a mark of Jewish identity. In particular three things became especially sensitive:

- the OT law;
- the call to be separate from everything unclean (including the unclean foreigner);
- the temple.

These concerns motivated the Pharisees, and also the community at Qumran, though they felt that the temple in Jerusalem had been fatally compromised. (See further in ch. 2.)

Longing for change The OT books, especially the prophetic books, spoke of a day coming when God's judgement would be removed from the people, when they would be free again, and there would be a new age of prosperity and salvation. The end of the Babylonian exile represented a partial fulfilment of that hope, but the experience since that time of living under the thumb of a variety of pagan super-powers left the Jews longing and praying for a more complete liberation, not least at Passover time when they recalled God's past deliverance from the superpower of Egypt.

The longing turned into action for some: individual leaders appeared, promising salvation and offering themselves as various sorts of messianic deliverers. People flocked to such people. In the NT itself there is mention of Judas and Theudas, not to mention John the Baptist and Jesus himself (Acts 5:36, 37). There were also periodic uprisings against the Romans – people hoped that the Maccabean experience of victory through faith and heroism would be repeated.

Religious confusion and division The situation encouraged a variety of religious responses, some justifying the status quo (at least tacitly), some advocating violent resistance, some maintaining religious purity but not violence, and others claiming that the Messiah or a Messiah had come. There was a level of tolerance within Judaism of different points of view, but a very limited level, and divisions could easily become violent, as they did between Jews and Samaritans. The most successful messianic movement was, of course, the Christian movement, and its very success made it the most divisive movement, threatening all sorts of people: its message of liberation from law and temple threatened the Pharisees and also the powerful temple authorities; its eventual inclusion of Gentiles threatened Jewish national identity.

Modern parallels? There are intriguing parallels between the situation of first-century Jewish Palestine and that in some modern Muslim countries: in first-century Palestine there was a struggle going on, at least culturally, between the pagan super-power and traditional Judaism. In many Muslim countries today modern Western secularism is the attractive, powerful paganism associated with the world super-power, America; it is very much in evidence in the capital cities of the world – bringing wealth to many and proving very attractive to many. But to the poor and pious, who often live in country areas (e.g. in Egypt), the secular threat is just that – a serious threat to their traditions, their culture, their family life. In that situation the fundamentalists flourish (compare the Pharisees), having great power with ordinary people; and so do the terrorists who attack tourist buses and other targets (compare the Jewish zealots – like Judas the Galilean – who were prepared to be violent in their opposition to Rome). Christians now, as then, are caught in a dilemma – being open to the charge of betraying the traditional faith and morals, even though they reject the secularism of the superpower.

ESSAY TOPICS

INTRODUCTORY
- What problems did the Romans face when ruling Jewish Palestine? What problems did the Jews have being ruled over by the Romans?

- Why did people like Herod and Pilate want to get rid of people like John the Baptist and Jesus?

INTERMEDIATE
- Why were the events of 167-164 BC of such importance to the Jews of Jesus' day, and indeed to Jesus himself?

FURTHER READING

INTRODUCTORY
F. F. Bruce *Israel and the Nations*, 3rd ed., revised by D. F. Payne, Carlisle: Paternoster, 1997/Downers Grove: IVP, 1998 (a reader-friendly history of Israel from OT times onwards).

J. Riches *The World of Jesus*, Cambridge: Cambridge University Press, 1990.

J. Stambauch & D. Balch *The Social World of the First Christians*, London: SPCK, 1986 (looks at the history and the social environment of Jesus and the first Christians).

G. Theissen *The Shadow of the Galilean*, London: SCM/Philadelphia: Fortress, 1987 (a brilliantly readable, semi-fictional account of Jesus' Palestine).

INTERMEDIATE
C. K. Barrett *The New Testament Background: Selected Documents*, 2nd ed. London: SPCK, 1987/New York: HarperSanFrancisco, 1995 (a useful collection of extracts from original documents).

E. Schürer *The History of the Jewish People in the Age of Jesus Christ*, 175 BC – AD 135, vol. 1. Edinburgh: T. & T. Clark, 1973 (a classic, thorough work, revised under the editorship of G. Vermes and F. Millar).

There are also editions of Josephus available, including *The Jewish War*, in Penguin, and the *War* and the *Antiquities* in the Loeb edition.

Chapter 2

JUDAISM IN FIRST-CENTURY PALESTINE

Jesus lived, taught and died in Palestine in the first century – and the church was born in that social, cultural and religious context. In order to understand Jesus and the early church well, we need to know about this setting. This chapter will introduce:

● key beliefs in Judaism at that time;
● significant groups within first-century Judaism.

Recently our picture of the Jewish context of Jesus' ministry has grown and developed, as scholars have learned more about the beliefs and lifestyles of the people of that period, both from archaeological discoveries (such as the Dead Sea Scrolls) and from re-reading the documents we have from the time. Scholars today speak of the 'second temple' period of Judaism, the time from the return from the Babylonian exile (sixth and fifth centuries BC) to AD 70. The first temple was Solomon's temple, built in the tenth century BC and destroyed by the Babylonian invaders in the sixth century (the OT book of Lamentations records the reaction of devout Jews to this cataclysmic event). The 'second temple' was the one built when the Jews returned from exile (the OT books of Ezra and Nehemiah describe the rebuilding process). By the time Jesus was born, Herod

the Great's (third) temple was being built, starting in 19 BC and finally being completed in AD 64 – just in time to be destroyed by the Romans in the Jewish War of AD 66-70. The Judaism of the second temple period, from the fifth century BC to the first century AD, is key to understanding Jesus' life and work.

Recent scholars sometimes speak of the Judaisms of the first century, for there was a considerable variety of belief and practice in that time among the Jews. Certainly there was a core of common beliefs and practices, which we shall look at next, but there were also at least four 'parties', each with its own distinctive understanding of how their faith was to be understood and lived out. (For the main groupings, see pp. 37–43.)

FIVE KEY MARKS OF SECOND TEMPLE JUDAISM

ONE TRUE GOD
First and foremost, Jewish people in the ancient world were marked out by their belief that there was only one true God, Yahweh (the name this God has in the OT, derived from the Hebrew verb meaning 'to

be'; see Exod. 3:13-15). This monotheism (belief in one God) contrasted sharply with the many gods of other faiths, whether the Greek and Roman gods known to us through mythology (Jupiter/Zeus, Mercury/ Hermes, etc.) or the many local deities in different parts of the ancient world. Although monotheistic faiths are most common today (particularly Christianity, Judaism and Islam), Jews were unusual in ancient times in holding this belief. Thus, a devout Jew would regularly recite the *Shema* (meaning 'Hear', the first word of this statement), a kind of Jewish 'creed':

> Hear, O Israel, the Lord our God is the only Lord. You shall love the Lord your God with all your heart, with all your soul, with all your mind and with all your strength. (Deut. 6:4-5; cf. Ps. 96:4-5)

With the belief in one true god went a rejection of the worship of other gods – in particular, of the worship of idols, which were physical representations of people, animals or plants treated as objects of prayer and religious devotion. Isa. 40–55 is particularly strong in its critique of idolatry, developing the second Mosaic commandment, 'You shall not make for yourself an idol, whether in the form of anything that is in heaven above, or that is on the earth beneath, or that is in the water

---

What do you think?
IDOLATRY

Read Isa. 40:18-20; 44:9-20 and Ps. 135:15-18. What are the criticisms of idolatry which these passages offer? How do they make the point that idolatry is foolish?

---

under the earth. You shall not bow down to them or worship them' (Exod. 20:4-5). The stinging caricature of idols in Isa. 44:9-20 is typical, portraying a craftsman who turns half of a tree into an idol to worship, and the other half into firewood.

It followed that Judaism rejected syncretism, the attempt to identify the gods of a people with the gods of another people. Syncretism had been around at least since the Israelites had entered the promised land in the second millennium BC, and was seen as a cause of both the Assyrian exile of Israel in 722 BC (Amos 5:25-27) and the Babylonian exile of Judah in 587 BC (Jer. 19:10-13). The book of Judith (probably second century BC) puts it graphically:

> For never in our generation, nor in these present days, has there been any tribe or family or people or town of ours that worships gods made with hands, as was done in days gone by. *That was why our ancestors were handed over to the sword and to pillage*, and so they suffered a great catastrophe before our enemies. (Judith 8:18-19, my italics)

The problem was that syncretism was a standard way of subduing a conquered people in the ancient world. Alexander the Great, the brilliant Greek general of the third century BC, and the Romans of the first centuries BC and AD, both operated this way: they would conquer a people and then identify the gods of that nation with their own gods – the top god would be regarded as being the same as Zeus (for Alexander) or Jupiter (for the Romans), and other gods would be identified with their Greek or Roman equivalents. This issue came to a head when Antiochus Epiphanes installed an altar to Zeus in the Jewish temple in

Jerusalem in 167 BC. From Antiochus' point of view, this was a logical step to take, since he identified Zeus, the highest god of his faith, with Yahweh, the highest (and only) god of Judaism. From the Jews' perspective, Antiochus could hardly have done anything more offensive, for he was implying that there was not only one true God. That, in combination with Antiochus making observing the Jewish law illegal, led directly to the successful Maccabean revolt – and may explain in part why the Romans of Jesus' day allowed the Jews to worship in their own way, for they wanted to avoid armed revolt in Judea.

A spin-off of Jewish monotheism was that they (and Christians later) were regarded by others as *atheists*. The charge of 'atheism' sounds strange to modern western ears, for atheism today is the belief that there is *no* god at all. But in the ancient world most religions had visible gods to worship – hence there were statues of the gods in pagan temples. Hence the Roman general Pompey was very surprised to find no statue of Yahweh when he went into the Jerusalem temple.

The monotheism of the Jews had two major characteristics, both of which made large truth claims over against other faiths: the Jews were *creational* and *providential* monotheists.

Creational monotheism

Central to Judaism was the belief that Yahweh was the creator of the world, seen particularly in the creation stories of Gen. 1–2, but also throughout the OT (e.g. Pss 89, 104). Judaism's claim that Yahweh was the creator of all people everywhere implied that everyone should worship him alone. In particular, believing in Yahweh as creator ruled out four views which were common in

the period of Jesus and the early Christians.

● *Henotheism* was a common belief in those times. This is the belief that each nation should worship its own god(s), without believing that there is only one true God. Gen. 1:1ff immediately opposes this view by its strong assertion that Yahweh is the creator God who alone made the whole world. This implies that all the nations should worship him as the only true God, and not their own god(s) – hence the prophetic critique of idolatry.

● *Pantheism* identified god with the natural order (in similar manner to some modern 'New Age' philosophies) – 'god' was a name for all that exists. On this view, 'god' was intimately involved in the created world, and it was legitimate to worship the created world. By contrast, Gen. 1:1 sets Yahweh apart from the universe: he created it and is distinct from it.

● *Epicureanism* was a Greek philosophy which included the belief that the gods were not interested or involved in human life. (Modern deism holds a similar view of God.) Thus prayer, worship and sacrifice were all pointless. More than that, creation was an accident, and events in the world follow laws derived from the movement of atoms. By contrast, Jewish creational monotheism included the belief that Yahweh was intimately involved in the world: he both created it and sustained it moment by moment (see also Isa. 40:26; Pss 65:9-13; 135:6-7). Hence the weather, for instance, was attributed to Yahweh's work.

● *Paganism* saw the universe as populated by a large number of divine beings, each with different areas which they controlled – the weather, the sea, the crops, particular nations, the stars or planets, etc. The Greek and Roman pantheons were like this, with many gods. With this belief went the view that these gods were capricious – their reactions depended on how they were feeling. So people sought ways to placate the gods in order to persuade them to act kindly. By contrast, Gen. 1 portrays Yahweh as the creator of these elements within the universe, including the sun, moon and stars (vv. 14-18; cf. Isa. 40:26), thus claiming that the pagan 'gods' were no gods at all.

Providential monotheism

Judaism was and is committed to the belief that this one true God reigns. He is the true ruler of the universe, and he orders its existence in line with his purposes (e.g. Pss 10:6; 22:28; 93:1; 96:10). God's usual way of reigning is to work in and through 'natural' events; hence he can be said to be responsible for the rise and fall of kings and emperors in *all* the nations (e.g. Isa. 40:22-24; 45:1-8). Indeed, Amos claims, 'Does a disaster befall a city unless the Lord has done it?' (3:6). Yahweh is no absentee landlord, but is working within the world to bring about his desires.

But that raised a large question: if God was truly ordering the events of the world, why was there so much evil in the world? Was Yahweh powerless to do anything about it or did he not care? Jews rejected both of those alternatives in favour of the belief in election, the second major mark of their faith.

GOD HAS CHOSEN ISRAEL

Election is the belief that the creator of the universe has chosen Israel to be his people, and has committed himself solemnly to them by a covenant. This is how Judaism understood God's response to evil, and it is worthwhile noticing that the biblical authors in both OT and NT are much more

interested in *what* God is doing about evil than in *where* evil came from. Philosophical questions about the origin of evil are rarely touched on in the Bible; rather, evil is recognized as a reality which God is acting to bring to an end.

The means Yahweh is using to bring evil to an end is the people of Israel. God called this people to be his own special people through their ancestor Abraham, in order that the creation order might be restored. In three key passages God promises to Abraham that he will have many descendants (Gen. 15:1-6), that the whole earth will be blessed through him and his family (Gen. 12:1-3), and that the nation descended from him will be given their own land (Gen. 15:17-21). Thus the purpose of calling Israel was not for the nation's own sake, but so that they might be a light to the world, enabling the world to respond to its creator God (e.g. Isa. 42:6; 49:6; 51:4).

Not only had Yahweh called the nation into being as his own people, he had saved them from danger time after time. The great Jewish festivals – many celebrated in the home – focus on the occasions when God had acted in history to keep his people safe, bringing them freedom (see pp. 35f.). The language used for this is often 'redeem' and 'redemption', which means 'to buy back': God redeemed the people from slavery in Egypt through the leadership of Moses at the Exodus. The return from the Babylonian exile of the sixth century BC was pictured using 'new Exodus' language, suggesting that God was doing again what he had done in the time of Moses (Isa. 40–55). Year by year, the festivals recalled the Jews to their destiny by reminding them graphically of how Yahweh had saved them.

The vision of the world being blessed through Israel had not been lost, however, and the later OT prophets pictured the nations coming to Jerusalem or to Zion, the mountain on which the city was built, to meet with God:

> Thus says the LORD of hosts: Peoples shall yet come, the inhabitants of many cities; the inhabitants of one city shall go to another, saying, 'Come, let us go to entreat the favour of the LORD, and to seek the LORD of hosts; I myself am going.' Many peoples and strong nations shall come to seek the LORD of hosts in Jerusalem, and to entreat the favour of the LORD. Thus says the LORD of hosts: In those days ten men from nations of every language shall take hold of a Jew, grasping his garment and saying, 'Let us go with you, for we have heard that God is with you.' (Zech. 8:20-23)

The expression of God's commitment to Israel was in the form of a covenant. This was a commitment marked by solemn oaths (cf. Gen. 15:17-21). Human covenants could be between equals, or between a conquering army and a conquered people; God's covenant with Israel is most like the second type – hence the later chapters of Deuteronomy promise good things to the people if they keep the terms of the covenant (28:1-14; 30:1-10) and bad things if they break the conditions of the covenant (27:14-26; 28:15-68; 29:17-28).

In this covenant arrangement, it is striking to modern westerners how little the individual is spoken about. A major cultural value inherent in God making a commitment to a nation is that of solidarity – and Jews (in common with most ancient people, and many in the non-western world today) saw themselves first and foremost as members of the people, their tribe and their clan, and only secondarily as individuals.

GOD HAS PROVIDED A WAY TO LIVE

The law (or torah) was God's gracious gift to the people he had chosen and redeemed, in order to show them how he wished his people to live (Deut. 7:7-11), and it was highly prized by first-century Jews. Israel was not meant to see keeping the law as a way of *becoming* the people of God, as is clear from the introduction to the ten commandments:

> I am the LORD your God, who brought you out of the land of Egypt, out of the house of slavery; you shall have no other gods before me. (Exod. 20:2-3)

The commandments are being given to a people who are *already* the people of God, for he has brought them out of slavery in Egypt to be his own people. They are given so that they may know how to conduct their national, family and individual lives in line with God's will. Keeping the law was a, arguably *the*, key marker of being a member of God's people, for the torah set Israel apart from the other nations.

During the Babylonian exile worship had begun to centre more on reading the torah and prayer than on the temple services – for there was no Jewish temple in Babylon. The return from exile established the centrality of the law to Jewish worship, particularly through the work of Ezra the scribe (see Neh. 8). This developed over the years into the institution of the synagogue, a meeting for worship focused on the reading of Scripture and prayer. It became particularly important in diaspora Judaism – for they lacked access to the Jerusalem temple – but was also important in the land of Israel itself, as we know from Jesus' regular attendance (Luke 4:16).

Three facets of the law were particularly important by the time of Jesus – namely circumcision, the Sabbath and the food laws – and these were treated as 'boundary markers' which showed who truly belonged to the one true God. In circumcizing baby boys on the eighth day a physical mark was being imposed on a child which identified him as Jewish, and the OT traces this ceremony back to Abraham, the father of the nation (Gen. 17:9-14). So when Antiochus made circumcision illegal in 167 BC (1 Macc. 1:60-61), he was directly attacking the distinctiveness of Judaism. Similarly, a concern among devout Jews about the impact of Greek culture was that it led to

THE 'NEW PERSPECTIVE' ON JUDAISM

This sketch of the Jews' view of their law represents a picture which has been redrawn in the last 25 years, particularly through the work of E. P. Sanders (notably in his key books Sanders 1977; Sanders 1992; for a helpful summary, see Dunn 1990, ch. 7). Prior to Sanders it was common for NT scholars to present Judaism as a religion of 'book keeping', which sought to do good deeds in order to earn God's favour. It is now widely argued that this picture of Judaism stems from reading debates in the NT about works and faith (particularly in Paul) through the spectacles of sixteenth-century debates between Luther and the Roman Church, and assuming that the questions Luther was addressing in sixteenth-century Germany were the same as those tackled by Paul in the first-century world. This approach can easily treat first-century Judaism as though it was attempting to accumulate 'merit' by keeping the law, so that those who do this will be welcomed by God at the Last Day – as Luther understood the Roman Church of his day to believe.

By contrast, Sanders re-reads the Jewish texts and finds a rather different picture, which he calls 'covenantal nomism'. Sanders argues for a distinction between keeping the law as the means of *getting into* a covenant relationship with God (which was the older view of Judaism) and keeping the law as the means of *maintaining* a covenant relationship with God which has been established by God's generosity and grace. Thus by 'covenantal nomism' he means:

> … the view that one's place in God's plan is established on the basis of the covenant and that the covenant requires as the proper response of man his obedience to its commandments, while providing means of atonement for transgression … *obedience maintains one's position in the covenant, but it does not earn God's grace as such.* It simply keeps an individual in the group which is the recipient of God's grace. (Sanders 1977, 75, 420)

While he has been very influential, not everyone is persuaded by Sanders. Since the literary sources we have are likely to come from highly educated circles within Judaism, it is certainly possible that there was a 'legalistic' stream within popular Judaism, as there can be in some popular forms of modern Christianity. Some also argue that the texts which Sanders reads within a 'covenantal nomism' framework may speak of the importance of keeping the law for final salvation. (See more fully D. Moo *The Epistle to the Romans*. New International Commentary on the NT. Grand Rapids/Cambridge: Eerdmans, 1996, 214-17.)

Nevertheless, recent interpretations of Jesus and Paul take Sanders' points very seriously, and work hard at ensuring that first-century Jewish beliefs are understood on their own terms, rather than through the eyes of later debates.

young Jewish men who trained in gymnasiums (where the athletes were naked) trying to remove the marks of circumcision so as to avoid ridicule because they were Jews:

> In those days certain renegades came out from Israel and misled many, saying, 'Let us go and make a covenant with the Gentiles around us, for since we separated from them many disasters have come upon us.' This proposal pleased them, and some of the people eagerly went to the king, who authorized them to observe the ordinances of the Gentiles. *So they built a gymnasium in Jerusalem, according to Gentile custom, and removed the marks of circumcision, and abandoned the holy covenant.* They joined with the Gentiles and sold themselves to do evil. (1 Macc. 1:11-15, italics mine)

Resting on the Sabbath day (Saturday) was also important to devout Jews, for that was commanded both in creation (Gen. 2:2-3) and in the ten commandments (Exod. 20:8-11). During the Maccabean revolt, one group of faithful Jews even refused to defend themselves on the Sabbath, and as a result were killed (1 Macc. 1:31-38).

The food laws required Jews to eat only 'kosher' meat, which came from certain kinds of animals and which had had the blood drained out of it first (see Lev. 11:1-23; Deut. 14:3-21). They were forbidden to eat meat from other animals, particularly pigs, which were regarded as 'unclean' (Deut. 14:8). Jews therefore refused to eat with non-Jews, for they could not be confident that the meat they were eating was 'kosher' (and this is the probable background to the disputes about Jewish Christians eating with Gentile Christians in Gal. 2:11-14). Again, Antiochus Epiphanes

made it illegal to keep these laws and therefore met with resistance from devout Jews (1 Macc. 1:62-63).

The Maccabean crisis was still very strong in folk memory in the time of Jesus as a period when commitment to keeping the law had preserved the nation's identity and led to deliverance by God from the Gentiles. Mattathias, the initiator of the revolt, used 'zeal for the law' as a slogan around which the people rallied:

> Thus [Mattathias] burned with zeal for the law, just as Phinehas did against Zimri son of Salu. Then Mattathias cried out in the town with a loud voice, saying: 'Let every one who is zealous for the law and supports the covenant come out with me!' … Now the days drew near for Mattathias to die, and he said to his sons: 'Arrogance and scorn have now become strong; it is a time of ruin and furious anger. Now, my children, show zeal for the law, and give your lives for the covenant of our ancestors.' (1 Macc. 2:26-27, 49-50)

Likewise, Judas Maccabeus, the key Jewish leader in the revolt, saw the law as one of the key things his troops fought to defend:

> So, committing the decision to the Creator of the world and exhorting his [Judas'] troops to *fight bravely to the death for the laws*, temple, city, country, and commonwealth, he pitched his camp near Modein. (2 Macc. 13:14, italics mine)

For faithful Jews, keeping the law was vital for two reasons: first, to maintain their standing within the community of God's people, those whom he would redeem when he acted to free Israel from her present bondage under the Romans. Second,

The Temple Mount AD 70
(elevation viewed from the south-west)

Reconstruction by Leon Ritmeyer (with permission)

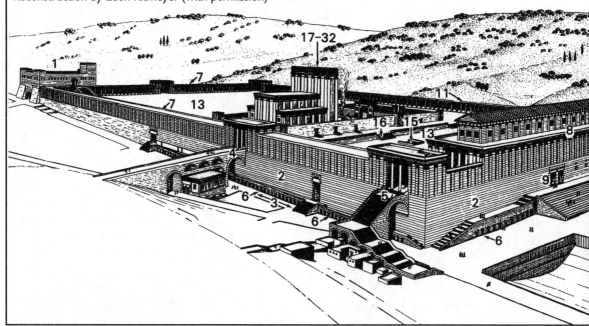

KEY TO THE PLANS OF HEROD'S TEMPLE

1 The Antonia fortress
2 Retaining wall
3 'West Wall Street'
4 'Wilson's Arch', spanning the Tyropoeon Valley
5 'Robinson's Arch', which leads to the street below
6 Shops
7 Porticoes (stoas)
8 The Royal Portico
9 The exit gate
10 The entrance gate
11 'Solomon's Portico' (pre-Herodian)
12 The Mount of Olives
13 The Court of the Gentiles
14 The entrance to the platform, connected by a tunnel to no. 10
15 The exit from the platform, connected by a tunnel to no. 9
16 Steps and balustrade prohibiting Gentiles
17 Inner platform and steps
18 Inner wall
19 First eastern gate, through which male Israelites entered

20 Southern and northern gates, through which female Israelites entered
21 Court of the Women
22 Inner porticoes (stoas)
23 Wall separating Court of the Women from male area
24 Second eastern gate, through which male Israelites entered. There may have been a barrier from 19 to 24, preventing men and women from mingling in the Women's Court, and there may have been a gallery on top of 23, allowing women to see the priests at work.
25 The altar for burnt sacrifices
26 Court for the (ordinary, male) Israelites
27 Parapet separating priests from ordinary Israelites
28 Court of the Priests
29 The façade and entrance to the sanctuary
30 The first chamber (with incense altar and candelabrum)
31 The holy of holies
32 Upper floors

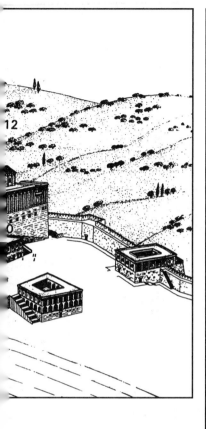

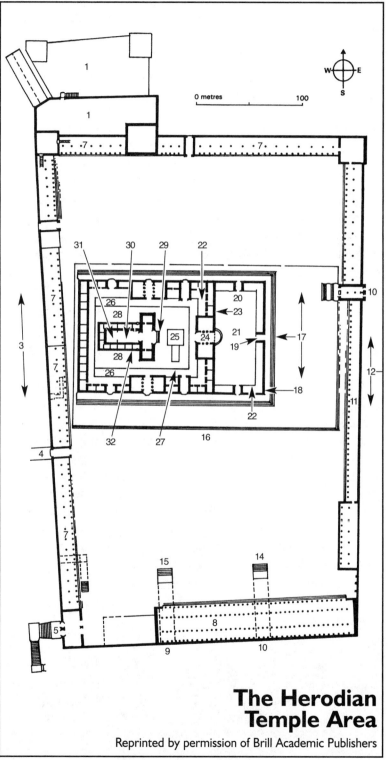

0 metres   100

The Herodian Temple Area

Reprinted by permission of Brill Academic Publishers

maintaining the distinctives of the torah – circumcision, the Sabbath and the food laws – preserved Jewish national identity at a time of pagan rule. So at the time of Jesus the law was central to Judaism; it would be hard to overstate its importance.

As Sanders clearly says above, this understanding of Judaism requires that there should be means for dealing with sin, and this was the role of animal sacrifices, particularly for Jews located in Israel itself. For Jews in the diaspora, spread around the Mediterranean basin, prayer and good works often took the place of sacrifice, since those Jews did not have ready access to the Jerusalem temple.

GOD HAS GIVEN THE PEOPLE A LAND, FOCUSED IN THE TEMPLE

A key element in God's covenant with Abraham was the promise of a land:

> Now the LORD said to Abram, 'Go from your country and your kindred and your father's house to the land that I will show you.' (Gen. 12:1)

> On that day the LORD made a covenant with Abram, saying, 'To your descendants I give this land, from the river of Egypt to the great river, the river Euphrates, the land of the Kenites, the Kenizzites, the Kadmonites, the Hittites, the Perizzites, the Rephaim, the Amorites, the Canaanites, the Girgashites, and the Jebusites.' (Gen. 15:18-21)

God renewed this promise with Moses at the time of the Exodus (Exod. 3:8), and it became a key element in Judaism. Thus, Deuteronomy records a warning that if the people were unfaithful to God, they would be scattered from the land (Deut. 28:64), as well as a promise that if they were exiled in another land and genuinely turned away from their misdeeds and wholeheartedly returned to God, God would bring them back to the land (Deut. 30:1-5; cf. 1 Kgs 8:33-34). It was through these promises that Jewish thinkers interpreted the exile in Babylon in the sixth century BC and the return some fifty years later – they saw the exile as God's punishment for them breaking the terms of the covenant, and the return to the land under Ezra and Nehemiah as God's gracious act of restoration and forgiveness.

Because the land was promised to them by God, the Jews saw it as holy – for God lived there among them (Numbers 35:34). So to rebel against God by failing to live as the law required was to make the land unclean. Equally, the situation in the first century AD, when Gentiles were in control of the land, was seen as making the land unclean (more fully, see Wright 1992, 226-7).

The temple

Within the land, the city of Jerusalem held a special place and within the city, the temple was seen as the jewel. The temple was on Mount Zion, and God had placed his 'name' there – hence the sense of loss during the Babylonian exile, when both city and temple were beyond reach, expressed so powerfully in Ps. 137 (see also 1 Kgs 8:48; 9:3; Isa. 18:7; Matt. 23:21).

The temple had a number of different sections (see plan pp. 32) which only certain groups were allowed to enter. Gentiles were allowed only in the Court of the Gentiles, a large open area which included the Royal Portico, where the traders and money changers probably operated (cf. Mark 11:15-17, esp. v. 17). A series of steps and a balustrade 1.5

metres high led up to another courtyard, within which the main buildings lay. Notices in Hebrew, Latin and Greek on the balustrade forbade Gentiles to go further, and warned that if they did they would likely be killed. Two doorways in the main buildings led into the Court of the Women, where female Jews could go, and a doorway from there led to the Court of Israel, into which only male Jews could go (although women could see into this area and the Court of the Priests, since there was probably a gallery where they could stand). A further parapet separated the Court of Israel from the Court of the Priests, into which only priests were allowed. In this court stood the altar of sacrifice, where animal sacrifices were offered daily. Up a set of steps and through a further doorway lay a chamber containing the incense altar, a table for the shewbread and a candleholder; only priests on duty were permitted in here. Finally, a curtain led into the holy of holies, an unadorned room; only the high priest was allowed to enter here, and only on one day each year. Most Jews saw this room – and the temple more widely – as the symbol of Yahweh living among his people (cf. Matt. 23:21).

The temple was central to the sacrificial system, one of the cornerstones of Judaism. Through the sacrifices offered there atonement and forgiveness were possible (e.g. Lev. 1:4; cf. Heb. 9:22). Sacrifice was a daily ritual performed by the priests, who were divided into 24 teams (or 'courses') on a weekly duty rota for offering sacrifice (cf. Luke 1:8, 23). (Sanders 1992, 78 estimates that there were about 20,000 priests and Levites at the time of Jesus.) The daily sacrifices climaxed in the annual ritual of the Day of Atonement (*Yom Kippur*), when the whole people spent the day fasting and sorrowing for their sins (see Lev. 23:26-32).

During that day the high priest entered into the Holy of Holies, and offered the blood from special sacrifices to atone for the people's sins during the previous year – the only time when anyone entered this place where God was thought specially to dwell.

The temple was supported by a temple tax of one half-shekel for each adult male, which Jews throughout the Roman empire paid annually (cf. Matt 17:24). The amount was roughly two days' wages for a labourer (Sanders 1992, 156).

The festivals

Each year there were three pilgrim festivals, when devout Jews would come to Jerusalem to worship, plus other festivals celebrated at home. Each commemorated a key action of God for his people. While not every Jew went every year to every pilgrim festival, most Palestinian Jews would try to be in Jerusalem for at least one a year, and diaspora Jews would plan to be in Jerusalem at least some times in their lives – and the most popular was Passover: Luke notes that Jesus' parents went each year for this festival (Luke 2:41). The population of the city would swell massively at festival time: Sanders (1992, 125-128) estimates conservatively that there were between 300,000 and 500,000 in the city for Passover, compared with a regular population of perhaps 120,000.

Passover (in March/April) celebrated God bringing the people out of slavery in Egypt, led by Moses – the event which the Jews saw as marking them as God's people. It lasted one day, but led into the week-long Festival of Unleavened Bread, when the Jews ate bread baked without yeast. Year by year this festival reinforced and heightened the Jews' hopes for a new liberation from the pagan Romans who occupied the land.

Fifty days later *Pentecost* or the *Festival of Weeks* (in May/June) was the Jewish 'harvest festival', when they gave thanks to God for the first crops from the land. This festival declared that the land given to the Jews was God's – and thus renewed and celebrated their sense of God's choice of them. There is some evidence that Pentecost was also celebrated as a festival of the giving of the law to Moses on Sinai, although this is not certain as early as the NT period.

The third major pilgrim festival was the *Festival of Tabernacles or Booths* (in September/October), taking place five days after the Day of Atonement. During an eight-day period people lived in booths made from branches (Lev. 23:42; Neh.8:15), culminating in a great celebration on the last day, when work was forbidden. During the festival Scripture was read aloud each day in the temple and many sacrifices were offered. This feast also marked the end of the harvest, and was therefore a joyful occasion.

The other festivals were celebrated in people's own towns and villages in the main. These included the two fasts, *Yom Kippur* (the Day of Atonement) and *Rosh Hashanah*, the New Year festival (September/October), and two other festivals, *Hanukkah* (November/December), a festival commemorating the rededication of the temple in 164 BC following the Maccabean revolt, and *Purim* (February/March), a celebration of God's deliverance of the Jews in Persia at the time of Queen Esther (Esth. 9:24-28).

The temple not the focus for all Jews

However, some Jews saw both the temple and its priesthood as corrupt, particularly because of the compromises with Gentile Roman rulers involved in the appointment of high priests. Such people looked forward to a day when pure worship would again be offered to God on the site of the temple. Prominent were the Essenes, who refused to attend the temple services and some of whom withdrew into their own 'monastic' communities, applying the priestly purity laws to their whole community (see p. 42).

HOPE FOR THE FUTURE

Given that at the time of Jesus Palestinian Jews were virtually prisoners in their own land, it is hardly surprising that most Jews looked to a future time when God would act to save them. They were acutely aware that the great promises of the prophets – particularly Isa. 40–66, Jeremiah and Ezekiel – about God blessing the people by a return from exile had only been partially fulfilled. Yes, they were back in their own land, and had been since the days of Ezra and Nehemiah in the fifth century BC, but they were under Gentile rule and did not have freedom to act as they wished in serving God (see more fully Wright 1992, esp. 268-70). These feelings were similar to those expressed in the days of Nehemiah:

> Here we are, slaves to this day – slaves in the land that you gave to our ancestors to enjoy its fruit and its good gifts. Its rich yield goes to the kings whom you have set over us because of our sins; they have power also over our bodies and over our livestock at their pleasure, and we are in great distress. (Neh.9:36-37)

Similarly, 2 Maccabees (written in the second or first century BC) presents a prayer that God would change the situation:

> Gather together our scattered people, set free those who are slaves among the Gentiles, look on those who are rejected and despised, and let the Gentiles know

that you are our God. Punish those who oppress and are insolent with pride. Plant your people in your holy place, as Moses promised. (2 Macc. 1:27-29)

Elements of hope

This expectation and longing that God would act had five key elements, which together made up this hope for the future or *eschatology*.

- **Hope for the restoration of all twelve tribes of Israel to the land**, and not just the two tribes of Judah and Benjamin. The ten northern tribes had been lost at the defeat and exile of the northern kingdom of Israel by the Assyrians in the eighth century BC, and faithful Jews longed for God to restore his people fully: '… you should be my servant to raise up the tribes of Jacob and to restore the survivors of Israel' (Isa. 49:6a).
- **The conversion, subjugation or destruction of the Gentiles**, so that the one true God's rule would be seen in all the world: 'I will give you as a light to the nations, that my salvation may reach to the end of the earth' (Isa. 49:6b); 'For the nation and kingdom that will not serve you shall perish; those nations shall be utterly laid waste' (Isa. 60:12). This generally did not lead them into outgoing 'evangelism' of Gentiles, but rather a hope that Gentiles would come to Jerusalem, to Mount Zion, to meet God there (e.g. Zech. 8:20-23; Isa. 2:1-3).
- **A new, purified or renewed temple**, for they were aware that the Jerusalem temple, great though it was, could not operate with the freedom the prophets had promised, for the land was polluted by the presence of pagan rulers. For example, 'The glory of Lebanon shall come to you, the cypress, the plane, and the pine, to beautify the place of my

sanctuary; and I will glorify where my feet rest' (Isa. 60:13; cf. 54:12), thus promising that God would bring the most beautiful materials from other nations to decorate the temple ('my sanctuary'), because that was the place where God lived ('where my feet rest').

- **Pure worship**, untainted by Gentiles living in the land as overlords. This vision was not simply (as we might say) of the services of the temple being offered rightly, but of the whole of life bringing honour to God. For example: 'Your people shall all be righteous; they shall possess the land forever. They are the shoot that I planted, the work of my hands, so that I might be glorified' (Isa. 60:12).
- **Messianic expectations** First-century Jews looked forward to God sending a figure or figures who would be the agent of God's deliverance of his people. This person was called 'Messiah', which means 'anointed one', and the dominant expression of this hope was a new king descended from David, the greatest Jewish king. Many – perhaps most – Jews looked for a military leader who would lead the fight to drive the Romans from the land. For others the hope was for a priestly figure who would restore pure worship. In pharisaic circles there seems to have been a hope for a legal and prophetic figure who would introduce true interpretation of the torah. The Qumran community looked for two messianic figures, one priestly and the other prophetic.

(See also pp. 108–11.)

PARTIES AND GROUPS WITHIN FIRST-CENTURY JUDAISM

The core beliefs of first-century Judaism gave rise to debates over *how* God would act to redeem and save his people. With these debates went a fierce argument over *which*

What do you think?
MESSIANIC HOPES

Consider the quotations below. What are the characteristics of the hoped-for Messiah in each?

Behold, O Lord, and raise up to them their king, the son of David, at the time in which you see, O God, that he may reign over Israel your servant. And gird him with strength, that he may shatter unrighteous rulers, and that he may purge Jerusalem from nations that trample her down to destruction. (Pss of Solomon 17:23f)

They shall depart from none of the counsels of the law to walk in the stubbornness of their hearts, but shall be ruled by the primitive precepts in which the men of the Community were first instructed until there shall come the Prophet and the Messiahs of Aaron and Israel. (1QS 9:10f)

In the time of King Herod, after Jesus was born in Bethlehem of Judea, wise men from the east came to Jerusalem, asking, 'Where is the child who has been born king of the Jews?' ... When King Herod heard this, he was frightened, and all Jerusalem with him; and calling together all the chief priests and scribes of the people, he inquired of them where the Messiah was to be born ... Then Herod secretly called for the wise men and learned from them the exact time when the star had appeared. Then he sent them to Bethlehem, saying, 'Go and search diligently for the child; and when you have found him, bring me word so that I may also go and pay him homage.' ... When Herod saw that he had been tricked by the wise men, he was infuriated, and he sent and killed all the children in and around Bethlehem who were two years old or under, according to the time that he had learned from the wise men. (Matt 2:1-4, 7f, 16)

And as for the lion that you saw rousing up out of the forest and roaring and speaking to the eagle and reproving him for his unrighteousness, and as for all his words that you have heard, this is the Messiah whom the Most High has kept until the end of days, who will arise from the posterity of David, and will come and speak to them; he will denounce them for their ungodliness and for their wickedness, and will cast up before them their contemptuous dealings. For first he will set them living before his judgement seat, and when he has reproved them, then he will destroy them. But he will deliver in mercy the remnant of my people, those who have been saved throughout my borders, and he will make them joyful until the end comes, the day of judgement, of which I spoke to you at the beginning. (4 Ezra 12:31-34)

And they said to me, 'Levi, your posterity shall be divided into three offices as a sign of the glory of the Lord who is coming. The first lot shall be great; no other shall be greater than it. The second shall be in the priestly role. But the third shall be granted a new name, because from Judah a king will arise and should found a new priesthood in accord with the gentile model and for all nations. His presence is beloved, as a prophet of the Most High, a descendant of Abraham, our father.' (Testament of Levi 8:11-15)

particular people God would save when he acted. Within Judaism there were sharp disagreements over both of these questions, and these disagreements gave rise to the various parties within Judaism.

Three of the four major groupings occur in the pages of the NT: the Pharisees, Sadducees and revolutionaries; the fourth is the Essenes. A greater source for knowledge of their beliefs is in the writings of Josephus. Overleaf is his description of them, in which he speaks of them as groups of philosophers, hoping thus to help his Graeco-Roman audience understand them better.

PHARISEES

The Pharisees were the largest of the groups within Judaism, possibly having about 6,000 members around the time of Jesus. They get a 'bad press' in the Gospels generally, and modern Christians have come to regard them as the 'bad guys' in the story of Jesus. But this was not how they were seen by the Jews of their day – rather, they were seen as highly religious and devout.

The roots of the pharisaic movement were in the Babylonian exile, when study of the Scriptures became central to Jewish life and worship because there was no temple where sacrifices could be offered. By Jesus' day they were highly significant in the life of the synagogues where Jews worshipped each Sabbath. The Pharisees' focus was on interpreting and applying the torah for everyday life. In doing this they placed great value on oral tradition, which they believed came from the time of Moses, especially concerning ritual purity and giving a tenth of one's property to God (tithing). The Pharisees met on Friday evenings (the beginning of the Jewish Sabbath) in small groups known as *Haburoth* to eat, study the

Scriptures and pray together.

While they accepted the priesthood of the Jerusalem temple, they believed that it was not pure, and so they sought to reform it. However, they had little political power within Judaism, so they had to work by persuasion: there were, for example, few Pharisees in the Sanhedrin, the main Jewish ruling council (Saul of Tarsus may have been one such, see Acts 26:10). The Pharisees' lack of political power may explain why Saul needed letters from the high priest in order to persecute Christians in another city (Acts 9:1-2). Their lack of political power also ties in with their need to collaborate with the Herodians in plotting against Jesus (Mark 3:6).

The Pharisees believed firmly in a future resurrection from the dead and in angelic beings (cf. Acts 23:8). Their hope was solid and earthly, and seems to have agreed with the mainstream Jewish hope (by contrast with the Sadducees, see below). They also looked forward to a messianic figure who would be a great teacher of the law, expressed particularly in the Psalms of Solomon, a book which seems to have come from pharisaic circles during the first century BC.

However, we should not regard the Pharisees simply as an 'other worldly' pietistic movement: in the first century AD some of them (the school of Shammai) were also heavily politicized. In common with other Jews they longed for the Romans to be removed from the land, and on occasion Pharisees were key figures in violent revolts or riots.

The Pharisees, then, were a separatist group, both in name – their name probably meant 'separatists' – and in theology and

Digging deeper:
JOSEPHUS ON THE JEWISH PARTIES

Make notes on the key characteristics of the parties according to Josephus from his description of them below (from *Antiquities* 18.1.2-6 =18:11-25, Whiston's translation). Then use a Bible concordance to find the references to the Pharisees in Luke and Acts, and compare what you have found about the Pharisees from Josephus with what Luke says. What does Josephus tell us that we don't know from Luke, and vice versa? What perspective does Luke have on the Pharisees?

The Jews had for a great while three sects of philosophy peculiar to themselves; the sect of the Essenes, and the sect of the Sadducees, and the third sort of opinions was that of those called Pharisees; of which sects, although I have already spoken in the second book of the Jewish War, yet will I a little touch upon them now.

Now, for the Pharisees, they live meanly, and despise delicacies in diet; and they follow the conduct of reason; and what that prescribes to them as good for them they do; and they think they ought earnestly to strive to observe reason's dictates for practice. They also pay a respect to such as are in years; nor are they so bold as to contradict them in any thing which they have introduced; and when they determine that all things are done by fate, they do not take away the freedom from men of acting as they think fit; since

their notion is, that it hath pleased God to make a temperament, whereby what he wills is done, but so that the will of man can act virtuously or viciously. They also believe that souls have an immortal rigour in them, and that under the earth there will be rewards or punishments, according as they have lived virtuously or viciously in this life; and the latter are to be detained in an everlasting prison, but that the former shall have power to revive and live again; on account of which doctrines they are able greatly to persuade the body of the people; and whatsoever they do about Divine worship, prayers, and sacrifices, they perform them according to their direction; insomuch that the cities give great attestations to them on account of their entire virtuous conduct, both in the actions of their lives and their discourses also.

But the doctrine of the Sadducees is this: That souls die with the bodies; nor do they regard the observation of any thing besides what the law enjoins them; for they think it an instance of virtue to dispute with those teachers of philosophy whom they frequent: but this doctrine is received but by a few, yet by those still of the greatest dignity. But they are able to do almost nothing of themselves; for when they become magistrates, as they are unwillingly and by force sometimes obliged to be, they addict themselves to the notions of the Pharisees, because the multitude would not otherwise bear them.

practice, seeking separation from impure Jews and from the pagans.

SADDUCEES

By contrast with the Pharisees, the Sadducees had their hands on the levers of political power. They were Jerusalem-based and very influential in the councils of the Jews (many members of the Sanhedrin were sadducean); they were the 'establishment' of their day. Many of the group were priests (although a good number of priests were not Sadducees) – quite possibly the name 'Sadducees' comes from the priestly family of 'Zadokites'. Generally their members were wealthy, and the result was that they were politically

The doctrine of the Essenes is this: That all things are best ascribed to God. They teach the immortality of souls, and esteem that the rewards of righteousness are to be earnestly striven for; and when they send what they have dedicated to God into the temple, they do not offer sacrifices because they have more pure lustrations of their own; on which account they are excluded from the common court of the temple, but offer their sacrifices themselves; yet is their course of life better than that of other men; and they entirely addict themselves to husbandry. It also deserves our admiration, how much they exceed all other men that addict themselves to virtue, and this in righteousness; and indeed to such a degree, that as it hath never appeared among any other men, neither Greeks nor barbarians, no, not for a little time, so hath it endured a long while among them. This is demonstrated by that institution of theirs, which will not suffer any thing to hinder them from having all things in common; so that a rich man enjoys no more of his own wealth than he who hath nothing at all. There are about four thousand men that live in this way, and neither marry wives, nor are desirous to keep servants; as thinking the latter tempts men to be unjust, and the former gives the handle to domestic quarrels; but as they live by themselve

certain stewards to receive the incomes of their revenues, and of the fruits of the ground; such as are good men and priests, who are to get their corn and their food ready for them. They none of them differ from others of the Essenes in their way of living, but do the most resemble those Dacae who are called Polistae [dwellers in cities].

But of the fourth sect of Jewish philosophy, Judas the Galilean was the author. These men agree in all other things with the Pharisaic notions; but they have an inviolable attachment to liberty, and say that God is to be their only Ruler and Lord. They also do not value dying any kinds of death, nor indeed do they heed the deaths of their relations and friends, nor can any such fear make them call any man Lord. And since this immovable resolution of theirs is well known to a great many, I shall speak no further about that matter; nor am I afraid that any thing I have said of them should be disbelieved, but rather fear, that what I have said is beneath the resolution they show when they undergo pain. And it was in Gessius Florus's time that the nation began to grow mad with this distemper, who was our procurator, and who occasioned the Jews to go wild with it by the abuse of his authority, and to make them revolt from the Romans. And these are the sects of Jewish philosophy.

quietist. They did not 'rock the boat' because their positions were secure under Roman rule; indeed, they collaborated closely with the Roman occupying power. This made them nervous of revolutionaries and of people who appeared to be anti-establishment.

When we find mention of the Sadducees in

Jewish literature (and in the NT) – and there are relatively few such references – their beliefs are often discussed, probably because they were thought unusual. They rejected the oral traditions which the Pharisees valued so much and, though they accepted the books of the OT as Scripture, in practice they only accepted beliefs which could be demonstrated from the first five books of our OT, the Pentateuch. They did not believe in resurrection from the dead or in angelic beings (cf. Acts 23:8) – hence the sadducean story about the woman who was wife to seven brothers successively (Mark 12:18-23), which was designed to mock the idea of resurrection. Indeed, the Sadducees seem to have had little future hope at all – not untypical of people who are very comfortable in this life!

ESSENES

The Essenes represent a radical wing of Jewish life and thought. They regarded the Jerusalem-based priesthood and temple as hopelessly corrupt and withdrew from it entirely. With their rejection of the temple went a form of worship without the normal sacrifices. They set up communities in various parts of the land similar in style to later monasteries. Most scholars regard the group of about 200 at Qumran, near the Dead Sea, as Essenes – this was the group which wrote and copied the Dead Sea Scrolls. There is also a strong possibility that there was an Essene quarter in Jerusalem during the time of Jesus (Capper 1995, esp. 341-50).

The rules of life in these communities were strict, applying the priestly purity laws to the whole group, including bathing before meals, and those who broke them could be expelled. They were strongly hierarchical, with unquestioning obedience to superiors being expected, and focused their community life on study of the Scriptures.

The Essenes had a two-part 'noviciate' lasting at least two years to prepare people to be full members of the community, for community life was very demanding. They were known as 'despisers of riches' and were highly ascetic, in some cases having no private property. Some – though not all –

were celibate. Common meals were a strong feature of their life together.

Biblical commentaries were an important product of the Qumran community, using a method known as 'pesher', which identified the testimony of Scripture with contemporary events. A key figure is the 'Teacher of Righteousness', a priest who seems to have been a founder and inspiration of the Essenes in the mid-second century BC.

They looked forward to a war between the 'sons of darkness' and the 'sons of light', through which Yahweh would establish pure worship and a reformed temple. However, they were not plotting to initiate violent revolution – they believed that God would act to bring this about through two messianic figures: the 'War Scroll' (1QM) describes their expectations. The Qumran group – and likely other Essenes too – believed that they were the only people whom Yahweh would redeem when he acted in this way. With this went a strong belief in resurrection and a future life.

THE 'FOURTH PHILOSOPHY': THE REVOLUTIONARIES

For several hundred years the land had been occupied by pagans, ranging from the invasions of the north by the Babylonians in the eighth century BC and of the south by the Persians in the sixth century BC, through to the Roman occupation at the time of Jesus. Given the importance for the Jews of the land as God's gift to them, it is hardly surprising that there was a strong under-current of armed revolt against the pagan occupying forces throughout this period. Add to that the burden of Roman taxes, which were widely resented, and we can see why this undercurrent came to the surface in revolt of various kinds at different times.

A key slogan for these groups seems to have been 'No king but God', thus opposing the claims of Yahweh to those of Caesar.

By the lifetime of Jesus there were a variety of groups who took arms to free the land from the pollution of the pagans. Josephus groups them together as 'the fourth philosophy'. One of the first identifiable groups was that led by Judas of Galilee in AD 6 (Josephus, *JW* 2:117-118 = 2.8.1; cf. Acts 5:37). This group was typical, in that there was a leader who claimed to be Messiah. Most such movements were suppressed by the Roman army killing both leader and followers, lest another should be chosen as leader.

A similar group was the Sicarii, a word meaning 'dagger-men', who killed leading Jewish officials whom they thought were collaborating with the Romans. According to Josephus (*JW* 2:254-7 = 2.13.3) they were active while Festus was procurator, 20–30 years after the death of Jesus (cf. Acts 21:38). Josephus attributes the beginning of the Jewish war against Rome of AD 66-74 to the actions of the Sicarii.

Many speak of 'Zealots' as a term for the revolutionary groups in this period. Strictly the term should be used only for the time of the Jewish war from AD 66 onwards, when there was a specific party of this name committed to violent revolution against the Romans. The term does seem to have been used earlier in a more general sense, for those who were 'zealous' for the torah and were willing to act violently for that cause (cf. Luke 6:15).

While generally the Romans did what they could to pacify the Jews – for it was in their interests to have a co-operative population in this outpost of the empire – a number of key actions were deliberately or accidentally highly provocative. Pontius Pilate was notorious in this regard (see pp. 18f. and Wright 1992, 174f.).

> **What do you think?**
> **THE REVOLUTIONARIES**
>
> Imagine yourself to be a first-century Jewish revolutionary. How would you respond to Jesus' answer about paying taxes (Luke 20:20-25) and why?

COMMON JUDAISM

Josephus reports that there were over 6,000 Pharisees at a time when the total population in the land was perhaps 500,000-600,000. The Jewish population of the Roman empire at this time is estimated at 3.5 million. It seems likely, therefore, that most Jews were not members of the parties at all, since they were too busy just surviving. Their religion was expressed in a number of ways which can be summed up as 'taking trouble over the torah' (cf. Rom. 10:2).

Thus those who identified themselves as Jews would keep the Sabbath and attend synagogue, pray, keep the food laws, circumcize their baby boys on the eighth day, keep the festivals and fasts, and go to Jerusalem for at least some festivals. Those in the diaspora would make it their aim to attend festivals in Jerusalem some times in their lives, regarding it as a sacred pilgrimage.

All would look forward to a day when Yahweh would again act to redeem them from the pagan Romans, so that they would be free in their land, free to keep the torah given to them by God. Their hope for this would focus on a Messiah, one who came from God to lead them into liberation. Into that setting, Jesus walked, announcing that the time had come and God's reign was arriving (Mark 1:15).

FURTHER READING

INTRODUCTORY
DJG articles: 'Apocalyptic', 'Dead Sea Scrolls', 'Judaism', 'Pharisees', 'Revolutionary Movements', 'Sanhedrin', 'Scribes', 'Taxes', 'Temple' (helpful survey articles)

L. L. Grabbe *An Introduction to First Century Judaism: Jewish Religion and History in the Second Temple Period*. Edinburgh: T. & T. Clark, 1996 (valuable brief overview).

INTERMEDIATE
B. J. Capper "The Palestinian Cultural Context of Earliest Christian Community of Goods." In *The Book of Acts in its Palestinian Setting* ed. R. Bauckham. The Book of Acts in its First-Century Setting, vol. 4. Grand Rapids/Carlisle: Eerdmans/Paternoster, 1995, 323-56 (a well-argued case for the presence of Essenes in Jerusalem).

J. D. G. Dunn *Jesus, Paul and the Law: Studies in Mark and Galatians*. London: SPCK/ Louisville: Westminster John Knox Press, 1990, ch. 7 (valuable summary of the 'new perspective' on Judaism).

J. D. G. Dunn *The Partings of the Ways: Between Christianity and Judaism and Their Significance for the Character of Christianity*. London: SCM/Philadelphia: Trinity Press International, 1991 (some helpful studies of particular parts of Jewish-Christian interface and conflict).

E. P. Sanders *Judaism: Practice and Belief 63 BCE-66 CE*. London: SCM/ Philadelphia: Trinity Press International, 1992 (a thorough and valuable study of Judaism in our period).

J. J. Scott, Jr *Customs and Controversies: Intertestamental Jewish Backgrounds of the New Testament*. Grand Rapids: Baker, 1995 (helpful survey of key areas).

J. C. VanderKam *The Dead Sea Scrolls Today*. Grand Rapids: Eerdmans/London: SPCK, 1994 (helpful introduction and overview of the Scrolls).

N. T. Wright *The New Testament and the People of God*. Christian Origins and the Question of God, vol. 1. London: SPCK/Philadelphia: Fortress, 1992, chs 7-10 (a judicious and well-written portrait of Jewish thought and life in our period).

TEXTS IN ENGLISH TRANSLATION
Some of these texts are also available on the Christian Classics Ethereal Library Web site, http://www.ccel.org

C. K. Barrett, ed. *The New Testament Background*, revised ed. London: SPCK, 1987/New York: HarperSanFrancisco, 1995 (an excellent collection of source material).

R. H. Charles, ed. *The Apocrypha and Pseudepigrapha of the Old Testament*, 2 vols. Oxford: Clarendon Press, 1913 (an older translation of many intertestamental Jewish texts).

J. H. Charlesworth, ed. *The Old Testament Pseudepigrapha*, 2 vols. New York: Doubleday, 1983, 1985 (a fuller modern collection of intertestamental Jewish texts).

H. Danby *The Mishnah*. London: Oxford University Press, 1933 (the standard older translation).

J. Neusner *The Mishnah: A New Translation*. New Haven & London: Yale University Press, 1988 (a good newer translation).

G. Vermes, ed. *The Complete Dead Sea Scrolls in English*. London: Allen Lane, 1997 (paperback ed: London/New York: Penguin, 1998) (readable and reliable translations of all the non-biblical scrolls by one of the top Scrolls scholars).

W. Whiston *The Works of Josephus*, revised ed. Peabody, MA: Hendrickson, 1987 (a new edition of an older translation).

C. D. Yonge *The Works of Philo*. Peabody, MA: Hendrickson, 1993 (a reprint of an older translation).

Section B

APPROACHING THE GOSPELS

Chapter 3

WHAT ARE THE GOSPELS?

In reading the Gospels we need to be alert to the kind of books that they are. In this chapter we shall:

- consider the meaning of the term 'gospel' in the ancient world and Christian use;
- see how far the NT Gospels are like other ancient books;
- see ways in which the NT Gospels are distinctive among ancient writings;
- examine the reasons for the writing of the four Gospels;
- look briefly at other Gospels which were not accepted into the NT by the early churches.

Matthew, Mark, Luke and John are the first books called 'Gospels': what does this mean? Why were they given this description? And what expectations would an ancient reader have of a book with this title? These questions add up to asking about the literary *genre* to which the Gospels belong. Three reasons demonstrate that this is important.

First, what readers expect to find in a book is determined by their initial perception of what kind of book it is. This expectation comes from reading the introduction to the book, seeing the writing style used and examining the literary structure. Thus, a modern reader will have a quite different approach to reading poetry compared to reading a newspaper report of a political event. Similarly, an ancient reader would expect different things from, for example, Thucydides' historical account of the Peloponnesian war and Aristotle's handbook for students on rhetoric.

Second, knowing something about the genre of a work can help us, reading centuries later, to enter into how the ancient author and ancient readers would experience the book. Genre forms an implicit 'contract' between writer and readers, with shared expectations, which enables good communication to take place – expectations which are modified as the readers read and re-read the book.

Third, a knowledge of genre means that we can recognize when something new is being done. Authors can and do break the bounds of established literary genres and introduce fresh elements or even new genres – and we shall see that some argue the Gospels do precisely this. We shall need to be alert to such novelties in considering the genre of the Gospels.

WHAT DOES 'GOSPEL' MEAN?

To the first Christians it would be a great surprise to find a book called 'gospel', since for them 'gospel' meant the gospel *message*. The word itself (Greek *euangelion*) means 'good news' and was used in Graeco-Roman literature for announcements such as the accession of a new emperor. In Jewish writings the cognate verb (Greek *euangelizomai*) is used in announcing the coming of Yahweh to save his people (e.g. Isa. 40:9; 52:7; Joel 2:32; Nah. 1:15).

GOOD NEWS OF AN EMPEROR

The emperor Augustus is praised in an inscription from Priene (c.9 BC):

> providence … created … the most perfect good for our lives … filling him [Augustus] with virtue for the benefit of mankind, sending us and those after us a saviour who put an end to war and established all things … and whereas the birthday of the god [i.e. Augustus] marked for the world the beginning of good tidings through his coming…

Translation from N. Lewis & M. Reinhold, eds, *Roman Civilization II*. New York: Harper & Row, 1955, 64.

Throughout Paul's letters, which are the oldest books of the NT, the noun 'gospel' means the Christian message about the coming, life, death and resurrection of Jesus which Paul and others preach (e.g. Rom. 1:1-4, 16; 1 Cor. 15:1; 2 Cor. 2:12), and the verb 'I proclaim good news' is used for announcing this message orally (e.g. Rom. 1:15; 1 Cor. 1:17; 9:16).

So how did a word associated with a spoken message become the title of a written book?

The first step towards answering this is to recognize that when Matthew, Mark, Luke and John first appeared in writing, they were not labelled as 'Gospels'. That title was attached to them later, when they were collected together, and each was seen as an expression of the one gospel (message) of Jesus, but told 'according to Matthew', 'according to Mark', etc.

To answer this question fully, we need to consider two main approaches to the genre of the Gospels. The first considers the similarities which the Gospels have with other forms of ancient writings; the second focuses on the distinctive features of the Gospels when compared with such works.

THE GOSPELS AS LIKE OTHER ANCIENT LITERATURE

There is a long tradition in scholarship of comparing the Gospels with other ancient writings, and for good reason. Looking for features which the Gospels share with other literature is natural, since if they were totally unlike any other books which were known in antiquity, it might have been harder for them to find acceptance by readers.

What do you think?
THE GOSPELS AND TODAY'S LITERATURE

From your knowledge of the Gospels, which forms of today's writing and literature do you think are most similar to them? If you were writing a modern 'Gospel' to explain the story and significance of Jesus to non-Christian readers, what form of literary presentation do you think would be most appropriate and why?

Christopher Evans imagines a librarian in the famous library in ancient Alexandria encountering Mark for the first time and having to decide with which other writings to shelve it. Like other ancient (and modern) literature, a book would not necessarily have a genre label attached to it (e.g. a modern novel does not usually have the word 'novel' on its cover), so the librarian would have to compare the style and contents of Mark with those found in other books.

Three particular kinds of literature might be considered as potential parallels to the Gospels, and therefore places for the librarian to put Mark and the others.

First, the 'acts' (Greek *praxeis*), which were books giving accounts of great historical figures and their deeds. In the second century AD Arrian wrote his *Anabasis* about the military campaigns and battles of Alexander the Great, the brilliant Greek general of the fourth century BC who conquered most of the known world. The Acts of the Apostles is an example of a Christian book using this title – and thus Luke may well be using two different genres of book in his two-volume work, Luke-Acts.

However, the Gospels contain a good deal of teaching by Jesus, and contain relatively little movement and few exploits of the kind which Greek readers would expect in such a book (principally political and military). Further, Jesus' trial for sedition and state execution would suggest that he was too doubtful and obscure a figure for treatment in such a book.

Second, the 'memoirs' (Greek *apomnēmoneumata*), which were collections of individual stories about, or sayings of, a famous person. Xenophon wrote his *Memoirs*

about the philosopher Socrates (c. 380 BC) and Plato had also written his *Dialogues* about Socrates (c. 380-350 BC). In about AD 150 Justin Martyr describes an early Christian meeting thus:

> And on the day called Sunday there is a meeting in one place of those who live in cities or the country, and *the memoirs of the apostles* or the writings of the prophets are read as long as time permits. (*Apology* 67.3, italics mine)

He also writes 'the memoirs of the apostles … are called Gospels' (*Apology* 66). Justin thus sees similarities between these Christian writings and the previous 'memoirs', although he is unique in describing the Gospels this way. He may choose this term because he writes for pagan readers who would know books called 'memoirs'.

Our Gospels, however, contain much that would be regarded as unnecessary to memoirs, including most of the action within them, as well as the account of the death of Jesus. Indeed, when we remember the percentage of each Gospel which is taken up with the last days of Jesus, his death and resurrection (almost 50% in Mark), and the relatively small amount taken up with Jesus' teachings (especially so in Mark), it is likely that an ancient reader would see Justin as stretching considerably the bounds of the term 'memoirs' in applying it to the four Gospels.

Third, the 'lives' (Greek *bioi*) of the ancient world. Plutarch was a famous biographer of the first century AD who wrote a number of *Parallel Lives* which compare and contrast two great figures. He sets out his aims as follows:

> *I am not a writer of histories but of biographies.* My readers therefore must excuse me if I

do not record all events or describe in detail, but only briefly touch upon, the noblest and the most famous. For the most conspicuous do not always or of necessity show *a man's virtues or failings*, but it often happens that some light occasion, a word or a jest, gives a clearer insight into character, than battles with their slaughter of tens of thousands and the greatest array of armies and sieges of cities. As painters produce a likeness by the representation of the countenance and the expression of the face, in which the *character is revealed*, without troubling themselves about the other parts of the body, so I must be allowed to look rather into *the signs of a man's character*, and by means of these to portray the life of each, leaving to others the description of great events and battles. (*Alexander* 1.1, italics mine)

Thus for Plutarch, and the Graeco-Roman biographical tradition, the 'lives' focused on the person, whereas 'acts' and other historical writings focused on events. A 'life' was written to provide an example or model by highlighting the person's character or *ethos* – and thus Plutarch says that he chooses the material for his biography in order to draw his readers' attention to that.

For a long time it used to be argued that the Gospels are not biographies, but this argument was usually based on a comparison with modern biographies. It is true that the Gospels lack the full coverage of modern biographies: they say little about Jesus' childhood and upbringing; they are very uneven in their coverage of his life, focusing particularly on his public ministry of about three years, and especially on the last period; and they do not tell us much about his psychological and personal development.

However, Richard Burridge has mounted a strong argument for considering the Gospels to be considered as ancient 'lives' (Burridge 1992). He studies a wide range of ancient 'lives' and establishes a set of features of this literary genre:

- **opening features:** there is usually a title and an opening formula;
- the **subject** of the biography tends to be the subject of a large proportion of the main verbs in the book, and is given the lion's share of the space, providing the focus on the subject which Plutarch describes;
- **external features** including the structure of the book, its style, etc., which enhance the focus on the subject;
- **internal features** such as the settings, the topics and content included, the values and attitudes espoused or promoted by the work, and the author's intention and purpose (whether stated explicitly or not).

When Burridge compares the four Gospels one by one with this pattern he finds each of these features to be present in a comparable form in each. This strongly suggests that an ancient reader hearing Mark and the others read aloud (the normal way that books were 'read' in the ancient world, cf. Acts 8:30) would recognize them as 'lives' of Jesus. To repeat our earlier point: this does not mean that we should think of them like modern biographies, but it does mean that the evangelists have chosen a vehicle which would be recognizable to a wide readership around the Mediterranean basin.

A weakness of Burridge's conclusion is that the 'lives' form a very wide category of books, and vary considerably in how much they aim to be true to what happened and how much they write stories which typify the person's character but which may not have happened. Nevertheless, Burridge has identified a key point which has moved the debate forward and which tells us that *the focus of the Gospels is Jesus*, the subject of the 'life'. This might sound blindingly obvious, but for much of the last hundred years the heart of Gospels scholarship has been in examining the communities supposed to be behind the Gospels, rather than their true subject. More recent scholarship (such as the work of N. T. Wright, M. Borg and S. McKnight) has begun to reverse this trend and to follow Burridge's lead by studying the Jesus whom the Gospels present.

THE GOSPELS AS UNLIKE OTHER ANCIENT LITERATURE

The alternative approach in scholarship has been to notice ways in which the Gospels are distinctive and different from other ancient books. A key figure is K. L. Schmidt, who published an essay 'The place of the Gospels in the history of literature' (1923), in which he claimed that the Gospels should be seen as 'folk literature' (as opposed to 'high literature') because the evangelists did not write in the 'I' of an eyewitness narrator and made use of stories and material from others (rather than carrying out the research entirely themselves). Schmidt assumed that the Gospels had been put together by the evangelists collecting stories about Jesus and then putting them together, rather like sticking newspaper cuttings into a scrapbook (this approach is called 'form criticism': see more fully pp. 70–4). This view treats the Gospels as preaching documents, gathering together the stories told in the early Christians' proclamation about Jesus.

The British scholar C. H. Dodd studied the evangelistic speeches in Acts in a very significant work (Dodd 1936), and argued that there was a fairly consistent pattern found in these speeches. Dodd's 'set piece' study was of Acts 10:34-43, Peter's speech in Cornelius' home in Caesarea, and he identified six key elements of the speech which formed the pattern of early Christian preaching:

- John the Baptist prepared the way for the coming of Jesus, v. 37;
- these events were promised in the OT Scriptures (here, 'the prophets'), v. 43;
- Jesus' ministry was powerful and empowered by God, vv. 38-39a;
- Jesus was arrested, tried and executed on a cross, v. 39b;
- God raised Jesus from the dead and he was seen by witnesses, vv. 40f.;
- those who follow Jesus are commanded to tell others about him (thus summarizing the response the message requires), v. 42.

The key step in Dodd's argument was to notice that these six points correspond to the major sections of Mark, and come in roughly the same sequence:

- John the Baptist appears in fulfilment of the OT (note the quotation from Isa. 40 in Mark 1:2f.), Mark 1:1-15;
- Jesus' ministry is outlined and described, Mark 1:16–8:30;
- An extended description of Jesus' movement to Jerusalem, where he is arrested, tried and dies on the cross, Mark 8:31–15:47;
- A brief description of the resurrection of Jesus, Mark 16:6 (perhaps plus a lost ending, see p. 201);
- Jesus' disciples are to go and tell others, Mark 16:7.

Digging deeper:
GOSPEL OUTLINES?

Compare Dodd's outline from Acts 10:34-43 with the contents of Mark. How far do you think Mark fits the outline? Is there material in Mark which is additional to the outline?

Compare the outline from Acts 10:34-43 with two other evangelistic sermons in Acts 3:12-26; 17:22-34 and with Paul's 'gospel outlines' in 1 Thess. 1:9f and 1 Cor. 15:1-7. What is similar to and different from the outline in each case? What explanation might there be for the similarities and differences?

While Dodd's picture does not fit completely at every point of detail, it does go a long way to explain why these books came to be called 'Gospels', for Dodd shows that they were each an extended narrative form of the gospel message which the early Christians proclaimed.

To add to this, R. P. Martin (1972, 27f) has examined Mark's opening verse to see how he 'titles' his book. Mark calls his book 'The beginning of the gospel of Jesus Christ, the son of God' (1:1). The word 'beginning' (Greek *archē*) could well have the sense of 'origin' or 'source' here. If that is so, Mark's book is an explanation of where the gospel message comes from, what the foundational events which the gospel message proclaims are. On this view the Gospels are the church's testimony about Jesus rather than biography, for biography's focus is on a *past* figure who is remembered, whereas Jesus was not 'remembered' by the early Christians – they experienced him as alive and present with them by the Spirit.

TRUTH IN BOTH VIEWS?

On balance it seems likely that there is truth in both approaches to the genre of the Gospels. It is likely that they would have similarities with other ancient literature, for such familiarity would help readers to engage with the book. Burridge demonstrates by detailed study that there are close resemblances between the four Gospels and ancient 'lives', and thereby shows that the focus of these books is on Jesus.

But it is also likely that there will be something novel about the Gospels, since they centre on what the early Christians believe God has done in and through Jesus. Dodd and Martin argue persuasively that the Gospels enshrine the church's proclamation of Jesus in narrative form – and thus show from a different perspective that these books are all about Jesus. C. F. D. Moule concludes judiciously:

> Here, then, in the Synoptic Gospels and Acts, each with its own peculiar emphasis, may be found the deposit of early Christian explanation: here are the voices of Christians explaining what led to their existence – how they themselves came to be: telling the story to themselves, that they may tell it to others, or even telling it directly to those others. (Moule 1981, 133)

WHY WERE THE GOSPELS WRITTEN?

So in order to understand the nature of the Gospels better, we shall ask what we know about the immediate causes of them being written down. On the usual dating of the four Gospels, it is held that Mark is the oldest and that he did not publish his book until the sixties AD. Why did it take so long before writing these books, and what other reasons led to the stories about Jesus taking written form? Broadly four reasons seem probable, within which scholars then debate the precise reasons for each individual Gospel being written.

First and most practically, the period of writing the Gospels was a time when *the original eyewitnesses were dying*. For example, Luke presents himself as part of this 'second generation' by separating 'us' and 'those who from the beginning were eyewitnesses' (Luke 1:2). This would give an urgency to preserving their personal knowledge of Jesus' ministry for future generations, and a

written form would be the most permanent. We might call this an *historical* reason.

Second, there was an *evangelistic* reason, namely *to communicate the gospel message to those who were not yet believers*. In the NT letters we get only the briefest summaries of the evangelistic message preached to non-believers (e.g. 1 Thess. 1:9f; 1 Cor. 15:1-7), whereas (as Dodd argued) it seems likely that the written Gospels provide extended narrative summaries of the contents of the Christian proclamation. John seems to say that this is his purpose (John 20:31; contrast 1 John 5:13, clarifying that the letter is for

---

JOHN 20:31: TEXT, TRANSLATION AND IMPLICATIONS

In the case of John 20:31, two issues in the Greek text affect our understanding (more fully see Carson 1991, 90f., 661-3). [If you don't have Greek, feel free to skip this box.]

Some ancient manuscripts have the verb meaning 'you may believe' in the present subjunctive tense (Greek *pisteuēte*); a strict translation would be 'you may believe (and go on believing)'. Others have the aorist subjunctive tense (Greek *pisteusēte*); a strict translation here would be 'you may come to believe'. In the former case, John's target audience are likely to be Christians already whose faith he is aiming to reinforce. In the latter case, John's intended readers are probably not yet believers, and he is seeking to persuade them to become Christians.

However, Carson's careful study shows that both aorist and present subjunctive tenses can be used both for continuing in faith and for coming to initial faith. John 11:15 has an aorist subjunctive used for the strengthening of the disciples' faith, and 6:29 has a present subjunctive used for the process of coming to initial faith and then continuing to believe. This means that the textual variant question is not decisive.

However, the presence of the definite article (*ho* in Greek = 'the') with 'Messiah' and not with 'Jesus' would normally mean that the last part of the sentence should be translated 'that the Messiah, the son of God, is Jesus', rather than 'that Jesus is the Messiah, the son of God'. This implies that the question John is answering is not, as the usual translation suggests, 'Who is Jesus?', resulting in the answer, 'He is the Messiah, the son of God.' Rather, the question John asks is, 'Who is the Messiah, the son of God?', and his answer is, 'Jesus.'

Certainly, John is likely to be writing to people who know what the term 'Messiah' means, and the fact that he uses 'son of God' alongside it (effectively as a kind of synonym) strongly suggests a target audience familiar with the Jewish Scriptures – likely a mixture of Jews and godfearers. If Carson's well-marshalled argument carries the day, they are likely to be non-believers, since Christians would already know the answer to the question, 'Who is the Messiah?'

Carson's view is in the minority in modern scholarship, principally because others, reading the whole of John, conclude that it would be most suited to strengthen the faith of those who are already believers, probably in a hostile environment. To my knowledge, no persuasive answer to his case on the translation of 20:31 has been made.

believers) and it may be part of Luke's agenda also, depending on whether 'Theophilus' is a believer or an enquirer (Luke 1:1-4).

Third, there was a *didactic* (or teaching) reason, *to teach those who followed Jesus* more about their faith and to help them grow in it. If 'Theophilus' was a believer already (Luke 1:3f.) it is likely that this was one of Luke's aims. Similarly the five major blocks of teaching material in Matthew (see p. 212) would be wonderfully appropriate for explaining Christian lifestyle to a congregation; the sermon on the mount (Matt. 5–7) looks particularly tailored to this end.

Fourth, there was a *geographical* reason, *to spread the eye-witness testimony further afield*. We know that the early Christians valued the oral passing on of the stories about Jesus into the second century (see p. 70), so writing them down did not necessarily supersede the oral traditions. However, it did allow them to spread around more easily, since written documents could be copied relatively cheaply and were light enough for a traveller to carry.

WHY THESE GOSPELS?

Christian tradition from at least the second century AD has identified Matthew, Mark, Luke and John as the accounts of Jesus that are important and authoritative historically (hence 'canonical' – in the list or canon of recognized books). However, there were other gospels, many of them written in the second century AD.

These so-called 'apocryphal gospels' are often attributed to an apostle, e.g. Peter or Thomas. Some, such as the *Infancy Gospel of Thomas*, focus on the birth of Jesus,

recounting tales of Jesus as a super-boy; some are just sayings of Jesus, notably the Coptic *Gospel of Thomas*; some are more comprehensive. Most scholars have seen the apocryphal gospels as historically valueless: they contain bizarre stories (the *Gospel of Peter*, for example, describes a huge Jesus coming out of the tomb followed by the cross); one leading scholar speaks of 'a field of rubble, largely produced by the pious or wild imaginations of certain second-century Christians.' (Meier 1991, 1:115)

However, some have argued recently that these gospels may after all be useful sources of historical information about Jesus, and were suppressed in the early Christian church by those who disliked their teaching.

The Gospels of particular interest include:

- various Jewish Christian gospels, such as *The Gospel of the Nazarenes*, *The Gospel of the Ebionites*, *The Gospel of the Hebrews* (the last resembling Matthew's Gospel). These gospels only exist now in fragmentary form.
- the so-called *Gospel of Peter*. The notable American scholar J. D. Crossan has taken a particular interest in this gospel, postulating an early *Cross Gospel*, on which it was based, from the fifties AD that was used by the canonical Gospels.
- *The Secret Gospel of Mark*. This gospel was contained in a letter supposedly written by the fourth-century church leader Clement of Alexandria which was discovered in 1958 (and subsequently lost!) by the American scholar Morton Smith. The gospel is purportedly Mark's more 'spiritual' account of Jesus, including some stories not found in canonical Mark, e.g. one that sounds like the Lazarus story of John 11, another in which the man of Mark 14:52

who fled away naked comes to Jesus for teaching.

- *The Gospel of Thomas* was found in a fourth-century Coptic library in 1945 at Nag Hammadi in Egypt. It is a collection of 114 sayings of Jesus, many paralleled in the canonical Gospels, but some quite different, e.g. Saying 77: 'Jesus said … "I am the all; the all came forth from me, and the all attained to me. Cleave a (piece of) wood, I am there. Raise up a stone, and you will find me there" ' (Schneemelcher 1991, 127); and Saying 114: 'Simon Peter said to them "Let Mariham (Mary) go out from among us, for women are not worthy of the life." Jesus said: "Look, I will lead her that I may make her male, in order that she too may become a living spirit resembling you males. For every woman who makes herself male will enter into the kingdom of heaven."' (Schneemelcher 1991, 129)

Scholars have debated endlessly over the historical value of Thomas: some see it as rivalling the canonical Gospels in importance; most see it (and even more the other apocryphal gospels) as at best a secondary source, of dubious value. Like other apocryphal gospels, Thomas is arguably (a) later than the canonical Gospels, (b) dependent – directly or indirectly – on them and (c) reflecting the ideas of second-century gnosticism.

SOME ISSUES FOR TODAY

- The Gospels are focused on Jesus and (according to Dodd) highlight the central themes of the early Christians' proclamation about him. It is worth reflecting on modern church life in the light of this focus, and asking how far these 'mainstream' themes are also at the heart of church life today. Or have other things taken their place?

- The Gospels present the key things which the early Christians wanted to say about Jesus to their world, expressed in forms which their readers would be likely to understand. In doing this, they created a form of literature which had some novel elements. This encourages today's Christians to be imaginative and creative in their presentation of the Christian message to this generation and, like their first-century forebears, find ways to take existing forms of communication and give them new twists in order to get the gospel message across.

ESSAY TOPICS

INTRODUCTORY

- Write an article for a 'thinking person's' magazine or newspaper (in the USA, e.g. *Time* magazine; in the UK, e.g. *The Independent* or *The Times*) outlining how scholars think about the genre of the Gospels, including the implications this has for how we read the Gospels today.

INTERMEDIATE

- Outline the purpose of *either* John *or* Luke after reading through the Gospel you choose and assessing: (i) the central elements of its teaching; and (ii) any explicit statements of purpose made by the author.

FURTHER READING

INTRODUCTORY

DJG articles: 'Gospel (genre)', 'Gospel (good news)' 'Gospels (Apocryphal)' (very good overview articles).

J. P. Meier *A Marginal Jew: Rethinking the Historical Jesus, vol. 1*. New York: Doubleday, 1991.

INTERMEDIATE

R. A. Burridge *What are the Gospels? A Comparison with Græco-Roman Biography.* SNTS Monograph Series 70. Cambridge: Cambridge University Press, 1992 (a modern classic, arguing the case for the Gospels being Græco-Roman 'lives').

D. A. Carson *The Gospel according to John.* Leicester: IVP/Grand Rapids: Eerdmans, 1991, 90f., 661-3 (on the nature of John).

J. D. Crossan *The Historical Jesus.* San Francisco: Harper, 1991 (significant book using Thomas and other apocryphal gospels extensively).

C. H. Dodd *The Apostolic Preaching and its Development.* London: Hodder & Stoughton, 1936/New York: Willett, Clark & Co, 1937 (the classic discussion of the nature of early Christian preaching, and the application of the conclusions to the Gospels).

R. P. Martin *Mark: Evangelist and Theologian.* Exeter: Paternoster/Grand Rapids: Zondervan, 1972, ch. 1 (valuable and clear discussion of the nature of Mark).

C. F. D. Moule *The Birth of the New Testament,* 3rd ed. London: A. & C. Black/San Francisco: Harper & Row, 1981, ch. V (careful and wise discussion of the origins and nature of the Gospels).

W. Schneemelcher, ed. *New Testament Apocrypha,* vol. 1. Cambridge: James Clarke/ Louisville: Westminster/John Knox, 1991 (the relevant texts).

See also the discussion of the purpose of each of the Gospels in the commentaries (see 'further reading' at the ends of chs 9–12).

Chapter 4

WHERE DID THE GOSPELS COME FROM?

The evangelists did not pull the stories in the Gospels out of thin air, nor did they write them immediately after the life, death and resurrection of Jesus: it is likely that they wrote some 30-60 years later. This chapter will explore:

● how scholars analyse the processes by which the Gospels were composed;
● how to use a Gospels synopsis as a tool to study the Gospels for yourself.

LUKE 1:1-4

[1]Since many have undertaken to set down an orderly account of the events that have been fulfilled among us, [2]just as they were handed on to us by those who from the beginning were eyewitnesses and servants of the word, [3]I too decided, after investigating everything carefully from the very first, to write an orderly account for you, most excellent Theophilus, [4]so that you may know the truth concerning the things about which you have been instructed.

Luke is unique in outlining his process of writing, and each of his stages of work and research correspond to a type of study of the Gospels. The oldest source is eyewitness testimony (v. 2). Some of the evangelists may have been eyewitnesses of the ministry of Jesus; all of them had access to stories about Jesus, his life and teaching, that come from eyewitnesses. In scholarly study of the Gospels, this leads to questions about how these stories were passed on and shaped during the period before the Gospels were written, and *form criticism* is the major tool used to attempt to answer them.

Second, others wrote about Jesus – the 'many' (v. 1). As we shall see, similarities of wording and sequence among Matthew, Mark and Luke lead most scholars to suppose that some sharing of stories is going on, whether by one author copying another, or by two or three Gospels sharing a common source or sources. *Source criticism* is about identifying the written sources used in putting the Gospels together.

Third, Luke makes his own contribution, of two kinds (v. 3). He does his own research, 'investigating everything from the very first', checking his sources, both oral and written. He also selects and organizes the stories into a sequence, and puts his own stamp on them by the way that he retells the stories for his readers: all of this is involved in writing 'an *orderly* account'. Scholars investigate these processes under the banner of *redaction criticism*.

In each of these kinds of study, there are phenomena in the books themselves which lead to the questions that scholars ask, and we shall outline these as we look at each form of study. Each is called 'criticism', which does not mean that scholars are criticizing the Gospels – rather it means they are making careful, thoughtful judgements about matters of history, literary presentation, text and language in the light of the evidence available, all of which are crucial to understanding the Gospels correctly.

This kind of study has focused on Matthew, Mark and Luke because there are close resemblances of sequence and actual wording among the stories in these three: John has a different style and contains much which is not found in the other three. These three are often called the *synoptic Gospels*, because of the arrangement in a *synopsis* where they are 'seen together' (the origin of 'synopsis'). The meaning of this name also draws attention to the shared perspective that these three have.

USING A GOSPELS SYNOPSIS

A major tool used to help in studying the Gospels is a synopsis. This sets out Matthew, Mark and Luke (and sometimes John too) in parallel columns, passage by passage, in order to allow detailed comparisons to be made between them. Some synopses use the Greek text; others use a fairly word-for-word English translation (such as the NRSV or RSV) to allow those without Greek to do this kind of study (see p. 80 for recommendations).

To find a particular passage in the synopsis you can use its index pages, which set the references for passages out in tabular form and give the page where each passage is found. More quickly, you can navigate using the reference across the top of each page of the body of the synopsis: references in **bold** indicate the passage(s) on that page; plain type references indicate the last passage from that Gospel prior to that page.

Once you have found a particular passage you can then (on a photocopy if the book is not your own!) mark the page to identify which words are exactly the same in two or three Gospels, and which show no agreement among the three. This is best done by underlining words which agree, and using a dotted underline for words which agree, but are not in exactly the same form. At a more sophisticated level, you could use four different colours for:
(a) agreements between all three Gospels;
(b) agreements between Mark and Matthew alone; (c) agreements between Mark and Luke alone; (d) agreements between Matthew and Luke alone. This allows you to see easily where the similarities and differences among the accounts come.

As we look at the different sorts of critical study of the Gospels, we shall use synopsis pages, or we shall suggest that you examine passages in parallel yourself.

SOURCE CRITICISM

We consider this first as the oldest of the forms of Gospels study. Two phenomena in the Gospels have led scholars to consider questions of the literary sources used by the evangelists: the agreements and the differences found when they are compared.

Matt. 22:22-33	Mark 12:18-27	Luke 20:27-40
23The same day some Sadducees came to him, saying there is no resurrection; and they asked him a question, saying, 24'Teacher, Moses said, "If a man dies childless, his brother shall marry the widow, and raise up children for his brother." 25Now there were seven brothers among us; the first married, and died childless, leaving the widow to his brother. 26The second did the same, so also the third, down to the seventh. 27Last of all, the woman herself died. 28In the resurrection, then, whose wife of the seven will she be? For all of them had married her.' 29Jesus answered them, 'You are wrong, because you know neither the scriptures nor the power of God. 30For in the resurrection they neither marry nor are given in marriage, but are like angels in heaven.	18Some Sadducees, who say there is no resurrection, came to him and asked him a question, saying, 19'Teacher, Moses wrote for us that "if a man's brother dies, leaving a wife but no child, the man shall marry the widow and raise up children for his brother." 20There were seven brothers; the first married and, when he died, left no children; 21and the second married her and died, leaving no children; and the third likewise; 22none of the seven left children. Last of all the woman herself died. 23In the resurrection whose wife will she be? For the seven had married her.' 24Jesus said to them, 'Is not this the reason you are wrong, that you know neither the scriptures nor the power of God? 25For when they rise from the dead, they neither marry nor are given in marriage, but are like angels in heaven.	27Some Sadducees, those who say there is no resurrection, came to him 28and asked him a question, 'Teacher, Moses wrote for us that if a man's brother dies, leaving a wife but no children, the man shall marry the widow and raise up children for his brother. 29Now there were seven brothers; the first married, and died childless; 30then the second 31and the third married her, and so in the same way all seven died childless. 32Finally the woman also died. 33In the resurrection, therefore, whose wife will the woman be? For the seven had married her.' 34Jesus said to them, 'Those who belong to this age marry and are given in marriage; 35but those who are considered worthy of a place in that age and in the resurrection from the dead neither marry nor are given in marriage. 36Indeed they cannot die anymore, because they are like angels and are children of God, being children of the resurrection. 37And the fact that the dead are raised Moses himself showed, in the story about the bush, where he speaks of the Lord as the God of Abraham, the God of Isaac, and the God of Jacob. 38Now he is God not of the dead, but of the living; for to him all of them are alive.' 39Then some of the scribes answered, 'Teacher, you have spoken well.' 40For they no longer dared to ask him another question.
31And as for the resurrection of the dead, have you not read what was said to you by God, 32"I am the God of Abraham, the God of Isaac, and the God of Jacob"? He is God not of the dead, but of the living.' 33And when the crowd heard it, they were astounded at his teaching.	26And as for the dead being raised, have you not read in the book of Moses, in the story about the bush, how God said to him, "I am the God of Abraham, the God of Isaac, and the God of Jacob"? 27He is God not of the dead, but of the living; you are quite wrong.'	

AGREEMENTS

In a number of passages Matthew, Mark and Luke agree very closely in *how they tell a story*. Consider the synopsis page showing Matt. 22:22-33 and its parallels (p. 59), where we have underlined places where two or three Gospels agree in their wording. Here the majority of the story is told in the same words. Such closeness suggests to most scholars that there has been some copying of one by another (or from a common source) going on.

The agreements are not just in the 'mainstream' of shared stories: they include asides to the reader, such as 'let the reader understand' (Matt. 24:15; Mark 13:14).

As well as agreements of wording in the so-called 'triple tradition' (where Matthew, Mark and Luke all tell a story), there are also agreements where only two Gospels tell a story (the 'double tradition'), notably where Matthew and Luke are the two. For example, there is very close agreement in the wording of Jesus' teaching on prayer (Matt. 7:7-11; Luke 11:9-13).

Further, there is *agreement in the sequence of the stories*, as well as their wording. Considering the stories in Mark 1:21–3:19 (see below) illustrates this point. Mark and Luke agree completely in order, and Matthew and Mark have broadly the same sequence of events.

DIFFERENCES

There are also *differences of wording*. If we examine the synopsis for Matt. 22:22-33 and parallels again (see above, p. 59), we see sections with no underlining at all, indicating that they are unique to that

AGREEMENTS IN SEQUENCE: AN EXAMPLE

Story	Matt.	Mark	Luke
Jesus' teaching in the synagogue in Capernaum		1:21f	4:31f.
Jesus' healing of the demonized man in the synagogue		1:23-28	4:33-37
Jesus' healing of Peter's mother-in-law	8:14f.	1:29-31	4:38f.
Jesus healing and exorcizing in the evening: summary	8:16f.	1:32-34	4:40f.
Jesus leaves Capernaum		1:35-38	4:42f.
Jesus preaching in Galilee: summary	4:23	1:39	4:44
The miraculous catch of fish			5:1-11
Jesus heals a leper	8:1-4	1:40-45	5:12-16
Jesus heals a paralysed man	9:1-8	2:1-12	5:17-26
Jesus calls Levi to follow him	9:9-13	2:13-17	5:27-32
A question about fasting	9:14-17	2:28-22	5:33-39
A question about plucking grain on the Sabbath	12:1-8	3:1-6	6:1-5
A question about healing on the Sabbath	12:9-14	3:1-6	6:6-11
Healing by the sea: summary	4:24f.; 12:15f.	3:7-12	6:17-19
Jesus chooses the twelve	10:1-4	3:13-19	6:12-16

Based on Stein 1988, 35.

Gospel (e.g. Matt. 22:28b-29a; Mark 12:25a; Luke 20:36). This makes it clear that, while copying has probably taken place, it has not been the kind which follows the source blindly: Matthew, Mark and Luke each tell the story in their own distinctive way.

There are also places throughout the synoptics where the wording of two Gospels agrees and the third is different. However, it is rare for the 'odd one out' to be Mark. In our example above, this only happens with short phrases: 'no children' (Matt. 22:24), 'Now', 'and died' (v. 25), 'After them all' (v. 27) and 'in the resurrection'(v. 30) – and the last two are not exact agreements between Matthew and Luke.

> ## What do you think?
>
> Study the story of Jesus healing the man with the withered hand (Mark 3:1-6; Matt. 12:9-14 and Luke 6:6-11) using a synopsis. Underline words which are in common between two or three Gospels, using a dotted underline where the words agree, but not exactly (see p. 58 above). Which version of the story do you think is likely to be the oldest, and why? What distinctive points are found in each account, and what might they suggest about the interests of each evangelist?

Similarly, there are *differences of sequence* when we look in detail. In the table of Mark 1:21–3:19 above (p. 60), Mark and Luke follow exactly the same sequence (Luke having an extra story at 5:1-11), whereas Matthew tells a number of these stories in a different order from them. More generally, where either Matthew or Luke have a different sequence, the other agrees with Mark's order: cases where they agree in having a different sequence of stories to Mark are almost impossible to find.

Each of the synoptic Gospels *has unique stories or sections* (e.g. Matt. 13:36-52; Luke 15:11-32), although in Mark they are few (e.g. 3:19b-21), since a very large proportion of Mark is paralleled in Matthew and/or Luke.

This combination of agreements and differences has set the 'synoptic problem' for scholars: what is the likeliest explanation of these phenomena in the Gospels? Numerous solutions have been proposed over the years, but one has become the 'mainstream' view and another is a significant minority view. We shall examine these two briefly before sketching one or two other significant ideas.

THE 'TWO SOURCE' HYPOTHESIS

The majority view in scholarship since the early 1900s has been the 'two source' or 'two document' hypothesis. This view holds that Mark was the first Gospel to be written, and that Matthew and Luke both used Mark as a source in composing their books. Further, Matthew and Luke also drew on a now lost source known as Q (from the German *Quelle*, meaning 'source'), to which Mark did not have access. Pictorially, the relationship looks like this:

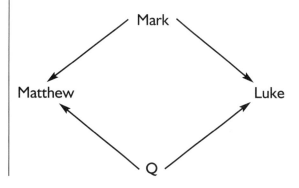

Markan priority

Five key arguments support the view that Mark wrote first.

Length Mark is the shortest of the synoptics. There are 661 verses in Mark, and 601 are paralleled in Matthew and/or Luke. 97% of the words in Mark are found in Matthew; 88% of the words in Mark are found in Luke. If Mark writes first, the others have supplemented his material with other stories. However, if Mark is using Matthew or Luke, it is very surprising that he has missed out so much material, including the birth of Jesus, the sermon on the mount, much teaching material (particularly surprising given Mark's stress on Jesus' teaching activities, e.g. 1:21f.; 2:13; 4:1f.; 6:2; 8:31; 12:35, 38) and the resurrection accounts.

It is logically possible that Mark is producing an abridged version of Matthew and/or Luke, but Mark's (Greek) version of stories he shares with the others is usually the longest: e.g. Mark 10:23-31 is 171 words in Greek; Matt. 19:23-30 is 154 words; Luke 18:24-30 is 120 words. So to claim that Mark is producing an abridged account is not really true – he tells fewer stories, but tells the individual stories at greater length. On the other hand, if Mark is first, the others have added in other stories and produced longer Gospels.

Agreements in the sequence of stories Mark and Matthew agree in order against Luke; Mark and Luke agree in order against Matthew; but Matthew and Luke virtually never agree in order against Mark. This is most easily explained by supposing that Matthew and Luke have independently chosen to depart from Mark's order.

Grammar and style Mark's Greek is 'rougher', written by a man who seems to be working in Greek as his second language, whereas Matthew and Luke have a smoother style. For example, Mark uses Aramaic words and expressions which the others omit (e.g. 'Boanerges' Mark 3:17; 'Talitha cum' Mark 5:41). Similarly, Mark uses a slang term for 'bed' (Greek *krabatton* 2:4), whereas Matthew and Luke use more refined terms (*klines* Matt. 9:2; *klinidion* Luke 5:19). In each case it is easier to understand why Matthew and Luke would change Mark than Mark change Matthew or Luke.

'Harder' wordings Mark reports stories which suggest a limitation on Jesus' power or influence. For example, in Mark 1:34 Jesus heals 'many', whereas Matt. 8:16 and Luke 4:40 have stronger statements that Jesus healed 'all' or 'every one of them'. At Nazareth, Mark 6:5f reports that Jesus '*could* not' do deeds of power there and relates this to the people's unbelief, whereas Matt. 13:58 says that Jesus '*did* not' do miracles because of their unbelief – suggesting that he could have done them, but chose not to. In each case Mark's balder statement is presented in a more nuanced or qualified form in Matthew and/or Luke. Again, it is easier to see why Mark's version might be edited in this way by Matthew and Luke, whereas it is harder to imagine Mark creating potential difficulties by introducing such language into accounts derived from Matthew or Luke.

Further, the portrait of the disciples is also frequently more critical in Mark. Only Mark reports that Jesus was 'indignant' with them (Mark 10:14; cf. Matt. 19:14; Luke 18:16). Mark says that James and John asked for the best seats in his kingdom (10:35), but Matthew has their mother ask on their

What do you think?
MATTHEW'S 'HEIGHTENED' CHRISTOLOGY

Compare the following passages (in a synopsis if you can), noticing the authors' use of titles for Jesus such as 'Master', 'Lord', 'Rabbi', 'Teacher', etc. Is there a consistent pattern of a 'heightened' presentation of Jesus (in using 'Lord' more frequently) in Matthew and Luke, as the two source hypothesis predicts?

Mark 9:17; Matt. 17:15; Luke 9:38
Mark 9:5; Matt. 17:4; Luke 9:33
Mark 13:35; Matt. 24:42; Luke 12:40

behalf (20:20). If Mark wrote first, it is easy to see that later writers might want to cover up some of the disciples' failings, since they were seen as great Christian leaders when the later Gospels were written.

Theology In a number of places the presentation of Jesus (Christology) appears 'heightened' in Matthew by comparison with Mark. For example, Matthew uses 'Lord' (Greek *kurios*) rather more of Jesus than Mark in triple tradition stories (see above).

Q

There are roughly 235 verses which Matthew and Luke share and Mark does not have. Four pieces of evidence are used to argue that these are derived from a common source known as Q.

Agreements in wording A number of these stories agree very closely in wording, in similar manner to the triple tradition stories. For example, compare the accounts of John the Baptist's preaching in Matt. 3:7-10 and Luke 3:7-9, which agree almost verbatim.

Agreements in sequence If we consider only the double tradition stories, they come in a similar sequence in Matthew and Luke. The table on p. 64 shows the sequence in Matthew in relation to the sequence in Luke: notice both the general trend of Matthew's sequence in agreeing with Luke and the significant exceptions (highlighted in **bold**).

'Doublets' These are stories or sayings found in both the triple tradition and the double tradition, such as Jesus' saying that those who have will receive more (triple tradition: Matt: 13:12; Mark 4:25; Luke 8:18; double tradition: Matt. 25:29; Luke 19:26). If Matthew and Luke were using Mark alone, it would be surprising to find such a saying in the double tradition – its repetition in a different setting suggests that Matthew and Luke have drawn it from two different sources.

Digging deeper:
MATTHEW'S ADDITIONS TO MARK'S STORIES (see p. 64)

Assuming that Mark wrote first, compare the following sets of passages (using a synopsis if you can). In Matthew's account, underline words which Mark and Matthew share in one colour, and words which Matthew has added to Mark's account in a different colour. Assuming that Luke is using Matthew and Mark, which of Matthew's added words has Luke missed out? Do you agree that these are surprising? How could they be explained on the two source hypothesis?

Matt. 8:16f.; Mark 1:32-34; Luke 4:40f
Matt. 12:1-8; Mark 2:23-28; Luke 6:1-5
Matt. 16:13-23; Mark 8:27-30; Luke 9:18-22

THE SEQUENCE OF Q

	Luke		Matthew	
1	3:7-9, 16f.	John the Baptist's preaching	3:7-12	1
2	4:2-13	Temptation of Jesus	4:2-11	2
3	6:20-23, 27-30, 32-36	Jesus' sermon I	5:3-6, 11f., 39-42, 45-48	3
4	6:37f., 41-49	Jesus' sermon II	7:1-5, 16-21, 24-27	7
5	7:1-10	Healing of the centurion's servant	8:5-13	9
6	7:18-35	John's disciples and Jesus	11:2-19	**13**
7	9:57-60	The cost of following Jesus	8:19-22	10
8	10:1-12	Mission of the seventy	9:37–10:15	11
9	10:13-15, 21f.	Woes, Jesus rejoicing in the Spirit	11:21-23, 25f.	14
10	11:1-4	Lord's prayer	6:9-13	**5**
11	11:9-13	Teaching on prayer	7:7-11	**8**
12	11:14-23	Jesus and Beelzebul	12:22-30	15
13	11:24-26	The returning unclean spirit	12:43-45	17
14	11:29-32	Jesus refuses to do a sign	12:38-32	**16**
15	11:33-35	Light sayings	5:15; 6:22f.	**4**
16	11:39-52	Jesus criticizes the Pharisees	23:4, 23-25	19
17	12:2-10	Teaching on acknowledging Jesus	10:26-33	**12**
18	12:22-34	Teaching on worry and trust	6:19-21, 25-33	**6**
19	12:39-46	The need to watch	24:43-51	**22**
20	13:18-21	The mustard seed and the yeast	13:31-33	**18**
21	13:34f.	Jesus mourns over Jerusalem	23:37-39	20
22	17:22-27	The coming of the son of man	24:26-28, 37-41	21
23	19:11-27	The parable of the talents/pounds	25:14-30	23

Based on Stein 1988, 105.

Coherence Generally the Q material forms a coherent body with quite a consistent theological perspective. Most of it is teaching of Jesus, rather than stories about Jesus. For a number of years some scholars objected to the idea of Q on the grounds that there was no document of this type, containing mainly teaching of Jesus, among the early Christian writings we have. The discovery of the Gospel of Thomas (see p. 55) put paid to this criticism, since it is similar to the kind of document Q is supposed to be, primarily teaching of Jesus (although Thomas is presented as sayings of the 'living' – presumably, risen – Jesus, rather than the earthly Jesus).

The case for Q goes on to claim that alternative explanations are unbelievable. The main alternatives are that Matthew used Luke and Mark, or that Luke used Matthew and Mark (see the 'Digging deeper' box on p. 63). Matthew and Luke each have their special material, unique to each, and that means that if one used the other's book, it is surprising that they left out so much.

MATTHEW'S SERMON ON THE MOUNT MATERIAL IN LUKE

	Matt.	Luke
The Beatitudes	5:3-12	6:20b-23
The salt of the earth	5:13	14:34-35a
The light of the world	5:14-16	8:16
The law and the prophets	5:17f.	16:16f.
On reconciliation	5:25f.	12:58f.
On adultery and divorce	5:32	16:18
On retaliation	5:39-42	6:29f.
On love for enemies	5:43-48	6:27f., 32-36
The Lord's prayer	6:9-13	11:2-4
On treasure in heaven	6:20f.	12:33f.
Good eyes	6:22f.	11:34f.
On serving two masters	6:24	16:13
On anxiety	6:25-34	12:22-32
On judging others	7:1, 3-5	6:37, 41f.
On answers to prayer	7:7-11	11:9-13
The golden rule	7:12	6:31
The two ways	7:13f.	13:23f.
A tree and its fruit	7:16f.	6:43f.
Obedience, not words only	7:21-23	6:46; 13:25-27
The two builders	7:24-27	6:47-49

Based on Stein 1988, 96.

In particular, if Luke used Matthew and Mark (the commoner view among those who disbelieve in Q but hold to the priority of Mark), then he broke up Matthew's large teaching blocks (e.g. see above on the sermon on the mount). For Luke to disperse Matthew's well-organized blocks into apparently arbitrary contexts would be surprising, for Luke makes much of writing in an orderly way (Luke 1:3).

As reconstructed by scholars, Q consists mostly of teaching of Jesus, and some scholars have studied the 'theology' of this hypothetical source, postulating an early Christian community which preserved it and lived by its teaching, and suggesting that there were stages in the formation and editing of Q (e.g. C. M. Tuckett, B. L. Mack). Others, perhaps wisely, have felt less confident about sketching a community on the basis of a document which is not extant.

CRITICISMS OF THE TWO SOURCE HYPOTHESIS

The relationships among the synoptic Gospels are not straightforward, and there is data which doesn't fit easily into the tidy picture of the two source hypothesis.

Regarding *the priority of Mark*, the omission of the substantial section Mark 6:45–8:26 by

65

Luke is somewhat surprising, given that Luke generally follows Mark's sequence of stories quite closely. Most significantly, the 'minor agreements', where Matthew and Luke agree in wording against Mark (e.g. compare Matt. 3:11f.; Mark 1:7f. and Luke 3:16-18), are harder to explain on this view, for they must mean that Matthew and Luke independently changed Mark's phrase to exactly the same different phrase. Critics of Markan priority (e.g. Farmer 1976) make this a major plank in their argument, and claim that the minor agreements are easier to understand on the basis that one Gospel used two of the others in writing. (See further on the Griesbach hypothesis below.)

Regarding Q, there is greater unevenness in the agreement in wording in the double tradition than in the triple tradition stories. While there are places where the wording is very close, there are other passages where the content is similar, but the wording is very different, such as the parable of the pounds/talents (Luke 19:12-27; Matt. 25:14-30). This may suggest that Q should not be thought of as one written document – and some scholars postulate a series of 'editions' of Q as a result, or that Q is a mixture of written and oral material, thus multiplying hypothetical documents.

Further, there are stories which appear in both Mark and Q, which has led some to argue for an 'overlap' between the two, including the stories of John the Baptist, the temptation of Jesus, the claim that Jesus colluded with Satan, the parable of the mustard seed and Jesus' commissioning of the disciples. However, there is exact agreement in the wording of some of these stories, which would mean that Mark and Q do not merely overlap, but actually agree verbatim in some 50 verses. This makes it harder to argue that Q as an independent source is a necessary hypothesis at this point, since here Q is, for all practical purposes, Mark! (See further Sanders & Davies 1989, 78-82.)

If we examine the sequence of the Q material in Matthew and Luke, there are numerous places where individual passages come in a different sequence (see p. 64). Since a prime argument for the use of a common *written* source is a common sequence, this weakens the case for Q being a document.

Farrer and Goulder have argued for dispensing with Q on the assumption that Luke used Mark and Matthew, and we shall consider this view in examining the Griesbach hypothesis. For most scholars who disbelieve in Q, the main reason for doing so is that they find another hypothesis more persuasive, and so we shall turn to examine other views.

THE GRIESBACH (OR 'TWO GOSPELS') HYPOTHESIS

W. R. Farmer (1964, 2nd ed. 1976) led a revival of the view that Matthew wrote first, Luke then used Matthew, and finally Mark produced a short version of the two longer Gospels – a very different view of Mark from the two source hypothesis! This 'two Gospels' hypothesis, as it has become known, originated with J. J. Griesbach in about 1784, and there is now a vigorous group of scholars who study the synoptic Gospels on the basis of it. Pictorially, the relationship looks like this:

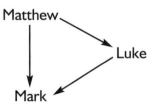

Arguments in favour

Six key arguments are used in support of this hypothesis.

Early testimony The universal testimony of early Christian writers outside the NT, including Irenaeus, Eusebius and Augustine, is that Matthew was written first.

Matthew's Jewishness Matthew frequently appears to show the strongest colouring of Jewish culture and settings. For example, he does not explain the Jewish washing customs (Matt. 15:1-20), presumably because he assumes his readers know about them, whereas Mark explains them (Mark 7:1-23). Given that the church became less Jewish and more Gentile as it grew over the years, it seems more likely that a strongly Jewish Gospel would be earlier.

Agreements in order and wording This view explains cases where two Gospels agree against the third:

- if Matthew and Mark agree against Luke, Mark has followed Matthew rather than Luke;
- if Luke and Mark agree against Matthew, Mark has followed Luke rather than Matthew;
- if Matthew and Luke agree against Mark, Mark deviates from both of his sources.

Markan redundancies In over two hundred places Mark, to our eyes, says things twice over: e.g. 'That evening, at sundown' (1:32). The parallel passages in Matthew and Luke contain the two elements of this phrase: Matt. 8:16 has 'That evening'; Luke 4:40 has 'as the sun was setting'. On the Griesbach hypothesis, Mark is incorporating both phrases into his account because he respects his sources and wants to harmonize them.

The 'minor agreements' The Griesbach hypothesis is strong in being able to explain passages where Matthew and Luke agree in wording against Mark. This can happen when Matthew and Luke share the same wording and Mark is different, or when Mark has wording which is missing in the others. On the Griesbach hypothesis, Mark is simply choosing to deviate from the wording of his two sources, perhaps because he has access to oral tradition (which was likely circulating in the churches throughout the period of the synoptic Gospels being written).

> ### What do you think?
> #### SOME 'MINOR AGREEMENTS'
>
> Compare the following sets of passages (using a synopsis if you can). Underline agreements in wording between Matthew and Luke where Mark has something different, and words which Mark uniquely has. Where do these come? How significant do you think they are for the Griesbach hypothesis? How could they be explained on the two source hypothesis?
>
> Matt. 9:1-8; Mark 2:1-12; Luke 5:17-26
> Matt. 14:13f.; Mark 6:31-34; Luke 9:10b-11

Alternating support In a number of places Matthew and Luke appear to 'alternate' in agreeing with Mark's sequence of events (see p. 68 for an example). This view has no difficulty in explaining this, for it marks occasions when Mark has chosen to switch between the sequence of Matthew and Luke. The two source hypothesis has to argue that this phenomenon means that Matthew and Luke have independently managed that, when one stops following Mark's sequence, the other straight away resumes Mark's order, and supporters of the Griesbach view see this as unlikely.

ALTERNATING SUPPORT: AN EXAMPLE

This example is based on Mark's sequence of events, and it can be seen that, when Matthew stops agreeing with Mark's order, Luke starts to do so, and when Luke stops agreeing with Mark's order, Matthew starts to do so.

Bold print indicates who agrees with Mark's sequence at each point. References in brackets indicate where Matthew or Luke disagrees with Mark's sequence; a dash indicates that the Gospel lacks the section.

Matthew	Mark	Luke
13:10-15	**4:10-12**	**8:9f.**
13:16f.	–	(10:23f.)
13:18-23	**4:13-20**	**8:11-15**
(13:12)	**4:21-25**	**8:16-18**
13:24-30	–	–
13:31f.	**4:30-32**	(13:18f.)
13:33	–	(13:20f.)
13:34f.	**4:33f.**	–
13:36-43	–	–
13:44-46	–	–
13:47-50	–	–
13:51f	–	–
(12:46-50)	(3:31-35)	8:19-21
(8:18, 23-27)	**4:35-41**	**8:22-25**
(8:28-34)	**5:1-20**	**8:26-39**
(9:18-26)	**5:21-43**	**8:40-56**
13:53-58	**6:1-6a**	(4:16-30)
(9:35; 10:1f.)	**6:6b-13**	**9:1-6**
14:1f.	**6:14-16**	**9:7-9**
14:3-12	**6:17-29**	–
14:13-21	**6:30-44**	**9:10-17**
14:22-33	**6:45-52**	–

Based on Sanders & Davies 1989, 88f.

Criticisms of the Griesbach hypothesis

This view has the beauty of simplicity, for it does not require belief in a hypothetical source, but serious questions have been raised against it.

Early church tradition is not agreed
Although the early writers seem agreed that Matthew wrote first, Papias claims that Mark had Peter as a source and wrote independently (see p. 205), and Origen and Augustine say that Luke wrote last, not Mark. Thus traditions need critical assessment, for they do not speak with one voice.

Why should Mark have missed out so much of importance? On the Griesbach hypothesis, Mark conserves and harmonizes his two sources, Matthew and Luke. However, he omits the birth of Jesus, the sermon on the mount (including the Lord's prayer), large amounts of teaching, and the resurrection narratives. This is hard to understand.

Why does Luke break up Matthew's teaching blocks? As we saw, Luke has most of the teaching found in Matthew's sermon on the mount (Matt. 5–7), but spread around his Gospel (see p. 65), and something similar happens with Matthew's four other teaching discourses (Matt. 10, 13, 18, 24–25). If Luke is using Matthew, this seems unusual behaviour.

Luke's rearrangement of Matthean material
Consider the material shared by Matthew and Luke, but not found in Mark (the Q material on the two source hypothesis). Apart from rare examples (such as the temptation of Jesus, Matt. 4:1-11; Luke 4:1-13), Luke and Matthew do not present this material in conjunction with the same Markan material, but locate it in different settings in their Gospels. In fact, on the

Griesbach hypothesis, in editing Matthew, Luke has systematically moved almost all this material from its Matthean contexts to somewhere else in his Gospel. This seems unlikely: a better explanation is that Luke is using Mark as a main source and other material to supplement Mark.

The Markan redundancies We saw above (p. 67) how these are seen by Griesbachian scholars; on the other hand, they can be explained on the two source hypothesis as showing places where Mark, as the more grammatically awkward and semitic writer, has used redundant language, and Matthew and Luke have improved Mark's style. Of over two hundred Markan redundancies, only seventeen have Matthew take one part of the redundant phrase and Luke take the other, which considerably reduces the strength of this argument for the two Gospels hypothesis.

OTHER VIEWS

A number of other hypotheses have been proposed (see Sanders & Davies 1989, chs 3–7 for a thorough review), but the two above have dominated discussion during the last hundred years. A significant alternative is Farrer's proposal (see his 'On Dispensing with Q' in Bellinzoni 1985, 321-56) developed by M. Goulder and M. Goodacre, that Mark is first, Matthew second, and Luke used both Mark and Matthew in writing his Gospel. This eliminates Q completely, and therefore avoids needing to postulate a hypothetical document, and produces this picture:

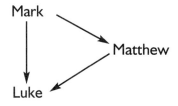

However, this view faces many of the same objections as the Griesbach hypothesis, for it still holds that Luke has edited Matthew in ways that appear hard to understand, and this has meant that, like the Griesbach view, it is not very widely held.

ORAL TRADITION AND THE SYNOPTIC PROBLEM

Where does this discussion get us? The majority view in scholarship remains Markan priority, and most still believe in a common source used by Matthew and Luke but unknown to Mark, although there are varying views on whether Q was written or oral, or a mixture of the two. In general, we assume that Mark wrote first in what follows, although for much of what we say that will make no great difference to our conclusions.

However, we know that the stories about Jesus circulated widely among the churches in oral form, and this means it is likely that (for example) Matthew knew the parable of the sower before he read it in Mark, as well as many other stories about Jesus. This complicates things considerably, for it means that sometimes Matthew or Luke may have a wording which is actually closer to Jesus than Mark. In these cases, Matthew or Luke is using words from oral tradition available to them. Thus, although we generally assume that Mark wrote first, we should not necessarily assume that his version of a story is closer to Jesus than the others. Source critics need to keep remembering the importance of oral tradition to the transmission of Jesus' teaching and the stories about him.

THE VALUE OF SOURCE CRITICISM

So why is source criticism worthwhile? Two main reasons suggest themselves.

First, recognizing the similarities and differences between the synoptics clarifies the expectations we can bring to reading them. The varying ways in which the synoptic evangelists report the teaching of Jesus show that they were not aiming at word-for-word reproduction of their sources. They paraphrase, expand and modify the material in order to help their readers understand its significance for them. They have different orders of events, which shows that the synoptic Gospels should not be treated as strictly chronological, although they follow the same broad sequence – again, they do this to communicate with their readers.

Second, recognizing the literary relationships among the synoptics enables us to see the emphases of each evangelist in their use of the material (see pp. 74ff. on redaction criticism), and this is a major benefit. Depending on the 'solution' we embrace, we can examine how, for example, Matthew has edited his Markan source, to find what emphases and theological interests Matthew offers. This allows us to see the particular perspectives of the different writers – a great gain. It also shows up places where an evangelist includes material which goes against his particular interests, and therefore makes the historicity of that material more likely.

FORM CRITICISM

Historically, form criticism developed after source criticism, and that is why we are considering it second. But form criticism focuses on the period *before* the Jesus stories were written down, the so-called 'oral period'. It was initiated by K. L. Schmidt, M. Dibelius (both 1919) and R. Bultmann (1921) in Germany, with a significant British contribution by V. Taylor (1935).

Eusebius reports Bishop Papias expressing the value which the early Christians placed on oral traditions about Jesus, at least alongside written material:

> … if ever anyone came who had followed the presbyters, I inquired into the words of the presbyters, what Andrew or Peter or Philip or Thomas or James or John or Matthew, or any other of the Lord's disciples, had said, and what Aristion and the presbyter John, the Lord's disciples, were saying. *For I did not suppose that information from books would help me so much as the word of a living and surviving voice.* (Eusebius *Hist. eccl.* 3.39.3-4, LCL, italics mine)

Form critics set out to investigate the transmission and development of the stories in the Gospels before they were written down. Two key phenomena in the Gospels are central to their investigations.

Loose links Schmidt identifies a number of 'seams' in Mark, where one story is joined to another, and notices how imprecise their wording is (e.g. Mark 2:18; 4:1, 26; 7:1; 8:1). This suggests that the evangelists were collectors of these traditions, rather like someone who puts pearls on a string to make a necklace, with the individual stories as the pearls: their contribution was simply to provide the overall framework for the story of Jesus and the brief links joining one story to another.

Stereotyped shapes The stories in the Gospels can be grouped, each group having a common 'shape' or form (hence the name 'form criticism'). Different scholars give different names to the forms:

Dibelius	Bultmann	Taylor	examples
Paradigms	Apophthegms	Pronouncement stories	Mark 6:1-4; 12:13-17
Tales	Miracle stories	Miracle stories	Mark 1:29-31; 5:1-20
Exhortations	Sayings	Sayings and parables	Luke 10:7, 23f.; Mark 7:15
Legends	Historical stories or legends	Stories about Jesus	Mark 1:9-11; 9:2-8; Matt. 4:1-11

For example, a pronouncement story:

- is independent of its context in the Gospels – it stands as a story in its own right;
- is brief and simple, giving minimal information about the participants – they are there only as 'foils' to Jesus;
- has religious, rather than literary/artistic colouring in the way it is told;
- climaxes in a word of Jesus, rather like the punch line of a joke;
- ends with a thought useful for preaching.

THE MODEL USED BY FORM CRITICS

These two key phenomena lead form critics to construct a model of how these stories were passed around and shaped during the oral period. They make five key claims.

The oral period Generally form critics believe that the Gospels were written during AD 70-100, and assume that the 'delay of the parousia' had led to traditions being written down – for those who are expecting the end of the world at any minute do not waste their time writing books!

Isolated units During the oral period, form critics claim that the stories of Jesus circulated as single, isolated units, rather than in groups or complexes. Acts 20:35 and 1 Cor. 7:10 provide examples of such individual sayings being used. The stories about Jesus, on this view, were told as preachers needed them, rather than as one continuous story. The exception to this is the passion narrative, which most form critics claim circulated as a unit (although Bultmann disagrees).

Stereotyped shapes As these individual stories were told again and again among the earliest Christians, form critics claim that the stories began to fall into set shapes or 'forms' and the wording became fairly fixed. This process gave rise to the particular forms they identified among the Gospels' stories.

'Natural selection' Form critics believe that the stories which survived were those which the early Christians found helped them in their situations. The German phrase *Sitz im Leben*, meaning 'life setting', is used to speak of the general situation for which a particular story or saying would be relevant, and a major concern of form critics is to reconstruct the *Sitz im Leben* of the stories of Jesus (either in the early church or, occasionally, in the ministry of Jesus). This might mean the situation which led to the preservation (and moulding) of the story or, in the hands of more radical form critics, the situation which caused the early Christians to *create* the story. Form critics claim that each form had its own *Sitz im Leben*. The pronouncement stories, for example, are thought to have been used as illustrations in the preaching of early missionaries.

Laws of tradition Based on studying German folklore, Greek literature, rabbinic writings and the apocryphal Gospels, form critics believe they can identify 'laws' about how stories developed as they were passed on orally. For example, they argue that shorter stories are probably earlier, for detail was likely to be added in later (e.g. the epileptic boy of Mark 9:17 becomes the 'only son' in Luke 9:38). On the basis of these laws, form critics attempt to reconstruct the actual event and strip away the later additions from the 'pure form' which they believe was more original.

What do you think?
A PRONOUNCEMENT STORY

Read Mark 2:23-28, classified as a pronouncement story. What is the 'punch line' at or near the end of the story? What is the central point of the story? Are there any later additions which form critics would want to remove? What life setting in the early churches might fit this story, and how would the main point be relevant to that setting?

(Further reading: Nineham 1963 or Taylor 1966 on 2:23-28 or Sanders & Davies 1989, 156.)

SOME PROBLEMS
'Form criticism' is used to describe two separate (but connected) tasks:

- the classification and analysis of the stories about Jesus by their literary form (much as OT scholars classify the different forms of Hebrew poetry);
- the attempt to make historical judgements about what in the Jesus stories is most likely to have come from Jesus, and what could be added by the early church.

Criticisms of form criticism tend to focus mainly on the second of these, and each of the form critics' major claims have been challenged.

- The oral period did not stop when the Gospels began to be written. The Papias quotation above shows that oral tradition was still valued in the early second century.

It is likely that oral tradition about Jesus was generally carefully passed on (see pp. 119f), not least since oriental memory is far more accurate than modern western memory, which has books, computers and the like to store information for later retrieval! This living oral tradition would then provide a check on the stories in the written Gospels.

- As well as continuing oral tradition, eye-witnesses of the ministry of Jesus were available at least until the writing of the earliest Gospels, and probably through to the writing of our last canonical Gospel, and their knowledge would act as a check and safeguard on the careful transmission of the traditions about Jesus – not least since they had been given that particular role (Acts 1:21f.; 2:42; 6:2, 4).
- It is possible that the disciples wrote some of Jesus' sayings down during his ministry, for this is a known practice among Jewish rabbis and their followers, and the Essene community at Qumran ensured that their scriptural interpretations were recorded in writing (cf. Luke 1:63, highlighting the widespread availability of wax tablets for writing).
- There is some possibility of pre-Markan collections of stories, such as Mark 2:1–3:6, which appear to be linked very closely together, and there may have been a framework of the story of Jesus circulating also (see pp. 51f.).
- Much of the classification of stories is too tidy: many stories do not fit neatly into one category and are classified as 'mixed' or 'formless'. In any case we need to beware value judgements which are built into the terminology used. As T. W. Manson wisely observed, '... a paragraph of Mark is not a penny the better or the worse as historical evidence for being labelled, "Apophthegm" or "Pronouncement Story" or "Paradigm".'

- When scholars step beyond a general description of a form's life setting to proposing a *specific* life setting for a particular story (as they sometimes do), there is the danger of a circular argument. A story can be said to be created by a particular need in the life of the early churches, but when we ask how we know of that need, the only answer is that the story shows that! This danger can be ameliorated by focusing on the needs we know the early churches to have had, from the NT letters. The NT letters also show us that the earliest Christians could respond to particular problems or issues without using words of Jesus to resolve them. In Galatians and 1 Pet. 3:14-18, where the use of a word of Jesus would have clinched the argument, no such thing appears. This suggests that the early Christians did not feel free to create words of Jesus to fit their needs.
- The 'laws' of tradition need handling with considerable care, for it is difficult to produce hard and fast laws. The most we can speak of are the *tendencies* of tradition, and even then we cannot be dogmatic: research suggests that stories can become longer or shorter, and add detail or lose it in the course of transmission in writing. For example, on the one hand Luke 8:42 gives more detail about Jairus' daughter than Mark 5:23, but on the other hand it is Mark alone who gives the name Bartimaeus to the blind man Jesus heals (Mark 10:46; contrast Matt. 20:29; Luke 18:35).
- Study of the transmission of written texts (such as the use of Mark by Matthew and Luke), which forms the basis of many 'laws of tradition', cannot teach us much with certainty about the transmission of *oral* traditions.

THE CONTRIBUTION OF FORM CRITICISM

Some ideas in this approach are valuable, not least in attempting to understand the oral period. It is helpful to reflect on the kinds of debates which early Christian preachers had with opponents and within the churches. Some awareness of the *Sitz im Leben* of a story or saying can be helpful, providing that it is used with caution – for the evangelists wrote to tell stories about Jesus in a way that related to the audience(s) of the ancient world, rather than to show us their *Sitz im Leben*.

In identifying different forms of Gospel stories, form criticism underlines the point that, for example, we should interpret a parable differently from an account of Jesus healing someone: the stories are structured differently and are often making a different point. Similarly, recognizing the focus of a pronouncement story on the 'punch line' at the end assists in seeing the point it makes.

Form criticism helps further in recognizing the true nature of the Gospels: its recognition that stories were preserved because they were helpful to the early Christians suggests that our Gospels give us the church's picture(s) of Jesus. The Gospels are not like modern biographies, which sketch the psychological development of the subject, and they tell us nothing about Jesus' height, looks or manner of speech. What we have is what the earliest Christians thought it was important to preserve.

Finally, the recognition that many stories can stand on their own as the basis of early Christian preaching highlights the 'gospel in a nutshell' in each story or saying, and looking for that kernel can be very helpful in interpreting the Gospel stories. Mark 3:1-6, a classic pronouncement story, focuses on the saying, 'Is it lawful to do good or to do harm on the Sabbath, to save life or to kill?' (v. 4), and thus challenges the Pharisees' interpretation of the Sabbath, leading to their plot to kill Jesus (v. 6).

REDACTION CRITICISM

Form criticism paints a picture of the evangelists as stringing stories together like pearls on a necklace. The writers make little contribution to the telling of the stories themselves, but only provide the framework and the links between stories. Redaction criticism began as a reaction to this, focusing on the contribution of the authors to the Gospels and asserting that the evangelists should be seen as creative authors in their own right. Its name comes from the German *Redaktionsgeschichte*, meaning 'editing history', and it focuses on the editing of the tradition by the evangelists. Bornkamm, one of the pioneers, puts it well (Bornkamm, Barth & Held 1963, p. 11):

> The synoptic writers show – all three and each in his own special way – by their editing and construction, by their selection, inclusion and omission, and not least by what at first sight appears an insignificant, but on closer examination is seen to be a characteristic treatment of the traditional material, *that they are by no means mere collectors and handers-on of the tradition, but are also interpreters of it.* (Italics mine)

Thus redaction criticism aims to identify the evangelists' own theology and perspective, with a view to sketching the situation from which each writes – for redaction critics assume that the emphases of each Gospel reflected the church out of which the evangelist wrote. Thus they speak of 'Mark's community' or similar phrases, and identify the problems of that church with the issues raised in Mark.

WHAT IS REDACTION?

There are a number of possibilities for editing a story, as the quotation from Bornkamm above makes clear. These include (assuming Markan priority in each case):

- **combining** two separate traditions into one story, e.g. the temptation of Jesus in Matt. 4:1-11 and Luke 4:1-13 looks like a combination of Mark's brief version (1:12f.) and a longer version from another source to which Mark did not have access.
- **expanding** a source, e.g. Matthew adds the story of Peter walking to Jesus on the water to Mark's shorter story (Matt. 14:22-33; Mark 6:45-52).
- **changing the setting** of a story or saying, e.g. Jesus' words of lament over Jerusalem are part of a general critique of the Pharisees in Matt. 23:37-39, whereas Luke places them much earlier in Jesus' ministry as a response to the Pharisees warning him about Herod (Luke 13:34f.).
- **omitting parts** of the story, e.g. Matthew seems to have cut out a lot of detail in his account of Jesus healing the epileptic boy (Matt. 17:14-21; Mark 9:14-29).
- **adding explanations** to a story, e.g. Mark makes it clear that he is explaining Jewish customs about washing vessels before meals or Corban to his readers (7:3f., 11).
- **altering to avoid misunderstanding**, e.g. Matthew seems to reword Mark's bald 'No one is good but God alone' so that it cannot be misunderstood as implying that Jesus is not God; Matthew has 'One there is who is good' (Mark 10:18; Matt. 19:17).
- **conserving** source material – a point often missed in focusing on things which the evangelist has changed. Where an evangelist reproduces wording from his source

without amendment, this shows that he accepts and agrees with the source. Such conservation is particularly noticeable in the actual words of Jesus, which often show much closer agreement between the Gospels than the words of their narrative setting, e.g. Jesus' words of lament over Jerusalem, although placed in different contexts, correspond very closely in wording (Matt. 23:37-39; Luke 13:34f.).

Scholars using this approach will study a passage using a synopsis to identify the editorial activity of each evangelist. With each small or large change they ask whether it is *stylistic*, simply part of the evangelist's writing style (e.g. Mark's frequent use of 'immediately'), or *redactional*, done with a theological purpose and showing the evangelist's own perspective. This is redaction criticism proper, 'reading horizontally' (a phrase of C. L. Blomberg) across a synopsis page to see the different emphases of the writers.

Once this has been done for a number of passages, scholars then put together the differences they notice to see if patterns emerge across whole Gospels. This is how major themes of each evangelist can be identified, such as Matthew's interest in fulfilment of the OT by Jesus or Luke's interest in prayer. Although this process is often also called redaction criticism, it should more properly be called *composition criticism*, which is looking at how an evangelist has composed his whole Gospel. (We suggest that 'redaction criticism' is best reserved as a description of work with a *particular passage*, highlighting the differences and emphases of each account.)

SOME COMPOSITION-CRITICAL OBSERVATIONS

Matthew describes Jesus as 'preaching, proclaiming and healing' twice (the only places in the NT where this combination is found), and these summary verses 'frame' a section of his Gospel where Jesus does precisely those things (4:23; 9:35).

Favourite words show a lot about an evangelist's perspective: John uses 'truth' 25 times (cf. Matt. once; Mark three times; Luke three times), 'life' 36 times (Matt. seven; Mark four; Luke five), and 'world' 78 times (Matt. nine; Mark three; Luke three).

Luke introduces references to Jesus praying in a number of stories he shares with Mark and/or Matthew (e.g. Luke 3:21; 5:16; 6:12; 9:18, 28f.; 11:1; 22:31f.; 23:46), highlighting a theme he will develop in Acts.

If Mark was written first, how can redaction criticism of Mark be done? In the cases of Matthew and Luke we have one of their sources at least – Mark – but this is not so with Mark. However, there are some avenues open to studying Mark's editorial activity. His 'seams', which join one story to another, often show his particular emphases (e.g. 1:21-23a highlights Jesus as teacher, a Markan emphasis). Likewise, his summaries show his concerns (e.g. 3:11f. on the theme of secrecy). Occasionally he tells us that he is commenting by introducing an explanatory clause with 'for…' (e.g. 14:27). Sometimes he edits by the way he presents two stories in 'sandwich' form, one wrapped around the other (see p. 195).

The last stage of the process is sometimes called finding the 'third *Sitz im Leben*'. The first life setting is that in the ministry of

Jesus; the second is the situation which caused the preservation (or, some would say, creation) of the story during the oral period; and the third is the church community implied by the story or Gospel in its edited form. This involves 'mirror-reading' the Gospels for the communities behind them, rather like reconstructing Paul's opponents in Galatia (about whom we know little outside Galatians) from Paul's letter to the church there.

AN EXAMPLE: THE STILLING OF THE STORM IN MARK AND MATTHEW

Matthew, Mark and Luke all report this story (Matt. 8:23-27; Mark 4:35-41; Luke 8:22-25); we shall focus on Mark's and Matthew's versions (see below).

Mark's story contains a number of touches which suggest that we are hearing eye-witness testimony:

- the time of day is specified 'when evening had come', v. 35;
- Jesus went 'just as he was', v. 36;
- there were 'other boats', v. 36;

- the cushion in the stern, which may be the boatman's cushioned seat, v. 38;
- the disciples' reproach to Jesus is specific: 'do you not care that we are perishing?', v.38;
- Jesus speaks directly to the wind and waves, v. 39;
- we are told that Jesus rebukes his disciples and the reason – their lack of faith, v. 40.

Mark focuses his story on Jesus' unique authority. He trusts God through the storm, sleeping peacefully (cf. Pss 3:5; 4:8), whereas the disciples panic and wake Jesus (v. 38). More, Jesus rebukes the wind and waves, using the same language as he uses to demons (v. 39, echoing 1:25), and they are still. No wonder the disciples are in awe and ask who he is (v. 41)!

Matthew has eliminated inessential details from Mark's story (on the assumption that Mark wrote first), including all of the eye-witness touches. Like Mark, he focuses on Jesus' unique authority, but in a heightened way: the disciples address Jesus as 'Lord' (v. 25, a Matthean favourite word, cf. Matt. 8:2,

Matt. 8:23-27	Mark 4:35-41
23And when he got into the boat, his disciples followed him. 24A windstorm arose on the sea, so great that the boat was being swamped by the waves; but he was asleep. 25And they went and woke him up, saying, 'Lord, save us! We are perishing!' 26And he said to them, 'Why are you afraid, you of little faith?' Then he got up and rebuked the winds and the sea; and there was a dead calm. 27They were amazed, saying, 'What sort of man is this, that even the winds and the sea obey him?'	35On that day, when evening had come, he said to them, 'Let us go across to the other side.' 36And leaving the crowd behind, they took him with them in the boat, just as he was. Other boats were with him. 37A great windstorm arose, and the waves beat into the boat, so that the boat was already being swamped. 38But he was in the stern, asleep on the cushion; and they woke him up and said to him, 'Teacher, do you not care that we are perishing?' 39He woke up and rebuked the wind, and said to the sea, 'Peace! Be still!' Then the wind ceased, and there was a dead calm. 40He said to them, 'Why are you afraid? Have you still no faith?' 41And they were filled with great awe and said to one another, 'Who then is this, that even the wind and the sea obey him?'

6, 8, 21, 25) and ask him to 'save' (v. 25, perhaps a word used in the worship of churches known to Matthew), and Matthew shares with Mark the Christological focus at the end of the story (v. 27; cf. Mark 4:41).

Matthew also has an interest in discipleship in this story (highlighted by G. Bornkamm in his 1948 article 'The Stilling of the Storm in Matthew' (Bornkamm, Barth & Held 1963, pp. 52–7). Thus he has located the story after 8:19-22, in which Jesus spells out the cost of following him to various would-be followers, by contrast with Luke, who places it elsewhere in his Gospel, not associated with the stilling of the storm (Luke 9:57-62). Matthew also uses 'follow' as a link word, having the disciples follow Jesus onto the boat (v. 23), whereas in Mark they take Jesus with him (Mark 4:36). These links put the stilling story in a situation requiring total discipleship.

Matthew uses the word for 'earthquake' (Greek *seismos*, v. 24) of the storm (it can be used of storms at sea), a word with 'eschatological' overtones of God's action, particularly in 'earth-shaking' situations (as we might say today). Matthew is less critical of the disciples: they have little faith (v. 26, a Matthean phrase: it is found four times in Matthew and only once elsewhere in the NT), rather than no faith (Mark 4:40) – and thus Jesus in Matthew is calling them to greater faith from a basis of some faith, even if it is little. And this saying of Jesus comes before he stills the storm, thus encouraging faith before he acts to save them, whereas Mark has Jesus being critical after the stilling – again, Matthew gives the disciples a chance to grow in following and trusting Jesus.

Thus a redaction-critical approach suggests that Matthew has adapted Mark's story by bringing out the theme of Jesus' authority

more sharply, and also by introducing a theme of discipleship. If this reflects the situation of Matthew's church (see pp. 78f. below for reservations about this question), then it suggests that they are under pressure, pictured by the storm, and Matthew is encouraging them to trust Jesus through it and to hang on to their faith in him through the trying circumstances they face.

> ### Digging deeper:
> ### DOING REDACTION CRITICISM
>
> Compare one of the following sets of parallel accounts (using a synopsis if possible), underlining words that agree (see p. 58). What differences of emphasis appear in the way that the different evangelists record the passage? After you have studied the passages for yourself, consult the commentaries to see whether they notice the same things as you, and what conclusions they draw.
> - Matt. 4:1-11; Mark 1:12-13; Luke 4:1-13;
> - Matt. 9:1-8; Mark 2:1-12; Luke 5:17-26;
> - Matt. 20:29-34; Mark 10:46-52; Luke 18:35-43.

STRENGTHS OF REDACTION CRITICISM

This approach is good at highlighting the evangelist's own contribution to the Gospels and helps us to see particular emphases in each writer. It treats the Gospels holistically, as portraits of Jesus, whereas form criticism has the danger of focusing so much on the individual stories that it can miss the big picture. It focuses on the purpose of the Gospels and asks what it is that each writer wants to communicate.

Further, a redaction-critical approach will assist in hearing the evangelists individually. Christians who see God's hand behind the writing of *four* Gospels will welcome this, for it allows us to see what each Gospel says about Jesus, and thus to get a fuller portrait than simply combining and harmonizing the various elements in each Gospel to get one story.

From the point of view of evaluating the historicity of the Gospel stories, material which goes against a writer's known redactional emphasis is more likely to be from Jesus, rather than the addition or invention of the evangelist.

SOME CRITICISMS

For many early practitioners, redaction criticism was wedded to a highly sceptical view of the historicity of the Gospels. Thus they were inclined to think that redaction was always invention, and doubted that most events reported in the Gospels had taken place at all. For some students of the NT, this ancestry taints redaction criticism and means that those who have a more positive view of the Gospels' historical value cannot use it. However, the differences between the Gospels are there, and therefore require study in order both to understand better what the writers are saying, and also to see the different emphases which come out in the ways the evangelists have told the stories. To tell a story in a way that highlights a particular emphasis need not involve creating fiction, as we can see from our study of the stilling of the storm above.

In order to do the detailed comparisons involved, scholars must decide about source-critical questions. Most redaction-critical study assumes Markan priority, but a significant minority use other assumptions. This means, of course, that the scholarly world divides into different camps for redaction-critical study, depending on their

solution to the synoptic problem – and it can thus be hard for the various groups to engage with each other.

More than that, because oral tradition continued to be available throughout the period of the writing of the Gospels, there are likely to be occasions when, for example, Matthew is preserving material which goes back to Jesus, rather than simply editing Mark's version of a story (see pp. 69).

Redaction critics tend to focus on the differences between the synoptics, in other words on the changes to the tradition only. But at times this may mislead, for sometimes the most significant thing is that one evangelist has taken over a story from another with relatively little editing, because they agree with the point(s) the story makes and want to incorporate it into their Gospel. Redaction-critical study can tend, also, to overdefine groups within earliest Christianity, each with their own individual emphases and beliefs represented by a particular evangelist's redactional emphases. This can mask the wide agreement there seems to have been among the early Christian groups over quite a large core of beliefs about Jesus, about God and about the Christian life.

Recently R. Bauckham (1997) has led a group of scholars who have criticized the redaction-critical attempt to reconstruct the early churches from the Gospels on the assumption that the issues in a Gospel reflect the issues, for example, Matthew's church faced. Bauckham observes that this approach treats the Gospels as if they were like the NT letters, which we know to have been written for particular groups of people, whereas the genre of the Gospels as 'lives' (see pp. 50f.) would mean that they should be seen to be aimed at quite a general readership. He then notes that the assumption of literary interdependence among the synoptic Gospels means that they must have circulated among the earliest Christian communities quite quickly, so that the later evangelists could use the earlier Gospels as sources – and this suggests that the evangelists wrote for a wide circulation.

Redaction-critical reconstructions of early Christian communities behind each Gospel tend to assume that the churches were quite isolated, held their own idiosyncratic 'theologies', and that there was considerable homogeneity in what was believed within individual churches. The second stage of Bauckham's argument seeks to show that, on the contrary, the earliest churches saw themselves as part of a network, and that regular communication went on among them.

Paul's collection (see 1 Cor. 16:1-4; 2 Cor. 8–9; Rom. 15:25-28) illustrates the point, and other lines of evidence point this way: there are phrases in the NT letters such as 'your brothers and sisters in all the world' (1 Pet. 5:9). Many Christian leaders travelled to different churches: Peter, Barnabas, Silas, Apollos, Philip, Priscilla and Aquila all moved around – to say nothing of Paul. Letters were sent from one church to another: 1 Pet. 5:13 sends greetings from the church in 'Babylon' to the churches receiving the letter, and 1 Clement and the Epistle of Polycarp (late first century or early second century AD) were church-to-church letters. In the days before a postal service, such letters were sent with a member of the sending church as courier, so the relationship between the churches was more than literary.

Not only was there a network of relationships between the earliest churches, but there is evidence of conflict and some diversity among these groups, which suggests that they communicated with each other – for you cannot disagree and debate with someone of whom you know nothing! We know from Acts and Galatians that the Judaizers travelled around to propagate their views in other churches. Such travelling means that it is unlikely that each church was theologically homogeneous, for there could be conflict within individual churches – of which Corinth is a prime example (e.g. 1 Cor. 1:10-13).

All this evidence points not to individual churches being isolated groups which developed in idiosyncratic ways, but rather that we should see the Gospels as being aimed at wider first-century society. Thus the redaction-critical quest to reconstruct individual churches behind each Gospel could be very misleading. Certainly the evangelists each have their own emphases and agendas, but these need not reflect the needs of particular churches to the extent that redaction critics sometimes claim.

AND NOW?

The heyday of redaction-critical study is over, and a wide variety of other ways of reading the Gospels have been developed. Most scholars still use source-, form- and redaction-critical tools in studying the synoptic Gospels, but without necessarily accepting the historical scepticism which some of the originators of these tools held. We shall turn next to consider how we can use these and other tools to interpret the Gospels better.

ESSAY TOPICS

INTRODUCTORY

● Assess the strengths and weaknesses of the 'two source hypothesis' concerning the origins of the synoptic Gospels.

● Offer a critical assessment of the contribution of redaction criticism to understanding the synoptic Gospels.

INTERMEDIATE

● Consider the Matthean and Lukan beatitudes and woes (Matt. 5:3-12; Luke 6:20-26) from the perspectives of source, form and redaction criticism.

FURTHER READING

* denotes books assuming knowledge of Greek; most can be used by all students.

GOSPELS SYNOPSES AND CHARTS

*K. Aland, ed. *Synopsis of the Four Gospels*. Stuttgart: United Bible Societies, 1976 (Greek and RSV on parallel pages; all four Gospels; another edition has just RSV).

A. Barr *A Diagram of Synoptic Relationships*. Edinburgh: T. & T. Clark, 1938 [2nd ed. 1995] (superb colour-coded chart of the synoptic Gospels to show where parallels occur).

B. H. Throckmorton, Jr, ed. *Gospel Parallels*, 5th ed. New York: Nelson, 1992 (NRSV; synoptic Gospels only).

INTRODUCTORY

DJG articles: 'Form Criticism', 'Redaction Criticism', 'Synoptic Problem', 'Tradition Criticism'.

INTERMEDIATE

Mark Goodacre's Web site http://www.ntgateway.com/ is a fine collection of NT resources, with excellent links and material, especially on source criticism.

R. Bauckham, ed. *The Gospels for All Christians*. Edinburgh/Grand Rapids: T. & T. Clark/Eerdmans, 1997 (a key book, arguing that the Gospels are aimed at a wide audience, and not merely at individual, small Christian communities).

A. J. Bellinzoni *The Two-Source Hypothesis: A Critical Appraisal*. Mercer: Mercer University Press, 1985 (valuable collection of key articles on all sides of the source-critical debate).

*G. Bornkamm, G. Barth & H. J. Held *Tradition and Interpretation in Matthew*. London: SCM/Philadelphia: Westminster Press, 1963 (key collection of pioneering redaction-critical essays).

W. R. Farmer *The Synoptic Problem*, 2nd ed. London/New York: Macmillan, 1976 (classic statement of the 'Griesbach' view that Mark is last).

D. E. Nineham *Saint Mark*. Harmondsworth: Penguin/New York: Seabury Press, 1963 (classic form- and redaction-critical commentary).

N. Perrin *What is Redaction Criticism?* Philadelphia: Fortress, 1969/London: SPCK, 1970 (clear introduction by a leading practitioner).

J. Rohde *Rediscovering the Teaching of the Evangelists*. London: SCM/Philadelphia: Westminster Press, 1968 (good survey of the work of redaction-critical scholars on the synoptic Gospels, although now dated).

E. P. Sanders & M. Davies *Studying the Synoptic Gospels*. London: SCM/Philadelphia: Trinity Press International, 1989 (good introduction to critical study of the synoptics for students).

R. H. Stein *The Synoptic Problem*. Grand Rapids: Baker, 1987/Leicester: IVP, 1988 (fine introduction to source, form and redaction criticism with good examples).

*V. Taylor *The Gospel according to St Mark*, 2nd ed. London: Macmillan, 1966 (classic form-critical commentary).

J. W. Wenham *Redating Matthew, Mark and Luke: A Fresh Assault on the Synoptic Problem*. London: Hodder & Stoughton, 1991/Downers Grove: IVP, 1992 (a stimulating study which proposes a much larger place for oral tradition than many approaches).

Chapter 5

UNDERSTANDING THE GOSPELS TODAY

Since the heyday of redaction criticism in the 1960s and 1970s a number of other approaches to reading the Gospels have been developed by scholars to help today's readers understand the Gospels for themselves. Some scholars are more interested in the ancient setting; others are particularly focused on using models and methods from today's world. In this chapter, which is likely to be more stretching work than the previous one, we shall:

- examine 'newer' approaches to reading the Gospels, focusing particularly on narrative criticism;
- outline a practical approach to studying a passage from the Gospels;
- consider how to interpret particular types of Gospel stories: parables, miracles and apocalyptic;
- discuss the implications of critical study of the Gospels for their historical reliability;
- think about how to read the Gospels today.

TOOLS FOR INTERPRETING THE GOSPELS

In broad terms there are three areas of focus for approaches to reading the Gospels (and almost any kind of literature). There are those which focus on the author, on the text and on the reader. This analysis uses a 'communication' model of writing, in which an author writes a text in order to communicate with readers:

$$\boxed{\text{author} \rightarrow \text{text} \rightarrow \text{reader}}$$

Author-centred approaches pay particular attention to the author's contribution and intention(s) in writing the text. This means that the key to interpreting the text is outside it, located in the author, his or her sources (written and oral) and the author's concerns and emphases. The classic historical-critical approaches (source, form and redaction criticism: see ch. 4) were concerned with precisely this area of study. They looked for the sources used by the author (source criticism seeking written sources, and form criticism oral sources) and how the author had organized and edited them into their final form (redaction criticism). The focus of attention in author-centred studies is therefore *behind* the text. The text is being used as a window, through which the reader looks both to see the historical world described and to reconstruct the story of the text's production. For these approaches, these two things are the 'meaning' being sought.

The difficulty that these approaches met was the so-called *intentional fallacy*, which highlights two issues. First, since the Gospels were written long ago, we have no knowledge of the intention of the author except through the text which he has left to us. We cannot ask Mark why he wrote something in the way that he did, or what he meant by a particular phrase or story. Indeed, with the Gospels we are in a much worse position than with studying, for example, Charles Dickens, for in his case we know quite a bit about his background and ideas from the prefaces of his books and the writings of his contemporaries about Dickens.

In the case of both Mark and Dickens we can, of course, work out some things about the authors' ideas by intelligent detective work on the text (looking for clues authors have left as to why they wrote), and by using our knowledge of the time and culture from other written and archaeological sources. Nevertheless, this criticism alerts us to a key potential difficulty.

The second issue is that scholars (initially in studying English literature, but later also in Biblical Studies) began to argue that, even where the intentions of the author are known, once the text is in the public domain, the author has no further control over it. Others may see connections or meanings in the text which were not 'intended' by the author – and on the other hand, the author may not have fully succeeded in carrying through his or her intentions in writing. Thus the proper object of study is not the author's intentions, which are inaccessible, but the text itself.

This is clearly making a valid point, although it needs to be qualified, for it should not be possible to make a text 'mean'

anything at all (see further on post-structuralism, pp. 93f.). In a wider sphere, we may think of the way in which biblical texts function in the churches. Christians often see connections between different biblical books which are highly unlikely to have been seen by the author, but which raise valid questions about the nature of Christian faith and life. One approach, 'canonical criticism' (developed initially by Brevard Childs), focuses on these questions and seeks to read individual books and passages in the context of the whole Bible.

Text-centred approaches pay great attention to the text itself, seeking to examine the 'world' which the text creates and attempting to understand the story of the text entirely within its own terms. In reading texts this way, the meaning is to be found *within* the text, and scholars working this way pay particular attention to literary genre, structure, and echoes of language and concepts within the text. Studying the text is viewed as an end in itself, rather than as the vehicle for studying something else (such as the historical Jesus).

Careful attention to the text in this way is clearly important since, without understanding the text on its own terms, there are greater possibilities for misunderstanding. But the Gospels present stories about historical figures and therefore claim to be telling of events which actually happened. This suggests that the historical information available to the authors would control what they wrote: sometimes they give a particular piece of information simply because that is the way it happened. In this respect, reading the Gospels is different from reading novels, and this limits the usefulness of text-centred approaches (as it does with other books narrating historical events). Nevertheless, asking how the text tells its story is crucial to reading well, as well as asking what that story is about.

The process of communication also involves those who read the text, and *reader-centred approaches* pay particular attention to the effects the text has on readers, and the effects readers have on the texts they read. These approaches look at the assumptions, conscious or unconscious, which the reader brings to the reading process – assumptions drawn from the background, culture, world-view, and traditions of reading learned by the reader. Every reader has such a 'pre-understanding' (which will be modified in the process of reading), and recent scholars tend to be more up front about this, by contrast with older approaches to scholarship, which effectively claimed that they were being 'objective' in their study. Thus scholars speak of the 'interpretative community(ies)' to which they belong, meaning groups which share a common approach to reading a text or texts. For example, Margaret Davies begins her 'reading' of Matthew:

> … let me tell the reader to which interpretative communities I belong. I am a British, female academic, a member of the Anglican church, but not of its evangelical wing, a member of the Labour Party and of several civil liberty groups. (M. Davies *Matthew*. Readings: A New Biblical Commentary. Sheffield: JSOT Press, 1993, 15).

Some reader-centred approaches ask how ancient readers would have experienced the text, and therefore use tools from ancient rhetoric (the art of persuasion and argument in the Græco-Roman world) to identify how a text would be persuasive for ancient readers. Others focus on today's readers, sometimes approaching with particular ideological presuppositions in order to see how the text looks from that perspective. Such 'ideological' approaches include feminism, the concerns of particular ethnic groups, or Marxism. Meaning in these approaches is found in the interaction between the reader and the text: some scholars therefore speak of the text as a mirror which enables the reader to reflect on his or her thoughts and beliefs.

What do you think?
YOUR PRE-UNDERSTANDING

What do you bring to reading the Gospels? For example:

- what values are most important to you in life?
- what methods of reading texts have you learned in your education so far?
- what kind of documents do you think the Gospels are: historical, fictional, theological, biased, inspired by God, etc.?
- do you share the Christian faith that the Gospels aim to communicate? If so, what Christian tradition or denomination do you come from, and what are the key ways of reading the Gospels used in that tradition?

Reflect on your answers to these questions with others who are studying the Gospels. (If you have a culturally mixed group this will be particularly valuable.) Try to help each other see the potential 'blind spots' in each of your approaches: what perspectives, ideas or emphases in the Gospels might you be in danger of missing because of your assumptions or world-view? Keep thinking about this as you study particular parts of the Gospels.

83

There is clearly value in identifying the pre-understanding we bring to reading a text, for it may limit what we hear from our reading by causing us to be deaf to particular ideas or literary techniques. However, a proper reading of the Gospels will also need to listen carefully to the texts in their own right and as historical sources, so that we respect the 'otherness' of these texts – they come from a different world from ours, and that is why careful historical study is important alongside text- and author-centred approaches. Hence, scholarship today includes all three kinds of approaches and most accept that each has valuable insights to offer in reading the Gospels, and that no one method is the only 'correct' way to read them.

The danger for the beginner is being bewildered by the variety of approaches. A key to avoiding this is to become more conscious of how each scholar approaches reading the Gospels, and more self-conscious about your own pre-understanding and preferred methods.

Our study will now focus on narrative criticism, as one of the most widely used of these newer approaches, although we shall also briefly consider a number of others, including rhetorical criticism, sociological approaches, structuralism, post-structuralism and deconstruction, reader-response approaches, and liberationist and feminist approaches.

NARRATIVE CRITICISM

Narrative criticism is a text-centred approach whose primary concern is to understand how the text works in its present, final form. It was pioneered in Gospels studies by Rhoads and Michie, one a biblical scholar and the other an English lit-erature scholar, in studying Mark. Other key writers have been Tannehill and Johnson (on Luke and Acts), Culpepper and Stibbe (on John), and Kingsbury (on Matthew). (See the 'further reading' at the end of chs 9–12 for full details.)

One of the first moves made by narrative critics is to think of the *implied author* of a text. This is not the real, historical author, but a portrait of the kind of person who would write this text, including what we can know of their values and beliefs from their text. To speak of the implied author highlights helpfully how limited our knowledge of the real author is: we know of Matthew only what he has chosen to show us through his book.

On the other side of the reading process lies the *implied reader*. As with the implied author, this is not an actual reader, but a portrait of the kind of person who would understand and respond to this text fully – sometimes called the *ideal reader*. For example, Mark's explanation of Jewish customs suggests that his implied reader is Gentile rather than Jewish (e.g. Mark 7:3f.; see pp. 204f.), whereas Matthew's implied reader needs no such explanation (cf. Matt. 15:1-3). Reading the text carefully will highlight the kind of response the implied author seeks from the implied reader.

Narrative critics frequently discuss the development of plot, point of view, characters and settings. We shall briefly look at examples of each of these.

Plot

Regarding plot, narrative critics highlight the way the story develops within the text in order to detect causes and effects. For example, Matt. 12:14 concludes two stories in Matt. 12:1-14: 'But the Pharisees went out and conspired against him, how to destroy him.' Reading the second story alone (vv. 9-14), where Jesus heals the man with the withered hand on the Sabbath, it is not clear why the Pharisees went out to conspire against Jesus, for they are not mentioned in that story. However, Matthew has constructed his plot carefully, for the first story (vv. 1-8) tells of Jesus responding to the Pharisees' criticism of his disciples for plucking grain on the Sabbath and this explains who 'they' are in the second story (vv. 9, 10, 11).

In studying plot the use of *narrative time* can be highly significant. Sometimes the duration of a story is important, for to slow down narrative time by telling a story at much greater length and in more detail than others often shows that the story is particularly significant. When John writes of the death and raising of Lazarus, he tells of Jesus hearing of his death and then travelling, totalling about four days, in 16 verses (John 11:1-16), but the following 28 verses cover only a few minutes (11:17-44). By slowing down narrative time, John focuses attention on the discussion between Jesus and the sisters and his raising of their brother – and we discover why within a short time, for verses 45-53 describe the differing reactions to Jesus' action: some believe in him, but the chief priests and Pharisees plot against him, wanting him dead.

Sometimes the *sequence* of stories is important, with a story told out of chronological sequence for particular effect. Mark presents the death of John the Baptist as a 'flashback' from King Herod's comment that Jesus is John raised from the dead (Mark 6:14-29). By contrast, Luke tells of the removal of John from the scene before Jesus' public ministry begins (Luke 3:19f.) because from there on he focuses attention upon Jesus – hence Luke only alludes briefly to John's death (Luke 9:9).

The *frequency* of a story being told can show its importance. Luke tells the story of Saul's encounter with the risen Jesus on the Damascus Road three times (Acts 9, 22 and 26) and thereby highlights it as important to his overall story in Acts.

> **What do you think?**
> **NARRATIVE TIME**
>
> Read the different accounts of Jesus' early life until the coming of John the Baptist in Matt. 1:18–3:1 and Luke 1:26-58; 2:1–3:2 and identify the speed at which narrative time is moving in different sections of these narratives. Which elements of the narratives are highlighted and which are passed over quickly? What do your discoveries suggest about the particular emphases of Matthew and Luke in telling these stories?

Finally regarding plot, it is worth looking for *conflict* within the story, clashes of wills, actions, ideas, desires or characters. In the Gospels, Jesus is frequently in conflict: with the Jewish leaders, his disciples (who fail to understand him, e.g. Mark 6:52; 9:32), demons, disease, death, nature and even himself in the Garden of Gethsemane (Mark 14:36). Each of these conflicts is resolved within the narrative, but some are left unresolved: we do not know, within the horizon of Acts, what finally happened over the conflict between Paul and Barnabas over John Mark (Acts 15:36-41).

Point of view

A TV advertisement for a national newspaper in Britain showed a close-up shot of a powerful-looking young man with shaven head running at high speed towards an elderly woman, giving the strong impression that he was going to attack her. At the last moment the camera angle changed and we saw the full picture: he was running in order to get her out of the way of a fast-moving car which was going to hit her as she crossed the street. We saw him pick her up and take her to safety. The advertisement went on to claim, of course, that the newspaper gave its readers the fuller picture of what was really going on!

The choice of the 'angle' from which the storyteller looks is crucial; the decision about point of view is the implied author's method of guiding the implied reader to see the narrative from the implied author's perspective. Here we see the world-view, the values and norms of the implied author. For example, the evangelists all present a world in which supernatural beings are real and miraculous healings happen – a point of view at variance with that of many modern westerners.

Sometimes we meet an *evaluative* point of view, in which the author offers us what he believes is God's perspective. This can happen by 'telling', by statements by the implied author about characters or situations: e.g. Zechariah and Elisabeth are 'righteous before God, living blamelessly according to all the commandments and regulations of the Lord' (Luke 1:6) – these are the 'good guys'! At other times we see an evaluative point of view more subtly by 'showing', by reliable characters, such as angels or Jesus or the OT Scriptures, speaking about a character (see the evaluations of John in Matt. 3:3, 13-15; 11:7-15; 21:32).

Characters

Characters are clearly important to the plot of a narrative, for they are the agents who move the story on. Some scholars speak of 'actants' in the Gospels (rather than 'actors') because some of these agents are not human – such as demons or angels (cf. the serpent in Gen. 3). *Characterization*, or how characters are portrayed, is important to understanding a narrative, for implied authors often show their point of view by which characters they approve of and which they do not.

In considering a character we need to ask whether they agree with the implied author's point of view; if so, they are 'reliable'. As we have seen, Matthew regards John the Baptist as reliable. By contrast, Matthew does not agree with the Pharisees' view of Jesus as working by the power of Beelzebul (Matt. 12:24) and he shows this partly by Jesus' critical answer (vv. 25-32) and partly by his overall characterization of the Pharisees, who are consistently Jesus' opponents in Matthew (e.g. 9:11, 34; 12:1, 14).

The implied reader is being invited to offer various responses to characters. Sometimes they are expected to *empathize*, to identify strongly with the character, perhaps because they see their own likeness in them, or want to be like the character. The disciples in Matthew invite empathy as people like the implied reader of this Gospel: they have little faith (6:30; 8:26; 14:31; 16:8); their spirits are willing to follow Jesus, but their flesh is weak (26:41); they fail (26:36, 40f., 43); and yet they grow in understanding (16:5-12, esp. v. 12), and they are called by Jesus to spread the news about him after his resurrection (28:16-20).

Alternatively, the implied reader may be invited to *sympathize*, to identify rather less intensely with the character. Mark's portrait of the disciples seems harsher than Matthew's, for he regularly highlights their mistakes and lack of understanding (e.g. Mark 6:37; 7:17f.; 8:4, 31-33; 9:18, 28f., 31f.). Nevertheless, Jesus is confident that they will ultimately come through and be faithful witnesses to him (Mark 13:9-13) – hence the implied reader is not being encouraged to be distant from the disciples, but to sympathize.

Occasionally, the implied reader is asked to show *antipathy* to a character and to feel alienated from them or hostile to them. The devil is one clear example in the Gospels, for he is Jesus' opponent (Luke 4:1-13), as is Judas, who betrays Jesus.

Digging deeper:
CHARACTERIZATION

Choose one of the following characters and study how the evangelist named presents and develops them (use a concordance or computer to find the places in the particular Gospel where the character occurs – and don't forget that a Gospels synopsis can help you spot particular emphases of your writer by comparing his account with the others). Is the implied author encouraging the implied reader to show empathy, sympathy or antipathy to the character?

● Peter in Matthew
● John the Baptist in John
● Mary the mother of Jesus in Luke

(*Further reading*: Powell 1993, ch. 5 gives a fuller discussion of characters, and he provides a good set of analytical questions for seeing how an author is characterizing a figure in the narrative (104).)

Settings

Locations can bring an atmosphere or feeling to a scene in a story in a remarkable way, including where, when and how the action takes place. Settings may be symbolic, reveal characters, determine conflict and provide a structure for the story.

On the whole the Gospels are economical in their provision of physical descriptions of spatial settings – strikingly, we would not know that there were tables in the temple if Jesus had not turned them over! But temporal settings – when or how long the action takes place – are much more significant. For John, 'night' is a potent symbol: Nicodemus comes to see Jesus at night, implying secrecy (3:2, 19-21) and Judas leaves at night, symbolizing that spiritual darkness has descended as he goes to betray Jesus (13:32).

Knowing something of the social conventions of a setting can be important for seeing how the implied author is guiding the implied reader to see a situation. Much of this kind of study is similar to that found in traditional historical criticism, and this fact is a corrective to those who regard narrative criticism as a new approach which is isolated and on its own.

Luke 7:36-50 offers a particularly striking example of the importance of understanding cultural settings. A modern westerner's picture of eating a meal involves sitting at chairs around a table, whereas here we should see a low table of food in the middle of a large room, surrounded by low couches on which the diners reclined with their heads nearest the central table. That was why the woman found it easy to anoint, wash and kiss Jesus' feet, for they were on his couch (v. 38). Further, the custom of hospitality in that culture is to greet a visitor with a kiss, to pour oil on the visitor's head and to wash the visitor's feet. But Simon fails to do all of these things, thus systematically insulting Jesus, by contrast with the woman, who demonstrates her welcome by her actions (vv. 44-46). (On this story, see the excellent study in Bailey 1980, ch. 1.)

Assessment

Narrative-critical approaches offer real strengths, for they enable readers to focus on the text of the Gospels, rather than hypothetical historical reconstructions. As a holistic approach, narrative criticism contrasts with source and form criticism. Both of them divide the text up into sections, depending on tensions within the text to find the different sources used by the author. By contrast, a narrative-critical reading of a Gospel passage will relate it to the other parts of the book from which it comes, and will usually expect consistent development and coherence within the book. This has great strengths, since it avoids some of the (sometimes arbitrary) reconstructions of hypotheses about the life setting of a story, and can provide insights into the text where the historical content is not certain: a solution to the synoptic problem is not required in order to do narrative criticism!

Narrative criticism also takes seriously the role of the reading process in engaging with a text, identifying what is required in order to make sense of a narrative. While it can be done in ways that are inaccessible to 'ordinary Bible readers', by becoming over-technical, many of the insights of narrative critics are available to those who are not scholars, and for Christian readers of the Gospels, this enables a more fruitful dialogue between scholars and such readers. However, narrative criticism developed out

of the study of modern fiction and Russian folk tales, and therefore some of the questions it asks and approaches it utilizes may not be appropriate to the Gospels as ancient literature. For example, narrative criticism puts on one side questions of history, since it is concerned with the way that stories work as stories. This puts limits on its value in studying texts which purport to be describing historical events: with the Gospels in particular it is also important to ask about their historicity and historical context, using what we know from ancient literary and archaeological sources.

This example highlights that narrative criticism is not a 'one size fits all' approach to studying the Gospels; most of its practitioners acknowledge that it needs other, complementary approaches in order fully to understand the Gospels (see Powell 1993, 98-101).

SOCIAL-SCIENTIFIC APPROACHES

Historical critics acknowledge the importance of understanding the social setting of the Gospels, both that from which the author writes and that which he or she addresses. Social-scientific approaches, which came to prominence in the 1970s, pay attention to the analysis of the social and cultural context(s) of the text and its environment using models, theories and perspectives from the modern social sciences. This is asking about the kind of society presupposed in order to make better sense of the text. The Gospels both reflect and react to ancient social contexts, and social-scientific studies consider both aspects. When the Society of Biblical Literature set up its first study group on 'The Social World of Early Christianity', four key tasks were outlined: (i) to describe the social facts of early Christianity and place it in its social setting; (ii) to develop a social history of early Christianity; (iii) to examine the social forces which led to the rise of Christianity and its institutions; (iv) to consider the early Christian 'symbolic universe', identifying how they saw the world and what structures and ideas supported that perspective.

In considering the contexts which the Gospels reflect and assume, issues can be highlighted to which other approaches are not so sensitive. For example, Theissen looks at the Jesus movement and sketches the Palestinian social, economic and cultural setting in which Jesus lived and draws parallels between Jesus' group and the travelling Cynic teachers. This approach helpfully highlights Gospel material concerned with travelling teachers, family ties, possessions and homelessness to which other approaches can be 'blind' (e.g. Matt. 8:19-22; Luke 14:26; Mark 10:28-31).

In using models from modern social sciences, scholars consider whether and how far a modern social movement can provide a 'grid' through which to understand an ancient movement. For example, Gager compared aspects of the early Christian movement to modern 'millenarian' cults which expect the end of the world any day. Gager used modern studies of these cults, noticing that they often grow out of a strong sense of social alienation and dispossession on the part of the members. Accordingly, Gager then considered the early church as a group who were marginalized within the power structures of the Roman empire, and for whom Jesus became a prophet who promised a better world. However, Gager argued, the eventual realization that the return of Jesus was not going to happen quickly caused adjustments to be made to the Christians' beliefs and led to

accommodation with the Roman state and its social structures.

While there are undoubted gains in such study, there can be a danger of reductionism, attempting to explain everything in early Christianity as a result of this or that part of the social environment. Equally, modern models of groups may not always fit the ancient world, and such models need to be used carefully, in tune with what we know of the ancient settings from more traditional historical and archaeological studies.

RHETORICAL CRITICISM

Rhetorical criticism is a group of reader-centred approaches which look for the persuasive strategies adopted by the writer. Generally, people write in order to persuade, whether to change a perspective, to push a decision about the future in a particular direction, to advocate a particular judgement about the past, or to encourage a group to maintain a stance or view already held. As we say, writers have an 'agenda' which they seek to communicate in order to achieve an effect. Broadly, rhetorical criticism of the Gospels and Acts covers two main approaches, one focusing on ancient forms of rhetoric, and the other looking from today's understanding of rhetoric.

Ancient rhetoric was a well-developed art which was taught as part of 'higher education' in the Graeco-Roman world. Every adult man needed to be able to speak persuasively, whether in the law court (where citizens often defended or prosecuted for themselves, rather than use a lawyer), the city's citizen assembly or senate (where decisions about the city's policy and future were made), or on formal occasions (such as funerals or weddings). Thus the rhetorical handbooks of Aristotle, Quintilian and Cicero were used in the schools to train young men how to speak, and they learned to imitate the best practice of the handbooks in composing and delivering speeches.

Rhetorical criticism using these models considers how the Gospels speak into a world well aware of this training. Kennedy has analysed NT passages, including the sermon on the mount (Matt. 5–7), from this perspective (Kennedy 1984, 39-63). He advocates a five step approach: (i) identify the rhetorical unit; (ii) analyze the rhetorical situation in which the speech is presented; (iii) identify the type of the speech, focusing on what kind of decision it seeks; (iv) analyse the use of evidence, structure and use of language; (v) consider how effectively the speech persuades.

In the case of the sermon on the mount, Kennedy sees the unit as Matt. 5–7, the rhetorical situation as Jesus addressing his disciples and the crowds who are drawn to him because of his healing activities (Matt. 4:24f.). The speech is deliberative, that is, it is designed to persuade the hearers to take a particular course of action, which is following Jesus (note 5:29f.; 7:24-27). Its structure begins with a statement (5:13-16), followed by a proposal (5:17-20), and the latter is unpacked in 5:21–7:20. The closing summarizes (7:21-23) and then appeals to the hearers for a response (7:24-27). The speech persuades by appealing to Jesus' authority (especially in 6:1-18, where he teaches without reference to other authorities) and to the hearers' emotions (7:24-27 paints a picture which would move people's feelings).

Others propose a broader consideration of rhetoric which takes account of

developments in understanding and analysis since ancient times, not least the so-called 'new rhetoric' of the 1960s onwards. This group of approaches often finds alliances with narrative or reader-response approaches to the text. Some speak of 'socio-rhetorical criticism' and highlight the social context(s) within which writers seek to persuade readers to share their views. Others advocate using reader-response tools to identify the kind of person that authors wish their readers to become (somewhat akin to analysis of the 'implied reader' in narrative criticism).

Witherington is an example of a scholar who attempts to use socio-rhetorical tools in analyzing NT texts, and his commentaries on John and Acts (see pp. 264, 299) are examples of his analysis of the persuasive power of these books.

As with narrative criticism, rhetorical criticism is frequently used in conjunction with other approaches to the Gospels. Thus a scholar who concludes, using source criticism, that Mark was written first will then examine how Matthew and Luke have adapted Mark's stories to their rhetorical ends, using tools from redaction criticism. The rhetorical part of the study will ask questions about what it is that Matthew and Luke are seeking to persuade readers to do or believe, and how they go about using their stories in order to do that.

READER-RESPONSE APPROACHES
Different people read books in different ways and notice different features of them; the history of NT scholarship provides a commentary on this, for different questions have been asked of the NT texts at different periods, in different countries and by different individual scholars. The process of

communication between author and reader involves the reader's own cultural setting, upbringing, beliefs, values and expectations. These can – and are – changed in the process of reading, but the reader is not a 'clean sheet' for the writer to communicate with. Thus reader-response approaches focus on the readerly end of the communication process, seeking to understand and analyse how readers make sense of texts. The English literature scholar Wolfgang Iser's work was influential in the development of such approaches in NT studies.

In narrative, authors leave 'gaps' in stories which readers must fill in for themselves. For example, 'the Word' is mentioned in John 1:1 without introduction or explanation (much as God enters the stage in Gen. 1:1). It is not until 1:17 that we are told that 'the Word' is Jesus. When Jesus leaves Cana after the miracle of the water become wine and goes to Capernaum (2:11f.), John tells us nothing of Jesus' route, his reasons for going to Capernaum, or of precisely how long he spends there ('a few days', v. 12). John's story is economical with such features and leaves the reader guessing at how to fill in these gaps: thus it invites readerly response. (I owe these examples to Stibbe 1994, 12f., 16f.)

Reader-response critics vary a great deal in how they approach the relationship of reader and text. Some see the reader's role as creating meaning, whereas others would be more cautious, believing that the text itself sets some limits on the meanings that can be legitimately attributed to it. The latter group therefore overlap with those practising narrative criticism, and historically reader-response approaches grew from that soil.

> **What do you think?**
> **GAP FILLING**
>
> Read the parable of the labourers in the vineyard (Matt. 20:1-16). Try to imagine reading this parable for the first time. What significant gaps are left in Jesus' telling of this parable at each stage of the story? What effect do these gaps have on how you read the parable at each stage? How might the gaps help the parable be effective in getting its point across?

Equally, there is variation in the kind of readers considered by different scholars. Some focus on ancient readers, and are therefore close to rhetorical critics, whereas others want to read the Gospels, for example, from a Marxist or feminist perspective. These approaches spill over into a number of ideologically based approaches.

'IDEOLOGICAL' APPROACHES
What unites this group of reader-centred approaches is their commitment to reading a text from a particular point of view. The chosen perspective is said to 'privilege' certain ways of thinking and seeing things, and certain questions to be asked. Often such approaches stem from the experience of a group who see themselves as marginalized by 'mainstream' scholarship. Hence liberationist approaches privilege the experience of poor people, historically stemming from such communities in South America, and read the Gospels through (usually) Marxist spectacles. Similarly, feminist critics concentrate on the experience and the situation of women from economic, social and political perspectives, and seek to read 'under the text' to hear the suppressed voices of women in texts which

came out of an ancient world where (it is argued) women were not powerful in the ruling classes.

There are a huge number of such approaches now, for each reader or group of readers can argue that their experience ought to be heard as a context for the meaning of the text which they find. Even within a field like feminist studies, there are several major streams of thought, depending on the kind of feminism which is being discussed: black or white, Western or two-thirds world, European or North American.

As we suggested above, it is helpful to be self-conscious as a reader about one's own pre-understanding and perspective, and ideologically based approaches have highlighted issues which would not otherwise have been seen, and which can relate powerfully to today's readers. Equally, ideological approaches reflect the fact that *everyone* has an agenda in reading a text, and it is wisest to be self-aware about that agenda (hence the quotation marks round 'ideological' in our heading, to suggest that to some extent all approaches are ideological). To read the texts self-consciously from particular perspectives is a valuable corrective to the classic historical approaches, which privileged the experience of white, middle-class western academics. For example, Luke's emphasis on Jesus' concern for the poor (see p. 237) can easily be treated as relatively unimportant by westerners for whom it presents a great challenge to their wealth and comfort.

Nevertheless, it is also important to place these approaches alongside others, for they will provide a corrective to readings of the text which are simply a reflection of the ideology of the reader and show no

sympathy for the text itself. Reading, when all is said and done, is an activity of entering into another's world of ideas (or symbolic universe). Only after that world has been seen, as far as possible, through the other's eyes can the reader begin to reflect on what he or she thinks of what they see.

What do you think?
YOUR IDEOLOGY AND READING

Reflect on your experience of reading books in general and the Gospels in particular. Offer examples of where: (a) you initially misunderstood or were puzzled by an author because you had not understood their world-view, and (b) your views were changed by reading. How far is the ideology you now bring to reading the Gospels open to change?

STRUCTURALISM

In the 1920s Vladimir Propp analysed Russian folk stories to see what patterns emerged from them. He found that the same basic structure of events came in story after story. In the 1950s and 1960s a group of French scholars undertook similar study of narratives with corresponding results, and thus the text-centred approach called structuralism was born. Its key insight is that patterns and structures recur in story-telling across a wide range of cultures and periods of history. Accordingly, structuralists approach Gospel stories looking for these so-called 'deep structures', including seeking polar opposites, such as rich and poor, strong and weak, good and evil, life and death. Thus it has little to do with traditional analysis of the literary structure of a story (such as we consider on p. 94).

A popular approach is A. J. Greimas' actantial analysis, in which he pictures every story as having six key 'actants' or figures: a sender, an object, a receiver, a subject who is delivering the object, and helper(s) and opponent(s) of the subject. For example, Wright analyses the parable of the wicked tenants (Mark 12:1-12) this way (Wright 1992, 69-77). Initially, the owner of the vineyard (sender) wants the tenants (subject) to provide fruit (object) for himself (receiver). In this task they are helped by the vineyard, but opposed by their own greed. As the story develops the owner (sender) requests fruit (object) from the tenants (receiver), and sends various messengers (subject) in order to achieve this. The messengers are helped by the owner's authorization, and opposed by the tenants; here the tenants are both receiver and opponents. Wright analyses each stage of the story, observing that in the end the owner (sender) seeks fruit (object) for his own benefit (receiver), but now from the new tenants (subject), who are helped by the vineyard and opposed by the old tenants.

Wright goes on to draw out the value of this analysis, including that it shows similarities to the story of Israel, for Israel's story in Jesus' day is of God (sender) aiming to rescue (object) Israel (receiver) by the gift of the torah (subject). The torah is opposed by the pagans, but helped by God's promises and his past actions to deliver the nation. Thus Wright argues that the parable is a subversive re-telling of Israel's story.

Awareness of structure and of polar opposite pairs can clearly be helpful in studying stories, but the danger it poses is that it can miss the specifics of a particular story by focusing on the patterns which it shares with other stories. As with other approaches, it can try to 'explain' everything and eliminate anything which does not fit its assumptions. Used with caution it can provide valuable insights.

POST-STRUCTURALISM AND DECONSTRUCTION

Post-structuralism grew out of a discontent with structuralism, in that it takes the insights of structuralism concerning basic structures, polar opposites and the like, but denies that there is any ultimate meaning to what is being discovered. Such scholars strongly affirm that texts are 'polyvalent', that there can be no definitive 'meaning' to a text – it can mean different things to different people, depending on their approach and ideology.

Deconstruction is a highly suspicious form of post-structuralism, for it looks for alternative views within a text which have been suppressed, and then argues that these meanings should take precedence. But in due course, a thoroughgoing deconstructionist will want to deconstruct the second set of meanings and replace them by a third, and a fourth and so on. Reading a text can become a never-ending game in which meaning is never achievable.

It must be said that both post-structuralist and deconstructionist theory are often expressed in highly technical language which is not easy to follow, and this alone makes them inaccessible to many students. When applied to the Gospels in practice, however, they can be entertaining and light: Moore's study of Jesus' meeting with the Samaritan woman (John 4) is witty, creative and thoughtful (Moore 1994, 43-64). For example, he makes a fascinating link between the living water the woman lacks and the water flowing from Jesus' side on the cross (John 4:7, 10f., 13-15; 19:34), and argues that John has moved from metaphorical uses of water with the woman and the promise of the Spirit (John 7:39) to a literal use at the end of the Gospel (19:34). However, it is clear that ultimately Moore does not think there is real truth to be had, admitting that a particular view he expresses 'could … be deconstructed in its turn, should space permit it or strategy require it' (Moore 1994, 62 n. 69). Those who believe there is real truth in the Gospels will find such an approach hard to stomach.

AN APPROACH TO EXEGESIS OF THE GOSPELS

What follows is an attempt to provide some questions to ask in studying a passage from the Gospels, illustrated by a study of Luke 5:1-11, the meeting of Jesus and the disciples centred on a large catch of fish. The process of studying a passage in this way is usually called *exegesis*, which means bringing out what is in the passage. The aim is, as far as possible, to enable today's reader to read the passage and to hear it as the intended readers of the first century would have heard it. The focus is therefore not on relating the passage to today's issues and concerns, although good exegesis prepares for that kind of reflection to go on by identifying the main thrust of the passage.

Digging deeper:
EXEGESIS

Choose one of the following passages and use each of the study steps below on it. Finally, pull your findings together into a form you can present to a group of fellow students of the Gospels, whether in writing or orally.

Matt. 9:27-34; Mark 3:1-6; Luke 7:11-17

THE PROCESS OF STUDY

The first thing to do is to read the passage carefully several times, including the surrounding section of the book, to familiarize yourself with the story. Read the passage in at least two different Bible versions (and if you have Greek, read the original too). At this stage do *not* read Bible commentaries or use a Study Bible which has notes to guide you: read the story for yourself, for you will learn a great deal more that way (we shall use reference books later in the process).

Look

As you do this, keep looking for points about translation, literary context, form, structure and focus:

Translation Are there any significant problems of translation here? (Using different versions will highlight this.) What consequences might a decision about these have for the meaning of the text?

Literary context What precedes and follows the passage? What is the relationship of the passage to the preceding and following sections of the book? For example, the passage could be offering a contrast, a comparison, a consequence, a repetition, or an illustration of the surrounding material.

Form What kind of story or teaching is this? What are the marks of that form and how are they seen in this passage? (See pp. 70f., 100–4.)

Structure What sections does the passage fall into? How are they related to each other? How does the story flow and develop? There may be, for example, cause and effect, means to an end, progression to a climax or challenge, general statements followed by specific instances, or the same idea repeated in different ways.

Focus What are the central ideas and themes? Some key clues here are the grammar and vocabulary of the passage.

- Who is performing the actions of the main verbs? Are the verbs singular or plural? Are they active or passive (in other words, is the subject doing the action of the verb or receiving the action of the verb)? If passive, who is doing this to the verb subject?
- Where do 'shift' words come, which lead into an explanation, a contrast or a new idea (e.g. but, therefore, for, because, yet, if, since, when, while, so that, in the same way)?
- What are the key words in the passage? Often these will be highlighted by being repeated or by being mentioned at prominent places in the story.
- Are there features which seem culturally alien to you as a reader? Note these for future reference.

Examining Luke 5:1-11 we discover that the translation seems straightforward, but that there are interesting points on other areas:

Literary context In Luke 4 Jesus has growing popularity, although he is working alone at this stage. 4:38 shows Simon experiencing Jesus healing his mother-in-law, so 5:1-11 is not his first meeting with Jesus. Following our story, 5:12–6:16 forms a series of stories of Jesus' continuing ministry in Galilee.

Form Bultmann claims that this story is a 'legend' or nature miracle (see p. 71), but such stories usually climax with a sense of wonder or awe being expressed. In this case, there is wonder (v. 9), but the story goes on to the fishermen leaving their boats and going with Jesus (v. 11). This suggests that this story's form is not a straightforward miracle story, but rather that it should be seen as a pronouncement story (see p. 71) focused on Jesus' call in v. 10b, or perhaps a 'call' story centred on v. 10b and the response in v. 11.

Structure The story breaks into three sections: vv. 1-3 set the scene by outlining the circumstances that lead to the key events; vv. 4-10a describe the central events, during which Simon and the others recognize Jesus through the miraculous catch of fish; vv. 10b-11 tell of the results which follow from the central events: the fishermen respond to Jesus' call by leaving everything to follow him.

Focus In vv. 1-4 Jesus is the subject of most of the main verbs: he is the centre of the action here, climaxing in his call to Simon to put the nets out into the deep water (v. 4). But in vv. 5-10a the verb actions are now performed by Simon and the others: Jesus does nothing – he does not appear again in the story until Simon falls at his knees (v. 8). The pattern of vv. 1-10a is repeated in vv. 10b-11, where Jesus speaks and then the fisherman respond.

A key shift word is 'Yet' in v. 5 (Greek *de*), for it highlights Simon's willingness to trust Jesus' instruction against his own experience and instincts as a fisherman.

There is an interesting change of language from Simon's initial address to Jesus as 'Master' (v. 5) to 'Lord' (v. 8) – the latter is likely to reflect a change in Simon's view of Jesus as a result of the catch of fish. There is also a fascinating switch from catching fish to catching people (vv. 4, 5, 6, 9, 10), identified by a change from a verb meaning 'snare, take prisoner' (v. 6, Greek *sunkleiō*) to one meaning 'take alive' (v. 10, Greek *zōgreō*).

95

In terms of the cultural context, we receive hints that they fish at night (v. 5) and that they use nets (vv. 4, 5), and Jesus' call to go 'into the deep water' (v. 4) suggests that they do not fish near land. It would be helpful to a modern westerner to find out more about fishing customs on the lakes of Palestine in this period.

Ask

There are a number of fact-finding questions to ask of the passage being studied:

- **Who** are the people involved, and what kind of relationship do they have? Is it friendly, antagonistic, open, closed, etc.?
- **Where** are they? What's the atmosphere of this setting?
- **When** does the action happen? What caused it to happen at this specific time? Is there any particular symbolism of the time?
- **What** is the central event or key theme? Is it a problem, an event influencing others, a conflict, a crisis, etc.?
- **How** does the writer seek to communicate the story? How are events described? Do previous events lead up to this story, or do subsequent events develop from it? Do words used reveal motives, feelings, ideas, etc.?
- **Why** do the events of the story happen? Are the reasons stated, explicitly or implicitly? Does the writer hint at the reasons by the links made with other stories?
- **So?** What results follow from this story? Are they expected or surprising within the overall narrative? What results would follow for the reader who accepts or rejects this story?

In the case of Luke 5:1-11 each of these questions leads to further understanding of the passage:

- The people are Jesus, Simon, the crowds (vv. 1, 3), Simon's partners (James and John, v. 10). The relationships vary: the crowds want to hear Jesus teach (v. 1); Simon knows Jesus a little already (4:38), and has some grasp of Jesus' authority (v. 5).
- The setting is by the lake of Gennesaret, possibly near Capernaum, since this is where Simon's home is (4:31, 38; see the map, p. 15). The atmosphere is positive and open towards Jesus, both from the crowds and Simon (vv. 1, 3, 5).
- This story takes place early in Jesus' ministry; previously he has worked alone (Luke 4). It is likely to take place in the morning, since the fishermen are cleaning their nets after a night's fishing (vv. 2, 5).
- The central event is the catch of fish (vv. 6f.), which leads to Simon recognizing both himself and Jesus (v. 8), and in turn this leads to Simon and the others leaving everything to follow Jesus (vv. 10f.).
- Luke tells this story skilfully: there is a change from Simon addressing Jesus as 'Master' (v. 5) to 'Lord' (v. 8). Peter's feelings are seen in his recognition that he is a 'sinful man' (v. 8) and his being 'amazed' (v. 9). There is a development from Simon's recognition of both himself and Jesus, to Jesus calling Simon and others to go with him.
- The reasons for the story's events can be summed up, then, by observing that the catch of fish is Jesus' method to catch Simon, James and John.
- The results which flow from this story are that Jesus has his key co-workers: a computer search for other passages in Luke where Simon/Peter is mentioned with James and John reveals that these are the 'close three' who are with Jesus at key moments of his ministry (6:14; 8:51; 9:28;

cf. Acts 1:13). For Luke's readers, this story invites them to identify with Simon in recognizing Jesus, seeing their own weakness and sin, and becoming people who follow Jesus too.

Note

Now we turn to identify particular emphases of the writer, using insights from redaction criticism (see pp. 74–7) and narrative criticism. The use of a Gospels synopsis will be valuable at this stage (see p. 58) in order to compare the passage with any parallels in the other Gospels, especially the other synoptics. As you look at the synopsis, seek out similarities and differences between the various accounts. In particular, look for: selection, arrangement and adaptation of the story. Adaptation can mean changing the focus, the proportions or the emphases of a passage – but it can also mean repetition without changes, suggesting that the later writer agrees with the earlier writer's emphases. Look also for particular emphases or themes known to be important for the writer (see chs 9-12 for the emphases of each of the evangelists).

A look at a synopsis for Luke 5:1-11 suggests that Matthew and Mark tell this story only briefly, if it is the same story (cf. Matt. 4:18-22; Mark 1:16-20). There is also a good sprinkling of favourite Lukan words here. Luke uses 'Lord' (v. 8) much more than the other evangelists, and his is the only Gospel containing 'Master' (seven times in total).

Luke 5:8 presents the first use of 'sinful' (Greek *hamartōlos*) in this Gospel, but it will occur 17 more times in Luke. The phrase 'sinful man' (v. 8) is found only once elsewhere in the NT, of Zacchaeus, again in Luke (19:7), and the theme of Jesus'

welcome of sinners is also a particular Lukan emphasis (see pp. 236f.).

'Amazement' (v. 8; Greek *thambos*) is another Lukan word, for it is only found elsewhere in the NT at Luke 4:36 and Acts 3:10. The Acts parallel may suggest that the miracle done through the apostles, healing the lame man at the Beautiful Gate of the temple, is the same kind as the huge catch of fish in Luke 5.

PULL THE IDEAS TOGETHER

Having gathered this material, now is the time to put order and structure on it, and to investigate outstanding questions – remember, up to now we haven't looked at Bible commentaries, but have worked with a Bible and a concordance (perhaps on a computer). But now the reference books come into their own, as we use them to help answer our questions – questions arising from reading the text for ourselves.

First, then, check any difficult or uncertain points. For meanings of words, a lexicon or Bible dictionary can help. For customs or cultural context, a Bible dictionary is valuable. For locations, a Bible atlas will give assistance. In Luke 5:1-11 we shall want to find out more about some of the words used (and I have made use of such research above in commenting on particular words), as well as investigating the location of this story and some of the fishing practices of this culture.

Second, and vitally important, seek to identify the *most important* idea or theme in the passage. What's the 'big idea' that the passage is conveying? How do the other components of the passage help readers to understand that? In Luke 5:1-11 the focus of the passage is at its end, in the call of Jesus to Simon, James and John to follow him and their immediate response.

Third, attempt to state your 'big idea' in one sentence. It is helpful with a narrative passage to answer the question: *Who is doing/ saying what, to whom, in what circumstances, for what reason(s) and with what results?* Be as objective and descriptive as you can in doing this, and avoid subjective, personal statements of what the passage might mean for today's readers or what it means 'to me'. That said, there is no one 'correct' way of putting this, so do choose words which are your way of writing or speaking. Summing up Luke 5:1-11, we might say: *Simon recognizes Jesus (as Lord) and himself (as a sinful man) as a result of the miraculous catch of fish. This leads to Simon and his friends responding immediately to Jesus' call to follow him.*

Finally, outline how the passage presents the 'big idea', showing how each section contributes and how the story develops. This is where you will make use of the detailed work that you have done earlier as you go through the passage verse by verse. Consider also how to relate points within the passage to key themes in the biblical book or author (with Luke you will also want to think about Acts) being considered. For Luke 5:1-11, we can outline the passage:

vv. 1f. Jesus sees the situation
v. 3   Jesus gains Simon's help in his people-work
v. 4   Jesus tests Simon with a greater challenge
vv. 5-7 Simon accepts Jesus' challenge and makes a huge catch of fish
vv. 8f. Simon recognizes Jesus and himself as a result of the catch
v. 10   Jesus calls Simon and the others to follow him
v. 11   They respond by immediately leaving everything to follow Jesus

PRESENTATION

The last stage of an exegetical study is to present the ideas to other people, whether in written or spoken form. Here it is vital to filter out anything which is not relevant to helping the audience to hear the passage through its central theme. Remember that interesting is not the same as relevant! One way to do this follows, but there are many possible ways in which the results of your study could be presented. Don't be afraid to be creative and imaginative in your presentation, whether in writing or orally.

First, set the scene for your study. Here you might identify some key problems in interpreting the passage or sketch some of the key scholarly approaches to the passage which you have found in your reading.

Second, set the passage in its literary contexts by commenting on why it belongs at this point in its Gospel. You might consider whether this is likely to be a traditional location or a deliberate choice by the writer to locate it here: an example of the latter may well be John's placing of Jesus' demonstration in the temple very early in his Gospel (John 2:13-22). In either case, what is the effect of placing the story at this point in Jesus' ministry?

Third, consider the *Sitz im Leben* (life setting) of the story. How does it fit within Jesus' ministry? Does it show signs of having been adapted by the evangelist as he writes, or by the process of oral transmission? Here the work of form and redaction criticism, along with narrative approaches, can be helpful.

Fourth, what is the central point of the story? Here you will state your 'big idea' for the passage and then lead your readers/hearers through the passage verse by verse so that they can see how each part contributes to this central theme. This is the stage at which you will use much of the detailed work of your research as you comment on the passage.

Finally, sum up and highlight again how you have responded to the issues you raised in your introduction. If your study is a written assignment, you will also want to give a bibliography of the books and reference tools you have used.

ESSAY TOPICS

INTRODUCTORY
● Offer a critical assessment of the contribution which narrative criticism makes to study of the Gospels with reference to its use on particular passages in the Gospels.

INTERMEDIATE
● Write an exegetical study of *either* Luke 9:28-36 or Matt. 8:5-13.

FURTHER READING

INTRODUCTORY
DJG articles 'Liberation Hermeneutics', 'Literary Criticism', 'Rhetorical Criticism', 'Sociological Approaches to the Gospels', 'Tradition Criticism'.

D. Marguerat & Y. Bourquin *How to Read Bible Stories*. London: SCM, 1999 (a superb introduction to narrative criticism – with pictures!).

M. A. Powell *What is Narrative Criticism?* Philadelphia: Fortress, 1991/London: SPCK, 1993 (a very fine, readable 'way in' to narrative criticism).

E. P. Sanders & M. Davies *Studying the Synoptic Gospels*. London: SCM/Philadelphia: Trinity Press International, 1989, chs 15-16 (introductions to structuralism,

deconstruction, rhetorical and narrative approaches).

INTERMEDIATE
K. E. Bailey *Poet and Peasant*. Grand Rapids: Eerdmans, 1976 (excellent studies of Luke's parables within their cultural setting).

K. E. Bailey *Through Peasant Eyes*. Grand Rapids: Eerdmans, 1980 (more excellent studies of Luke's parables within their cultural setting).

J. H. Elliott *Social-Scientific Criticism of the New Testament*. London: SPCK, 1995 [US edition: *What is Social-Scientific Criticism?* Philadelphia: Fortress, 1993] (useful overview).

G. D. Fee *New Testament Exegesis*, revised ed. Louisville, KY: Westminster John Knox Press/Leominster: Gracewing, 1993 (valuable, reasonably detailed introduction to exegesis).

E. S. Fiorenza, ed. *Searching the Scriptures, vol. 2: A Feminist Commentary*. New York: Crossroad/London: SCM, 1994 (a stimulating set of feminist approaches to particular books).

D. Horrell, ed. *Social-Scientific Approaches to New Testament Interpretation*. Edinburgh: T. & T. Clark, 1999 (valuable set of key essays with a good overview in Horrell's introductory essay).

G. A. Kennedy *New Testament Interpretation through Rhetorical Criticism*. Chapel Hill: University of North Carolina Press, 1984 (the best introduction to NT rhetorical criticism).

S. McKnight *Interpreting the Synoptic Gospels*. Guides to NT Exegesis 2. Grand Rapids: Baker Book House, 1988 (helpful introduction to exegesis of the synoptics).

S. D. Moore *Poststructuralism and the New Testament*. Minneapolis: Fortress Press, 1994 (key work by one of the leading deconstructionists).

M. W. G. Stibbe *John's Gospel*. NT Readings. London/New York: Routledge, 1994 (a careful reader-response approach to John).

D. Tidball *An Introduction to the Sociology of the New Testament*. Exeter: Paternoster, 1983 [US edn. *The Social Context of the New Testament*. Grand Rapids: Academie Books, 1984], esp. chs 1–4 (valuable survey of key issues).

N. T. Wright *The New Testament and the People of God*. London: SPCK/Philadelphia: Fortress Press, 1992, pp. 69-80 (useful 'way in' to Greimas' actantial analysis).

METHODS OF INTERPRETATION: PARABLES, MIRACLES, APOCALYPTIC

This section explores some of the issues raised by:

- Jesus' parables, including the question of allegory and the interpretation of Mark 4:11-12;
- the miracles of Jesus, in relation to other miracle-workers and to his teaching about the kingdom of God;
- apocalyptic imagery, with special reference to Mark 13 and Dan. 7.

THE PARABLES OF JESUS

One of the most attractive features of Jesus is his teaching through stories and vivid pictorial images. The parables give an insight into Jesus as someone who observed, appreciated and reflected creatively on the world around him.

The word 'parable' is a Greek word meaning something like 'comparison'; the underlying Hebrew/Aramaic word – *mashal/mathla*, has a breadth of meaning, denoting all sorts of proverbial or figurative uses of language. The word is used of the OT book of 'Proverbs'. Some NT parables are proverb-like, e.g. 'You are the salt of the earth' (Matt. 5:13); others are full-blown stories, e.g. the prodigal son (Luke 15:11-32).

Historical bedrock?

According to Mark most of Jesus' public teaching was in parables (4:33), and all the Gospels show his extensive use of them. (In John we find figurative discourses, e.g. the good shepherd and the vine in chs 10 and 15, rather than pithy story-parables.) Other Jewish teachers used parables, but they seem to have been particularly characteristic of Jesus.

The parables themselves are widely recognized as deriving from Jesus. But the interpretations given or implied in the Gospels are often seen as coming from the church, not Jesus. So Matthew and Luke have interpreted the parable of the lost sheep differently (Matt. 18:10-14; Luke 15:3-7) in line with their respective interests. The interpretation of the parable of the sower (Mark 4:13-20, cf. Matt. 13:18-23; Luke 8:11-15) is regarded as Christian reflection on preaching, rather than as what Jesus intended to say through the parable. A few scholars go further still in ascribing some of the parables to the evangelists – they say that Luke's parables, for example on the theme of money, reflect his own interests so heavily as to be suspect.

Digging deeper:
THE INTERPRETATION OF THE SOWER

Many scholars have seen the interpretation of the parable of the sower as a church interpretation reflecting its experience of Christian ministry rather than as Jesus' own teaching. Other scholars have argued that it is very like Jesus' teaching found elsewhere in the Gospels. Compare the interpretation in Matt. 13:18-23 with the sermon on the mount in Matt. 5–7. What themes and ideas do they have in common?

This last argument is not persuasive: Jesus clearly used many more parables than those recorded in Mark (4:33). Inevitably those which Luke has added to Mark will reflect his special interests; and if Luke's interests coincided significantly with Jesus' own, then there is no problem in recognizing parables like the prodigal son and the good Samaritan as very Lukan, and yet also as coming from Jesus. Something similar may be said about other parts of Jesus' teaching which scholars ascribe to the evangelists' redaction rather than to Jesus: thus, with the parable of the lost sheep, it is quite likely that Jesus used the parable in different ways on different occasions, and almost inevitable that both Matthew and Luke will have selected the form of the parable that fitted their interests.

Interpreting the parables

Very few of Jesus' parables are explained in the Gospels – most leave us to guess the precise meaning. In Mark 4, for example, we have a collection of parables. The first is the sower, which is explained, but later there is the parable of the mustard seed (4:30-32). How should this be understood? It clearly describes the kingdom as something that is small at first, but vast at last. But how many of the details are significant? Is it about the growth of the kingdom? Are the big branches, the birds and the shade significant? Are the birds the same as the birds in the sower, where they represented the devil taking the word of God from people's hearts?

For much of church history the favoured method of interpretation has been allegorical, with every detail of the parables being given significance. A good example is the interpretation of the parable of the good Samaritan by Augustine, a North African bishop who lived around AD 400 (see below).

Wonderfully edifying teaching was derived through such interpretation. But there are major historical and literary problems:

- the explanations sound more like later Christian doctrine than teaching of Jesus in his first-century context;
- they treat the parables as messages to be decoded and not as the forceful stories that they seem to be;
- the method lacks any clear control, allowing interpreters to read almost anything into the parables.

Adolf Jülicher (1899) argued that Jesus' parables were not complex allegories requiring esoteric decoding, but simple stories with one point. His view fitted the

What do you think?
AUGUSTINE'S INTERPRETATION

The man (Adam) going down from Jerusalem (the city of heavenly peace) fell among robbers (the devil and his angels) who left him half dead (spiritually dead). The priest (the OT priesthood) did not help, the Levite (the OT prophets) did not help, the Good Samaritan (Christ) helped, binding up wounds (stopping sin), pouring in oil (hope) and wine (exhortation to spiritual work), put him on the beast (the body of Christ), took him to the inn (the church), paid two coins (the two commands to love God and neighbour) to the innkeeper (Paul) until his return (Jesus' resurrection).

(From Augustine, *Quæstiones Evangelionum* II. 19, as in R. H. Stein, *An Introduction to the Parables of Jesus.* Philadelphia: Westminster Press, 1981, 46.)

What do you think of this interpretation? If you have doubts about it, why?

then prevalent understanding of Jesus as an enlightened teacher of attractive religious and moral truths about the love of God, love of neighbour, use of talents, etc.

Jülicher's one-point-parable approach was dominant for a good part of the twentieth century. But although his reaction to the fanciful and anachronistic excesses of the older interpretation was justified, his view of Jesus and of the parables raised its own problems. It did not do justice to:

● the literary shape and form of the parables, since some, such as the sower, are evidently not simple one-point stories. Not surprisingly Jülicher and others like him regarded the interpretations of the parables found in the Gospels (e.g. of the sower and of the tares) as derived not from Jesus, but from the church.
● Jesus in his historical context: as a Jewish teacher of that time, he is entirely likely to have made use of enigmatic and allusive sayings.

More recent scholars such as C.H. Dodd (*The Parables of the Kingdom*, 2nd ed. London: Nisbet, 1961) and J. Jeremias (1963) have pointed out that Jesus' parables are not proclaiming general moral truths, but the eschatological kingdom of God, this being the core of his message. Even more recently Madeleine Boucher (*The Mysterious Parable*. Washington: Catholic Biblical Association, 1977) and Craig Blomberg (1989) argue that the parables are not simple one-point stories, but something richer and more subtle.

Modern literary appreciation of the parables has focused not just on their ideas or message, but also on how they convey their message. J. Jeremias, perhaps the most influential German scholar to write on parables in the modern period, speaks of

them as 'weapons', and others have pointed out that parables do not just convey theological information – they involve and challenge the hearer. An inexact parallel would be the modern TV advertisement, which involves, intrigues and then makes a demand on the watcher. The good Samaritan, for example, would have evoked the interest and sympathies of Jesus' Jewish hearers, who knew the Jerusalem-Jericho road and its dangers, and who would have had mixed feelings about religious people such as the priest and the Levite, but for whom theappearance of a Samaritan as the hero of the story would have posed a powerful challenge. The parable does not just convey information about loving one's neighbour; it brings into sharp focus the challenge of Jesus to love even one's enemy, and provokes a reaction. Scholars have spoken of a 'language event' on the grounds that a parable creates a new situation or a new relationship.

What do you think?
PARABLES AND THEIR AUDIENCES

Some parables are encouragements or exhortations to disciples or would-be disciples, some are warnings to unbelievers. Look at the following parables, and consider:

● is the audience mentioned?
● what is the point of the parable, and does it address the audience?
● what is the hearers' response likely to have been?

Matt. 3:10; 5:13-15; 13:31-33; 21:28-46; 24:42-51; Luke 12:13-21; 18:9-14.

In recent years the shift in scholarly interest away from historical approaches towards more purely literary approaches has been reflected in parable studies. There has been a tendency to deny that we can know the meaning of Jesus, but to claim that it does not matter; parables are works of art – like a painting – which are open to any number of different interpretations. However, a retreat from history into subjectivism, though understandable, is neither necessary historically, nor desirable from a Christian point of view that emphasizes revelation through history.

How then should parables be interpreted?

The historical context of Jesus We need to pay attention to the political, social and religious context. Mustard seeds, Samaritans and tax collectors all make sense and make a point in Jesus' context.

The context of Jesus' teaching as a whole The parables need to be interpreted in the context of his teaching about the kingdom of God, not in terms of modern liberal, existentialist, or other thinking.

The literary shape and dynamic of the parables Neither the detailed allegorism of the church fathers nor the one-simple-point method of Jülicher does justice to the form of all of the parables, e.g. the sower is more complex than the pearl, and interpretation must be sensitive to the different dynamic of the different parables. The interpretation of the sower may be a model for interpreting the parables generally, since it has a simple focus on seed in soil and on different responses to hearing the word of the kingdom, but still makes a variety of points about that theme.

The clues given directly or indirectly in the Gospels about the meaning of the parables

---

MARK 4:11-12

'To you the mystery of the kingdom of God has been given. But to those outside everything happens in parables, so that looking they may look and not see and hearing they may hear and not understand, lest they turn and it be forgiven them.'

These words of Jesus in reply to a question from the disciples about his parables are some of the most difficult in the Gospels. It could look as though Jesus is saying that his parables are meant to stop people understanding about the kingdom of God. This has seemed so unlikely to have been Jesus' meaning, that scholars have proposed all sorts of explanations, including:

- The saying does not go back to Jesus at all, but comes from the church – the early Christians couldn't understand the Jews' failure to believe in Jesus the Messiah, so they came up with the explanation that this was all in the plan of God, and that Jesus' parables were designed to stop the Jews believing.
- The saying has been mistranslated from the original Aramaic which Jesus spoke.
- Teaching through puzzling riddles, visions and parables was a familiar teaching method among the Jews, and fitted in with Jesus' refusal to go the route of populist leader and his determination to go the way of the cross. (See pp.180f. on the 'messianic secret'.)
- Jesus is commenting on the way some people got very little out of a parable like the sower, just hearing it as a story, whereas those who wanted to go deeper asked Jesus about its meaning and learned a lot from it about God and his kingdom. Jesus sees his ministry and his parables as bringing God's salvation and his judgement (such as the prophet spoke of in Isa. 6).

The last two suggestions seem most likely to be what Mark intended.

For differing approaches to these verses see C. H. Dodd *The Parables of the Kingdom*, 2nd ed. London: Nisbet, 1961; Jeremias (1963); Wenham (1989) and commentaries on Mark.

What do you think?

Look at two of Jesus' short parables, Matt. 13:45,46 and Luke 15:8-10, and reflect on the social context, the form and emphasis of the respective parables, and the hints given in the Gospels about their meaning. Then try to sum up in a sentence or two what Jesus probably meant.

are important – direct clues like the interpretation of the sower, indirect clues through the context or brief explanatory comments. We should not be too quick to assume that (deliberately or accidentally) the Gospel writers have lost Jesus' meaning. Of course, they have also selected and used the parables in their own distinctive ways, and it is right and proper to consider the function and force of the particular parable for a particular evangelist.

THE MIRACLES OF JESUS

Probably the thing that marked Jesus out the most from other religious leaders of his day was the way that he 'went around doing good and healing' (Acts 10:38). His reputation as a healer drew crowds, and even his opponents recognized his spiritual power, explaining it as demon-inspired (Mark 3:22; later Jews spoke of Jesus' magical powers).

The Gospels describe a range of miracles performed by Jesus: he healed 'all manner of diseases', including blind, deaf, dumb and lame people. He cleansed people suffering from 'leprosy', a skin disease that made a person an outcast in society. He cast out demons from the possessed – an aspect of his ministry to which he appears to have attached considerable theological

importance (e.g. Matt. 12:22-32). A few instances of Jesus raising the dead to life are also recorded (Mark 5:21-41; Luke 7:11-17; John 11): raising the dead is in a different category from the other healings, and yet there is something in common between healing a man who has been blind or crippled all his life and raising the dead.

Jesus typically accomplished his healings by a word of command, e.g. 'Little girl get up', 'Come out of him' (Mark 5:41; 1:25). They were sometimes accompanied by a physical gesture: Jesus touched the untouchable leper, cleansing him as opposed to being made unclean by him (Mark 1:41); he took Jairus's dead daughter by the hand (Mark 5:41); he put saliva on the blind man's eyes (Mark 8:23). But often words were enough, and sometimes he healed at a distance (Matt. 8:13).

CLEANNESS/UNCLEANNESS

We think of cleanness and uncleanness as something physical (clean clothes) or ethical (a dirty joke). In the OT there is also ritual cleanness and uncleanness: it is necessary to be 'clean' to enter the presence of God and to be part of the worshipping people of God. Certain foods (e.g. pork) and certain physical conditions (e.g. internal bleeding and 'leprosy') made people unclean (see Lev. 11–15). There were cleansing rituals in the OT. The NT sees Jesus as overcoming uncleanness (e.g. Mark 7:19; Acts 10:9-28; Rom. 14:14).

Jesus' power astonished people. But an important ingredient in the miracles was faith: he healed in response to people's faith, he was limited by lack of faith, he called for the exercise of faith, and in John's Gospel his miracles are signs to which the proper response is faith (Mark 4:40; 5:34; 6:5; 11:24; John 2:11; 20:30-31).

There are connections between sickness, sin, society and the spiritual – sometimes implied, sometimes explicit. There are conditions which are clearly spiritual, such as demon possession; sometimes illness is associated with Satan's work (e.g. Luke 13:11); sometimes there seems to be a connection with people's sin, and they need forgiveness not just healing (Mark 2:5); sometimes no connection is made between disease and sin or spirits (John 9:2,3). Often the social and the physical go together: leprosy and some forms of demon possession cut the victim off from society, and other conditions force the ill person into poverty and begging.

As well as the healing of disease and death, Jesus is described in the Gospels as exercising remarkable power over nature. His 'nature miracles' include feeding 5,000 and 4,000 people using a few loaves and fishes, exercising control over the sea, turning water into wine, etc. (Mark 4:35-41; 6:30-42; 7:45-52; 8:1-10; John 2:1-11; 21:4-8). Although there is a distinction between Jesus' healings and these miracles, they have something in common: Jesus meets acute human need, largely through the power of his word. Jesus' rebuking of the storm is reminiscent of his rebuking of demons.

The form of the miracle stories is quite similar:

- a description of the sickness or the problem,
- the request to Jesus for help, Jesus' response (e.g. a word of healing),
- the result and people's reactions.

Modern scholars may find certain categories of miracle (e.g. healings) easier to accept than others (e.g. walking on water), but although the Gospels themselves can distinguish healing, cleansing, exorcising, raising the dead, and nature miracles, there is not a sharp theological or other kind of distinction made.

The Gospels record other supernatural events in connection with Jesus, notably his birth, baptism, transfiguration and resurrection. These events are things that happen to Jesus rather than things Jesus does for others, but although they are distinct, they are theologically related revelations of divine power associated with Jesus.

Approaches to the miracles and their interpretation

Rationalism

In the last 200 years people have found the whole concept of miracle difficult. Science and reason have been seen as the touchstones for truth, and claimed events that appear to defy the 'laws' of science have been dismissed by some as fictional, and seen by others as logically and historically improbable and unverifiable.

In face of this rationalistic argument, attempts have been made to explain the Gospel miracles:

- **naturalistically** Jesus' healings were psychosomatic; his raisings of the dead were resuscitations of apparently dead people;
- **symbolically or mythologically** What sounds improbable history, for example the turning of the water into wine (John 2:1-10), makes better sense as religious symbolism (compare Mark 3:19-22). The Gospels, it is argued, have clothed Jesus with OT and pagan miraculous powers, so that he feeds people miraculously (like Elisha in 2 Kings 4) and produces large quantities of wine (like the Greek god

Dionysus). We therefore misinterpret the texts if we try to take them literally; it is necessary to translate the mythological language into more appropriate modern categories (see further in ch. 6 below).

There are problems with these explanations:

- The evangelists certainly see theological significance and OT themes in Jesus' miracles, but (a) that does not mean that they did not also see them as real miracles – on the contrary, they wrote their gospels because they believed that Jesus was extraordinary! – and (b) the fact that the miracles have theological significance increases their historical credibility rather than the opposite, because it means that they make sense in the context of Jesus' ministry and are not weird and inexplicable events.
- The motivation for the rationalistic interpretations has to do with a questionable modern world-view. Science and history need to work methodologically with assumptions about regularity and cause and effect, but to absolutize those working-principles so as to deny the supernatural is secular dogma, not good science or history.
- The general evidence for Jesus doing miracles and, in particular, for his resurrection is very strong.

(See further in ch 6.)

'History of religions' approaches
Scholars in recent years have become more positive about Jesus as miracle-worker, thanks to a better and more sympathetic appreciation of his religious and social context. The so-called 'history of religions' approach found parallels to the Christian picture of Jesus in Hellenistic ideas about semi-divine figures, who were seen as having miraculous powers and some sort of divine status (e.g. Hercules). It is not clear, however, that there was a clear Hellenistic category of 'divine man' into which Jesus would naturally fit (see p. 203).

But as scholars have noted, there were various miracle-workers contemporary or nearly contemporary with Jesus such as Apollonius of Tyana (in Cappadocia). Within Palestine itself there were exorcists and 'charismatic wonder-workers', and Jesus has been seen as one of these (see especially Vermes 1983).

HONI AND HANINA

Honi the circle-drawer lived in the first century BC. Josephus describes him as 'a righteous man and dear to God', who 'in a rainless period prayed to God to end the drought, and God had heard his prayer' (*Ant.* 14.22-4 (= 14.2.1)). The Mishnah in more detail describes how he drew a circle and told God, '"I swear by thy great name that I will not stir hence until thou have pity on thy children." Rain began falling drop by drop. He said, "Not for such rain have I prayed, but for rain that will fill the cisterns, pits and caverns." It began to rain with violence. He said, "Not for such rain have I prayed, but for rain of goodwill, blessing and graciousness." Then it rained in moderation.' (*m.Ta'an*.3:8)

(translation: H. Danby The Mishnah, London: Oxford University Press, 1933, p. 198)

Hanina ben Dosa, a Galilean who lived in the first century AD, is described as a man of great devotion. The evidence we have for his miraculous work dates from long after his time, but apparently he was famous for his long-distance healings. Once he prayed for the ill son of rabbi Gamaliel, saying, 'Go, the fever has left him.' The boy was found to have recovered at that moment. (*b.Ber.*34b) He is also credited with controlling the weather, once halting a downpour when he was walking home. (*b.Ta'an.*24b)

What do you think?

Matt. 12:22-30; Luke 7:11-17

What does a close reading of these passages tell us about miracle-working and ideas of miracle in Jesus' world? Who was doing miracles? How could they be explained?

This view is partly supported by the Gospels themselves, since they refer to Jewish exorcists and to 'doctors' other than Jesus (Matt. 12:27; Luke 8:43). On the other hand, the Gospels clearly see Jesus as in a category of his own (note also his opponents' verdict, Mark 3:22). The evidence outside the NT for other Jewish healers comparable to Jesus (in terms of the nature, scope and rationale of his miracles) is scanty.

Modern sociological and anthropological study of illness has also recently contributed to discussion of Jesus' miracles, showing how in many societies the physical, social and spiritual aspects of disease are inextricable from each other. Modern western society has recently begun to recognize this, and it is interesting to note increasing openness towards alternative medicine and spiritual healing.

Jesus and modern miracles

A different, but related, question about Jesus' miracles has been raised by modern Christian pentecostal and charismatic movements, since they claim that the miracles associated with Jesus continue today. This claim, if substantiated, would clearly undercut arguments that 'these things do not happen today'.

The problem is that many Christians have not had the same experiences, and the question is whether:

● the pentecostals/charismatics have rediscovered something within the Christian tradition which others have forgotten or lost;

● the modern experiences are actually comparable to those ascribed to Jesus in the Gospels, or whether they come into some broader category of faith healing;

● the NT sees the miraculous side of the ministry of Jesus and of the apostles as unique or as something to be continued in the later church.

There is an attractive simplicity to the view that Jesus sent the disciples out to continue his healing ministry by his Spirit and with his authority, so that we should expect miracles today (Mark 6:7-13; John 20:21-23). On the other hand, the NT gives the impression that Jesus and his miracles (culminating in his resurrection) are unparalleled in scope and power. The church continues that work in what we might call a lower key (though John 14:12 might suggest otherwise).

Jesus' miracles and the kingdom of God

One modern tendency is to interpret the miracles of Jesus as though they were parables, i.e. to give them symbolic rather than historical importance. This does not do justice to the Gospels, where half of the point is that the miracles happened! On the other hand, the Gospels make it clear that Jesus did not do miracles for the sake of it, but for the sake of the kingdom of God and in the context of faith. Jesus refused to do signs when his opponents demanded them, seeing the demand as an expression of unbelief (Mark 8:11-13; cf. Matt. 4:6-7). Furthermore, Jesus is portrayed as seeking to keep his miracles and his messiahship secret (Mark 1:34, 44; 3:12; 5:43). This 'messianic secrecy' has been much discussed. It is plausibly explained by Jesus' determination not to be distracted from his mission of suffering by people's attempts to turn him into a popular wonder-worker or political leader (Mark 1:35-39; John 6:15; see further pp. 180f.).

What do you think?

Matt. 11:2-6, 16-24

Why do you think John the Baptist asked his question? What is the significance of Jesus' answer? Compare Isa. 35:5f.; 61:1f.

What then was the function of his miracles? According to the Gospels Jesus' miracles are done through the power of the Holy Spirit, and are signs of the inbreaking, restorative rule of God, which was promised in the OT and which he was proclaiming and embodying. He was bringing God's healing to society and overthrowing the pretender to the throne of this world, Satan (Matt. 11:2-6; 12:22-32; Mark 3:29, 30; cf. Luke 4:14; Acts 10:38).

John's Gospel sees Jesus' miracles as signs of Jesus' own divinity. In Jesus the new age of God's dwelling among his people had come, for those willing to recognize it (1:14; 2:12).

The Gospels record particular controversy over Jesus' healing on the Sabbath, and suggest that Jesus saw himself as 'fulfilling' the true purpose of the Sabbath and also of the OT 'jubilee' year, by bringing release and refreshment to burdened and bound people (Luke 4:16-21; 13:10-16; Matt. 12:1-14; Mark 2:27).

It turns out that the miracles do resemble the parables, in being powerful pictures of God's salvation come in Jesus. They need to be interpreted in the Palestinian context of Jesus and within the context of Jesus' own teaching of the kingdom.

APOCALYPTIC IMAGERY

The cartoon is a powerful means of communication: the political cartoonist may positively portray the Prime Minister as a lion breaking out of a cage, or as a dejected football goalie who has just conceded a goal. Such pictures make a vivid point.

The Bible has something like the cartoon in so-called apocalyptic literature, where a message is conveyed through pictorial images. The two most important apocalyptic books in the Bible are Daniel in the OT and Revelation in the NT. Both are full of strange imagery and symbolism: there are curious animals (e.g. lions with eagles' wings), and curious people and happenings (e.g. a man with a sword coming out of his mouth, a woman shut up in a basket carried away by an eagle).

To appreciate the meaning of the political cartoon the reader usually needs some knowledge of the political scene being described, though sometimes there will also be a caption that gives a clue. So the meaning of the apocalyptic imagery of the Bible is sometimes explained, but often depends on the reader's knowledge of what is being pictured. In Rev. 17 there is a great prostitute whose name is 'Babylon the Great' and who sits on seven hills. The reader would immediately have recognized this as a picture of Rome, the great pagan city, which was built on seven hills, and which the author of Revelation sees as extravagantly and seductively immoral.

The word 'apocalypse' means 'a revelation', and the so-called 'apocalyptic' literature is typically in the form of visions or dreams, seen as revelation from God; often the prophet is transported mentally to heaven, and is shown things there. He sees the strange images – like a sci-fi film – and records them as God's word for the people. Like a foreign language, they need to be translated, and often the translation or interpretation is given in the vision by an angelic interpreter.

A typical apocalyptic vision, which is of great importance for the gospels, is that of Dan. 7, where Daniel sees:

Scene 1: A churning windswept sea, out of which emerge four terrible animals: a lion with eagle's wings; a lopsided bear; a leopard with four wings on its back and four heads; an indescribably terrible beast with huge teeth and ten horns, one of them with eyes and a mouth.
Scene 2: A court, presided over by a very old man ('the Ancient of Days'). Judgement is given against the four beasts, who are either destroyed or disarmed, with their power being taken away.
Scene 3: A figure resembling a human being ('like a son of man') comes with clouds to the Ancient of Days, and is given the glory, power and kingdom that the animals had previously.

What does this mean? Daniel himself asks this, and is given the interpretation: the four beasts are four kings or kingdoms, whose power is going to be taken away by God (the Ancient One); authority and dominion is going to be given instead to 'the saints of the Most High', in other words to God's people, who are represented in the vision by the human figure, the 'one like a son of man'.

Scholars debate the meaning of various parts of the vision, but the general thrust of it – as a cartoon-prophecy about the future triumph of God's people Israel over pagan empires and forces – is clear.

Jesus' figurative teaching, as we have seen, is mostly in the form of down-to-earth parables, not in the form of strange visions. But he can speak of God's 'mysteries' being revealed to the disciples, in a way that is reminiscent of apocalyptic literature (Matt. 13:11), and of 'seeing Satan fall like lightning from heaven' (Luke 10:18). Most interestingly, he uses the language of Dan. 7, speaking of himself as the son of man coming on the clouds of heaven (Mark 13:26; 14:62).

MARK 13:30 AND THE NEARNESS OF THE DAY

Mark 13:30 – 'This generation will not pass away until all these things have taken place' – has been seen by scholars as a reflection of the mistaken thinking of Jesus or the early Christians about the timing of the second coming. However, various alternative interpretations have been offered.

It has been argued:
- Mark 13 does not refer to the second coming much, if at all. The description of the son of man coming on clouds is apocalyptic language figuratively referring to the political catastrophe that happened in AD 70. Jesus was not mistaken.
- The coming of the son of man is indeed the second coming of Jesus, but the discourse of Mark 13 speaks both of that day, and also (rather confusingly) of catastrophe coming on Jerusalem before that day. 'These things' (v. 30) which will happen in a generation are the things that will precede the second coming (v. 29); the time of the second coming is unknown (v. 32).

(For further study on this verse, see Beasley-Murray 1993; Geddert 1989.)

The passage that most resembles Dan. 7 and other Jewish apocalyptic literature is Mark 13, where Jesus speaks of the future – of sufferings and plagues before the end, of a 'desolating sacrilege' in Jerusalem (that very phrase being found in Dan. 9:27; 11:31), of the heavens being shaken, and of the heavenly coming of the son of man to gather his elect (13:14-27).

This chapter provokes two questions which are much discussed:

● Does the teaching go back to Jesus? Some have seen the apocalyptic core of the chapter as Jewish teaching, a 'little apocalypse', that Christians then adopted (perhaps in the face of the events of AD 39, when the emperor Caligula tried to have his statue erected in the Jerusalem temple, or in the period of the Jewish War AD 66-70) and ascribed to Jesus. This suggestion, propounded by T. Colani in 1864, may originally have been motivated by a dislike of apocalyptic and by a desire to make Jesus a reasonable teacher of human brotherhood. Also, it saved Jesus from being mistaken, since Mark 13:30 appears to have Jesus expecting the second coming within the lifetime of his contemporaries. However, the arguments against the authenticity of the teaching are more than outweighed by the evidence that Danielic thinking (e.g. about the kingdom of God and the 'son of man') was extremely important to Jesus. (On scholarly debate of this question, see Beasley-Murray 1993.)

● How much is Jesus speaking literally, and how much is he using apocalyptic cartoon language? Much of the chapter, e.g. the references to plagues, famines, the persecution of Christians and the preaching of the gospel, sounds straightforward. The 'desolating sacrilege', on the other hand, is language that is deliberately enigmatic, hence the call – 'let the reader understand' (Mark 13:14). In Daniel the phrase evokes the events of 167 BC, when Antiochus Epiphanes desecrated the Jerusalem temple (Dan. 9:27; 11:31; 12:11; cf. 1 Macc. 1:54). Jesus is anticipating something similar in the future. But what of the shaking of the sun, moon and stars? Was Jesus perhaps using poetic language as is used in the OT to refer to what we might call 'earth-shattering' events within history? (See Isa. 13:10; 34:4; cf. Ezek. 32:7f.) Similarly when Jesus refers to the son of man coming on the clouds of heaven, is Jesus predicting his own return to earth, or is he speaking pictorially of the vindication of God's people, using the Danielic imagery? (For further study of this see esp. Caird 1980.)

No doubt there is a large figurative element in the language used by Jesus. And yet, given Jesus' frequent use of the expression 'son of man' for himself, it is hard to avoid the conclusion that he is speaking of his own triumphant return (as he does in his parables) to complete the work that he has begun.

ESSAY TOPICS

INTRODUCTORY

● Look through one synoptic Gospel, and write an essay on the miracles in that Gospel. Note all the miracles referred to. Put them into categories, e.g. 'healings'. What do you think the Gospel writer saw as their significance? Are any of them harder to believe in than others? If so, why?

● Prepare three Bible studies on 'parables in Luke's Gospel'. Choose parables on different themes, and write notes and questions to bring out the background and the meaning of the parables in Luke's context.

INTERMEDIATE

● What is the meaning of the parable of the unjust steward (Luke 16:1-10)? In answering this: (a) consider (with the help of commentaries) the historical/social background (e.g. what was a steward?); (b) look for the main points and don't over-interpret (Jesus did not intend his hearers to imitate the steward in everything!); (c) consider the hints that Luke gives as to his interpretation (e.g. vv. 1-13, 19-31; also 14:12-14).

FURTHER READING

INTRODUCTORY

DJG article: 'Miracles and Miracle Stories'.

K. R. Snodgrass, 'From Allegorizing to Allegorizing: A History of the Interpretation of the Parables of Jesus', in R. N. Longe-necker *The Challenge of Jesus' Parables*. Grand Rapids/Cambridge: Eerdmans, 2000, 3–29.

N. T. Wright *The New Testament and the People of God*. London: SPCK Philadelphia: Fortress, 1992, 280–99 (a discussion of apocalyptic).

INTERMEDIATE

D. Allison *The End of the Ages has Come*. Philadelphia: Fortress, 1985 (a leading scholar explains the eschatological/apocalyptic background to the NT).

K. Bailey *Poet and Peasant and Through Peasant Eyes*. Grand Rapids: Eerdmans, 1983 (fascinating for its explanation of the cultural background to the parables).

G. R. Beasley-Murray *Jesus and the Last Days*. Peabody: Hendrickson, 1993 (the standard work on Jesus and the future).

C. Blomberg *Interpreting the Parables*. Downers Grove: IVP, 1989 (excellent discussion of history and principles of interpretation).

C. Brown *Miracles and the Critical Mind*. Grand Rapids: Eerdmans, 1985.

M. L. Brown *Israel's Divine Healer*. Michigan: Zondervan/Carlisle: Paternoster, 1995.

G. B. Caird *The Language and Imagery of the Bible*. London: Duckworth, 1980 (a fascinating discussion, including of parables and apocalyptic).

T. Geddert *Watchwords, Mark 13 in Markan Eschatology*. Sheffield: JSOT, 1989.

S. J. Hultgren *The Parables of Jesus*. Grand Rapids: Eerdmans, 2000.

J. Jeremias *The Parables of Jesus*, 2nd ed. London: SCM, 1963 (originally a classic German work).

G. Twelftree *Jesus the Miracle Worker*. Downers Grove: IVP, 1999.

G. Vermes *Jesus and the World of Judaism*. London: SCM, 1983/Philadelphia: Fortress, 1984.

D. Wenham *The Parables of Jesus*. Downers Grove: IVP, 1989 (a popular exposition of all the parables).

THE HISTORICITY OF THE GOSPELS

The Gospels tell an astonishing story, but is it history or fiction, or something in between? This section looks at what is involved in this question, and in particular:

● explains why some people have doubts about the history;
● why others argue for the historicity of the Gospels.

A SUBJECTIVE ISSUE?

If you go to your local shopping centre around Christmas and ask people 'Are the Bible stories of Jesus' birth true?', you will get a lot of different answers: some say yes; some, perhaps the majority, say no and put the stories into the category of fairy tales; and some are agnostic. Even in church congregations you would get different answers to the question.

Two hundred years ago most people in a country like Britain would have accepted the stories without serious question. Why the difference? Is it that today we are more intelligent? We have more knowledge available to us, that is true. But the main reason for the change is that Western society over the past two hundred years has gone through a rationalistic phase. People have doubts about all sorts of traditional beliefs and do not accept what cannot be rationally or scientifically proved.

Things, however, may now be changing again, with modern 'scientific' rationalism giving way to post-modernism and a renewed openness to things supernatural and spiritual. People now have all sorts of surprising beliefs (as they would have been regarded not long ago), and ideas of aliens, spirits, angels and virgin births are after all more acceptable in some circles.

Digging deeper

Talk with friends (or do a survey in your college or town!), asking questions such as:

(1) Do you believe that miracles happen today? Why do you believe this? If you do believe in miracles, what sort of miracles do you think happen?
(2) Do you believe that Jesus did miracles? Why do you think this?

Collect your answers, and see if any pattern emerges with different ages, educational backgrounds, etc.

The point is that opinions, including scholarly opinions, about the historicity of the Gospels are affected by subjective factors. Westerners, influenced by the secularism of their society, may find it hard to believe the miracles of the Gospels; people from other more religious parts of the world (whether Christian or not) may have much less difficulty, as I experienced first-hand when teaching in India some years ago.

Even on an individual level, the person who considers the Gospels as an unbeliever may find them quite incredible, but that same person may undergo a conversion experience and find the same documents quite compellingly believable.

So is it all a matter of faith, as some would say? Certainly there is a big subjective element in how we human beings assess all sorts of things. We all have vested interests: the unbeliever may not want to accept Jesus as Lord; the believer, who has 'experienced Jesus' in the present, expects to find Jesus a miraculous figure in the Bible; and the scholar is often influenced by scholarly fashion.

However, this does not mean that everything is hopelessly subjective. Although no historian is perfectly objective, it is possible to weigh up historical evidence and arguments, whether it is about a recent (almost mythological!) figure such as Diana, Princess of Wales, or

What do you think?
OBJECTIVITY IN THE LAW COURT

Can law courts be at all objective? What factors make it difficult? How far do the racial or religious views of lawyers or members of juries affect their judgement? What steps can be taken to ensure maximum objectivity?

When you read the Gospels and think about the stories, what subjective factors influence you? What can you do about this, if anything?

about ancient heroes such as Julius Caesar, or about Jesus Christ. It is possible to weigh the evidence, and to be persuaded by the evidence to change one's mind, including about the historicity of the Gospels. The subjective and objective are inextricably present in the mind of every critic, but it is not entirely a one-way relationship.

WHAT SORT OF DOCUMENTS?

A key question is that of genre, i.e. of the literary character of the Gospels. Many ordinary Christians see the Gospels simply as true stories about Jesus (as 'gospel truth'), like the news we get in the newspaper or see on the TV (or at least what we may think we are getting, since the media are often far from objective). But it is possible that the Gospels are rather different – that they are edifying, mythological tales about Jesus, which should not be understood as serious history. Or that they are something between history and fiction, for example, just as children's Bibles tell the stories of Jesus with all sorts of interesting elaboration (e.g. commenting on the weather and people's feelings), so the Gospels could be elaborated history. Scholars have compared Jewish 'midrash', which was (in part at least) the retelling of OT stories with a lot of fanciful elaboration. So the question 'What sort of documents are the Gospels?' is a very important one (see further in ch. 3 above).

There is a strong case for saying that the Gospels are historical biography in intention.

What do you think?

Read Luke 1:1-4 carefully. What does this passage suggest to us about Luke's historical method, intentions and sources?

Luke certainly starts his Gospel with a serious statement about his intention to write a reliable account of Jesus' life and teaching (1:1-4). Whether that statement should be taken at face value may be judged in part by the contents of his Gospel (and its companion volume, Acts); indeed, questions of genre will partly be judged by particular evidence in the Gospels themselves.

WHAT SOURCES OF INFORMATION DID THEY HAVE?

Even if the evangelists intended to write historically accurate accounts, their success in doing so would inevitably have depended in part on their sources of information. I might write a history of the Second World War: if I based it on my recollections of what a senile grandfather told me when I was a child, it would be historically worthless; if I based it on recent interviews with intelligent and alert eyewitnesses of the war and on contemporary records of the events (not just from one side, of course), it would stand much more chance of being accurate and valuable.

The earliest information from outside the Gospels themselves about how they were written dates back to the second century AD, when the Gospels are associated with Matthew, Mark, Luke and John. Matthew and John, as apostles of Jesus, represent first-hand sources of information about Jesus; Mark and Luke are people who had close contact with the apostles, Mark being associated in early church tradition with Peter. The Gospels have thus traditionally been regarded as first-hand reminiscences of the apostles, or something very like that.

However, this opinion has been widely discounted in modern scholarship, many arguing that the internal evidence of the Gospels themselves (see below) tells against their being eyewitness accounts. Matthew and Luke are thought to have depended on Mark for much of their account of Jesus, and Mark's account is seen as based on a chain of uncertainly reliable oral tradition; we have more faith than history in the Gospels.

EARLY TESTIMONY ABOUT THE GOSPELS

Papias, Bishop of Hierapolis in the early second century, is reported as saying: 'Mark became Peter's interpreter and wrote accurately all that he remembered … Matthew collected the oracles in the Hebrew language, and each interpreted as best he could'. (Eusebius *Hist.eccl.* 3.39.12-16 LCL translation)

Irenaeus, Bishop of Lyons later in the second century, said: 'Matthew among the Hebrews issued a writing of the Gospel in their own tongue, while Peter and Paul were preaching the gospel at Rome and founding the Church. After their decease Mark, the disciple and interpreter of Peter, also handed down to us in writing what Peter had preached. Then Luke, the follower of Paul, recorded in a book the Gospel as it was preached to him. Finally, John, the disciple of the Lord, who had also lain on his breast, himself published the Gospel, while he was residing at Ephesus in Asia'. (*Haer.* III.1.4, translation Cyril Richardson, Library of Christian Classics Vol 1, London: SCM, 1953, 370)

This scholarly view has not been universally accepted. There is evidence that supports the early church traditions. Most notably the way that Luke in his second volume Acts drops unselfconsciously into the first person 'we' (16:10 etc.) supports the tradition that Luke's Gospel was written by a companion of Paul. Luke in his prologue does refer to others who have written before him (and Mark may have been one of those), but he says that he has himself researched his

Gospel carefully, drawing on eyewitness tradition. Whether he succeeded in his intention of writing accurately is another question, and takes us on to the evidence of the contents of the Gospels. (See further in ch. 10 on Luke.)

DOUBTS ABOUT THE HISTORICITY OF THE CONTENTS

Scholars' opinions on the question of the genre and to some extent of the sources of the Gospels are inevitably and rightly influenced a great deal by their view of the actual contents of the Gospels.

Those who are sceptical about the Gospels as historical documents notice:

The miraculous nature of the accounts The overtly supernatural nature of the Gospel stories – with angels and demons all over the place and with Jesus doing extraordinary things, such as turning water into wine and walking on the surface of the Sea of Galilee – seems a clear indication to many readers that we are dealing with religious mythology and the sort of legends that grow up around great religious figures. We discuss this point further on pp. 106ff. and in ch. 6.

The differences between the Gospels Probably the most important argument against the historicity of the Gospels is the way they diverge from each other in relating the same life (of Jesus) and even the same events.

The outstanding example of this is the way John differs from the synoptics in the events described, the chronology of Jesus' ministry, the style of Jesus' teaching, and in the portrayal of Jesus' divinity. (See further in ch. 12 on John.) The conclusion reached by many scholars is that John is a highly theological work, which is of little value historically. The author elaborated sayings and stories of Jesus in his own style and with his own theological emphases.

But what is widely seen as true of John has increasingly been argued as true of the synoptics. And although the comparison of John and the synoptics has usually led to a historical devaluing of John, the argument can go in the other direction. The synoptics' portrayal of Jesus during his ministry making only one journey to Jerusalem – in order to die – not several journeys as in John, is arguably a stylized portrayal, designed to give focus to the cross as supremely significant.

But also the comparison of the synoptic Gospels with each other raises historical questions: Mark has Jesus send out the 12 with sandals and a stick; Matthew and Luke have Jesus prohibit such equipment (Mark 6:8, 9; Matt. 10:10; Luke 9:3). Matthew and Luke describe Jesus' birth very differently – no wise men in Luke, no shepherds in Matthew – and all the evangelists describe Jesus' resurrection differently, so that various scholars have concluded that the accounts are irreconcilable historically.

Such divergences (with or without the additional evidence of the miraculous contents already discussed) point to the Gospels being at best partially accurate.

The theological slant of the Gospels The comparison of the Gospels with each other not only raises historical problems, but also points to the Gospels being documents motivated more by faith and theology than by a concern for accurate history, as many would argue. This is widely believed about John, but it is also the conclusion of both

form and redaction critics in regard to the synoptic Gospels (see further on form and redaction criticism in ch. 4). A simple example is the parable of the lost sheep, which in Luke 15 illustrates Jesus' compassion on sinners and in Matt. 18 is about reaching out to the erring church member. It makes good sense to say that the parable was passed down in the oral tradition of the church, as form critics argue, and that it has been used and shaped by Luke and Matthew in line with their particular theological interests, as redaction critics argue (Luke being interested in the outsider, Matthew in matters of church life and discipline).

Repeatedly differences between the Gospels can be explained in this way. The conclusion of many scholars is that the Gospels are not the reminiscences of eyewitnesses, but something more like church preaching; the stories and sayings of Jesus have not been carefully preserved for historical purposes, but freely adapted for theological and pastoral purposes. We are nearer to midrash – at least in the infancy narratives of Matthew and Luke, but probably elsewhere too – than to modern history.

Disagreements with other historical sources There is relatively little contradiction between the Gospels and non-biblical historical sources, which is hardly surprising since there is little direct overlap in what they describe. However, there are some historical problems in the Gospels, arising out of a comparison with Græco-Roman sources. Most famous is Luke's reference to the census called by the Syrian governor Quirinius that brought Mary and Joseph to Bethlehem, at the time of Jesus' birth, according to Luke (2:1-4). The main difficulty here is that Quirinius is known to have conducted his census in AD 6, whereas both Matthew and Luke say that Jesus was born in the days of Herod the king, who died in 4 BC. Quirinius was not governor at that time. Furthermore, Luke's portrayal of the 'whole world' being taxed is problematic, since there is no other evidence of such a universal registration at that time. It looks as though Luke has an inaccurate under-standing of the chronology and of the exact sequence of events around the time of Jesus' birth, and that he used the census as an explanation of how Jesus of Nazareth could have qualified as the Messiah and been born in Bethlehem.

THE QUIRINIUS ISSUE

Explanations offered:

- Luke is confused and mistaken about the dates.
- Although Quirinius was not governor of Syria until AD 6, he was active as a senior Roman military official in the East Mediterranean before that, and it is suggested that he may have been involved with organizing a census in that period.
- Luke says: 'This was the first census, when Quirinius was governor.' Does he imply that there was more than one census? The Greek could be translated: 'This was the census *before* the one that took place in the time of Quirinius.'

At the other end of the Gospel story the description of Jesus' trial raises historical questions. The portrayal of the Sanhedrin trying someone at night is problematic, since such trials were illegal, at least under rabbinic law as defined after the NT period (Mark 14:53). As for Pilate's offer to release a prisoner of the people's choice at Passover time, there is no evidence outside the Bible of any such custom, and it is thought unlikely that the Jews would have had such a privilege (Mark 15:6).

Such difficulties are not massive evidence against the historicity of the Gospels; even the Quirinius reference is not a definite mistake. But there is a cumulative case with that historical difficulty occurring in a passage where the level of the miraculous is especially high, where Luke diverges widely from Matthew, and where Luke's own theology is very much in evidence.

ARGUMENTS FOR HISTORICITY FROM THE CONTENTS

Convergences between the Gospels and other historical evidence Although the Gospels and Josephus do not describe many of the same events, they do describe the

---

RELEVANT ARCHAEOLOGY

There have been many important recent archaeological finds, relevant to the NT, the most significant being the Dead Sea Scrolls (see chs 1 and 2). Among other interesting finds are:

- The Pilate Inscription, found at Caesarea in 1961. This fragmentary stone inscription refers to the Roman emperor Tiberius and then to: *(Pon)tius Pilatus, (Praef)ectus Iud(a)e(ae)* = Pontius Pilate, govenor of Judea
- The family tomb of Caiaphas, the high priest (see in ch. 1 above).
- Archaeologists have excavated a first-century house in Capernaum, which they believe may well have been Peter's home. (See Charlesworth 1988.)
- The 'Jesus Boat', found near Magdala in 1986, is a wooden fishing boat, 9 metres long, 2.5 metres wide, which was almost certainly in use in the first century AD. The boat, which was preserved in mud until its recent discovery, shows us what sort of boat Jesus' disciples would have used on Galilee, though the particular boat cannot be shown to have any link with Jesus.

---

same world in ways that often converge. Thus the impression we get of the Herod family, of Pilate and even of John the Baptist is very similar in the Gospels and Josephus (see ch. 1). Whether it is the political scene, the trial of Jesus or the world of Galilee and of Jesus' fishermen disciples, the Gospel narratives make historical sense, and are not theological romances written for Greek-speaking readers.

Historical elements in the Gospels A similar point has to do with the contents of the Gospels themselves, which arguably reflect Jesus' Palestinian context, rather than a later Greek-speaking, Christian context. Not only are there Aramaic words and Semitic ways of speaking that probably go back to Jesus (e.g. the word 'Abba', the prefacing of solemn sayings with 'Amen'), but other key ingredients in the Gospel picture of Jesus (e.g. the idea of the kingdom of God, the description of Jesus himself as 'Son of man'), make most sense in Jesus' Jewish context, as do many of the debates described in the Gospels, e.g. about the Sabbath.

What do you think?
ABBA

Mark 14:36; Gal. 4:6; Rom. 8:15

Abba was the family word for 'father' (somewhat similar to 'Dad'), and it was not normally used by Jews of God. Why do you suppose that Paul, when writing in Greek to people who spoke Greek, speaks of Christians crying out 'Abba'?

Even in John's Gospel the vigorous debate about Jesus as Messiah only makes sense in a Jewish context, and plausibly in a Palestinian one (e.g. 7:25-44).

There are also particular sayings of Jesus that seem unlikely to come from the church, such as Mark 13:32, where Jesus declares his ignorance of God's plan for the future, and Matt. 24:43, where he compares his own future coming to the arrival of a thief in the night. There are other things, such as Jesus' counter-cultural mixing with women (e.g. John 4:27; Luke 10:38-42) and the discovery of his tomb by women (rather than by the male leaders of the church), which seem likely to be historical.

It is striking how little some of the concerns of the later Christian, Greek-speaking church obtrude in the Gospels: for example, in Paul's letters, written mostly in the fifties and sixties AD, big issues include the Gentile mission, and the Spirit and spiritual gifts. It is remarkable how in their Gospels Mark and Luke, both arguably writing for Gentile readers, have Jesus saying very little about those issues. The Gospels reflect Jesus' context, not the later church context.

ARAMAISMS/HEBRAISMS

Some examples of Aramaic/Hebrew words and expressions in Mark and the other Gospels:

- '*Talitha cumi*' = 'Little girl, get up' in Aramaic (Mark 5:41).
- '*Ephphatha*' = 'Be opened' in Aramaic (7:34).
- '*Abba*' = 'Father' in Aramaic (14:36).
- '*Eloi, Eloi, lama sabachthani*' = 'My God, my God, why have you forsaken me?' in Aramaic (15:34).
- In Matt. 16:18 Simon is named Peter or *Cephas* in Aramaic (cf. I Cor. 1:12), meaning rock.
- '*Amen*, I say to you' is one of Jesus' distinctive ways of addressing his hearers. '*Amen*' is a Hebrew affirmation, used by Jesus to emphasize his authority.
- Expressions like 'son of...' (son of man, sons of darkness) are typical of Hebrew and Aramaic, but not of Greek.

A rather different point that has impressed readers of the Gospels is the vividness of many of the stories. This has plausibly been seen as evidence that they come from eye-witnesses, but might simply reflect that the evangelists and others in the early church were good storytellers.

A few of the vivid stories:

- The four men letting their friend down through the roof to Jesus (Mark 2:1-12)
- The stilling of the storm (Mark 4:35-41)
- The healing of legion (Mark 5:1-20)
- The denials of Peter (Mark 15:66-72)
- The walk to Emmaus (Luke 24:13-35)
- The healing of the man born blind (John 9)
- The race to the tomb (John 20:1-8)

Historical integrity In other ways the Gospel writers show what may be seen as historical integrity. One of the remarkable things is how the disciples of Jesus, most of whom went on to be leaders in the early Christian church, are repeatedly described in the Gospels as failing Jesus. From the extreme of Judas, who betrayed Jesus, to Peter, who denied him, to James and John, who wanted to call down fire from heaven on their enemies and to achieve the top places in Jesus' regime, the disciples seem almost all to be disastrous followers of Jesus (e.g. Mark 10:35-37; 14:10-11, 66-72; Luke 9:54).

The proposal of some scholars (e.g. T. Weeden *ZNW* 59, 1968, 145-58) that the evangelists are deliberately attacking the apostles for reasons of their own is not persuasive, since they are clearly seen as privileged and chosen leaders. Rather we have striking historical honesty, which has been seen by conservative scholars as confirming the early tradition associating a Gospel like Mark with Peter, since Peter might well have been so honest.

> **What do you think?**
> **THE FAILURE OF THE DISCIPLES**
>
> Although they are called privileged followers of Jesus, the disciples constantly fail and misunderstand Jesus, e.g. Mark 4:13; 8:33; 10:13, 35; 14:10-11, 37, 40, 50, 66-72; Luke 9:54.
>
> How can we explain the mixed picture that we get? Are the Gospel writers confused, hostile to the disciples, or something else?

Authorial intent In favour of taking the Gospels historically are the expressions of historical intent on the part of the evangelists. Most important in this is Luke, since in his prologue in 1:1-4 he strongly affirms his historical ambitions and methods.

This may be formal, and not actually achieved, but in Luke's second volume, Acts, he achieves some remarkable historical accuracy (see ch. 13 on Acts), which suggests that his statement of intent is to be taken seriously. John's Gospel, in a more indirect way, shows great interest in eyewitness testimony and truthfulness (5:31-47; 19:35; 21:24).

Convergence of different NT writings and oral tradition Although there are some historically problematic differences between the Gospels, the fact that we have four different and partly independent accounts of Jesus, all dated by scholars within the first century AD, all agreeing very substantially in their portrayal of Jesus, is significant.

Paul is a further witness. He wrote his famous letters to various churches (such as the Romans, the Corinthians) mainly in the fifties and sixties AD. And he shows himself

Digging deeper:

LAST SUPPER

Compare the accounts of the supper in 1 Cor. 11; Matt. 26; Mark 14 and Luke 22. What differences and similarities do you notice? How can these be explained?

DIVORCE

Compare 1 Cor. 7:10,11, where Paul says that he is reproducing the teaching of 'the Lord', with Mark 10:2-12. What points of agreement and convergence do you note?

familiar with a wide variety of Gospel stories and sayings of Jesus. Most significant are his references to the Last Supper and the resurrection, since he refers to the traditions as ones 'he received and passed on', thus probably taking us back to the thirties AD (1 Cor. 11:23; 15:1).

These observations do not mean that the differences between the Gospels are never problematic. But sometimes scholars notice the differences and overlook the similarities; they also forget that Jesus, like any good teacher, will often have repeated himself, using the same teaching in different contexts, sometimes in exactly the same words, sometimes varying what he said. He could perfectly well have used the parable of the lost sheep more than once, to make slightly different points.

It is worth adding a note on oral tradition at this point. The traditions Paul refers to in 1 Cor. 11, 15 were presumably oral traditions, and his evidence points to the conclusion that stories and sayings of Jesus were systematically taught and learned in the earliest days of the church. So the writers of the Gospels were not drawing on vague memory, but on a living oral tradition, which went right back to the time of Jesus. Oral tradition and memorization were important in the Jewish world of the time (unlike in many modern writing/computer-based societies), and people could and did remember a good deal with great accuracy.

Historical impact The substantial accuracy of the Gospel tradition may be confirmed by the astonishing impact of the Christian movement in the first century. Other religious movements came and went, mostly fizzling out when their leader died. But the Christian movement in a very few years 'turned the world upside down' (and caused riots in Rome as early as AD 49, if the references to rioting 'at the instigation of Chrestus' by the Roman historian Suetonius are correctly interpreted in this way (*Claud.* 25.4; Acts 17:6). It also produced a remarkable body of literature in the NT. It is hard to explain this, unless Jesus was more than an average healer or revolutionary leader. The historian cannot deny that something remarkable happened, and there is no particularly plausible explanation of what happened to rival the explanation suggested by the Gospels themselves.

A final comment is in order. Those who argue that the Gospels are substantially historical are not claiming that they are simple, uninterpreted descriptions of the words and actions of Jesus. After all:
● there has been a process of translation – the Gospels are in Greek, whereas most or all of Jesus' teaching was in Aramaic;
● there has been a process of interpretation, the evangelists not simply relaying the words and describing the actions of Jesus,

119

but paraphrasing and bringing out the meaning of Jesus' words and actions in a way that will be relevant to their readers;

● there has also been a process of selection, the different evangelists choosing different things to mention and emphasize.

ESSAY TOPICS

INTRODUCTORY

● Write a debate on 'Are the Gospels historically reliable?', giving (a) the case for unreliability, explaining the five strongest arguments in your view; (b) the case for reliability, also with five reasons; (c) your own comments on the arguments in both directions and your conclusions. Illustrate your answer from the Gospels themselves.

INTERMEDIATE

● How can we explain the different accounts of Jesus' resurrection in the Gospels? Compare for yourself the accounts in Matt. 28; Mark 16:1-8; Luke 24; John 20,21; Acts 1:1-11 and 1 Cor. 15:4-8, listing the different appearances of the risen Jesus mentioned. Why do you suppose that some scholars consider them incompatible and irreconcilable? Can you see ways in which they may be sensibly reconciled?

FURTHER READING

INTRODUCTORY

P. Barnett *Is the New Testament History?* Carlisle: Paternoster, 1998 (a reprint of an older version).

J. D. G. Dunn *The Evidence for Jesus.* London: SCM/Philadelphia: Westminster, 1985.

INTERMEDIATE

DJG article 'Archaeology and Geography'.

K. E. Bailey, 'Informal Controlled Oral Tradition and the Synoptic Gospels', *AJT* 5

(1991) 34-54, reprinted in *Themelios* 20 (1995) 4-11 (an article arguing that Middle-Eastern oral tradition combined historical accuracy and narrative flexibility).

C. Blomberg *The Historical Reliability of the Gospels.* Leicester/Downers Grove: IVP, 1987 (a wide-ranging discussion, representing a conservative approach to the question).

J. H. Charlesworth *Jesus within Judaism.* London: SPCK/New York: Doubleday, 1988.

N. Perrin *What is Redaction Criticism?* Philadelphia: Fortress, 1969/London: SPCK, 1970 (a readable explanation of a more sceptical approach).

USING THE GOSPELS TODAY

This section:

● discusses approaches to differences between the Gospels and the question of 'harmonization';
● makes a few suggestions about using the Gospels today.

The writers of the Gospels believed that Jesus was relevant to generations and cultures other than his own, which is why they wrote their Gospels. We live in another time and a very different culture. How are we to explain Jesus today?

The four Gospels are our earliest records of Jesus' life and ministry. In thinking about their use today, our starting point must be that they are associated with the disciples whom Jesus himself authorized to represent him. Christians have accordingly seen them as having the inspiration and authority of Jesus behind them.

WHAT ARE WE TO MAKE OF FOUR DIFFERENT GOSPELS?

Some people have wished there was only one

Gospel, and indeed have tried to produce one jumbo Gospel out of the four that we have.

Tatian's 'Diatessaron' is the earliest and most famous of such 'harmonies'. It was written probably in Syriac about AD 170. It was a 'combination and collection' of the four Gospels (so Eusebius, *Hist. eccl.* 4.196), though quite probably influenced by other traditions. It was popular in the early church, even being regarded as the standard Gospel text in Syria as late as the fifth century.

However, having four Gospels is a positive thing, not a problem, because no one account of a person like Jesus will do him justice; four angles are better than one! Furthermore, having four Gospels may remind us that Jesus, though himself a man who worked and expressed himself in one particular time and place, is a man for every time and place, whose message needs not to be synthesized into some universal form, but to be translated and applied to different contexts.

But what are we to do with Gospel differences, and in particular with those places where the Gospels appear to contradict each other?

Many readers have been perplexed by the different genealogies of Jesus in Matt.1:1-16 and Luke 2:23-38; by the contradictory instructions about taking sandals and a stick given to the twelve in Mark 6:8, 9; Matt. 10:10 and Luke 9:3; by the different timing of the Passover and the crucifixion in John's Gospel (e.g. 19:14) and in the synoptics (e.g. Mark 14:12), as well as by other divergences in the accounts of Jesus' death and resurrection.

Some scholars think this shows the historical unreliability of the Gospels, and have concluded either that the Gospels are not inspired Scripture at all, or that their inspiration lies more in their theological teaching than in their historical accuracy.

Others argue that the historical evidence does not demand a sceptical conclusion. Many harmonizing explanations of the differences have been proposed. Some harmonization is elaborately ingenious, as with the explanation that Peter actually denied Jesus six times (the different Gospels recording different denials). Such harmonization has, not surprisingly, been ridiculed as a desperate attempt to protect a particular doctrine of Scripture. Some scholars reject all harmonizing. However, any historian faced with divergent accounts of the same events would be well advised to see if accounts somehow complement each other. The Christian who sees the Gospels as inspired by God will be the more inclined to look for such complementarity.

But harmonizing needs to be honest. No one is served by a forced harmonization. Often we may only be able to propose how different accounts might possibly fit together, thus there are various possible explanations of why John's dating of the crucifixion differs from that of the synoptics, several of which are possible, none of which are certainly correct (see ch. 12 on John).

Sometimes the modern reader will simply have to admit ignorance, and that there seems to be a contradiction, for which we have no plausible explanation at present. Sometimes the answer may lie not in trying to get two accounts to fit together like pieces of a jigsaw, but in recognizing that the Gospel writers have edited their material in ways that produce discrepancies: thus it is possible that Mark was writing his Gospel for

121

Romans, and that he wished to interpret Jesus' instruction to the disciples about taking nothing for the journey intelligently for the Roman context; for them a staff and sandals were essential and allowable within the spirit of Jesus' teaching. Similarly some argue that Mark included women divorcing their husbands in Jesus' prohibition of divorce, because Roman women could divorce their husbands, whereas it was not normal Jewish practice (Mark 10:12; cf. Matt. 19:9; Luke 16:18).

WHAT ABOUT TEACHING AND USING THE GOSPELS TODAY?

Should we work from one Gospel at a time, or bring the four different accounts of, for example, the feeding of the 5,000 together and preach on them all together? The answer is perhaps both/and rather than either/or. If we have been given four Gospels (as opposed to one jumbo Gospel), we should respect their individuality and not mix them up or synthesize them. On the other hand, if the whole of Scripture has been given us by God, then we should interpret Scripture by Scripture, and read one Gospel in the light of the others. In practice that will mean listening carefully to each Gospel and appreciating its perspective, but consulting the other Gospels to see if they throw helpful light on each other. Apart from anything else, if Matthew and Luke used Mark, then they are the very earliest interpretations of Mark that we have, and it may be highly informative to see how they have understood their Markan source. We would usually be well advised to preach from one particular Gospel, explaining its emphases and themes, but not to ignore light on a passage that we may gain from the others.

Purists may argue that we should stick to one Gospel at a time, others that we should always work with all four. But perhaps part of the conclusion to be drawn from our four Gospels is that there are different ways of looking at the same Jesus and different ways of presenting him to different readers, so we need not get too hung up about purity of method. Like the evangelists we will want to hear the historical Jesus, not a Jesus of our imagining, but like them we should be guided not just by our historical sources, but also by the situation and needs of those whom we are addressing.

An example: how to 'preach' Jesus and the Gospels

If we start at the beginning of the NT we will find in Matt. 1:1-17 a genealogy of Jesus that may seem remote in the extreme from the interests and needs of his twenty-first century readers. How can we hear that passage as relevant to today?

The model of translation is helpful. In our use of the NT we need to translate the text, not just from Greek into English, but in such a way that this ancient text speaks today. A good translation (a) is faithful to the original meaning in the original language, and (b) makes the meaning clear and intelligible in the new language. We will not make the Bible text relevant by changing its meaning, but should help people to see the relevance without changing the meaning.

The Christian belief in incarnation is significant at this point, since the idea of God becoming human in a particular historical context (first-century Palestine), though it seems very strange to some people, speaks of a God who does not communicate in abstractions, but who comes to us where we are and speaks in 'our language'. It is therefore not just a practical necessity that our teaching should be related to where people are today, but a theological imperative. If we are followers of Jesus, whom John famously calls 'the Word', we must be into communication.

This means that, when faced with a passage like Matt. 1:1-17, we will want to understand what Matthew meant and what his hearers will have heard. They were probably Jewish Christians for whom the figures of Abraham and David were particularly important figures, and who will also have had a special interest in the number seven (which is so important in Matt. 1:1-17 and which was seen by Jews as a perfect number). Matthew was expressing in ways that spoke to his hearers that Jesus was the fulfilment of God's plan for his people Israel and for the world, and that he had brought the day of God's righteousness and perfection. Translating that for our modern world may not be easy, but the story is told of someone who was converted to Christianity from Hinduism by reading this very passage, because it brought home to him the good news that history is not meaningless or circular (as in some religions), and that God is working out his purpose in history. The passage is equally relevant to an age that tends to be very individualistic and that emphasizes personal salvation and fulfilment: the Bible affirms the individual, but sees God as bringing us together as his people.

So our task is to make sense of the Bible story, but then to hear and help others to hear what the passage says to us today. To put it differently, our task is to help people relate the Bible's story of God's dealings with people in the past with their own story and life. A recent popular book asks *What would Jesus say to…?*, and then proceeds to suggest what Jesus might say to famous modern people (including Prince Charles and Richard Branson!). In using the Bible today, we need to hear what Jesus *did* do and say in his context, and then to reflect on what Jesus *would* do and say to people today, and then, having heard, to bear fruit in action.

ESSAY TOPIC

● You have been asked to write a short article responding to a letter in the local newspaper which argues that the Bible is full of contradictions and totally irrelevant to our modern world. What will you say?

FURTHER READING

DJG article 'Preaching from the Gospels' (where further bibliography may be found).

UNDERSTANDING JESUS

Chapter 6

THE QUEST FOR THE HISTORICAL JESUS

In this chapter we look at the modern 'quest':

● noting some of the important individuals and movements, from Reimarus in the eighteenth century to the present day;
● commenting on some of the issues that scholars have wrestled with, including the question of criteria and method.

Who was Jesus – really? What do we know about him? How reliable is the portrait of Jesus that we find in the Gospels? These questions go back to the very beginning of Christianity. During Jesus' lifetime, there was debate about who he was. After his lifetime the debate went on between the followers of Jesus and unbelievers, with, for example, non-Christian Jews offering explanations of Jesus' miracles and resurrection. As for the Gospels, there was reflection early on about how the four Gospels relate to each other – John's Gospel was described by one of the church fathers as a 'spiritual' Gospel.

But although the question of Jesus has never gone away, it has resurfaced acutely in the modern period, since the Enlightenment, and it is the modern debate that is usually referred to as 'the quest for the historical Jesus'.

INDIVIDUALS AND MOVEMENTS

RATIONALISM AND HERMANN SAMUEL REIMARUS

The seventeenth and eithteenth centuries were the time of the so-called Enlightenment in Europe, when all sorts of new ideas emerged and many received traditions were questioned, including traditions of the church. Among the influential movements were 'deism' and 'rationalism'. Deism rejected the idea of a God who intervenes in human affairs, preferring to think of God as the one who set things going, e.g. winding up a clock and then leaving it. Rationalism saw reason as supreme, and sought to test everything by its supposed reasonableness. Many Christian traditions, notably miracle stories, were found wanting.

A man who brought these sorts of attitudes into Christian theological debate and who is often regarded as the founder of modern critical studies of Jesus and the Gospels was Hermann Samuel Reimarus, professor of oriental languages at Hamburg University. He wrote a book, which was only published after his death (between 1774 and 1778), in which he argued that many of the Gospel miracle stories, such as Jesus walking on water, are absurd. He regarded Jesus as a mistaken Jewish prophet who wanted to found an earthly kingdom, whose life ended in failure in crucifixion, who was then turned into a spiritual and divine saviour by his followers. They stole his body from its tomb and invented the idea of the resurrection, as well as the notion that his death had atoning significance.

Reimarus' book caused outrage in traditional Christian circles, and he was not widely followed in his ideas. But he opened up a debate about miracles, the resurrection and the truthfulness of the Gospels, which has gone on ever since, with various of his ideas finding occasional endorsement. Reimarus also established for many a distinction between the Jesus of Christian faith as expressed in the Gospels and the Jesus of history. Even if most scholars have not endorsed his definition of the differences, they have agreed that there is a gap, if not a gulf, between the 'Jesus of history' and the 'Christ of faith'. The quest for the historical Jesus is the attempt to cross that gulf.

H. G. PAULUS AND MIRACLES

Reimarus' explanation of the Gospel miracles as fraudulent was unacceptable to many, and yet the rationalistic unease with miracle was widely shared. One way of dealing with this, advocated by H. G. Paulus (1828) and others, was to offer naturalistic explanations of the miracles. Thus Jesus did not actually walk on the water but only appeared to be doing so; he did not actually multiply the loaves and fishes to feed thousands of people, but inspired others to share what they had with those who were hungry. Such explanations of the miracles of Jesus have continued to be offered by scholars, most influentially by William Barclay the notable Scottish scholar (e.g. *The*

Digging deeper:
THE RESURRECTION OF JESUS

Various explanations have been offered of the resurrection, including:

- the disciples stole the body and fabricated the notion of the resurrection;
- Jesus only swooned on the cross, and revived in the cool of the cave tomb;
- the disciples on Easter day went to the wrong tomb, and on finding it empty concluded that Jesus had risen from the dead;
- one or more of the disciples had a hallucination, and supposed that they had seen Jesus. This story spread, and later engendered the idea of the tomb being empty;
- Jesus did rise from the dead.

What arguments would you offer for and against these views, on the basis of the following NT texts: Matt. 28; Mark 16; Luke 24; John 20–21; I Cor. 15:1-11?

(For contrasting views see G. Lüdemann *The Resurrection of Jesus*. London: SCM, 1994; P. Walker *The Weekend that Changed the World*. London: Marshall, 1999.)

Gospel of Matthew, vol 2. Edinburgh: St Andrews, 1958, 113-15), and also by G. Theissen (1987, 120).

DAVID STRAUSS AND MYTH

This sort of interpretation was firmly rejected as a highly improbable reading of the text by David Strauss (1808-74), who instead offered a mythological interpretation. According to this, the miraculous element in the Gospels is to be seen as part of a pre-scientific way of thinking and speaking. People used to explain thunderstorms as the gods being angry, and mental illness as demon possession. The Gospel writers used mythological and miraculous categories, derived in part from the OT, in order to explain Jesus. So the stories should not be taken as modern history, but read as ancient myth. A good example is the turning of water to wine, clearly a symbolic rather than historical story, according to this view.

This explanation of Gospel miracles was taken up by the famous Marburg scholar Rudolf Bultmann (1884-1976), who found much of the NT to be expressed in mythological terms. The mythological elements need to be 'demythologized' if modern people are to appreciate them. Just as we need to translate the Greek of the NT if we are to understand the texts, so we need to translate that myth into modern categories that convey the meaning for today. Bultmann taught at the time when existentialism (a philosophy associated with the German Martin Heidegger and others) was influential, and he interpreted the NT in existential categories. (See on this Bultmann's essays, *Kerygma and Myth*. New York: Harper, 1961.)

The mythological explanation of miracles is one, like the naturalistic one, that has continued to command some support. It is probably true to say that modern scholars use both explanations, finding some miracles easy to explain naturally (as psychosomatic healings, etc.), but others (such as the nature miracles) as more amenable to mythological explanation.

THE LIBERAL LIVES OF JESUS
The attempt to explain Jesus in non-miraculous terms went with a tendency to

---

What do you think?

If a man came out of a bar late on a Saturday night and told you that he had seen six Martians outside his house that morning, how would you assess his testimony? If you read in a reputable newspaper of a papal visit to South America and of various people being healed in response to the Pope's prayers, how would you react? What criteria do we use in assessing such stories? How might they be relevant or irrelevant to the Gospel miracle stories?

---

make Jesus out to be a 'reasonable' man in other respects. Thus the tendency was to downplay the angry, strange or apocalyptic elements in Jesus' teaching, or to ascribe those to his followers rather than to Jesus himself, and to portray Jesus as a wonderful, loving teacher, whose message focused on God as Father, on love and human brother-hood, with all men and women being God's children.

Famous liberal studies of Jesus include *The Life of Jesus* by Ernest Renan, published in 1863, a beautiful, sentimental and influential book, and *The Essence of Christianity*, lectures given by Adolf von Harnack in 1899-1900.

ALBERT SCHWEITZER AND THE ESCHATOLOGICAL JESUS
One of the greatest names in the history of the quest is that of Albert Schweitzer, who was famous not just as a theologian, but also as a fine organist and as a missionary to Africa. Perhaps his most important writing was *The Quest of the Historical Jesus* (1910), which traced the history of the quest from Reimarus up to William Wrede. Wrede was a contemporary of Schweitzer, who in 1901

wrote an influential book on the messianic secret in Mark, in which he argued that the strong emphasis in Mark's Gospel on Jesus keeping his messiahship secret was Markan theological fiction, not history. (See p. 193 on Mark.)

Schweitzer's contribution was twofold. First, he analysed the work of his predecessors, and showed how subjective people's portrayal of Jesus was. The scholars who earnestly looked down the well of history in order to see Jesus in fact saw the reflection of their own faces staring up at them, to quote Schweitzer's contemporary George Tyrrell talking about Harnack. Schweitzer insisted that we must not find a Jesus of our own liking, but let Jesus be the alien figure that he was.

Schweitzer's second contribution was to endorse and strengthen the case of his predecessor J. Weiss, who insisted that Jesus was a Jewish apocalyptic prophet (not a nineteenth-century liberal). Schweitzer saw Jesus as an apocalyptic Jewish prophet, who hoped that the end of the world would come in his ministry (e.g. Matt. 10:23). His disappointment, when it didn't, led him to precipitate his own death, hoping that that would force God's hand and make the wheel of history turn to its climax. Again he was disappointed, and he died crying out in despair at his sense of divine abandonment.

> 'Jesus … lays hold of the wheel of the world to set it moving on that last revolution which is to bring all ordinary history to a close. It refuses to turn, and He throws himself upon it. Then it does turn and crushes Him. Instead of bringing in the eschatological conditions, He has destroyed them. The wheel rolls onwards, and the mangled body of the one immeasurably great Man, who was strong enough to think of Himself as the spiritual ruler of mankind and to bend history to His purpose, is hanging upon it still. That is His victory and His reign.' (1911, 369)

RUDOLF BULTMANN, MYTH AND EXISTENTIALISM

Rudolf Bultmann, whom we have mentioned already, was one of the giants of German NT criticism. He was influenced by Schweitzer, and agreed that Jesus was an eschatological prophet. He was also influenced (a) by the new form-critical movement, and by W. Wrede, regarding the Gospels as highly theological and not very historical documents, and (b) by the work of various scholars (e.g. W. Bousset 1865-1920 and R. Reitzenstein 1861-1931) on the religious context of the NT. They explained how various of the ideas and practices described in the NT (e.g. the eucharist) could be seen as borrowed from Hellenistic cults and religions. Bultmann used this 'history of religions' approach in interpreting the NT. Thus John's Gospel, for example, represented a distinctly Hellenized portrait of Jesus, drawing on Greek redeemer myths.

It was probably a combination of things – including his sceptical conclusions about the Gospels and his agreement with Schweitzer that the historical Jesus was a rather uncongenial Jewish apocalyptist – which led Bultmann to argue that the question of the historical Jesus was unimportant for faith; faith only needed to know that Jesus died. Schweitzer had commented that it is not just Jesus as historically known, but as spiritually risen within men, who is significant for our time (1911, 399). Bultmann argued that faith arises out of the NT proclamation (Greek: *kerygma*) of Jesus (in particular of his death and resurrection), but the message

SOME MYSTERY RELIGIONS

There were various popular mystery religions in NT times, but our information about them is limited (partly because they were secretive). Typically they involved a religious story around which the cult was based, initiation ceremonies and other rituals (including washings), and meals.

The Eleusinian mysteries were popular in the Roman empire of NT times. The name is taken from Eleusis, a suburb of Athens. The cult myth is about the goddess Persephone being abducted while picking flowers by the god of the underworld, Pluto, but being rescued by her mother Demeter and restored to the world for two-thirds of each year. The myth is related to the annual 'death' of the seed in the ground and its coming to life again in the crops. The ceremonies included washing in the sea, a procession from Athens to Eleusis, a dramatic enactment of the myth, and a feast of barley, wine and other sacred things.

The Egyptian cults of Isis and Osiris celebrated Isis the great mother goddess and her husband Osiris (or Sarapis), the god of the underworld. His death and revivification, due to the heroic efforts of Isis, were celebrated each year, and he was seen as saviour of his devotees, bringing them hope of future life.

Mithraism came originally from Iran, and was based on the myth of Mithras killing a sacred bull, and thus releasing life-giving powers on earth. The worshippers (only men in this case) were organized into associations, and their rituals included complicated initiation into seven ascending grades.

proclaimed is theological rather than historical. Faith is commitment to the God proclaimed, not acceptance of historical facts. Indeed faith based on historical evidence and arguments is not real faith in Bultmann's view.

THE NEW QUEST

Bultmann's position would have ended the quest as a theologically significant enterprise, had it been accepted. However, Bultmann's own followers, without wishing to abandon his critical method and (often) sceptical conclusions, did not accept that Christian faith can be built on almost no knowledge of Jesus. They believed that there had to be at least some significant continuity between the historical Jesus and the Christ of faith, and they argued that such continuity could be established, even with a rigorously critical method. E. Käsemann argued this notably (1953); others agreed, G. Bornkamm noting the striking authority of Jesus' ministry (1956) and E. Fuchs the way that Jesus welcomed sinners (1960). The so-called 'new quest' of Bultmann's followers produced some significant books and ideas, but came up with quite meagre historical findings, thanks largely to the sceptical methodology used (see below on the criterion of dissimilarity). The approach is represented in some of the very recent German literature.

THE JESUS SEMINAR

Some of the most significant recent developments in the quest have been in the English-speaking world. The mantle of Bultmann and his followers has been assumed by the American Jesus Seminar, which has brought together a very large number of mainly North American scholars to debate and (notoriously) to vote on the authenticity of the different Gospel sayings and stories of Jesus. The scholars have been invited to vote with coloured balls on particular Gospel stories – a red ball for something definitely going back to Jesus, a pink one for something probably coming from him, a grey one for something unlikely to come from Jesus but perhaps reflecting some of his ideas, and a black one for something definitely not.

The results of the seminar's work are complete so far as the sayings of Jesus are concerned, and they have tended towards seeing Jesus as a cynic teacher rather than a Jewish eschatological prophet. The Cynics were a Greek philosophical school, founded by Diogenes of Sinope (in Northern Turkey) in the fourth century BC, who advocated simple lifestyle and rejected the establishment. This view of Jesus is derived particularly from the so-called Q traditions of Matthew and Luke and from the non-canonical Gospel of Thomas. The scholars particularly associated with this sort of view include J. D. Crossan and R. Funk (1991, 1993).

The Seminar's work has been criticized from all sorts of angles: for the populist voting system (though this is arguably just a reliable way of assessing a scholarly consensus); for the doubtful estimate of the Gospel sources; and for its improbable conclusions. It has been argued that, no less than their predecessors, the Americans have ended up portraying Jesus in their own image – as a reasonable, non-violent anti-establishment figure.

THE THIRD QUEST

Reaching very different conclusions are the so-called 'third quest' scholars. They are not an organized group like the Jesus Seminar, but they represent a similar approach, all emphasizing Jesus' Jewishness and interpreting Jesus in the context of second temple Judaism. Geza Vermes in his *Jesus the Jew* writes as a Jew, and identifies Jesus as a Jewish charismatic wonder-worker (1983). G. Theissen in *The Shadow of the Galilean* and other books tries to locate Jesus

sociologically, and sees him as a popular itinerant prophet (1987). E. P. Sanders in *Jesus and Judaism* sees Jesus as representing 'restorationist eschatology', i.e. as a prophetic figure who looked for the imminent divine restoration of Israel and Jerusalem (1985). N. T. Wright in *Jesus and the Victory of God* argues that Jesus saw himself as God's Messiah who was bringing the end of the exile to the people of God (1996).

The third quest is marked both by an emphasis on Jesus in the context of Judaism, and also by a relatively positive approach to the Gospel traditions. Both the Bultmann school and also the Jesus Seminar have been wedded to a sceptical method, demanding a rigorous and arguably impossible level of historical proof for the historicity of individual sayings of Jesus (see below on criteria). The third quest scholars are more willing to consider a wide variety of Gospel traditions as making sense in Jesus' context.

If the Jesus Seminar looks like slightly left-wing anti-establishment Americanism, the third quest may be seen as part of the post-Second World War trend to affirm Judaism, and not to be antisemitic. In NT studies there has been a major swing away from looking for Hellenism and Hellenistic ideas in the NT (as represented by Bultmann and others) to seeing Jesus – and also Paul, John and other NT authors – in a thoroughly Jewish context.

OTHER MODERN VIEWS OF JESUS

Not surprisingly the last century saw Jesus interpreted in a Marxist perspective, South American liberation theologians taking the lead in portraying Jesus as a revolutionary whose bias was to the poor (e.g. J. L. Segundo 1985). Most have seen him as a non-violent revolutionary like India's Mahatma Gandhi, but others have argued that the Gospels conceal the embarrassing fact that Jesus did identify with those who wanted to overthrow Roman rule by force, and that he was executed as a threat to the state and status quo (e.g. S. G. F. Brandon *Jesus and the Zealots*. Manchester: Manchester UP, 1967).

Feminism has also offered perspectives on Jesus, numerous scholars highlighting Jesus' positive and enlightened attitude towards women, e.g. to the Samaritan woman at the well, to Mary and Martha, etc. Jesus has been seen as representing a much more liberated attitude to women than was typical of Jewish rabbis of the day, even though he stayed with convention in appointing twelve male apostles. Some scholars believe that the Gospel writers, being less liberated than Jesus, have masked Jesus' truly revolutionary approach. Most notable of feminist scholars is E. S. Fiorenza (1983).

What do you think?

What features of Jesus, as described in the Gospels, lend themselves to explanation in terms of Jesus as a Marxist freedom fighter; as a proto-feminist? What features tell against these views?

ISSUES

PRESUPPOSITIONS AND SUBJECTIVITY

It is quite clear from our last remarks about the Jesus Seminar and the third quest as well as about Marxism and feminism how subjective factors have been very important in the quest, as Schweitzer rightly pointed out. The conclusion could be, and has been with some modern commentators, that the

quest is impossible, and that there can never be anything but the reflection of the historian when we look down the well of history.

But this conclusion is not necessary. We will never escape our subjectivity, but that does not mean that we can have no measure of objectivity in thinking about historical matters, any more than a police investigation into a crime today can have no objectivity. It does mean that we need to be:

● well aware of the influences on people (and suspicious of claims to neutrality/objectivity), taking these into account as far as possible;
● aware of our own subjective agendas as far as possible;
● listening to people who come from different angles than ours, recognizing the value in different approaches (whether Jewish, Marxist, feminist);
● concerned to allow Jesus to be alien from our own perspective;
● humble and provisional in our conclusions.

MIRACLES

Presuppositions about miracles have been among the dominant factors in historical studies of Jesus, with rationalist assumptions about the impossibility of miracle being openly aired by some of the most influential scholars, e.g. Schweitzer, Bultmann. Such assumptions are arguably weakening thanks to (a) the recognition that miracle-working of some sort was a feature of the Jewish world of Jesus, not unique to him, and (b) the decline of scientific rationalism in our society and the rise of interest in the 'spiritual' and supernatural dimensions of life. However, many scholars continue tacitly or openly to operate with the assumption that the more startling of the Gospel miracles could not have happened, which inevitably entails the conclusion that the Gospels are not reliable historical sources.

The issues that are raised by this include the validity or otherwise of a rationalistic outlook, and the fact that this assumption quite clearly contradicts the views of the Gospel writers (see further on miracles in ch. 5).

SOURCES

Alongside the discussion of the historical Jesus, and inextricably related to it, is the question of the nature and sources of the Gospels. Conclusions about the one subject (e.g. the historical Jesus) have inevitable implications for the other (the Gospels) and vice versa. Thus a rationalist who denies that Jesus could do miracles must have a negative view of the Gospels as historical sources, and will not be inclined to believe the early church traditions about the apostolic origin of the Gospels. On the other hand, those early church traditions are one factor to consider in weighing the historical value of the Gospel testimony to Jesus. In the history of research on Jesus, the development of the two source theory was important, giving priority to Mark and the postulated sayings source Q: the theory led to a devaluing of Matthew and Luke as historical sources, including their infancy and resurrection narratives, and to scepticism about the early church testimony concerning those Gospels. The theory of Markan priority came into favour at around the time the 'liberal' view of Jesus came to the fore (e.g. in the work of someone like H. J. Holtzmann 1863). Mark was perceived to give a more natural and believable account of Jesus, perhaps based on Peter's preaching, and Q was almost totally lacking in miracle. These judgements of the Gospels were doubtful in all sorts of ways: Mark and Q are not substantially less miraculous in outlook than Matthew and Luke, and the likelihood that Matthew and Luke used Mark does not mean that they did not have other important independent sources (written or oral). (See W. R. Farmer *The Synoptic Problem*. New York: Macmillan, 1964, for a critical account of the Markan priority theory, and ch. 4 above.)

In recent discussion the question of sources has again become important, members of the Jesus Seminar and others tending to give priority to Q (or to early versions of Q) and also to the Gospel of Thomas over the canonical Gospels as we have them. These source critical views fit in with the picture of Jesus which the Jesus Seminar has produced. But the confidence in Thomas as a historical source is hazardous, and their views of Q are distinctly speculative.

It is not only questions of Gospel sources that have a bearing on questions of history, but also questions of genre, since clearly the view that the Gospels are something like midrash or myth must be attractive to anyone with a rationalist outlook, whereas the view that they have a historical or biographical purpose is less so.

THE RELIGIOUS CONTEXT

One of the biggest issues in discussion of Jesus has been the issue of his context and of how he and the Gospel writers related to their respective contexts.

The recognition that Jesus and his followers did not live in glorious isolation from the world around them (associated with the history of religions approach) has been important for the quest for the historical Jesus in two respects at least:

● in assessing the Gospels, since it has been argued that their writings and portrayal of Jesus reflect their context, e.g. the distinctiveness of John's Gospel has often been seen as due to John's Hellenistic environment. The Last Supper story has been hellenistically explained: Jesus supposedly ate a simple fellowship meal with his followers, but this got turned into a sacramental meal associated with Jesus' death and resurrection by the Greek-speaking church, influenced by the mystery religions. These particular ideas of Greek influence on the Gospels have now fallen rather out of fashion, and the tendency, including with John's Gospel, is to emphasize Jewish, not Hellenistic, background and to explain many things in the Gospels in terms of the tensions between Jews and Christians in the first century, as their movements diverged.

● in assessing Jesus himself. The Jesus movement has been related to other contemporary religious movements, and Jesus has been seen as a cynic preacher, a Jewish charismatic healer, a 'sign prophet' (like the Theudas mentioned in the book of Acts 5:36) and as a zealot.

The variety of opinions makes clear how speculative many of the suggestions have been. Often scholars pick on one strand of Jesus' teaching (e.g. on his cynic-like renunciation of wealth) but play down another (e.g. his Jewish eschatological emphasis on fulfilment and the kingdom of God). Trying to make Jesus fit into some preconceived mould is fatally reductionist, because Jesus was clearly someone who did not fit into routine categories: on the one hand, he caused great offence and got himself crucified; on the other hand, he inspired a movement that did not disintegrate when he was killed, but rather it spread all over the Roman world in a short time. Jesus was clearly out of the ordinary. (On this point see further Wright 1996.)

CRITERIA AND METHOD

We have seen how subjective much of the quest has been, with scholars regularly ending up with a Jesus after their own image. It is desirable, in the light of this, to try and define criteria that are as objective as possible for determining what in the Gospels is historical and what is not.

Various criteria have been proposed:

Multiple attestation Given scholarly doubts about the historical reliability of some of the traditions of Jesus found in the Gospels, one obvious question to ask is: is this tradition only found in one Gospel, or in more than one? The simple logic is that, if it is attested by several NT writings, then this is in its favour. (Some scholars would include the Gospel of Thomas with the NT writings as a relevant witness.) There is, however, a problem with this criterion: if, for example, we argue that the feeding of the 5,000 has a high claim to being historical, being attested in the four canonical Gospels, the immediate objection could be that the other evangelists were using Mark as a source, so what appears to be four witnesses is really only one. This objection is not a total knockout blow to the proposed criterion: even if it is correct that the other evangelists used Mark, it is also clear that they had their own non-Markan sources, and very likely that they knew a story such as the feeding of the 5,000 independently of Mark. However, a simple adding up of the number of Gospels attesting something is not a particularly strong argument for historicity; nor, conversely, is the fact that something is found in only one Gospel any argument against its historicity.

Scholars have suggested other forms of multiple attestation. So although adding up the number of Gospels describing something may prove little, if a story or saying is found in more than one of the Gospel sources which scholars postulate (e.g. in Mark, Q, M, L), then this is possibly more significant. For example, the story of Jesus' baptism by John the Baptist is found in Mark and in so-called Q (a Mark-Q overlap), and there is some reason to think that Matthew, Luke and John may all have other independent traditions relating to John the Baptist and Jesus. Similarly Jesus' parable of the mustard seed appears in a Markan and a Q form, thus in our two oldest Gospel sources, as they are usually taken to be (Mark 4:30-32; Luke 13:18, 19).

This argument has some attraction, but its force is only as strong as the source-critical assumptions/arguments it is built on. If those scholars are right who deny the Q hypothesis and who say that Luke used Matthew, then the argument about the parable of the mustard seed would look shaky, since Matthew may have taken the parable from Mark adapting it somewhat, and Luke may then have followed Matthew. (In fact, in this case and with some others, even without the Q hypothesis, we might conclude that Matthew and Luke have an independent version of Mark's story, in which case the argument could stand.)

There is also evidence from Paul's letters of sayings and stories of Jesus, with which he and his readers were familiar (e.g. the teaching of Jesus on divorce 1 Cor. 7:10, 11; the story of the Last Supper 1 Cor. 11:23-26). Most of this evidence is allusive, since Paul does not often quote Jesus directly, but it is possible to cite Paul as a witness to all sorts of Gospel traditions (from the infancy narratives onwards). (For a detailed discussion of Paul and Jesus, see Wenham 1995.)

Yet another form of multiple attestation that has been proposed looks for ideas or themes

Digging deeper

Paul does not often mention stories or sayings of Jesus in his letters, but there are all sorts of possible echoes. You may like to look up the following and see if you think Paul is quoting from what he knows of Jesus:

1 Cor. 7:9,10 on marriage and divorce	Compare Mark 10:11,12
1 Cor. 9:4,14 on the Christian worker being paid	Compare Luke 10:7
1 Cor. 11:23-26 on the institution of the Last Supper	Compare Mark 14:22-25
1 Cor. 15:3-6 on Jesus' death and resurrection	Compare Luke 24, esp. vv. 34-36
1 Thess. 4:13-17 on the second coming of Jesus	Compare Matt. 24:29–25:13
Rom. 12:14 on non-retaliation	Compare Matt. 6:44; Luke 6:28
Rom. 14:14 on all foods being clean	Compare Mark 7:14-19
Gal. 4:4 on Jesus being born of a woman under the law	Compare Luke 1–2
Gal. 1:11-16; 2:7 on being an apostle (like Peter) receiving a revelation	Compare Matt. 16:16-18
2 Cor. 3:18–4:5 on 'transfiguration' – ours and Jesus'	Compare Matt. 17:1-8

that are found in different types of Gospel teaching: thus the 'kingdom of God' is a theme that permeates all sorts of Jesus' teaching (parables, miracle stories, etc.) and is seen therefore as having huge historical probability.

Dissimilarity A criterion that has been very important, not least in German scholarship, has been the criterion of dissimilarity. This criterion asks whether a saying of Jesus found in the Gospels is dissimilar from the Judaism of Jesus' day and dissimilar to the teaching of the later Christian church; if it is dissimilar to both, then it is surely a saying of Jesus. This criterion presupposes that the Gospel portrait of Jesus has been influenced both by Judaism and by the Christianity of the early church, ideas and sayings from both directions having got into the Gospel traditions. So if we eliminate all that is possibly Jewish or 'Christian', then what remains has a high claim to authenticity. An example would be Jesus' friendship with sinners, which contrasts with the Jewish and the early Christian striving to keep their respective communities pure.

The criterion, though widely depended on, is problematic:

● It is very difficult to assert confidently that any individual feature in Jesus' teaching is without parallel in first-century Judaism and Christianity, since we have only quite limited knowledge of second temple Judaism and of earliest Christianity. Thus, for example, Jesus' uncompromising teaching on divorce (as recorded in Mark) is distinct from most contemporary Jewish teaching, but the finding of the Dead Sea Scrolls in 1947 showed that at least one other Jewish group was equally negative about divorce. Jesus' addressing of God as 'Abba' was seen as unique, but now some

evidence has been adduced to show that others may possibly have used the address (see J. D. G. Dunn *Christology in the Making*. London: SCM, 1989, 26-9).

● Eliminating all that Jesus had in common with Judaism, and all that he had in common with the church that followed him and took his name, is clearly a draconian measure, which is likely to leave us not with the heart of Jesus' teaching, but with odd and eccentric snippets of teaching (which happen not to have been taken up by the church). Admittedly those who depend on the criterion see it as a solid starting point, on which they can build (via the criterion of coherence; see below). But it is questionable whether it is a good foundation, reliable enough to be of any use.

This is not to deny that Jesus must have been distinct from contemporary Judaism in some important ways, since otherwise his impact would not have been what it was. And it is reasonable to look for things that made Jesus distinct from his contemporaries, and which may have contributed to his success as a teacher and/or to his crucifixion. His ministry to sinners fits into that category, as do his claims to divine authority when healing and forgiving sins. It is also not to deny that there are ideas in the Gospels that do not appear to have been important in the early church (e.g. Jesus as 'son of man'), and which for that and perhaps other reasons seem likely to go back to Jesus rather than to the church.

On the other hand, it is important to emphasize that this sort of argument should not be used to suggest that things which are common to the Jesus of the Gospels and the later church do not go back to him: thus Jesus very probably used the word 'lord' of himself, but it was a title taken up by the early church, which became very important to them.

Going against the grain This is a different kind of criterion of dissimilarity. The argument is that, if a Gospel contains a saying or story of Jesus which is contrary to the evangelist's own particular interests or tendencies, then this is likely to be a tradition that is being passed on, not something coming from the evangelist himself. Behind this argument lies the assumption that the evangelists have put into the Gospels a lot of their own ideas and emphases – a lot of 'redaction'; one indication of non-redactional material is, clearly, things that do not reflect the evangelist's own concerns. Thus Matthew's Gospel was written, at least in the form we have it, by someone who was strongly committed to the Gentile mission of the church, as is clear from the great commission of Matt. 28:16-20. So the sayings in Matthew's Gospel which restrict the mission of Jesus and his disciples to 'lost sheep of the house of Israel' (namely 10:5; 15:24) are a probably received tradition, not Matthew's redaction.

There is some weight in this argument. And yet Matthew cannot have seen the sayings of 10:5 and 15:24 as contradicting his own outlook; after all, he, like all the evangelists, was writing selectively and need not have included sayings that he saw as misleading, mistaken or going against his grain. The probability is that Matthew did understand Jesus' mission as first to the Jews, then to the Gentiles, and that he saw 10:5 and 15:24 in that context. Still it is arguable that they represent a perspective that he would not have invented.

More generally there are features of the Gospel narratives which seem unlikely to have been invented by the early Christians, for example:

- the negative things said about the disciples and their failures, even though they were seen as Jesus' chosen successors;
- the baptism of Jesus by John the Baptist, which was seen as problematic to some of the early Christians who wished to assert the superiority of Jesus;
- the honest things said about Jesus' humanity (e.g. Mark 7:5);
- the humiliating death of Jesus, which was in the words of Paul 'a stumbling block to Jews and foolishness to the Greeks' (1 Cor. 1:23).

Aramaisms There are particular words in the Gospels, such as 'Abba', 'talitha cumi', 'eloi, eloi, lama sabachthani', which are Aramaic, the common language of Palestine in Jesus' day (Mark 5:41; 14:36; 15:34). Their appearance in the Greek Gospels is most simply explained in terms of Jesus' own usage. The same may be said of the way Jesus prefaces many of his important sayings with 'Amen', though this is Hebrew rather than Aramaic: 'Amen I say to you'. There are also many expressions in the Gospels which are in Greek but which sound Semitic, including such central concepts as 'kingdom of God', 'son of man'. It is clear that the roots of these traditions are in a Jewish and probably Palestinian environment.

This is not a conclusive proof that particular sayings go back to Jesus himself. After all, the earliest Christian church was the Aramaic-speaking church in Jerusalem, and Semitisms could have come from them. Furthermore, it is possible that some expressions, which may have entered the Christian tradition with Jesus, were then used creatively by the evangelists in their portrayal of Jesus: thus Jesus' 'Amen, I say to' becomes, 'Amen,

Amen, I say to you' in John's Gospel, and is used to introduce sayings of Jesus that would often be seen as Johannine rather than as historical (e.g. 3:3). It is possible that John used the phraseology of Jesus deliberately in creating new sayings of Jesus.

This observation does not entirely undermine the argument about Semitisms. Given that the Gospels claim to be conveying teaching of Jesus, and given some of the general arguments about the historical plausibility of the Gospel texts – e.g. based on a comparison with Josephus – the presence of Semitisms is what we might expect in texts that accurately describe the history of Jesus.

Coherence Lastly, we need to mention the criterion of coherence, which is ancillary to the other criteria. If any of the other criteria enable us even to identify some sayings or stories of Jesus that are probably historical, then we may build on that, and include other sayings and stories, which may not 'pass the test' in their own right, but which fit in with the emerging picture.

The criteria that we have described are all limited in their value; that is clear when one sees how differing scholars can use the same criteria, but still come up with quite different conclusions. Some scholars doubt if the criteria have any value. We have suggested that there is a grain of truth in many of them, but that they are not cogent proofs, and can only contribute to a cumulative argument about particular texts.

Alternative approaches

E. P. Sanders is sceptical about establishing anything with regard to the sayings of Jesus through the received criteria, and proposes instead a historical approach which focuses on events. He argues that there are certain events that are indisputable – e.g. that Jesus was baptized by John the Baptist, that he had disciples, that he was crucified – and that the way to historical reconstruction is through those events, seen in the Jewish context of Jesus' day (1993/1996).

N. T. Wright is positive about the value of the sayings traditions, but equally sceptical about some of the minute judgements made by scholars about individual sayings, calling their approach a way of 'frustration and tears'. He suggests that the proper method is to look at the Jesus tradition as a whole in the context of first-century Judaism, and to see if sense can be made of it. The way to weigh a historical hypothesis is by seeing how much it explains. He advocates what he calls a double similarity and dissimilarity approach, arguing, as we did above, that a historical account of Jesus must explain Jesus in a way that makes sense in the context of first-century Judaism and first-century Christianity, but in a way that also explains how Jesus got crucified and why he had such an impact (1996, 133 and passim).

Wright's approach has much to be said for it. Historians working with the writings of people like Julius Caesar and Josephus are much more open to their historical sources than sceptical Gospel critics – they do not insist on weighing individual sayings and stories with a criterion such as that of dissimilarity (which would indeed be the death knell of much ancient history). The Gospels are prima facie evidence for what the historical Jesus said and did (despite scholars who occasionally say of a Gospel story that 'there is no evidence that Jesus did this'); they describe the same real Palestinian world as does Josephus, and they deserve to be taken at least as seriously.

But does Wright's approach yield a coherent and historically persuasive picture of the historical Jesus? He believes it does, agreeing with E. P. Sanders and B. Meyer that Jesus should be seen as a prophetic figure, announcing 'restorationist eschatology', and more specifically as a messianic figure announcing the end of the Jewish exile and the return of God to his people. Wright may not be right in all respects, but his approach to the Gospel texts is particularly fruitful and illuminating.

HISTORY MATTERS

At various times scholars have effectively despaired of making progress in the quest for the historical Jesus, with someone like Bultmann denying that it is important for faith. Bultmann's own followers were right to say that Christianity is (uniquely) based on history and on the conviction that God has revealed himself in Jesus. However, despite that reaction, we see today (a) some scholars doubting again if we can get back to the historical Jesus and (b) a post-modern theology emerging, that affirms the value of the Christian stories for those to whom they speak, but which does not need or want a unique Jesus. Such an approach may suit the mood of our times; it does not suit the NT's own convictions and claims.

ESSAY TOPICS

INTRODUCTORY

- What have been the main questions and issues addressed in the scholarly quest for the historical Jesus? Are there parallels in modern popular discussion of Jesus?
- Write a dialogue between a sceptic and a Christian on the subject 'Knowing about Jesus is impossible historically; it all depends on faith'.

INTERMEDIATE

- Who was Jesus and what was he like? Explain what seems to you the strongest historical evidence and arguments.

- Why are scholars so divided in their views on the historical Jesus? Is there any way forward for the 'quest'?

- 'Looking down the well – lessons from the quest for the historical Jesus.' Prepare a talk on this topic for a church study group, encouraging them to be self-critical about their own views of Jesus and open to different perspectives.

FURTHER READING

INTRODUCTORY

E. P. Sanders and M. Davies *Studying the Synoptic Gospels*. London: SCM/Philadelphia: Trinity Press International, 1989.

N. T. Wright, 'Jesus, Quest for the Historical' in D. N. Freedman, ed. *Anchor Bible Dictionary 3*. New York: Doubleday, 1992, 796–802.

N. T. Wright and M. Borg *The Meaning of Jesus*. New York: HarperSanFrancisco, 1998/ London: SPCK, 1999 (particularly useful, being a dialogue between two important modern scholars).

INTERMEDIATE

J. D. Crossan *The Historical Jesus*. San Francisco: HarperCollins/Edinburgh: Clark, 1991 (most important representative of Jesus Seminar approach).

R. W. Funk & R. W. Hoover *The Five Gospels*. New York: Poleridge, 1993 (the Jesus Seminar findings).

J. P. Meier *A Marginal Jew*. New York: Doubleday, 1991 (important, three-volume work).

S. Neill & N. T. Wright *The Interpretation of the NT 1861-1986*. Oxford/New York: OUP, 1988 (very useful historical survey).

M. A. Powell *Jesus as a Figure in History: How Modern Historians View the Man From Galilee*. Louisville: Westminster John Knox, 1998/ Oxford: Lion, 2000.

E. P. Sanders *The Historical Figure of Jesus*. London/New York: Penguin 1993/1996.

A. Schweitzer *The Quest of the Historical Jesus*. 2nd ed. London: Black, 1910 (historical classic).

G. Theissen and A. Merz *The Historical Jesus*. London: SCM/Minneapolis: Fortress, 1998 (an excellent guide to issues).

D.Wenham *Paul: Follower of Jesus or Founder of Christianity?* Grand Rapids: Eerdmans, 1995 (arguing for Paul's knowledge of Jesus' teaching).

B. Witherington *The Jesus Quest*. Leicester/ Downers Grove: IVP, 1995 (a valuable survey of views).

N. T. Wright *Jesus and the Victory of God*. London: SPCK/Philadelphia: Fortress, 1996 (useful for its survey and for the author's own thesis).

Chapter 7

THE LIFE OF JESUS
IN THE LIGHT OF HISTORY

Jesus of Nazareth changed the world for ever. But what do we know about him? In previous chapters we have discussed many of the issues raised by this historical question. In this chapter we offer an answer to the question based on the Gospels and taking critical perspectives into account.

BIRTH AND BEGINNINGS

We have two very different accounts of the birth of Jesus, one in Matthew's Gospel, one in Luke's. But, though different, both accounts agree that (a) Jesus was born in the days of Herod the Great (who died about 4 BC), (b) in Bethlehem, (c) as the first child of a woman called Mary, who was engaged but not yet married to Joseph, and (d) that he was subsequently brought up in Nazareth in Galilee.

Nazareth was apparently a small and undistinguished village, and the family was not wealthy. (Luke 2:24 has them offering a poor person's sacrifice.) Joseph is described as a carpenter (or stonemason), though he could trace his ancestry back to the royal line of David, and it appears that Jesus did the obvious thing and grew up as his father's apprentice. But, whereas Mary features significantly in the story of Jesus, Joseph only appears in the story of Jesus the 12-year-old in the temple, which has suggested to some that Joseph died when Jesus was relatively young; hence references to Jesus as the 'son of Mary' in Mark 6:3 (though note John 6:42). Mary may have been just a teenager when Jesus was born. The name Jesus was common enough, being an abbreviation of the name Joshua (which meant 'Yahweh is salvation' in Hebrew).

The relative lack of interest in Joseph in the stories of Jesus may be because he was known not actually to have been Jesus' father. The Gospels suggest that Jesus was conceived in his mother miraculously without the intervention of a father; early Jewish polemic claimed that he was illegitimate. Modern scholars have raised all sorts of historical questions about the stories of Jesus' birth, arguing that the stories of supernatural conception, angelic appearances etc. are closer to religious myth than history. The expression 'midrash' is sometimes used, referring to a Jewish genre of story telling, which involved fanciful elaboration of the facts. So the Gospel accounts of Jesus' birth owe more to theological imagination (and reflection on OT stories such as the story of Moses) than to historical facts. It is pointed out that it is hard to reconcile the different stories of Matthew and Luke and that other parts of the NT (including our oldest Gospel Mark) fail to refer to the virginal conception.

MIDRASH

Midrash is a Hebrew word, meaning something like 'searching', and is used to describe the Jewish traditions that grew up interpreting and commenting on the OT. The rabbis distinguished two types of midrash – halakah, i.e. commentary on the OT laws, and haggadah, commentary on the OT stories. Haggadic midrash often involved the retelling of OT stories freely, with imaginative details and legendary ideas being added in. For example, in one of the Dead Sea Scrolls Noah's birth is described: the baby is a wonderful, unearthly child, and his father wonders if the child's real father was an angel! (IQapGenII).

However, it is unlikely that Matthew or Luke thought they were writing mythically rather than historically. Matthew's description of oriental astrologers interpreting the stars in terms of a royal birth is historically plausible, and there were various major astronomical events around the time of Jesus' birth, including the appearance of comets in 11 and 4 BC, and the conjunction of Saturn, Jupiter and Venus in 7 BC. Matthew's description of Herod's furious and brutal reaction to the suggestion of the birth of a new 'king of the Jews' agrees entirely with what we know of Herod the Great from other sources, and the comment that Joseph and Mary went to Galilee after the birth to keep out of the way of Archelaus is again historically plausible (e.g. Josephus *JW* 1:431-2:116 = 1.22.1–2.7.4). As for Luke, he precedes his account of Jesus' birth with a

strong statement of historical intent (1:1-4), and his account is punctuated with references to secular history. His reference in 2:1-2 to the census organized by Quirinius is historically problematic, since the census we know about took place after the deposing of Archelaus in AD 6 not in the time of Herod. However, Luke is clearly writing with a historical interest, whether or not he is accurate at this particular point.

The divergencies of Matthew and Luke are not all easy to explain, but they make their agreement on the central points of the story of Jesus' birth the more striking. The silence of other NT writers on Jesus' birth may be less total than is sometimes supposed, thus Paul speaks of Jesus' birth of a woman and has no reference to his father (e.g. Gal. 4:4).

The conclusion must be that the stories of Jesus' birth could be intended as theological affirmations about God coming among his people rather than historical narratives, but it is entirely possible that God's coming among his people was as miraculous as Jesus' later life. (For full discussion of the infancy narratives see Brown 1977.)

Digging deeper

Compare the infancy narratives of Matthew (1:18–2:23) and Luke (chs 1–2). Note all the ingredients that are in common, and the main differences. Consider how the similarities and differences might be explained.

We have no information about Jesus' childhood or adolescence, except for Luke's story of Jesus going up to Jerusalem with his family for the Passover festival when he was 12 years old. He displayed there a remarkable consciousness of a relationship with God as 'my father' (Luke 2:41-52), as well perhaps as a near-teenage boy's growing independence from his parents. The absence of other information probably points to a normal childhood which did not evoke particular comment, but also reflects the normal tendency of ancient historians not to dwell on a person's childhood.

JOHN THE BAPTIST

Jesus' public ministry began in association with John the Baptist. All the Gospels agree about this, and it is one of the least disputed facts about the history of Jesus.

John is known to us not only from the Gospels, but also from Josephus. He was a prophetic

figure who lived in the inhospitable Judean desert, who announced the coming of the day of the Lord, as promised in the OT, and who called people to prepare by turning away from their sins and undergoing a baptism in the river Jordan – a river with huge theological and historical significance for the Jews (Josh. 3; 2 Kgs 2).

John may well have had links at some time with the Qumran community, which produced the famous Dead Sea Scrolls. He had much in common with them (see p. 5). A major difference was that they were an enclosed community doing their own thing, whereas John attracted and excited a big and popular following, which was why Herod Antipas was nervous about him, especially when John denounced him and his wife Herodias.

Jesus was baptized by John. Historically this is almost certain, since the church would hardly have invented a story about Jesus 'joining' the movement of another religious leader. There is evidence of some embarrassment in Christian circles about the idea of Jesus becoming a 'follower' of John, submitting to his baptism, especially because it was a baptism for forgiveness of sins; there is also some evidence of followers of John arguing the superiority of John over Jesus because of the baptism (John 1:20). The Gospels go out of their way to explain that:

- Jesus was the 'stronger' messianic figure whom John himself looked forward to (e.g. Mark 1:7-9);
- John acknowledged the greatness of Jesus (e.g. John 1:25-31);
- Jesus underwent the baptism in order to identify with John's announcement of God's day of righteousness, not because of his own sinfulness (Matt. 3:15). (The NT

What do you think?

Compare the account of John in Luke 3:3-20 with that of Josephus Ant.18.116-119 (= 18.5.2):

'John, surnamed the Baptist … he was a good man and had exhorted the Jews to lead righteous lives, to practise justice towards their fellows and piety towards God, and so doing to join in baptism. In his view this was a necessary preliminary if baptism was to be acceptable to God. They must not employ it to gain pardon for whatever sins they committed, but as a consecration of the body implying that the soul was already thoroughly cleansed by right behaviour. When others too joined the crowds about him, because they were aroused to the highest degree by his sermons, Herod became alarmed.'

What similarities and differences do you notice?

portrays Jesus as someone who taught but also exemplified moral perfection and sinlessness, see John 8:46; 2 Cor. 5:20.)

The baptism appears to have been an important spiritual experience for Jesus. What is described in the Gospels as the descent of the Holy Spirit in the form of a dove and the announcement of a heavenly voice 'This is my beloved son' might these days be called a charismatic experience of the Spirit, and Jesus' ministry was going on to be a charismatically powerful ministry of healing as well as teaching. But it was a charismatic experience with a particular focus, in that it brought to Jesus:

- a sense of messianic mission. The words 'You are my son' evoke all sorts of OT ideas, notably the idea of Israel as God's son and also the idea of Israel's king being adopted as God's son. For the evangelists the baptism could be seen as a coronation, with Jesus being like the OT kings Saul and David – anointed and empowered by the Spirit of God for the task of leading Israel (e.g. 1 Sam. 10:5-11; 16:13; 1 Chr. 17:13; Ps. 2:7). It is likely that it had precisely this sort of connotation to Jesus himself.
- a particular awareness of his special relationship to God as his Father. It is clear that Jesus had such an awareness, the strongest evidence for this being his use of the word 'Abba' in prayer (Mark 14:36; cf. Gal. 4:6; Rom. 8:15).

Two things seem to have followed Jesus' baptism, the first being a different and more negative spiritual experience. The Gospels describe Jesus being led by God's Spirit into the wilderness which surrounded the Jordan river and being 'tempted' or 'tested' by the devil. It is as though his call to mission as the divine Son is immediately challenged – at the very outset he is confronted with the spiritual nature of his ministry. He will be involved in a cosmic conflict between God and the powers of evil. One of the most important dimensions to his ministry will be casting out demons from people: this is explained in the Gospels in terms of the power of the Spirit of God and of the coming of the kingdom of God (Matt. 12:28).

But the second thing is that Jesus began a ministry rather like John's – in Judea, with a focus on baptizing people. This John-like ministry is only described in the Fourth Gospel (3:22–4:3). It looks as though this early phase of Jesus' ministry may have become something of an embarrassment to the church, when people were comparing Jesus and John, since it made Jesus seem like John, and the Christians wanted to emphasize Jesus' superiority (cf. John 3:26). Certainly later the church when it wanted to emphasize the difference between John and Jesus and Jesus' superiority.

What do you think?

Read John 3:22–4:3. What in this passage suggests that there may have been some tension over Jesus' baptizing ministry, in relation to John the Baptist? How does the Gospel writer counter misunderstandings?

This parallel ministry does not appear to have lasted long. John was soon arrested by Herod, and Jesus moved to Galilee, where the main part of his ministry now began (Mark 1:14).

But Jesus' close association with John should not be forgotten. Jesus himself compared his ministry to John's on more than one occasion (Matt. 11:18, 19; 21:23-27; Mark 9:9-13) and others too made the connection (including Herod, Matt. 14:2). The Gospels, even if they are cautious about making too much of the links, make it clear that Jesus' ministry was very much in continuity with that of John: Luke makes the point by describing the birth of the two in tandem (Luke 1–2); Matthew actually has John preach the same message about the kingdom of God that Jesus will (Matt. 3:2); Matthew has John's disciples come to tell Jesus about John's death (Matt. 14:12); the Fourth Gospel has John direct his disciples to Jesus (John 1:29). Both were prophetic leaders, unmarried as far as we know, with a large popular following.

GALILEE

The bulk of Jesus' ministry took place in Galilee, and appears to have been based at Capernaum, the village on the shore of the Sea of Galilee where Jesus' disciples Simon and Andrew lived and worked. But his ministry was itinerant, and he went on occasions into the region north of Galilee, into the trans-Jordan area, through Samaria, and to Jerusalem (which John's Gospel has Jesus visit several times). Galilee was ruled by Herod Antipas and was administratively separate from Judea, which was ruled by a Roman governor. Religiously, however, it was predominantly Jewish, though Herod built up the Gentile cities of Sepphoris and Tiberias. It may be significant that the Gospels have no record of Jesus visiting these large cities; Jesus appears largely to have limited his ministry to those whom he calls 'the lost sheep of the house of Israel' (Matt. 10:5; 15:24), with notable exceptions. There was some strong Jewish nationalism in Galilee, associated not least with Judas the

Galilean, who led anti-Roman revolts in 4 BC and AD 6.

Luke informs us that Jesus was about 30 years old when he began his public ministry, and this would indicate a date of about AD 26/27 (Luke 3:23). Scholars have debated the length of Jesus' ministry: a reading of the synoptic Gospels would allow the conclusion that it lasted only a year or so, but John's Gospel describes Jesus going to various festivals in Jerusalem, and points to a ministry of two or three years' length. (On the date of the crucifixion, see below.)

Jesus' ministry was prophetic. He was known for his powerful teaching, which the Gospels contrast with the teaching of the scribes (Mark 1:22 etc.). The scribes were the professional teachers of the Jewish law, who explained the Scriptures. Jesus had a charismatic authority, like the OT prophets, although they proclaimed 'thus says the Lord', whereas Jesus claimed a personal authority and said 'Truly I say to you...'. (The word for 'truly' is *Amen*, which is actually a Hebrew word. Its retention in our Greek Gospels suggests that it was a distinctive usage of Jesus.)

Like OT prophets, Jesus spoke of the will of God, the judgement of God and of God's future purpose for his people. In these respects he was similar to John the Baptist, but whereas John's message appears to have focused on judgement and his lifestyle to have been thoroughly ascetic, Jesus' message focused on the good news of salvation and he was noted for his eating and drinking with people (Matt. 11:18, 19; Luke 7:33, 34), though he was ascetic in some respects, e.g. in his celibacy.

John's ascetic message went with his baptism of repentance; Jesus' message of salvation went with a ministry of healing – spiritual, social and physical. He was noted for his eating with 'tax collectors and sinners' and was criticized for this by the religious leaders of the day, notably by the Pharisees. He failed to keep himself 'pure' in the way advocated by Pharisees and Essenes, but saw himself as a doctor among the sick, bringing back the lost sheep (like the tax collector Zacchaeus) into the fold of God's people (Mark 2:17; Luke 19:10).

Socially Jesus identified with the poor especially, announcing the good news of God's salvation to them, denouncing the selfishness of the rich (e.g. Matt. 11:5; Luke 6:20-26). Practically Jesus brought relief to the poor by inspiring rich people like Zacchaeus to generous giving, by himself feeding the hungry, and by ministering to the physical needs of the sick and needy.

Miracle-workers and exorcists were not unknown in Jesus' world, and he has been compared to other Jewish charismatic wonder-workers. Certain of his miracles are reminiscent of those ascribed to OT prophets Elijah and Elisha, but Jesus appears to have outstripped ancient and contemporary prophets in the range and power of his miracles: casting out fierce demons, healing all sorts of diseases, even raising the dead, and taking control of forces of nature – so calming storms, feeding thousands, etc. The miracles are not seen as 'signs' to impress people, but as the fulfilment of OT promises and as manifestations of the kingdom of God, which Jesus preached – thus almost as parabolic in portraying the kingdom as free from Satan, from sickness, hunger and storm. (See further on miracles in ch. 5.)

The source of this power seems to have been in Jesus' experience of the Spirit. There is a mystical side to Jesus and his ministry: he is described by Luke as 'exulting in spirit' and bursting into praise (Luke 10:21). The climax of this 'mystical' side of Jesus may be seen in the mysterious event of the transfiguration, where Jesus' appearance was temporarily transformed by light and a divine voice was heard (cf. Mark 9:2-8). Basic to Jesus' experience and ministry appears to have been his prayer, to which he devoted himself and which his disciples observed as something important to him (Mark 1:35; Luke 11:1 etc.).

What do you think?

The Gospels suggest that people debated a lot over what to make of Jesus. Read Matt. 11:1-6; 12:22-29. What views of Jesus are being propounded, and what responses does Jesus give?

The response to Jesus appears to have been mixed. First, there were his disciples whom he specifically invited to 'follow' him. Some of his earliest and closest disciples were two sets of brothers, Simon and Andrew, James and John, all of them fishermen. Simon, James and John seem to have been particularly close to Jesus, being present at his transfiguration, in Gethsemane, and on other occasions. But they were part of a wider team of twelve, whom Jesus called to work with him and for him. The number twelve reminds us of the tribes of Israel in the OT, and suggests that Jesus saw his ministry in terms of fulfilling God's purpose of restoring the people of Israel (hence also his statements about only going to the lost sheep of Israel, Matt.10:5; 15:24, cf. Matt. 19:28). Jesus had a wider group of followers than just the twelve: Luke describes him as sending 70 (or 72) people out on one particular mission, the number possibly signifying the nations of the world. But there were other sympathizers and friends who provided for Jesus and his followers, whether financially, or in terms of hospitality (e.g. Luke 8:1-3; also the family of Mary, Martha and Lazarus, e.g. John 11).

The Gospels suggest that the followers of Jesus were often notable more for their enthusiasm than for their understanding of his mission. They wanted Jesus to be a popular messiah, who would take power in Jerusalem; he had a very different concept. It is striking how honest the Gospel accounts are at showing the failure, sometimes abject, of Jesus' disciples, with one of them abandoning Jesus altogether and betraying him, another denying him publicly, and others showing levels of incomprehension (e.g. Mark 10:35; Luke 9:54 etc.).

Second, there were very large numbers of people who were interested in Jesus and his message. The Gospels describe crowds of several thousand coming to see and listen to Jesus, some of them sharing the disciples' hope that Jesus would be a king who would bring liberation to the nation (John 6:15).

Third, there were those who were hostile to Jesus, primarily, it appears, the Pharisees and the scribes. The Pharisees were a highly influential religious group. They stood for (a) scrupulousness in keeping the OT law, which led them to promulgate detailed subsidiary regulations to help people keep the law, and (b) purity, expressed in ceremonial washing and in strict separation from other people who might be considered unclean. They saw themselves as maintaining the traditions of the people, in the face of the paganism of the Græco-Roman culture. Jesus offered an utterly different religious approach, sticking much more loosely to

strict Jewish tradition (e.g. being relaxed in his observance of the Sabbath), mixing with sinners and advocating love not hatred towards 'the enemy'. The conflict of ideologies would contribute significantly to the sequence of events that would lead ultimately to Jesus' death.

THE ROAD TO JERUSALEM

The picture that we get from the Gospels is of Jesus engaging in an itinerant ministry, centred on Galilee (the region around the lake), but extending to the surrounding areas, and occasionally going further afield, e.g. to Jerusalem for festivals (as in John; cf. Luke 2) and also into the northern parts of Palestine (Mark 7:24-31; 8:27–9:30).

Matthew and Mark describe Jesus going into northern Palestine, shortly after the execution of John the Baptist by Herod Antipas. Whether that execution was seen by Jesus as posing a threat to his life cannot be proved, but it is possible that a combination of events (including possibly his meeting with a Gentile woman, Mark 7:24-31; Matt. 15:21-28) were important for Jesus. In any case there is evidence in all the Gospels of a particular turning point being reached for Jesus at a place called Caesarea Philippi (in northern Palestine), where Jesus, who was facing considerable opposition to his ministry, questioned his disciples about their faith, and where Peter affirmed or reaffirmed the disciples' faith in Jesus as the Messiah. Before this point Jesus' focus seems to have been on teaching and healing, but from now on his focus is on a vocation of suffering (cf. Mark 8:27-38; also John 6:69 etc.). The Gospels describe him as then setting his face to go to Jerusalem and journeying there with striking deliberation (Mark 10:32; Luke 9:51 etc.).

LAST DAYS IN JERUSALEM

Jesus' arrival in Jerusalem was hailed by his followers with enthusiasm, and Jesus appears to have fuelled their excitement by arranging to ride into Jerusalem on a donkey. This was the first of a number of striking symbolic actions to characterize Jesus' last days. In this case the symbolism was to do with Zech. 9:9, which refers to Zion's king arriving in the city on a donkey (not, significantly, on a proud warhorse).

Jesus' next significant action was to enter the temple, and to drive out the money-changers and traders who were doing business there. The significance of this provocative act is debated: was Jesus cleansing the temple to make it a place of pure prayer for all nations? Was he expressing divine judgement on the corruption of those managing the sacred institution and its sacrifices? Was he doing both, and also fulfilling the OT prophecy about the Lord coming to his temple (Mal. 3:1; Zech. 14:21)? Whatever his exact motives, his action was offensive to those in power in the temple. The Gospels portray Jesus as engaged in serious argument less now with the Pharisees, and more with the Jewish authorities in Jerusalem, who find him a dangerous challenge to the status quo (e.g. John 11:48-50).

Jesus' third symbolic action was at the Passover meal with his disciples – the so-called Last Supper. Diverging from the standard liturgy, Jesus gave bread and wine to his disciples 'in remembrance of me'. It is clear that the meal was intended as a sort of farewell to his disciples, with the giving of the bread and wine being an acted parable of his coming death. One of the historical questions surrounding the Last Supper is whether it was a regular Passover meal (as suggested by the synoptic Gospels) or whether Jesus and his disciples met before the regular Passover (as John's Gospel may suggest) or whether Passover was celebrated on different days by different religious groups. (See further p. 249 on John's Gospel.) Whichever is the case, the Last Supper is a very early attested event, since Paul can refer to it in his first letter to the Corinthians as a tradition which he had 'received' and then passed on to the Corinthians (11:23); 1 Corinthians was written in about AD 55, and Paul probably 'received' the tradition in the thirties.

The meal was followed, later on that evening, by Jesus' arrest in a garden or olive orchard, just outside Jerusalem across the Kidron Valley, where he used to meet with his disciples. The temple authorities, led by ex-disciple Judas, arrived at night in this Garden of Gethsemane and took Jesus in custody.

They then tried Jesus. To be more accurate, there seem to have been a series of trials,

---

PASSION PREDICTIONS

In Mark there are three similarly constructed 'passion predictions' in 9:31; 10:31; 10:32-34. Each time Jesus' disciples show a failure to comprehend his teaching, and each time Jesus challenges them to the way of suffering and service. Scholars have argued that the predictions are 'prophecies after the event', i.e. church reflections on Jesus' death rather than words of the historical Jesus. But there is nothing implausible in the idea of Jesus anticipating his death and finding his vocation in that (see ch. 8). For a scholarly discussion of the predictions, see H. F. Bayer *Jesus' Predictions of Vindication and Resurrection*. Tübingen: Mohr, 1986.

QUESTIONS ABOUT
THE LAST SUPPER

There are many historical questions associated with the Last Supper. Whether it was a regular Passover meal is one, whether it was originally anything to do with Jesus' coming death is another. Some scholars believe that it was a fellowship meal, such as Jesus regularly had with his followers, and that this last fellowship meal came to be invested with sacrificial and sacramental overtones by the early church (possibly under the influence of Greek mystery religions), as they looked back on the events and sought to make sense of Jesus' death. However, such views go against the testimony of different NT authors, and take insufficient account of the evidence that points in a rather coherent way to Jesus (a) interpreting his ministry as fulfilment of OT promises and prophecies, (b) seeing himself as bringing a new Exodus-style liberation for God's people and (c) understanding that liberation to involve a Passover sacrifice and the sacrifice of the one called 'the servant of the Lord' in the book of Isaiah (Isa. 52, 53; cf. Mark 10:45; Luke 4:16-21; and see pp. 158ff.). For a variety of scholarly views, see Jeremias 1966; Marshall 1980; B. D. Chilton *A Feast of Meanings*. Leiden: Brill, 1994 – a scholarly case for a less traditional view of the origins of the eucharist.

whether official or informal. The high priests and the Jewish leaders found Jesus guilty for his threats against the temple and for his messianic claims. But then they brought him to Pilate and charged him with treason against Rome. Pilate was extremely vulnerable to pressure from the Jews, having repeatedly mishandled his governorship. The Gospels suggest that he was not personally convinced of Jesus' guilt, but that he was pressurized by the Jewish leaders, who threatened to denounce him to Rome should he not do what they wanted. Luke says that Pilate consulted Herod Antipas, who was in Jerusalem for the Passover and who had never previously seen this famous Galilean subject, and that he was equally unconvinced of Jesus' guilt. However, there was a prima facie case against Jesus (who had after all been preaching about 'the kingdom of God'), and there had been other disturbances in Jerusalem at the time. So eventually Pilate agreed to have Jesus crucified on the charge that he claimed to be 'king of the Jews'.

Digging deeper

What pressures will Pilate as the Roman governor have faced in making his decision about Jesus? Remember Pilate's past dealings with the Jews (pp. 18f.) and the volatile nature of Passover time, and compare Luke 23:1-25; John 19:1-16.

Historians have debated numerous questions about the trial of Jesus, questioning whether the Jewish Sanhedrin could legally have tried Jesus formally at night, noting that the custom of releasing one prisoner to the Jews at the time of Passover is not attested outside the Gospels, and speculating as to whether the Gospels have shifted the responsibility for the death of Jesus from the Romans on to the Jews (whether out of hostility to the Jews, or in order to counter the idea that Christianity was politically subversive). On the other hand, the picture portrayed of a city, highly charged with nationalist emotion at Passover time, of intrigue in the highest places, of Jews upset with Jesus for their own religious reasons and wanting to get rid of him, and of a power struggle between the Jews and their weakened Roman governor Pilate, is thoroughly plausible.

Crucifixion was a well-known Roman penalty. It was a slow and brutal process of execution, normally reserved for rebels and slaves. The prisoner was typically beaten with a whip studded with nails. He would be expected to carry the cross beam of his cross to the place of execution. There he would be stripped, and then have his wrists tied or nailed to the cross beam, before being lifted off the ground (not necessarily very high) on to the upright, where his body would rest on a small peg, and ankles be bent sideways and nailed to the upright. The prisoner would then die very slowly over a period of hours or even days, the pain being exacerbated by the shame of hanging naked, in a public place, exposed to the ridicule of people passing by or coming to watch. Jesus is said to have been crucified at a place called Golgotha (meaning 'skull'), which was probably just outside the west walls of the city (on the site of the present Church of the Holy Sepulchre), along with two others. The others are described as 'robbers' or 'criminals' by the Gospels; the word 'robber' could suggest a brigand, but is also a word used by Josephus to refer to nationalist guerrilla fighters.

Jesus apparently died quite quickly on a Friday, which historians have tried to pinpoint on the basis of known dates of Passover at that approximate time. There is a difference of opinion as to whether the calendrical evidence favours AD 27, 33 or most likely 30.

Jesus was buried, not in the common grave where victims of crucifixion were frequently interred, but in a private rock tomb (a natural or artificial cave) near the place of his execution, thanks to the intervention of some sympathizers.

On the following Sunday the tomb was found empty by women who had gone to anoint the body, and Jesus himself was seen on several occasions by a variety of people, individuals such as Peter and groups of his disciples. Subsequently he was seen by quite large numbers of his disciples, before finally departing from the disciples and 'ascending to heaven'.

Such is the testimony of the Gospels.

The resurrection stories raise all sort of questions, not least because of the considerable differences between the Gospels. One influential view is that the idea of Jesus' resurrection started with one or more individual visionary experience, and that the story then grew, with the idea of the tomb being empty coming later (e.g. recently G. Lüdemann 1994). However, a less sceptical approach notes among other things:

- the resurrection of Jesus is widely attested, including by Paul who cites it as a received tradition in 1 Cor. 15:3-6;
- something bigger than an individual hallucination would have been needed to start the explosive Christian movement;
- the stories of the empty tomb have a ring of truth about them –
  (1) an invented story would have been open to simple disproof by the production of Jesus' body (whereas Jesus' opponents accused the disciples of stealing the body); (2) in a culture where the testimony of women was not highly regarded it is unlikely that anyone would have invented a story with women finding the empty tomb, rather than Jesus' male disciples.

The appearances of Jesus seem to have been quite numerous, and to have gone on for a period of weeks, but then to have come to an end in what Luke describes as Jesus' 'ascension' to heaven (Luke 24:50; Acts 1:9).

The ascension is only described in Luke and Acts, but something of that sort is probably presupposed by other NT writers. Certainly Paul sees the resurrection appearances as happening together and for a limited time, so that his own claimed sighting of the risen Christ is clearly irregular (1 Cor. 15:8).

If the story of Jesus ends with the ascension, in another sense it continues into the history of the church and, from the point of view of the NT, into the story of the book of Acts.

ESSAY TOPICS

INTRODUCTORY

● 'The real Jesus was very different from the Jesus of popular imagination and folklore.' Write an essay bringing out some of the important and neglected parts of Jesus' life.

INTERMEDIATE

● Jesus and the Jewish Passover. Describe in your essay what the Jewish Passover was like in the time of Jesus, and discuss how that historical context throws light on Jesus' crucifixion and on his actions leading up to his crucifixion.

● You have been asked to talk on 'The value of biblical studies for understanding Jesus' to a group of young Christians who are suspicious of all academic study of the Bible. They say, 'We believe it and just want to live it out.' What would you say?

FURTHER READING

INTRODUCTORY

P. Barnett *Bethlehem to Patmos: The NT Story*. Downers Grove: IVP/Carlisle: Paternoster, 1998.

N. T. Wright & M. Borg *The Meaning of Jesus*. New York: HarperCollins/London: SPCK, 1999.

INTERMEDIATE

DJG article 'Birth of Jesus'.

M. Bockmuehl *This Jesus*. Downers Grove: IVP/Edinburgh: Clark, 1994.

R. Brown *The Birth of the Messiah*. London: Chapman, 1977 (standard work).

R. Brown *The Death of the Messiah*. 2 vols. New York: Doubleday/ London: Chapman, 1994 (masterly discussion).

J. Jeremias *The Eucharistic Words of Jesus*. Philadelphia: Trinity Press International/ London: SCM, 1966 (a standard work).

G. Lüdemann *The Resurrection of Jesus*. Minneapolis: Fortress/London: SCM, 1994 (a sceptical explanation).

I. H. Marshall *Last Supper and Lord's Supper*. Grand Rapids: Eerdmans/Exeter: Paternoster, 1980 (a very good and accessible summary).

G. Theissen & A. Merz *The Historical Jesus*. London: SCM/Philadelphia: Fortress, 1998, ch. 6 on 'The Chronological Framework of the Life of Jesus', ch. 14 on 'Jesus as Martyr: The Passion of Jesus' and ch. 15 on 'The Risen Jesus'.

P. Walker *The Weekend that Changed the World*. Louisville: Westminster John Knox/ London: Harper, 1999 (popular discussion of the Easter weekend).

Chapter 8

THE TEACHING AND AIMS OF JESUS

In this chapter we shall think about:

- why Jesus died;
- central themes of Jesus' teaching;
- Jesus' ministry among 'ordinary people';
- who Jesus thought he was and how he saw his mission.

To understand Jesus requires a grasp of his story (considered in ch. 7) and his own beliefs about who he was and what he was doing (the focus of this chapter). In order to do this, we shall begin at the end of the story, by asking why Jesus died, for the NT writers agree that this event is the heart of what he came to do. In the light of what we can learn about his death, and particularly his own understanding of his death, we shall then look at the major themes of his teaching and actions, particularly the kingdom of God, his mission to Israel, his ethics, and his keeping company with 'sinners' and offer of forgiveness to them. Finally, we shall ask about his own self-understanding, identifying what we can say about who he thought he was.

Throughout our discussion we shall focus on the synoptic Gospels, referring to John where this fills out the picture we gain from the others. We shall also be paying attention to Jesus in his particular historical situation, which will not always be the same as the church's later beliefs about Jesus. It is not that the early Christians were wrong in their formulation of their faith in Jesus, but the resurrection of Jesus dramatically changed the way Jesus was seen. In what follows we shall be looking mostly from a pre-resurrection perspective, which will, of course, help in understanding the roots from which the full flower of later Christian faith grew.

In what follows, we shall assume that the synoptics present an essentially trustworthy portrait of Jesus, in line with our discussion of their historical reliability (see pp. 112–21), although we shall discuss the authenticity of some particular sayings or actions of Jesus.

WHY DID JESUS DIE?

The final visit of Jesus to Jerusalem began with a demonstration as Jesus arrived in the city, and continued with a dramatic action in the temple. By the end of these events, his opponents, especially the Jewish leadership, were ready to dispose of him – two significant charges at his trial were that he claimed to be a king (Mark 15:2), which was the meaning of his entry, and that he had said that he would destroy the temple (Mark 14:58; cf. John 2:19-22), a central theme of his action in the temple (contrast John 11:47-52, which links the plot against Jesus with his raising Lazarus from the dead, an event not reported in the synoptics). Let us consider these events in more detail.

JESUS' ARRIVAL IN JERUSALEM

Jesus' 'triumphal entry', riding into the city on a donkey while his disciples and the crowds acclaimed him, is one of the few events recorded in all four Gospels (Matt. 21:1-9; Mark 11:1-10; Luke 19:28-40; John 12:12-19). Arriving in Jerusalem a week or more before Passover, as Jesus did, was normal practice. This was because people had to be ritually clean to eat the passover meal, and it took a week to become ritually clean if a person became unclean (e.g. through contact with a dead body; cf. Num. 5:2; 6:5f., 11; 9:6f., 10f.; 31:19f.). But to ride a donkey into the city was unusual for Passover pilgrims, for they normally entered the city on foot – so by arriving this way Jesus was separating himself from the run-of-the-mill Passover pilgrims. His commandeering of the donkey in the manner of a king underlines this (Mark 11:2f.; cf. 1 Sam. 8:16f.). There are OT overtones to Jesus' arrival which reinforce this point:

- the vision of a king arriving on a donkey (Zech. 9:9f.; quoted in Matt. 21:5; John 12:15);
- David's return to Jerusalem on a donkey after the rebellion and death of his son Absalom (2 Sam. 15:30; 16:1f.).

A donkey was not the usual means of transport for a king: a horse was more usual (cf. Esth. 6:8). To arrive on a donkey symbolized arriving in peace, rather than war (as David had), and therefore made a statement about the kind of kingship Jesus might be claiming for himself. This sort of kingship ran contrary to the hopes of many Jews, who longed for political liberation from the Romans – as Jesus himself says earlier (Luke 13:34f.).

The crowd's actions and cries show that they recognized the kingly overtones of Jesus' arrival (cf. 2 Kgs. 9:13; 1 Macc. 13:49-51). All four Gospels have them call a blessing on the one ('king' in Luke) who comes in the name of the Lord (echoing Ps. 118:26, from one of the 'Hallel' psalms used by pilgrims travelling to the holy city), and all four report kingly language about Jesus in the cries, whether Mark's 'the coming kingdom of our father David' (11:10), Matthew's description of Jesus as 'son of David' (21:9), or Luke and John calling Jesus 'king' (Luke 19:38; John 12:13). But what kind of king has Jesus come to Jerusalem to be?

JESUS' DEMONSTRATION IN THE TEMPLE

Jesus' general attitude to the temple appears positive: he speaks about it as 'the house of God' (Luke 6:4), he assumes that offerings there are legitimate (Matt. 5:23f.), and he likely attends festivals there prior to the final Passover (Luke 2:41-51; cf. John 4:45; 7:10). That said, his offer of forgiveness apart from the sacrificial system implicitly undermines the place of the temple (see p. 167) and he also asserts that 'something greater than the temple is here' (Matt. 12:6).

Jesus' action in the temple, turning over the tables and throwing out the money-changers and traders, is reported by all four Gospels (Matt. 21:10-17; Mark 11:11, 15-17; Luke 19:45f.; John 2:13-17), although John locates the event very early in Jesus' ministry, rather than during his final visit to Jerusalem. Scholars generally agree that the synoptic timing is likely to be correct and that John has placed the story early in order to emphasize the challenge of Jesus to the established order (although there is a significant minority view that Jesus did something like this twice in his life).

There is no evidence that the sale of sacrificial animals took place in the temple itself prior to AD 30. Traditionally the animals were bought and sold on the Mount of Olives, a short distance away, and there is evidence of controversy about the market in the temple, which suggests that it was an innovation introduced by Caiaphas as high priest shortly before Jesus' visit (for the evidence, see W. Lane *Commentary on the Gospel of Mark*. New International Commentary on the NT. Grand Rapids: Eerdmans/London: Marshall Morgan & Scott, 1974, 403f.). Most likely they operated in the court of the Gentiles under the shade of a colonnade (see (7) and (8) on map, pp. 32f.). However, the effect of Jesus' actions would have been limited in scope, for to prevent all trading going on for any length of time would require a group of armed assistants. It seems likely that, not long after Jesus' demonstration, the trading was continuing as normal.

This means that his action should be seen as symbolic. It has often been called a 'cleansing' of the temple, and some continue to claim that it should be seen as a call to reform the temple by removing the innovative commercialism brought in by the high priest and the corruption of the merchants. But a cleansing would be more likely to be symbolized in a Jewish setting by pouring out water, similar to events at the feast of tabernacles (cf. John 7:2, 37-39): there is

likely to be more to Jesus' action than this.

What then is the point of this action? First, it has strong messianic overtones, for the Davidic Messiah was expected to purify and renew the temple (Zech. 6:12f.; 14:21; Mal. 3:1-4); thus it was 'an implicit presentation of credentials' by Jesus (B. F. Meyer).

Second, the overturning of tables also symbolizes and warns of the destruction of the temple in two ways: the physical act of overthrowing tables suggests the physical fall of the temple, and the attack on the sellers of unblemished animals and birds required for sacrifices could be an implicit attack on the sacrificial system – for that system could not function without a supply of such animals and birds.

This reading of the demonstration fits well with Jesus' warnings of the destruction of the temple elsewhere (Mark 13:1f.; cf. Acts 6:14), the claim at the trial that Jesus had said that he would destroy the temple (Mark 14:58), and Jesus' quotation of the words 'den of robbers' from Jeremiah's sermon warning of the destruction of the temple (Jer. 7:11; Mark 11:17). It also coheres with John presenting Jesus as speaking at this time of himself as the replacement for the temple (John 2:21f.).

The 'destruction' view can be combined with elements of the 'cleansing' view by observing that Jesus' demonstration highlighted the corruption of temple religion, and also presaged the inevitable divine judgement which would follow in the fall of the temple in AD 70.

Some thirty years later, in AD 62, Jesus ben Ananias was flogged to death because he prophesied the temple's destruction

(Josephus, *JW* 6.5.3 [= 6:300-304]), and so it is no surprise that Jesus of Nazareth's action precipitated the final plot against him by the Jewish authorities – for he was attacking Judaism as they understood it and announcing its demise.

THE FINAL STEPS

The synoptic Gospels then report a series of debates between Jesus and various groups of senior Jews (Mark 11:27–12:40 and parallels), and by the end of these Jesus has offended all the significant players in the plot to kill him: the chief priests, the scribes, the elders, the Pharisees, the Herodians and the Sadducees (Mark 11:27; 12:13, 18, 28, 35, 38). The plot picks up speed as Jesus is arrested and tried by the Jewish authorities, charged with two key things: (1) blasphemy, that is, claiming prerogatives that belong to God alone; and (2) claiming to be a messianic kingly figure (Mark 14:61-64; we shall return to this passage in considering Jesus' view of himself, pp. 179f.). The Roman trial also focuses on the question of kingship (Mark 15:2, 9, 12, 18-20), and Jesus is mocked on the cross as 'Messiah, king of Israel' (Mark 15:32). The inscription on the cross also identifies the charge against Jesus as claiming to be king of the Jews, and that is unlikely to have been invented, for it was not universal practice for the charge against a prisoner to be nailed above them (Matt. 27:37; Mark 15:26; Luke 23:38; John 19:19f.).

For S. G. F. Brandon (*Jesus and the Zealots*. Manchester: Manchester University Press, 1967) this evidence suggests that Jesus was, in fact, a revolutionary. However, subsequent events show the Romans not to have treated Jesus' followers in the normal way they reacted to a revolutionary group, namely to round them up and kill them all. Rather, they allowed Jesus' disciples to remain in the city and to continue as a group, even recruiting new members (the opposition in the early chapters of Acts is entirely Jewish). This shows clearly that they were not perceived as a military or political threat to Roman power.

JESUS' PERSPECTIVE

Jesus must have done and said things which allowed the authorities, both Jewish and Roman, to make a charge against him at least appear plausible. But how did he himself see his death? The Gospels present a strong theme of Jesus' own expectation of his suffering and death, along with the disciples' lack of understanding of what Jesus says about this. This theme is particularly strong in the later parts of Jesus' ministry (notably the three predictions in Mark 8:31; 9:31; 10:33 and parallels), but it is present from the earliest days too, although more cryptic and hidden (e.g. Mark 2:20).

This expectation fulfils Scripture for Jesus, who speaks of his suffering using phrases such as 'it is written' (e.g. Mark 9:12; 14:21, 49). Indeed, it is *necessary* (Greek *dei*, Mark 8:31; Matt. 26:54; Luke 13:33; 17:25; 24:25-27). This theme illuminates passages which focus on Jesus' choice to go to Jerusalem: he leads the way there (e.g. Luke 9:51; Mark 10:32).

But in order to understand Jesus' death fully we need to look at three images of its meaning from his teaching. First, he presents his death as *experiencing God's judgement on sin*, particularly in imaging it as drinking a cup (Mark 10:38; 14:36). The cup alludes to OT passages about God's punishment for human evil and disobedience to him (see p. 159).

Jesus dies on the cross drinking the cup of God's anger against sin, but because he is innocent he takes the words of the innocent

What do you think?
THE CUP

Look up these OT passages, which use the image of the cup, and summarize how they use this picture and the points they make from it about what God is doing or will do.

Ps. 75:8; Isa. 51:17-23; Jer. 25:15-28; 49:12; 51:7; Lam. 4:21-22; Ezek. 23:31-34; Hab. 2:16; Zech. 12:2

How do they illuminate the use of the cup as a metaphor in the teaching of Jesus about his death in passages such as Mark 10:38; 14:36; John 18:11?

sufferer of Ps. 22:1 on his lips, 'My God, my God, why have you forsaken me' (Mark 15:34).

Second, his death is a *ransom* (Greek *lutron*, Mark 10:45) and accomplishes redemption (Greek *lutrōsis*, *apolutrōsis*) – words used in both Jewish and Græco-Roman contexts in connection with buying back something which has fallen into another's hands. In Græco-Roman texts it is used for the ransom price paid to recover a prisoner of war from the captors or to free a slave. In the OT it is used for compensation paid to a family in one of two situations. First, when an animal has killed one of their members, for the animal was considered to become the property of the dead person's family (Exod. 30:28-30). Second, for a relative's repurchase of land which had been sold to pay a family member's debt (Lev. 25:25). Supremely 'redemption' was used by the Jews in connection with God's redemption of the nation from slavery in Egypt (e.g. Exod. 6:6; Deut. 7:8), celebrated annually at Passover. In using 'ransom' language Jesus says that

his death will accomplish a new exodus, a new liberation for the people of God.

Third, Jesus speaks of himself as *the servant of God*, a figure alluded to in sayings throughout his teaching, notably Mark 10:45, where 'for many' echoes Isa. 53:12 'he poured himself out to death, and was numbered with the transgressors; yet he bore the sins of many'. As often, the echo of just a few words is designed to help readers hear the whole context of the phrase – here Isa. 52:13–53:12, the account of the suffering of the faithful servant of God who bears others' evil and wrongdoing and makes many righteous (53:11). Jesus is aligning himself with this figure. The context in Isa. 52 (as in the whole of Isa. 40–55) is of Israel returning from the Babylonian exile, an exile caused by the people's sin (Isa. 40:1). The servant bears the people's sin (Isa. 53:4-6), and thus wins them forgiveness and liberation (Isa. 53:10-12). So in alluding to this material, Jesus sees his death as the forgiveness-bringing event which brings about the new exodus into liberation. (I owe these suggestions to David Wenham.)

These three images come together in the last meal Jesus eats with his followers before he is arrested, where he takes the Jewish Passover meal and reinterprets it through the lens of his own forthcoming suffering. There are two main versions of this story in the NT, one found in Mark 14:22-25 and Matt. 26:26-29, and the other in Luke 22:15-20 and 1 Cor. 11:23-25; the older form may well be Paul's, written earlier than the Gospels' accounts.

Through his actions and words with the bread and wine Jesus makes clear that, just as the Passover marked God's action to redeem the people from slavery in Egypt, so his forthcoming death will redeem the people from their present slavery: his death will bring 'forgiveness of sins' (Matt. 26:28; cf. Isa. 40:2, part of a key passage speaking of the return from the Babylonian exile as a 'new exodus'). He identifies the bread as symbolizing his body which will be killed, and the cup of wine as symbolizing his blood which will be shed (1 Cor. 11:24f.; Luke 22:19f.). And this is 'for many' (Mark 14:24), likely echoing the language of the servant's suffering (Isa. 53:12) again.

The 'covenant' language which Jesus uses echoes Exod. 24:8 and Jer. 31:31-34, passages speaking of the Mosaic covenant and God's promise of a new covenant – again showing that Jesus' intention in going to die was to bring about a new exodus, a new deliverance. But for Jesus the real enemy is not the Romans, but sin and evil, which are the fundamental causes of human imprisonment. Jesus will 'tie up the strong man' who is Satan (Mark 3:27) by engaging him in hand-to-hand combat on the cross.

Doing and saying these things in the context of a meal centred on a Passover lamb which had died in place of the firstborn of the household (Exod. 12:21-27), the disciples would come to think of Jesus as taking the role of the sacrificial lamb, dying so that the people did not have to die. The implication, taken with the demonstration in the temple, is that it would no longer be through the temple sacrifices that people would approach Yahweh, but through the broken body of Jesus.

JESUS AND THE KINGDOM OF GOD

We now step back into the ministry of Jesus to listen to his teaching, which will add to our sketch of his aims and purpose. There is very wide agreement in scholarship that the kingdom of God is central to Jesus' teaching (Matthew normally speaks of 'the kingdom of heaven', using 'heaven' to avoid speaking the name of God, a common practice among Jews; cf. Luke 15:21). To see how Jesus used the phrase, we first look at Jewish expectations.

GOD'S REIGN IN THE OT AND JUDAISM

Within the OT, although the phrase 'the kingdom of God' is not found, two central themes about Yahweh's kingship recur. First and foremost, Yahweh is king of the whole world, an implication of creational monotheism (Pss 97:1; 99:1; 95:3; see pp. 27f.). Thus he rules the world for the good of its people.

But second, Yahweh is king of Israel in particular and rules with the good of this nation in mind (Num. 23:21; Isa. 43:15; see pp. 28f.). Hence he calls upon Pharaoh to let Israel go because Yahweh alone is the nation's true king and the Egyptian king cannot claim to rule the people (note the use of 'my people' in Exod. 3:7, 10; 5:1). At the time of Jesus the Jews had a sense of God's rule having been hijacked, for they were not free in their own land, and they looked forward to God's rule being seen over the whole earth.

These two themes come together at the end of the OT period, when Daniel prophesies that a kingdom set up by God will overcome the pagan nations (Dan. 2, esp. vv. 31-45). The creator God will bring the whole of his world under his rule.

By the time of Jesus this led to a variety of future expectations of God's rule among different groups within Judaism. Nevertheless, there was a common core of expectation, which had two major components. First, the day will come when

Yahweh's rule over the whole world will be clear for all to see (Isa. 45:23; Zech. 14:9; cf. Dan. 7:13f.).

Second, that day will inaugurate the 'age to come', a time when the world will be as God intended. This hope involved the renewal of creation, rather than its removal and replacement (hence Jews at the time of Jesus would have been very unlikely to have spoken of 'going to heaven'). The precise form of this hope varied among the Jewish groupings. Generally it was seen as a time of great upheaval when the righteous would be vindicated (either Israel or the righteous within Israel) and the unrighteous would be punished by God (cf. Dan. 12:1-3). The Pharisees saw it as a time when the law would be fully obeyed. The revolutionaries believed that God's rule would be established by military means. The Qumran sectarians, in common with many apocalyptic writers, also thought there would be a battle, but held that God would initiate it and bring it to a successful conclusion. Frequently a messianic figure was involved as a key agent in God bringing in the new age.

The 'kingdom of God' is sometimes a *realm* where God reigns – especially Israel – but also it sums up *the fact that* God reigns. Some express the second of these themes by translating as 'the *kingly rule* of God' (see Luke 11:20, where that rendition makes more sense than a 'realm' view). The focus in both cases is on Yahweh as the ruler who will be obeyed. Thus in the Lord's prayer, 'your kingdom come' is parallel to and interpreted by 'your will be done' (Matt. 6:10): God's rule is seen when he is obeyed.

JESUS AND THE KINGDOM

Against this backcloth Jesus arrived on the scene announcing, 'The time is fulfilled, and the kingdom of God has come near' (Mark 1:15; cf. Matt. 4:23). Where does his view of God's kingdom fit within Jewish thought? The varied expectations that we outlined above show the need for Jesus to define *his* beliefs, so that he would be understood rightly by his contemporaries – hence a number of his parables begin, 'The kingdom of God/heaven is like…' (e.g. Matt. 13:31, 33, 44, 45, 47, 52).

Jesus' use of fulfilment language links with his widespread use of OT Scripture as a major source for understanding his own ministry (see pp. 175f.), and suggests that he saw his ministry as God acting to bring about promises made by the prophets, particularly (since he then speaks of the kingdom) those concerning God's reign being seen over all the world, and the vindication and restoration of Israel. Some of this teaching seems to assume that the kingdom is already present in Jesus' ministry, while elsewhere he teaches that the kingdom is yet to come. We shall examine these two aspects to his message before analysing scholarly debate on this varied material.

God's reign in Jesus' ministry

A number of sayings, actions and parables point to Jesus' belief that God's reign was active in his ministry. Follow these passages in a Bible as we study them.

Matt. 12:28; Luke 11:20 In response to the claim that he casts out demons by demonic power ('by Beelzebul'), Jesus speaks of his exorcisms as demonstrating that 'the kingdom of God has come upon you' (cf. Jesus' claim that his exorcisms show that he is the one who has tied up the strong man who is Satan, Mark 3:20-30, esp. v. 27). The Greek word translated 'has come upon' (*ephthasen*) has the sense 'to come before, precede' or 'to have just come' and strongly suggests that God's reign is seen when Jesus frees people from demonization – a somewhat different version of 'kingly rule' to the political views held by the Romans, Herod and the Jewish high priests.

Luke 16:16 (cf. Matt. 11:12) By stating that from John the Baptist's time onwards 'the good news of the kingdom is preached, and everyone tries to enter it by force', Jesus again implies that God's kingdom is present in his ministry – for it is now after John's time.

Luke 17:20f. Here Jesus responds to the Pharisees' question about when the kingdom comes by the startling claim that 'the kingdom of God is among you'. Older translations have 'within you' but, though the Greek *entos humin* can be translated that way, it is unlikely that Jesus would tell his opponents that the kingdom was within *them*. Rather it is most probable that Jesus speaks of the presence of God's rule in his ministry. It is also possible that Jesus may be implying that the reign of God is 'within your grasp' (Wright 1996, 469), which would further strengthen the idea that the kingdom is present.

Mark 1:15 In the context of the three preceding sayings, this saying should also be seen as speaking of the presence of God's reign in Jesus' ministry. In it 'the time is fulfilled' parallels and therefore interprets 'the kingdom of God has come near', showing that Jesus' announcement is of the kingdom's arrival, not merely of its imminence. The verb translated here 'has come near' is also used in Mark 14:42 (the

only other use in this tense in Mark), where Jesus says that his betrayer 'is at hand', leading into Judas' immediate arrival in 14:43. Assuming the verb is being used similarly in 1:15, Jesus is announcing that God's reign is on the point of arriving as he begins his public ministry.

Luke 4:21 Jesus states emphatically in Nazareth, 'Today this Scripture has been fulfilled in your hearing', having read the prophet's announcement of the coming of key signs of the messianic age of God's reign – freedom for captives, sight for blind, liberty for oppressed, and good news for poor (Isa. 61:1f.). Thus Jesus' healing ministry (and, even more so, his raising of the dead!) is a sign of the presence of God's reign. More than that, it is evidence that the prophetic promises of a new exodus were finally happening. Isa. 61:1f. and 35:5f. (the latter cited by Jesus in Luke 7:22 concerning his ministry) are both integral to prophecies about return from the Babylonian exile, but pictured using imagery from the exodus from Egypt – notice in the Isaianic contexts the language of the renewal of the wilderness, a road through the desert, and return to Zion/Jerusalem to rebuild the city. This 'new exodus' motif shows that Jesus understands God's redeeming reign to be present in his actions – it is through Jesus' ministry that God is now acting in fulfilment of the prophetic word. Jewish expectation was that Isa. 61:1f. spoke of the messianic age to come; Jesus announces its arrival.

Among the parables of Jesus, several strongly suggest the presence of the kingdom in Jesus' ministry, especially:
- the treasure in the field and the pearl merchant (Matt. 13:44-46);
- the banquet (Luke 14:15-24) and the wedding (Matt. 22:1-14); in both cases the

invitation is issued *now* and requires a response here and now;
● the lamp under the bushel (Mark 4:21).

To this evidence we may add some sayings of Jesus which claim that the time of fulfilment has arrived, notably Jesus' statement that the prophets and kings looked forward to what the disciples now see (Luke 10:23; Matt. 13:16f.), and Jesus' answer to the criticism of his disciples not fasting which sees his presence as that of the long-awaited bridegroom (Mark 2:18-20 and parallels). Where Jesus was, there the kingdom of God was present.

God's coming reign

On the other hand, there are a number of themes in the teaching of Jesus which suggest that the reign of God will not be seen (at least in full) until the future.

Among the sayings of Jesus, most striking is the Lord's prayer, containing the petition 'your kingdom come' (Matt. 6:10; Luke 11:2), a pointless request unless God's reign is not yet fully seen. 'There are some standing here who will not taste death until they see that the kingdom of God has come with power' (Mark 9:1) implies that when Jesus spoke the kingdom had not come in that way. Jesus' striking claim that people from east and west will eat with the Jewish patriarchs in the kingdom (Matt. 8:11f.; Luke 13:28f.) presupposes the standard Jewish this age/age to come picture, and locates Jesus' hearers firmly in this age, with the age to come still in the future. Further, Jesus can speak of entering the kingdom as a future event (Mark 9:47; 10:15, 23; Matt. 7:21). Even the notoriously difficult 'this generation will not pass away until all these things have taken place' (Mark 13:30) clearly implies that the things of which Jesus speaks have not all taken place during his ministry.

> ## Digging deeper:
> ### WHAT ABOUT MARK 13?
>
> The synoptic Gospels each record a significant speech by Jesus about the future (Mark 13; Matt. 24; Luke 21) and there are a number of major interpretations of this speech; it is:
>
> ● entirely focused on the fall of Jerusalem; on this view the 'apocalyptic' language (e.g. Mark 13:24-27) is being used to speak of this-world events and to show their cosmic significance (e.g. Wright 1996, 339-67).
> ● about the end of this world and the coming of the son of man, which Jesus expected imminently, following on the destruction of the temple (and Jesus was disappointed that it did not happen) (e.g. Sanders 1984, 71-6 or Sanders 1993, ch. 11).
> ● describing both the fall of Jerusalem and the events of the End (e.g. Ladd 1994, 196-211). Sometimes this is described as 'prophetic telescoping', like looking at two mountains from a distance with the result that they appear very close together – whereas they are in fact some distance apart. The events of the fall of the city and Jesus' parousia are interpreted through the same lens and imagery.
>
> Read these chapters carefully, in a synopsis if possible, and compare the question(s) to which Jesus responds and the answers which he gives. What are the strongest arguments for each of the positions outlined above? What are the biggest problems each position has with these chapters? Which view do you find most persuasive and why?

A number of Jesus' parables speak of growth and thus involve a future aspect to their picture of the reign of God – for if the kingdom grows, it cannot be fully present yet:

- the mustard seed (Mark 4:30-32 and parallels);
- the yeast (Matt. 13:33; Luke 13:20f.);
- the sower (Mark 4:1-9, 13-20 and parallels);
- the seed growing secretly (Mark 4:26-29);
- the wheat and the weeds (Matt. 13:24-30, 36-43).

Further, there are parables of judgement which locate the judgement in a time yet to come, rather than the present:

- the faithful and unfaithful servants (Matt. 24:45-51; Luke 12:41-48);
- the ten bridesmaids/virgins (Matt. 25:1-13);
- the talents/pounds (Matt. 25:14-30; Luke 19:11-27) – the latter is specifically said to be told 'because they supposed that the kingdom of God was to appear immediately' (Luke 19:11).

The kingdom: present and/or future?

The debate on the kingdom as present or future has led to a huge volume of scholarly writing over the last 150 years, focused in five basic views of Jesus' beliefs about the kingdom. All speak of 'eschatology'.

Futurist (or 'consistent eschatology') J. Weiss (1892) and A. Schweitzer (1906) argued that Jesus held an entirely apocalyptic view of God's reign. They believed that Jesus held to the standard Jewish 'this age/age to come' model, and saw his ministry as bringing about the crisis which would lead to the inauguration of the age to come, in which the present space-time universe would be destroyed and a new world – God's kingdom – would begin (see further pp. 129f.). This view, with variants, is held by modern scholars such as E. P. Sanders and P. M. Casey.

ESCHATOLOGY: A MATTER OF DEFINITION

Dictionaries generally define 'eschatology' (derived from the Greek *eschatos*, meaning 'end') as study of the 'last things' – traditionally heaven, hell, death and judgement – and this is how the word is used in study of Christian doctrine (or systematic theology). However, NT scholars use 'eschatology' in various senses, which are not necessarily anything to do with the 'end of the world' in the popular sense, including:

- in a Jewish context, of the transformation of the world when God moves it from this age to the age to come;
- concerning the parousia, the coming of the son of man and the presence/coming of the kingdom of God;
- in discussion of the OT prophets, of their hopes for Yahweh's action for Israel in the future;
- of general ultimate hopes and expectations;
- qualitatively, of events in and through which God is at work and his purposes are being achieved;
- of events whose significance is drawn from the end towards which they are going.

It is therefore important, when reading scholars, to ask in what sense they use this word. Often the context in which they use it will make that clear.

(See further: I. H. Marshall "Slippery Words: I. Eschatology." *Expository Times* 89 (1977-78) 264-9 or G. B. Caird *The Language and Imagery of the Bible*. London: Duckworth, 1980, ch. 14.)

Realized eschatology This view is most closely associated with the British scholar C. H. Dodd (1935), who argued that *all* of Jesus' teaching about the kingdom was related to the present crisis of his ministry. Thus the parables of judgement speak of response in the present crisis, rather than of a judgement to come at a much later time. The kingdom is then viewed as a timeless reality which has invaded history in the ministry of Jesus, and no portion of it is to come in the future.

Mediating views In the debate which followed Dodd's work, scholars sought ways of portraying the kingdom as both present and future, recognizing that there are Gospel texts which stubbornly resist both an entirely future and an entirely present view. Particularly significant is J. Jeremias' work on the parables (1954): he spoke of *eschatology in process of realization*, arguing that signs of the kingdom appeared in Jesus' teaching and actions, but the kingdom itself was to come – and Jesus' expectation was that this coming would be seen imminently, in his own resurrection and parousia. A. M. Hunter used the phrase *inaugurated eschatology* to describe this view.

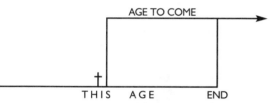

Another way of handling this 'already but not yet' shape of the kingdom is to see the relationship in terms of *salvation history*. O. Cullmann (1946) and G. E. Ladd (1952) proposed that the reign of God is climactically active in Jesus' ministry, as it was from time to time in God's redeeming acts for his people during the OT period, but that there is more to come at the end of history. Jesus' expectation was not of an imminent 'end of the world'. In terms of the Jewish categories, the age to come has broken into this age, but this age still continues until the End (see the diagram above). Cullmann portrays this scheme as a war in which the decisive battle has been fought (in the death and resurrection of Jesus), and therefore the result of the war is not in doubt, but the fighting must continue until the war is finally over.

Historical M. Borg and N. T. Wright (and their teacher, G. B. Caird) argue that, in classic Jewish manner, Jesus uses powerful symbols to interpret and explain this-worldly events. For example, when he speaks of the sun and moon being darkened and stars falling from heaven (e.g. Matt. 24:29), Jesus is not speaking of a literal end of the space-time universe, but is using this imagery to interpret historical events and invest them with cosmic significance. In particular, Wright argues that Jesus' teaching on the imminence of the kingdom should be understood in terms of the soon-to-come fall of Jerusalem. This event would be the vindication of Jesus, pictured as 'the son of man' who was taken to God in vindication (Mark 13:26) (see also pp. 175, 183f.). On this view, Jesus did not speak of his 'second coming' at all prior to his death (although Wright argues that the earliest Christians believed this on the basis of Jesus' post-resurrection teaching). Language that sounds like 'second coming' to our ears is in fact about Yahweh coming to Jerusalem in and through the ministry of Jesus, to bring judgement and salvation.

Others (e.g. France 1985, 333-6) combine a historical and a salvation-historical view, proposing that the main focus of Mark 13 and parallels is the fall of Jerusalem, but also that Jesus did speak of his 'second coming' during his lifetime. France points to the double question in Matthew's version of the passage as showing this, at least for Matt. 24: 'when will *this* [i.e. the fall of the temple] be, and what will be *the sign of your coming and of the end of the age?*'(v. 3). This means that 'all these things' which will happen before 'this generation' passes away (Matt. 24:34) are the events of the fall of the city, but 'that day', about which 'no one knows' (Matt. 24:36) is the day of Jesus' parousia.

What do you think?
THE TIMING OF THE KINGDOM

Which of the views above of the timing of the kingdom's presence do you find most persuasive and why? What evidence is hardest for this view to fit in?

Deciding between the various views is not easy. Futurist and realized eschatology are opposites, and ultimately each has to explain away or reinterpret the evidence which most strongly supports the opposing view. This suggests that one of the mediating positions has the best claim to describing Jesus' teaching. In fact, there is a consensus in scholarship that the formula 'now and not yet' describes Jesus' view, although there is not full agreement on how this combination works out in detail. The historical view remains a minority view, although it is influential.

THE CHARACTER OF THE KINGDOM

In announcing the presence of God's reign in his ministry Jesus was heralding a new order of things. Luke particularly highlights the reversal of the present order, but this is a theme throughout Jesus' teaching: the first shall be last and the last shall be first (Mark 10:31; Luke 13:30; Matt. 19:30; 20:16). This reversal means that those considered outside God's care now come within his care.

WELCOME FOR 'SINNERS'
In particular, those regarded as 'sinners' were welcomed by Jesus. Generally 'sinners' were outsiders to Judaism: all Gentiles were regarded that way (cf. Gal. 2:15), as the intertestamental writers of Jubilees and the Psalms of Solomon make clear:

He will rouse up against them the sinners of the nations who have no mercy or grace for them ... And they will cause turmoil in Israel and sin against Jacob; In those days, they will cry out and call and pray to be saved from the hand of the sinners, the gentiles. (Jub. 23:23f.)

Arrogantly the sinner broke down the strong walls with a battering ram and you did not interfere. Gentile foreigners went up to your place of sacrifice; they arrogantly trampled [it] with their sandals. (Pss. Sol. 2:1-2)

'Sinner' was also used *within* Judaism of those who were seen as apostate Jews, including those who collaborated with pagans such as the Romans (e.g. tax collectors). In the second-century BC Maccabean revolt, Jewish collaborators with the pagans were described thus:

... a sinful people, men who were renegades (1 Macc. 1:34)

... they struck down sinners in their anger and renegades in their wrath (1 Macc. 2:44)

The Qumran sectarians regarded those Jews from whom they had separated similarly, describing them in ways which mark them as outsiders:

'they sought smooth things' (CD 1:13-21); 'the men of the lot of Belial' (1QS 2:4f.); 'an assembly of deceit and a horde of Satan' (1QH 2:8-19); 'And they, teachers of lies and seers of falsehood, have schemed against me a devilish scheme, to exchange the Law engraved on my heart by Thee for the smooth things (which they speak) to Thy people' (1QH 4:6-8).

Dunn summarizes well:

Evidently within the Judaism of Jesus' day there were various groups who regarded themselves as alone loyal to the covenant and law, and who denounced their fellow Jews as being disloyal. And key and characteristic terms in the several polemics were 'righteous' and 'sinner'. (J. D. G. Dunn *The Partings of the Ways*. London: SCM/Philadelphia: Trinity Press International, 1991, 105, italics his.)

Groups such as the Pharisees and the revolutionaries use such terms (e.g. Luke 7:39) to mark themselves out as the true people of God, whom he would redeem when he acts. With that demarcation goes the belief that when God saves his people, the 'sinners' will be judged and condemned.

In this setting Jesus' actions are astonishing (e.g. Matt. 9:11; Mark 2:16). He shares table fellowship with 'sinners' in a culture where to share a meal was to welcome the guest in honour and to accept the guest's good standing in the community – more, within Judaism it was to recognize the guest as sharing fellowship with Yahweh (hence the rumpus over Jewish believers eating with Gentiles, Gal. 2:11f.). The evangelists present Jesus not only as accepting (and even soliciting) such outsiders' invitations to eat with them (e.g. Luke 5:29; 19:5-7), but also acting as the host who welcomes such people to his own table (e.g. Matt. 9:10; Mark 2:15).

The Pharisees' complaint against Jesus is not that he spent time with 'sinners' – after all, they would be delighted if he persuaded the sinners to turn from their way of life, go to the temple and offer sacrifices, and live according to the torah. Their criticism is that he spends time with sinners, promises them forgiveness (e.g. Luke 7:47-49; Mark 2:5-12),

and thus shows that he includes such people in God's reign, *without requiring return to the torah* by offering sacrifice. To act in this way amounts to the claim that Jesus himself can do what the temple and priesthood were designed to do, namely offer the forgiveness of God (see pp. 156–8).

Jesus defends his actions in several ways. It is likely that the shepherd of Ezek. 34 lies behind his teaching at key points (I owe this observation to Max Turner). Ezekiel compares the bad shepherds who have allowed the nation to become lost (vv. 2-10), and whom God will remove from their work, with God himself, who will be the true shepherd of Israel (vv. 11-16). The bad shepherds have failed to strengthen, heal and bind up the sheep (v. 4). Jesus' reply to the Pharisees' criticism is, 'Those who are well have no need of a physician, but those who are sick; I came not to call the righteous, but sinners' (Mark 2:17). Of course a doctor will be found among sick people, as the shepherd will bind up injured sheep (Ezek. 34:4, 16) – Jesus thus takes the role of Yahweh as the true shepherd of Israel. Not only that, but the bad shepherds of Ezek. 34:2-10 are identified as the Pharisees, who have failed to help the 'sinners'.

In the parable of the great supper (Luke 14:15-23) Jesus pointedly speaks of people who reject the kingdom invitation and are replaced by outsiders, 'the poor, the crippled, the blind and the lame' (v. 21) and those from the roads and the lanes (v. 23). The Pharisees and others who reject God's invitation in Jesus will lose their place at supper to these 'sinners'.

Jesus tells three parables of lost things (sheep, coin and son; Luke 15:3-32) in response to the Pharisees' and scribes' criticism of Jesus eating with sinners (Luke 15:1f.), and may well reflect God's shepherding search for the lost (Ezek. 34:16 again). The note of rejoicing in each story (vv. 6, 9, 23f.) shows the response to his ministry for which Jesus hopes. The elder brother (vv. 25-32) represents the Pharisees and scribes, who prefer to carp and criticize rather than to rejoice. This final story is left open, for Jesus does not say what the elder brother does: it is left for the hearers – the Pharisees and scribes – to decide whether they will join in the party and rejoice as God rejoices, or reject God's invitation to them.

Both Jesus' actions and his defence of those actions are deeply offensive to those who see the only way to God as through the Jewish covenant, torah and temple sacrifices, and lead to outright hostility from the religious establishment. To offer forgiveness and welcome sinners apart from the temple is highly provocative and will ultimately lead to his arrest, trial and death.

THE KINGDOM OF THE FATHER
Why does Jesus think and act this way? It is partly because of his sense of his own identity (see pp. 174–8) and partly because of his understanding of God.

Jesus characteristically regards God as 'my father' (e.g. Luke 2:49; 22:29; Matt. 7:21), and prays to God as 'abba (Mark 14:36), an intimate family term used by children to their father (and used by children of all ages, including adults – it is not a child*ish* term). Jesus also teaches his disciples to view and address God that way, notably in the Lord's prayer, beginning '(Our) father' (Matt. 6:9; Luke 11:2). In Gal. 4:6 and Rom. 8:15 Paul clearly echoes this usage – a remarkable example of an Aramaic word being used in predominantly Greek-speaking churches, for

which the best explanation is that using 'abba to address God stemmed from Jesus himself.

J. Jeremias proposed that this form of address to God was an innovation by Jesus. G. Vermes (1973, 210-13) has provided one or two examples of other Jews speaking of God this way, but their paucity shows that it was very uncommon, and therefore distinctive of Jesus. To describe God as 'father' in Judaism, including the OT, was particularly associated with his acts of redemption (e.g. Deut. 32:6; Isa. 63:16; Hos. 11:1; Mal. 2:10), which suggests that Jesus' choice of this language reflected his sense that God was *now* acting to redeem, in and through Jesus' own ministry.

However, Jesus does not teach a universal fatherhood of all people, or even all Jews, but only of those who follow Jesus – in the synoptic Gospels it is only in Jesus' prayers and in teaching with his followers that Jesus speaks of God this way. So Jesus' followers are the 'little flock' who receive the kingdom from their father (Luke 12:32); they are the righteous who will shine like the sun in their father's kingdom (Matt. 13:43).

THE RESPONSE REQUIRED
The presence of the reign of God in Jesus' ministry invites a response, as the parable of the great supper makes clear (Luke 14:15-24; cf. Matt. 22:1-10). What sort of response does Jesus seek?

Positively, the heart of response is to follow Jesus. Jesus spells this out as receiving the kingdom as a child, with entire trust (Mark 10:14f.). Strikingly, in a culture which does not value children in their own right, but only as potential adults, Jesus tells adults to be like children (and never tells children to be like adults!). In terms of Jesus' announcement of the reign of God, this is to 'believe' (Mark 1:15) – it is to trust one's life entirely into the hands of Jesus in the confidence that in and through him God is now acting decisively to save Israel. For some this means leaving everything and going with Jesus; there are other followers of Jesus who sometimes did not travel with him (e.g. the 'great crowd of disciples', Luke 6:17). For all it means a new lifestyle, characterized by being like God – including in his generosity to the poor (Matt. 5:48; cf. God's demand of Israel to 'be holy as I am holy', Lev. 19:2; 20:26).

Negatively, responding means renouncing anything which hinders. Thus those who follow Jesus must deny themselves, even to the point of losing their lives (Mark 8:34f.). With typical Jewish overstatement Jesus calls on people to cut off a hand or foot, or to pull out an eye, rather than lose their entry ticket to the reign of God (Mark 9:43-48). To believe that in Jesus Yahweh is acting to redeem the nation – and the world – means rejecting the old ways. This includes:

- renouncing reliance on personal wealth (Mark 10:17-31);
- not relying on keeping the commandments as a marker of covenant membership (Mark 10:17-22);
- not worrying about bodily needs, for God will provide (Matt. 6:24-34);
- rejecting ostentatious titles and behaviour, for they deny humble dependence on God (Matt. 23:5-12);
- placing family and friends lower in priority than God's reign: in Jewish parlance, they are to be 'hated' (Luke 14:26 – cf. Jesus doing this, Mark 3:31-35).

All of these demands are strongly counter-cultural; they run against beliefs that the Jews were the apple of God's eye, that

Digging deeper:
RESPONDING TO JESUS' DEMANDS

Write (and perform, if you get the opportunity) a short drama sketch based on one of the above stories, transposing it into today's terms, in order to bring out how shocking Jesus' demands are.

riches are a mark of God's blessing, that keeping torah is the marker of the true people of God, and that loyalty to the family, clan, tribe and nation is paramount.

This total demand reflects the total offer Jesus makes, vividly portrayed in the two brief parables of the pearl merchant and the treasure in the field (Matt. 13:44-46), both focusing on the need to 'sell everything' to obtain the kingdom, which is of enormous value.

JESUS' ETHICS AND HIS VIEW OF THE TORAH

What, then, does life in the kingdom look like? How are Jesus' followers to live? And what is the relationship of his ethical teaching to the demands of the torah, the Jewish law? These questions are hotly debated in scholarship.

JESUS' TEACHING ABOUT THE TORAH

Jesus' practice seems to have been to maintain Jewish customs: he attends synagogue regularly (Luke 4:16), he joins in the festivals (Luke 2:41; Mark 14:12-16), he fasts (Matt. 4:2), he has clothing with 'fringes' on the edges (Mark 6:56; Luke 8:44; cf. Num. 15:38-41), and he pays the temple tax (Matt. 17:24-27). Further, he uses the torah as the basis of his answers to

What do you think?
JESUS AND SCRIPTURE

Jesus frequently uses the phrase 'it is written' (Greek normally *gegraptai*) when he refers to Scripture. Read the verses below, which are all the places in the Gospels where this phrase is found on the lips of Jesus. What picture of his view of the role(s) and authority of the OT emerges?

Matt. 4:4, 7, 10; 11:10; 21:13; 26:24; 26:31; Mark 7:6; 9:12f.; 11:17; 14:21, 27; Luke 4:4, 8; 7:27; 10:26; 18:31; 19:46; 20:17; 21:22; 22:37; 24:44, 46; John 6:45; 8:17; 10:34

questions put to him (e.g. Mark 2:25; 12:10, 26). He points to the commandments in response to the rich man who asks how to inherit eternal life (Mark 10:17-19), and he commends the lawyer who summarizes the torah in the commands to love God and neighbour (Luke 10:25-28). Matthew also reports Jesus making a very strong statement about the OT (Matt. 5:17-20):

17Do not think that I have come to abolish the law or the prophets; I have come not to abolish but to fulfil. 18For truly I tell you, until heaven and earth pass away, not one letter, not one stroke of a letter, will pass from the law until all is accomplished. 19Therefore, whoever breaks one of the least of these commandments, and teaches others to do the same, will be called least in the kingdom of heaven; but whoever does them and teaches them will be called great in the kingdom of heaven. 20For I tell you, unless your righteousness exceeds that of the scribes and Pharisees, you will never enter the kingdom of heaven.

Because this statement sounds so strongly Jewish and Matthew is reckoned to be a 'Jewish' Gospel, some view it as likely to be inauthentic and to reflect debates in Matthew's setting about the continuing role of the torah for Christians. However, there is a partial parallel in Luke 16:17, and it is probable that Jesus' behaviour (such as eating with 'sinners'), when the common people compared it with the Pharisees' and scribes' somewhat different lifestyle, would lead to questions about his attitude to the torah. In that life setting it would be natural for Jesus to teach in exactly the way these verses describe. The fact that this teaching seems, on the surface, to be out of tune with some of Jesus' teaching and actions on the continuing validity of the torah (see below on 'Jesus' criticisms of the torah', pp. 171f.), also speaks for its authenticity – for it would be unlikely that a later Christian church would invent sayings which *created* such tensions.

So what is Jesus saying here? There are three major issues in interpreting these verses: the meaning of 'fulfil' (v. 17), the time meant by 'until all is accomplished' (v. 18), and the question of which 'commandments' Jesus refers to (v. 19).

Fulfilment The verb 'fulfil' (Greek *pleroō*) is a favourite of Matthew, especially when he notes 'this happened to fulfil what had been spoken through the prophet…' (e.g. 1:22; 2:15, 17, 23; 4:14). In those 'formula quotations' it means bringing a promise into being, rather than providing the full, intended meaning of the prophet's words. Given the practice of Jesus, including touching people with leprosy (which caused ritual uncleanness), and the early church's understanding that he had abolished the food laws (Mark 7:19), it is highly unlikely that 'fulfil' means something like 'confirm and establish'.

In the thirteenth century, Thomas Aquinas drew a distinction between the moral, ceremonial and civil aspects of the OT law: the civil and ceremonial laws related to the nation of Israel (and were therefore abolished as far as the church went), while the moral laws continued to have force for Christians. However, this distinction is unlikely to be recognized by first-century Jews – they see Scripture as one, unified entity.

It seems likeliest that when Jesus speaks of fulfilling the law and the prophets, he is presenting himself as the reality to which they point. This is the same sense in which the verb 'fulfil' is used in the 'formula quotations' in Matt. 1–4 (cf. also 26:54, 56). Thus Jesus sees his own ministry as the time in which the promises of Scripture are being realized – not least in his own obedience to the torah – and himself as the key to understanding the law and the prophets. Jesus thus asserts that his teaching does not undermine the ethical standards of the torah, but raises them higher (Matt. 5:20).

Accomplished Some suggest that Jesus means 'until the end of this age', but that would simply repeat v. 18a, and would also be a unique use of these words (the same Greek phrase is used in Matt. 24:34 meaning 'until all these things have taken place'). Equally, it would be surprising for this phrase to mean 'until everything contained in the law has been done', for the Greek verb used (*ginomai*) refers to events happening, rather than things being 'done'. Most probably Jesus means 'when everything it looks forward to has arrived' (thus translating the phrase in the same sense as

in 24:34, and linking the sense to v. 17, as 'for' at the beginning of v. 18 requires). This reading means that some parts of Scripture do not have validity beyond that time.

Commandments R. J. Banks (*Jesus and the Law in the Synoptic Tradition*. SNTS Monograph Series 28. Cambridge: Cambridge University Press, 1975) has proposed that Jesus means *his* commandments here, but this is unlikely following hot on the heels of the clear reference to the OT in vv. 17f. If Jesus means his teaching, and Matthew understands him this way, it would surely be clearer that there was a change of subject. There is a linking 'therefore' at the beginning of v. 19 (omitted by NIV) which shows that the same subject is still in view; that fact implies that Jesus is criticizing those who break the *OT* commandments. But v. 20 goes on to make it clear that Jesus is not advocating the same nit-picking attitude to Scripture as that of the scribes and Pharisees – he calls his followers to a righteousness which is deeper.

The net result of this (rather detailed) study of Matt. 5:17-20 is that Jesus is very positive about the torah, but is not saying that every word of the law is eternally valid. The torah points beyond itself to a time of fulfilment – the time of Jesus – and its role changes because of what God is now doing in and through Jesus.

JESUS' CRITICISMS OF THE TORAH

Jesus is accused of breaking the torah on a number of occasions, particularly by the Pharisees when he healed on the Sabbath (e.g. Mark 3:1-6). But Jesus rejects this accusation, turning it back on his accusers by asking them whether it was all right to do good on the Sabbath (Mark 3:4) – and thus

Digging deeper:
THE ANTITHESES

Study the six 'antitheses' in Matt. 5:21-48, which share a common pattern of 'You have heard … but I say …' (hence the name 'antithesis', meaning 'opposite idea'). The relationship between the two elements of each antithesis could be:

- 'you have heard, and in agreement with that, I say…';
- 'you have heard, but in addition to that, I say…';
- 'you have heard, but in contrast to that, I say…'.

For each antithesis, which of the above do you think is closest to Jesus' attitude, and why? Use a cross-reference Bible or a Bible concordance (so that you can check the source and actual wording of the 'You have heard' part in the OT) and commentaries to help you in considering this question.

claims that he is not in fact breaking torah. But were there times when he did do so?

Certainly Jesus broke with traditions added by the scribes and Pharisees about how the law was to be interpreted (the so-called 'halakah'), including Sabbath observance (see below), Corban (a practice of dedicating an object or money to God, Mark 7:9-13; cf. Num. 30:2) and the purity laws (rejecting the need to wash hands and vessels for ritual purity reasons, Mark 7:1-8).

Mark reports that Jesus 'declared all foods clean' (7:19), but if Jesus had publicly said this during his ministry, his opponents would have had a clear-cut case of him contradicting the torah, and there is no sign in the Gospels that they did have such evidence. So it is likely that we are seeing Mark's explanation of an implication of Jesus' teaching which the church recognized after the resurrection.

When Jesus discusses divorce (Mark 10:2-12; Matt. 19:3-12), he interprets the limited situation proposed by the Pharisees from Deut. 24:1-4 (alluded to in Mark 10:4; Matt. 19:7) through the original intention of God in creation (Gen. 1:27; 2:24, cited in Mark 10:6f.; Matt. 19:4f.). In fact, Deut. 24:1-4 *assumes* divorce rather than permitting it, for it legislates specifically for a situation where a man has divorced his first wife, married another, divorced the second wife and now wishes to remarry the first wife. By contrast, Jesus looks to a situation where people no longer suffer from 'hardness of heart' (Mark 10:5), and divorce legislation will no longer be necessary.

We see a similar technique, interpreting one part of Scripture through the lens of another, in Jesus' response to criticism of his disciples plucking and grinding corn on the Sabbath (Mark 2:23-28 and parallels). Here Jesus cites David's actions in eating the bread of the presence, kept for the priests (according to the law), when he and his soldiers were in need (1 Sam. 21:1-6). Jesus argues that, since David broke the law over who could eat the priestly bread because of hunger, so it was appropriate for his disciples to 'work' on the Sabbath by plucking corn to eat. This argument is rooted in Scripture, but also hints that Jesus brings something new, and in that setting his followers are no longer bound by some regulations about the Sabbath.

WAS JESUS CONSISTENT?
What, then, can we say about Jesus' attitude to the Jewish law? On one hand it appears that he supports the torah, but on the other he seems to undermine it.

Some scholars argue that this tension does not come from the teaching of Jesus, but rather reflects Matthew's conservative Jewish view of the torah in debate with Mark's more radical view. However, there is evidence within Matthew of the more radical view. For example, Matthew agrees with Mark in having Jesus' teaching that the Sabbath is for people (in response to the question about his disciples plucking corn), and Matthew even strengthens this teaching by having Jesus say, 'Something greater than the temple is here' (Mark 2:23-28; Matt. 12:1-8). Matthew also has a version of Mark's sayings which indicate that handwashing and ceremonial purity are not the most crucial thing (Mark 7:14-23; Matt. 15:10f., 15-20). Further, when Matthew's Jesus speaks of the importance of listening to the scribes and Pharisees, he speaks with heavy irony (e.g. Matt. 23:2f is followed by vv. 4-12, which identify the hypocrisy of the scribes and Pharisees).

Both strands of teaching about the torah have a good claim to authenticity: can the tension between them be resolved? A. E. Harvey (1990, esp. chs 3-4) notes that the form of Jesus' ethical teaching is not strictly 'legal', for by and large it could not be applied in a strictly 'legal' way. How would a court of law assess whether a man was looking 'with lust' at a woman (Matt. 5:28)? If a person's right eye caused them to sin and they tore it out, in accordance with Mark 9:47, why would their remaining left eye not cause them to sin? This kind of teaching has more in common with OT and Jewish wisdom teaching, which sets out ideals and is designed to persuade people to live in certain ways – but is not meant to be treated as laws. Thus Jesus' teaching is not like that of the Pharisees, who seek to extend the torah's meaning to every area of life by adding interpretative oral tradition (e.g. the tithing of herbs, Matt. 23:23). Rather, Jesus aims to challenge people's basic patterns of behaviour.

For example, Jesus says, 'You have heard that it was said, "An eye for an eye and a tooth for a tooth." But I say to you, Do not resist an evildoer. But if anyone strikes you on the right cheek, turn the other also' (Matt. 5:38f.). This statement is not in a legally applicable form at all, for Jesus' aim is to challenge the issue behind the OT legislation, which is the desire for revenge.

Jesus does not, in fact, live literally by this teaching, for he does resist evil people at times: he teaches against the scribes and Pharisees (Matt. 23). Further, he does not offer the other cheek when struck during his trial, but (in effect) challenges the injustice of the action (John 18:21-23).

The OT law (Jesus cites words from Exod. 21:24; Deut. 19:21) limited revenge to the same level as the injury caused. At least by the time of Jesus this law seems not to have been carried out literally, but a system of financial penalties had replaced the literal taking of a body part from the other person. Jesus goes behind the law to the desire for revenge which it presupposes, arguing (in effect) that to return violence for violence will only perpetuate that way of living. By contrast, Jesus' followers are to be peace-makers (Matt. 5:9) and therefore will not seek revenge.

Such teaching identifies Jesus as a teacher in the wisdom tradition, rather than someone presenting new rules for living which were to be enforced by the law courts. Indeed, Jesus was not in any official position which would allow him to offer a 'new law', but he was able to speak with personal authority in the new setting of the presence of the kingdom of God. Thus where he seems to endorse the torah, he is affirming that it represents God's will *in the situation for which it was given*.

Where Jesus goes beyond or even rejects the torah, he is reinterpreting it for the new setting where the kingdom is arriving – a situation different from that for which the torah was given, and therefore a situation in which some of its requirements were no longer necessary or appropriate. That said, what he teaches is to be seen as fulfilment of the torah (Matt. 5:17-20). The key to understanding Jesus' teaching is to know what the time is – it is the time of fulfilment, the time of the kingdom (Mark 1:15).

Digging deeper:
THE SERMON ON THE MOUNT:
A NEW TORAH?

Read the sermon on the mount (Matt. 5–7) at a sitting, noticing in particular its structure and major themes. How far do you think Jesus regarded the sermon on the mount as a 'new torah'? Specifically:

● What are the instructions Jesus gives here?
● Are they suitable for use as 'law'?
● Are they suitable as 'principles for conduct' for Jesus' followers?

If the sermon is not a 'new torah', how would you best explain its purpose and its relationship with the kingdom teaching of Jesus?

(Further reading: *DJG* articles 'Ethics of Jesus', 'Rich and Poor', 'Sermon on the Mount'; Harvey 1990, chs 4-5; Wright 1996, 268-97.)

WHO DID JESUS THINK HE WAS?

All that we have seen of Jesus and his death, teaching and beliefs raises the question of his sense of his own identity: who does he think he is, and what is his role in the inbreaking of the kingdom of God which he announces? Traditionally in NT scholarship this question has been answered by studying the 'titles' Jesus uses about himself, and we shall shortly consider them. But first we need to reflect on what we know of Jesus' mission and his aims.

JESUS AS ISRAEL

A central question to Judaism of Jesus' day is, 'Who is a true Jew?' We have seen debate on this among the various groups within Judaism (pp. 37–44) and we have discussed Jesus' concern for the 'sinners' (pp. 166–8). Central to the answers given to this question is the issue of purity. The Pharisees and scribes attempt to apply the torah to every situation of daily life by adding new laws, in order to safeguard their purity and to avoid being in danger of transgressing the torah. The revolutionaries plan to throw out the Romans, for they make the land impure. The Essenes attempt to apply the priestly purity laws to their whole community, and the Qumran group also withdraw into a 'monastic' community separated from the people of the land.

As we have seen in discussing Jesus' contact with the 'sinners', he regards his purity as spreading to those with whom he comes into contact, rather than being made impure by that contact. This suggests that his gathering of people around him is highly important to understanding his aims. In particular, Jesus presents himself in a number of ways as the *true Israel*. Three pieces of evidence lead to this conclusion.

First, a central charge at Jesus' trial is that he claims to be 'king of the Jews' (Mark 15:2, 26, 32, etc.). A careful reading of the Gospels, however, shows that Jesus never speaks of himself explicitly in this way: rather the reverse, for he speaks of Jerusalem as 'the city of the great king' (Matt. 5:35), thus identifying Yahweh as king. Thus something about his teaching and ministry must have led his opponents to see him as claiming kingship (see further on 'Messiah' below), and we saw above that his arrival in Jerusalem on a donkey and his demonstration in the temple both point in this direction.

Second, Jesus' actions and teaching identify him using three images from the OT which each combine individual and representative features: the servant of Yahweh, the son of man and the king. In each case, the OT figure in some sense represents Israel.

The *servant* figure of the later chapters of Isaiah (esp. 42:1-4; 49:1-6; 50:4-9; 52:13–53:12) underlies much of Jesus' teaching about his own role. The heavenly voice at Jesus' baptism and transfiguration echoes Isa. 42:1 (Mark 1:11; 9:7; although using 'son' [Greek *huios*] rather than 'servant'). Jesus speaks of himself as giving his life 'for many' (Mark 10:45; 14:24; see p. 159). Isa. 49:3 makes it clear, however, that the servant is Israel: 'he said to me, "You are my servant, Israel, in whom I will be glorified."' Thus the servant is both to fulfil the task of the nation and to be the one who will 'bring Jacob back to him … that Israel might be gathered to him' (Isa. 49:5). Jesus is to be all that the nation was intended to be, in order to renew the nation's identity as the people of God.

The *son of man* figure focuses these ideas

further (see pp. 183f.). It is widely agreed that Jesus used 'the son of man' as a means of speaking of himself and his mission, and the likeliest source of this image is Dan. 7:13f., 18:

> As I watched in the night visions, I saw one like a son of man coming with the clouds of heaven. And he came to the Ancient of Days and was presented before him. To him was given dominion and glory and kingship, that all peoples, nations, and languages should serve him. His dominion is an everlasting dominion that shall not pass away, and his kingship is one that shall never be destroyed … But the holy ones of the Most High shall receive the kingdom and possess the king- dom forever – forever and ever. (Edited NRSV)

This mysterious figure is an individual who comes to God on the clouds and is vindicated by being given authority over the nations. He is a human being – hence the name 'son of man' – but he is more than an individual, for v. 18 states that 'the holy ones of the Most High', the true people of God, receive this authority. Thus the 'son of man' represents the people of God. The setting of Dan. 7:1-8 reinforces this understanding, for there the pagan nations who oppress Israel are pictured as wild animals, by contrast with a human figure, the son of man, who represents Israel as God's true humanity. (On this passage, see more fully Wright 1992, 291-7.) So, as with the servant, this image used by Jesus of himself is both individual and representative of Israel.

The *king* image is present, as we have argued (p. 156), in Jesus' arrival in Jerusalem (esp. Matt. 21:5, quoting Zech. 9:9). But the king is not simply an individual: he represents the nation. When the tribes come to David at Hebron and anoint him as king, they say, 'We are your bone and flesh' (2 Sam. 5:1), thus identifying him with the nation and the nation with him. Likewise, for God to describe the king of Israel as 'the son of God' (2 Sam. 7:12-14; Pss 2:7; 89:26f.) evokes the image of Israel as God's son (e.g. Exod. 4:22f.; Jer. 3:19f.; Hos. 11:1), and adds a further layer of individual/corporate imagery to our picture.

These three images each present Jesus as an individual who represents Israel, as one who in some measure at least is what Israel is meant to be. The third area to notice is that Jesus applies OT passages about Israel to himself. Here are three types of examples.

During the wilderness temptation period Matthew and Luke report debates between Jesus and the devil (Matt. 4:1-11; Luke 4:1-13). In response to the devil's proposals Jesus quotes Scripture, Deut. 8:3 (Matt. 4:4; Luke 4:4); 6:16 (Matt. 4:7; Luke 4:12) and 6:13 (Matt. 4:10; Luke 4:8). The section of Deuteronomy quoted by Jesus describes the wilderness wanderings after the Israelites left Egypt: just as Israel spent 40 years in the wilderness, Jesus spends 40 days there – but the Israelites gave in to temptation, for they built and worshipped a golden calf, whereas Jesus succeeds in withstanding the devil's temptations. This perhaps suggests that Jesus spent time meditating on this section of Deuteronomy during his wilderness temptation period.

On a number of occasions Jesus' teaching echoes psalms about Israel's suffering. He quotes Ps. 118:22f., concerning the rejected stone, and applies it to himself (Mark 12:10f.), whereas the psalm is about a surprising victory by Israel (although

interpreted messianically by some Jews). On the cross Jesus uses words from Ps. 22:1 about his own suffering (Mark 15:34), again a psalm usually thought to be about the nation. In similar vein Jesus echoes the image of the friend who betrays from Ps. 41:9 (Mark 14:18) and the refrain 'Why are you cast down, O my soul?' from Pss 42:5, 11; 43:5 (Mark 14:34) – in each case psalms concerned with the nation's situation.

Finally, the words of Hos. 6:2, 'After two days he will revive us; on the third day he will raise us up, that we may live before him', offer the nearest OT parallel to Jesus' announcement of his resurrection (e.g. Luke 18:31-33; 24:46), and scholars accept the influence of these words on Jesus at this point. But in the OT setting, Hos. 6 is about Israel's restoration in the near future, evoked by the 'third day'. Thus, 'It is not so much that Israel was a type of Jesus, but Jesus *is* Israel' (France 1971, 55, his italics).

JESUS, HIS DISCIPLES AND THE RENEWED ISRAEL

Taken together, this evidence strongly suggests that Jesus sees himself as the true Israel who has come in order to see the nation renewed, in similar manner to the mission of the Isaianic servant. But not only does he use 'Israel' language of himself, he invokes it in relation to his disciples and those whom he meets.

When Jesus calls disciples to follow him (e.g. Mark 1:16-20), he is doing something remarkable for, by contrast, disciples of the Jewish teachers generally took the initiative in choosing their own rabbi. The personal attachment to himself which Jesus seeks from his followers also contrasts with the Jewish rabbis, who mainly seek their disciples' attachment to the torah. This suggests that John's portrayal of the disciples returning to their previous occupations after Jesus' death (John 21:2f.) is authentic, for the one thing which held them together – following Jesus – had gone.

Not only does Jesus call people into a personal attachment to him, he selects twelve with a particular privilege of being with him and sent out by him (Mark 3:14). These twelve represent the twelve tribes of Israel (Matt. 19:28; Luke 22:30), showing that Jesus is bringing a renewed Israel into being. In doing this Jesus echoes Ezek. 37:15-28, which speaks of the restoration of the twelve tribes under a Davidic king (esp. vv. 22, 24f.) – and the prophet is dealing with a similar situation to the time of Jesus where there are only the two southern tribes of Benjamin and Judah left (for the ten northern tribes were lost after the Assyrian invasion of the northern kingdom in 722 BC). Thus the choice of the twelve makes a statement both about Jesus' mission – to renew Israel – and about Jesus' identity – he is the kingly figure who is at the heart of the renewal process.

It is highly ironic that it is Israel's rejection of Jesus which will bring about the renewal of the nation, as the barbed parable of the tenants suggests (Mark 12:1-12). The parable speaks of the beloved son of the vineyard's owner being killed, and this resulting in the tenants being thrown out. The story is interpreted by the quotation from Ps. 118:22f. (Mark 12:10), which sees Jesus as the stone rejected by the builders which is now placed in the most crucial place in the whole building. Further, the Jewish authorities recognize that Jesus tells this story against them (Mark 12:12): they recognize that Jesus portrays them as the tenants who will be replaced by others.

Just as Jesus applies OT passages about Israel to himself (see p. 176), he identifies his followers as the subject of the OT. He speaks of his disciples using 'remnant' language which the OT authors apply to a faithful group within Israel, such as 'little flock' (Luke 12:32); Jesus also refers to himself as 'shepherd' (Mark 14:27; cf. Zech. 13:7; John 10). He echoes the call, 'Be holy as I am holy' (Lev. 19:2; 20:26) in teaching his disciples (Matt. 5:48).

Not only this, but Jesus makes provision for the continuance of his group of followers after his departure. Thus he describes mechanisms for discipline (Matt. 16:18f.) and gives the command to repeat the actions with bread and wine at the Last Supper (Luke 22:19; 1 Cor. 11:14f.).

G. E. Ladd summarizes well:

> Jesus … saw in the circle of those who received his message the sons of the kingdom, the true Israel, the people of God … a new fellowship brought into being by Jesus as the true people of God who, having received the messianic salvation, were to take the place of the rebellious nation as the true Israel (Ladd 1974, 261)

Jesus' reshaping of Israel

As Jesus travels, teaches, heals and works, he seems deliberately to seek and help those who are on the edges of Israel as the powerful and the leaders understand the nation to be, and draws these marginalized people into his community (cf. Luke 4:16-30). Strikingly, he can use 'Israel' language in this process.

The woman bent double, whom Jesus heals, he calls a 'daughter of Abraham' (Luke

13:16), echoing language previously used of heroic women who resisted paganism to the point of death (e.g. 4 Macc. 15:28; 18:20), but now applied to someone whom Jesus restores to the community after 18 years of exclusion by her disability (cf. Lev. 21:16-23).

Similarly, Zacchaeus the tax collector is restored to the community after his repentance with the words, 'he too is a son of Abraham' (Luke 19:9). As with the woman bent double, Zacchaeus is returning from social exclusion, in his case because he collaborated with the hated Roman occupying forces.

What do you think?
RESTORATION TO ISRAEL

Some of Jesus' other miracles also overcome barriers to belonging to the people of God. Consider the following stories against their OT background and identify in what way Jesus is restoring the person to full participation in Israel:
Luke 17:11-19; see Lev. 13–14; Num. 5:1-4
Mark 5:25-34; see Lev. 12:1-8; 15:19-30

If you have opportunity, consult commentaries on the Gospel passages.

Not only adults, but children are included too (see pp. 168f.), and even Gentiles. Jesus never seeks out Gentiles during his ministry, but he welcomes and helps them when they seek him to ask his assistance. The Syrophoenician woman debates wittily with him, overcoming his initial reluctance to help her daughter (Mark 7:24-30). The centurion's servant is healed by Jesus at a distance and with a word (Luke 7:1-10; Matt. 8:5-13; cf. John 4:46-54) – and Jesus commends this Gentile's faith as exemplary (Luke 7:9; Matt. 8:10). Jesus delivers a demonized man in Gerasa, a Gentile area, as can be seen from the herd of pigs kept there (Mark 5:1-20). It would have been all too easy for the early church, which was committed to a mission among Gentiles, to 'read back' their concerns into the ministry of Jesus by inventing stories about him encountering Gentiles and welcoming them. The presence of so few such stories argues strongly for their historicity.

THE AIMS OF JESUS

We can thus summarize what Jesus understands his mission to be: he sees himself as sent by Yahweh as the key agent of the renewal of Israel. Noticeably, Jesus (and the NT authors) never use 'new Israel' language, which would imply a radical break with the 'old Israel'. Jesus is bringing about the prophesied restoration and new exodus described by, especially, Isa. 40 onwards. He is the one around whom the nation is being reshaped, reconstituted, and being his committed follower is what determines membership in this renewed Israel. Hence he proclaims and enacts the forgiveness of sins and sinners apart from the ceremonies of the temple, and he liberates people from oppressive evil powers.

For Jesus to act and speak in ways which made it clear that he believed all this would inevitably provoke opposition from those most secure in the present situation – the Jerusalem leadership who worked hand-in-glove with the Romans, especially the high priests and the Sadducees, who formed the largest group within the Sanhedrin. It is historically highly probable that Jesus thus foresaw that his beliefs would lead to his arrest, suffering and death – as the Gospels record (Mark 8:31; 9:31; 10:33; etc.). Not only that, but Jesus saw his suffering and death as having a key role in his mission to redeem Israel, as his words at the Last Supper indicate (see pp. 159f.).

JESUS AS MESSIAH

What kind of person would be at the heart of such a restoration movement within Judaism? The most natural Jewish answer is 'some kind of Messiah' – but what kind? As we outlined (p. 37), there are a variety of hopes for a messianic figure in first-century Judaism.

The Hebrew word *mashiach* means 'anointed one', as does the Greek *christos* – hence the use of 'Christ' in some English translations of the NT. Priests, kings and prophets were all anointed: the first two literally, for oil was poured over them at their appointment (e.g. Exod. 29:7; 1 Sam. 9:27–10:1), and the last metaphorically, for prophets also were chosen by God for his service. Generally, then, a Messiah was a figure anointed, that is empowered and called by God to carry out a God-given task. Three passages are central for Jesus' understanding of his messianic task, and each represent rare cases of the explicit use of messianic language.

Mark 8:27-30; Luke 9:18-21; Matt. 16:13-20

Characteristically, Jesus wants people to come to their own understanding of his identity: hence he asks his followers who others say he is, and then who they say he is. Some scholars argue that Peter's answer, 'You are the Messiah' (Mark 8:29), is inauthentic, because it reads back the church's later beliefs into the lifetime of Jesus. However, the geographical setting is specific (Mark 8:27), which is unusual for Mark and suggests that at least the setting is historical. Further, the precise time link with the transfiguration (Mark 9:2) has no

theological purpose, which also supports historicity. Most of all, it seems highly unlikely that the early church would invent a scene in which Jesus calls one of his leading disciples – and by Mark's time a key leader in the church – 'Satan' (Mark 8:33). These arguments add up to a strong case for authenticity.

But what does Jesus' response mean (Mark 8:31)? Jesus reinterprets Peter's term 'Messiah' in terms of 'the son of man' and of forthcoming suffering and death, thus indicating that his conception of the Messiah's role requires careful definition – as we might expect, given the variety of views around at the time. What is striking is that a suffering Messiah features nowhere in Jewish thought at this date, or later: a crucified Messiah is a contradiction in terms. Thus Jesus' beliefs about his messianic role introduce a new element into Jewish thinking.

Mark 14:53-64; Luke 22:54-71; Matt. 26:57-68

During his trial Jesus is asked outright by the high priest whether he is 'the Messiah, the son of the Blessed One' (Mark 14:61), and he responds in words which vary in the three synoptics: 'I am' (Mark 14:62); 'You have said so' (Matt. 26:64); 'You say that I am' (Luke 22:70). Jesus would answer in Aramaic, the language of the Jews, and each of our three Greek Gospels has interpreted the words with a different nuance. Jesus may be politely agreeing with the high priest, meaning, 'I agree with what you have said', or he may be saying, 'Yes, but that's not how I would put it'.

However, Jesus' next words seal his fate (Mark 14:62), for he identifies himself as 'the son of man' of Dan. 7:13f. who is vindicated by God, a figure who (as we saw earlier) represents Israel, the true people of God – and thus Jesus renews his claim to be reconstituting the nation around himself, which implies the rejection of the present national leadership, in line with the parable of the tenants (Mark 12:1-12), and the end of the temple.

The verdict of the high priest, that Jesus is blaspheming (Mark 14:63), shows that he has said something which offends the religious establishment deeply. There is evidence of at least some first-century Jews believing in a second 'power' in heaven alongside Yahweh, and for Jesus to claim that he will be 'seated at the right hand of the Power and coming with the clouds of heaven' is to say that he will be at the side of Yahweh in similar manner: hence the verdict of blasphemy.

Mark 15:2-5; Luke 23:2-5; Matt. 27:11-14
Jesus' reply to Pilate's question, 'Are you the king of the Jews?' (Mark 15:2) is worded precisely the same in all three synoptics: 'You say so' (Mark 15:2), perhaps reflecting an answer given in Greek before this Roman court. Pilate does not immediately conclude that Jesus is guilty (esp. Luke 23:4), which shows that this answer is not a clear 'Yes', at least at this stage of the Roman trial.

In what sense, then, does Jesus see himself as Messiah? Certainly not as a violent revolutionary, for he tells his followers not to fight (Luke 22:49-51). Jesus' self-understanding includes the following elements, which run across the various Gospel sources, and thus have a strong claim to authenticity:

- his consciousness of being God's son seen, for example, in the voice from heaven (Mark 1:9-11; 9:7);

- his sense of being the agent of the presence of God's reign or kingdom (Mark 1:15; Luke 10:9; 11:20);

- his actions which fulfil OT prophecies of God's eschatological action (Luke 4:18f.; 7:22; cf. Isa. 61:1f.);

- his requirement that human attachment to himself was the condition of entry to the reign of God (Mark 1:14f., 16-20; 10:17-31);

- his dispensing of divine forgiveness to sinners and opening the way for the poor into God's reign (Mark 2:5-7; Luke 6:20; 7:36-50), thus fulfilling key Isaianic prophecies (e.g. Isa. 40:1f.; 44:22; 53:10-12; 61:1f.);

- his entry into Jerusalem in kingly fashion, fulfilling Zech. 9:9 (Mark 11:1-10 and parallels);

- his role in restoration and renewal of the temple and his prophecy of its destruction and replacement (Mark 11:15-17; 13:1f.; see pp. 156-8);

- his implication that he participates in the Davidic kingship (e.g. Mark 12:35-37).

Taken together, this is an impressive body of evidence which strongly supports the claim that Jesus understood himself to be Messiah, as well as indicating something of the shape of his understanding of messiahship. To it we can add the frequency of 'Christ' as a name for Jesus in the early churches (e.g. in the NT letters), for it is unlikely that the early Christians would use this term from Hebrew without having some reason to think that Jesus thought of himself as Messiah.

But if Jesus saw himself this way, why did he not explicitly claim to be Messiah during his ministry? Four points add up to an answer.

First, we have already noted the variety of views of messiahship around in the first century, and this alone would mean that Jesus would have had to define his concept of the Messiah's role over against the others. Because the other views were around, for Jesus to say that he was the Messiah explicitly would have a high risk of misunderstanding, and this forms a partial explanation for his hesitancy about using the word.

Second, for these reasons Jesus' preference seems to have been for other terms for himself, particularly 'the son of man', but also the servant of Yahweh, because he could bring out from them an emphasis on the need for his suffering and death – whereas the idea of a suffering Messiah was anathema in first-century Judaism.

Third, there would be great political danger in explicitly claiming messiahship, for it would lead rapidly to arrest by the Romans. Jesus shows signs of not wishing to precipitate a crisis too early (cf. the way John speaks of Jesus' 'hour' not having come yet, e.g. John 7:30).

Fourth, there was a tradition within Judaism that no one could claim to be Messiah without having done the work of the Messiah (Longenecker 1970, 71-73). This pattern is seen in the Teacher of Righteousness, the founder of the Qumran community, and Bar Kochba, who led a Jewish rebellion of the second century AD against the Romans. On this view, Jesus could not claim to be Messiah prior to accomplishing what he saw as the Messiah's task, which he conceived in terms of going to Jerusalem to suffer and die to redeem the people. This is why it was not until after his resurrection that the early Christians spoke of him openly as Messiah (esp. Acts 2:32-36).

So it is highly likely that Jesus conceived of himself in messianic terms, but had a particular interpretation of the role of the Messiah involving suffering and death for the nation. Because he held this view he preferred other terms to describe himself. We turn, then, to consider two of these terms: 'the son of God' and 'the son of man'.

JESUS AS THE SON OF GOD

For Jesus to speak of himself as God's son would not necessarily be understood as claiming to be divine in first-century Judaism. The OT speaks of the nation (Hos. 11:1f.) and the king (e.g. Ps. 2:7, from a coronation psalm) as God's son. And, as we saw, Jesus taught his disciples to address God as 'Father', thus giving those men the status of God's sons.

Each of these threads of usage, however, echoes themes we have seen earlier in Jesus' understanding of his mission. To think of himself as God's son echoes Jesus' understanding of himself as the true Israel and as the king/Messiah who represents the nation. In a Jewish way of thinking, for Jesus to be 'the son of God' can be another way of speaking of him as Messiah. To describe his disciples as 'sons of God' means that they are associated with him as members of his renewed Israel.

There seems to be more to this phrase than this when applied to Jesus, though, for it is notable how frequently it is the demons who recognize Jesus this way (e.g. Mark 3:11; 5:7), and they do not address others (such as the disciples) as 'the son of God' or even 'son of God'.

Jesus' sonship is not of the same kind as that of the disciples, however, just as they are not Israel in the same way as he is Israel. Jesus

181

What do you think?
GOD AS JESUS' FATHER

Jesus' address to God as 'abba (Mark 14:36) is, as we saw, not entirely unique to him in form, but in content, implying a great intimacy with God, it is highly unusual. Use a Bible concordance (book or computer) to look up the places in the synoptic Gospels where Jesus speaks of God either as 'my father' or 'the father', noting the distribution of them: (a) among the Gospels; (b) in the different sections of Jesus' ministry (birth stories, Galilean ministry, journey to Jerusalem, in Jerusalem, after his death).

What patterns of meaning emerge? In what kinds of teaching does Jesus speak of God this way? What are the results and meaning of Jesus' sonship in practice for him and for others?

speaks of God as 'my father' (see the box above) and 'your father' (e.g. Matt. 5:16, 45, 48; Mark 11:25; Luke 12:32) – but never of 'our father', where 'our' means Jesus plus the disciples.

He also speaks of himself as the unique revealer of the Father in Matt. 11:27 and Luke 10:22: 'All things have been handed over to me by my Father; and no one knows the son except the Father, and no one knows the Father except the son and anyone to whom the son chooses to reveal him.' Here there is no obvious link with messiahship, and the strong language concerning Jesus' intimacy with the Father is sometimes claimed as evidence that it is inauthentic.

Two factors suggest that this saying is likely to be from Jesus. First, its form reflects the lack of the reciprocal pronoun 'one another'

in Aramaic, so that Jesus cannot directly say 'the Father and the son know one another'. Second, the first part of the verse is not about the authority Jesus receives after the resurrection (cf. Matt. 28:19), but it is about what has been *revealed* to Jesus (see Matt. 11:25). Given that the first part is about God revealing himself fully to Jesus, it is most likely that the second part is about Jesus revealing God to others – something Jesus can do uniquely because of his intimate sonship. Thus Jesus' sonship is unique, and reflects his 'totalitarian' claims, such as:

● the need to acknowledge him before people in order to be acknowledged before the Father (Matt. 10:32f.);
● the blessing on the one who is not offended at him (Matt. 11:6);
● the parable of the two house builders, making it clear that obedience to what he says is the crucial thing (Matt. 7:24-27; Luke 6:47-49);
● the claim that the way to be saved is to lose one's life for Jesus' sake (Mark 8:34-38);
● his statement that heaven and earth will disappear and his words will still stand (Mark 13:31; Matt. 24:35; Luke 21:33).

While the synoptic Gospels do not speak in terms of Jesus' divine nature when they use 'son of God' terminology, they do imply an intimacy of relationship with Yahweh, a ready obedience to the will of Yahweh, and a personal authority which is on a level with that of Yahweh. They suggest that the coming of God to redeem his people, expected from the OT, is happening in Jesus, and that God is present with his people. They use language from a Jewish framework, therefore, in the way they speak of Jesus' divine sonship, a sonship which was made clearer by the resurrection of Jesus (e.g. Rom. 1:3f.) and which would allow the

182

early Christians to speak of their adoption as God's sons and daughters through Jesus and by the Spirit (e.g. Gal. 4:6).

JESUS AS THE SON OF MAN (see also p. 175)
'The son of man' is unique among the descriptions of Jesus, for it is the only one found exclusively on the lips of Jesus in the Gospels – indeed, it is found rarely outside the Gospels (only four times in the rest of the NT, contrasting with over 90 times in the Gospels). It seems to have been a favourite self-designation of Jesus, and is used by him more frequently than any other description of himself.

We noted (p. 175) that Dan. 7:13f. is a key source for understanding Jesus' use of the term. Jesus was not alone in using this phrase: others are clearly influenced by Dan. 7 (esp. 1 Enoch 37–71 and 4 Ezra 13, which both use the phrase of a messianic figure). However, the phrase can also be an Aramaic form of self-reference, meaning something like 'a man like myself' and used to make statements which are true of the speaker and of people in general. Some of Jesus' 'son of man' sayings might be understood by this means, e.g. Mark 2:28 states that 'the son of man is lord even of the Sabbath' following on Jesus' pronouncement that the Sabbath was made for people in general. If 'the son of man' in v. 28 means 'people in general, including Jesus', then it means that people have authority over the Sabbath. On occasions it seems to be used of a more specific group of people which includes the speaker.

However, there are other 'son of man' sayings which speak of Jesus' future and clearly allude to Dan. 7, especially Mark 8:38; 13:26; 14:62 (and parallels). In these cases Jesus is comparing himself to the son of man as a representative figure who comes

to the Ancient of Days and is vindicated. Noticeably, the 'coming' involved is coming *to God* with the clouds, rather than floating to earth on the clouds. This suggests that when Jesus takes up the Dan. 7 'son of man' language he is speaking of his future vindication. N. T. Wright in particular argues that it is unlikely that Jesus speaks of his 'second coming' by his allusions to Dan. 7, but rather that he speaks of his vindication, which Wright believes will be seen in the fall of Jerusalem in AD 70 (Wright 1996, 513-19). It is problematic for Wright's view that the earliest Christians, when they speak of Jesus' vindication, do it in terms of Jesus' resurrection (e.g. Acts 2:23f., 32f., 36), rather than a forthcoming fall of the city.

The Dan. 7 allusion also raises the question of the nature of the son of man, for when 1 Enoch and 4 Ezra take up this figure, their son of man appears divine, in line with the great authority invested in him by the Ancient of Days (Dan. 7:14). Further, he is closely associated with God, for clouds are a frequent OT image for the divine presence (e.g. Exod. 13:21f.; 19:9, 16; 2 Chron. 5:13f.). It is possible, perhaps probable, then, that we should see 'the son of man' in Jewish usage as being a figure closely associated with God – to the extent of becoming a 'second power' alongside Yahweh in the heavens. Such a background makes good sense of sayings about the son of man's present and future authority (e.g. Mark 2:10, 28; 8:38; 13:26; 14:62), and suggests that Jesus' use of this term speaks of his authority without having the danger of misunderstanding associated with 'Messiah'.

Alongside the stress on the son of man's authority and power goes frequent teaching on the son of man's forthcoming suffering (e.g. Mark 8:31; 9:12, 31; 10:33). While Jesus as the son of man exercises divine authority, he exercises it in weakness and suffering. But this suffering will lead to his vindication and the fresh recognition of his authority, as the Dan. 7 allusion in Jesus' sayings about the son of man's future makes clear.

It is hardly surprising that the earliest Christians rapidly ceased to use this term, for its strongly Jewish flavour and the allusive nature of the connection with Dan. 7 meant that the Gentiles with whom they spoke of Jesus would find it hard to understand. Modern readers of the Gospels have similar problems – which suggests that today's Christians would be wise to use other terms in speaking of Jesus too. A common mistake that is made is to think that 'son of man' refers to Jesus' humanity and 'son of God' to his divinity, whereas we have seen that both phrases seem to have both elements at least to some degree.

SUMMING UP: JESUS AND THE PURPOSES OF YAHWEH

How, then, can we sum up Jesus' own sense of his identity and mission? Jesus under-stands himself within a thoroughly Jewish framework, using imagery used in both the OT and later Jewish writings, but brings this imagery together in a fresh way. There is lit-tle evidence that (prior to Jesus) the images of the suffering servant, the Messiah, the son of man and the son of God were widely used together of the same person: with Jesus a startling confluence of ideas emerges which retells the story of Israel.

Jesus comes to renew Israel, to restore the nation to its mission to be Yahweh's vehicle for blessing the world, as God had long before promised to Abram (Gen. 12:3). However, as the people of Israel grew

numerically they treated God's choice of the nation as though it were mere favouritism, like a parent having a favourite child who was spoilt by being given more than other children. Within the OT prophets and in later Jewish writings the idea develops that not all who are ethnically Jewish are truly members of Israel, expressed by speaking of the need for people's hearts to be circumcized (e.g. Jer. 4:4; 9:25) or there being a 'remnant' who remain faithful to Yahweh within Israel (e.g. Isa. 10:20-22; 37:31f.; Zeph. 3:12f.). This comes to focus in the promise of a new covenant in which people's hearts are changed, the torah becomes internalized and they receive forgiveness (Jer. 31:31-34; cf. Ezek. 36:22-32).

Jesus, it seems, is at the heart of these processes, for he is the one true Israelite – he is the faithful remnant who lives under and brings in the reign of God. He teaches that the problems lie in people's hearts, which means their thoughts and wills (e.g. Mark 7:21; 10:5), and his ethical teaching presupposes a renewal of the heart (see p. 172). And he is the one through whom the covenant renewal will happen, as his words at the Last Supper clearly indicate (Luke 22:20; 1 Cor. 11:25). Ultimately, Jesus comes to believe that it is through his death and vindication in the resurrection that Yahweh's purposes for Israel and the world will be achieved, and he goes to die in this expectation.

More than that, Jesus' welcome of Gentiles who come to him and his commission of his followers after his resurrection to go to all nations (Matt. 28:18-20) shows him seeing promises of blessing to Gentiles which begin with the promise to Abram (Gen. 12:3) and stretch through the OT (e.g. Zech. 8:20-23;

Isa. 49:6). Out of the other side of his resurrection comes a people of God which fulfils Yahweh's promise to Abram and includes the Gentiles – but how that comes about is told by Acts, rather than the Gospels.

SOME ISSUES FOR TODAY

● The picture of Jesus we have reconstructed is very Jewish, whereas for much of Christian history 'the Jews' have been vilified as the race who crucified Jesus. This distancing from Judaism is reflected in many pictures of Jesus throughout Christian history as a white European with blue eyes and blond hair. Today's readers of the Gospels, especially Christian readers, need to pay careful attention to this phenomenon in order to see the Jewish roots of their faith and to portray Jesus rightly. This should result in both greater respect for Jewish people today, and a consequent desire that Jewish people hear and respond to Jesus for themselves.

● The OT basis of much of Jesus' teaching challenges the ignorance of the OT among many Christian readers, who regard it as much less important than the NT. Jesus' positive view of the OT, along with the fact that the NT will largely be misunderstood without the OT, invites and summons Christians to know the OT, including its big themes and ideas, well enough to pick up allusions and citations from the OT in the teaching and ministry of Jesus.

● Jesus' understanding of God embraces distance and intimacy, for he recognizes Yahweh as king of the universe and calls his followers to obedience, but at the same time he teaches them to speak to God as 'abba, using an intimate family form of address. Christians easily slide into paying attention to one of these characteristics of God at the expense of the other. Jesus' incorporation of his followers into an extended form of his sonship of God brings believers into a relationship with God which combines respect and intimacy, and prompts reflection on the way Christians regard God. In particular, it invites readers to think on the balance of their own prayers in relation to those of Jesus.

● Christians easily focus on the church as the heart of God's purposes and action, whereas Jesus focuses on God's reign or kingdom. Jesus' announcement of the presence of the kingdom offers a challenge to see God at work in the whole of world history, and not simply inside the walls of churches.

● Jesus' expectation that God would vindicate him is fulfilled in his resurrection and is yet to be fulfilled in the final renewal of creation at the End. The End of all things has barely featured in church history and Christian teaching and preaching, except at times of suffering and persecution. This lack calls for serious thought, for it suggests that Christian believers can easily become like the Sadducees, so comfortable in this world that they have no place in their thinking and living for its ultimate renewal at the End, and for understanding and living in the light of God's judgement to come on that day.

ESSAY TOPICS

INTRODUCTORY

● Outline Jesus' view of the OT Scriptures in relation to himself and his mission.

● 'I think it highly probable that Jesus himself intended the action [in the Jerusalem Temple] to predict the destruction of the Temple, rather than to symbolize its need of purification.' (E. P. Sanders) How far do you agree with this assessment of Jesus' actions in the temple reported in Mark 11:15-17 and parallels?

● Write a letter to a friend who knows little about the Bible (so avoid technical language and scholarly jargon!) to explain what we know about how Jesus himself saw his role and mission.

INTERMEDIATE

● How far do you agree with N. T. Wright's view that, prior to his resurrection, Jesus expected his vindication to be seen in the fall of Jerusalem, rather than in a 'second coming' at a later date?

● Which, if any, of the main phrases used to describe Jesus (Messiah, son of God, son of man, king, servant, etc.) are most central to an accurate understanding of his sense of his own identity?

FURTHER READING

INTRODUCTORY

M. J. Borg & N. T. Wright *The Meaning of Jesus: Two Visions*. New York: HarperSanFrancisco, 1998/London: SPCK, 1999 (a readable 'debate' between scholars holding different views).

R. T. France *Jesus the Radical: A Portrait of the Man They Crucified*. 2nd ed. Leicester: IVP, 1989 [US edition: *I Came to Set the Earth on Fire*. Downers Grove: IVP, 1975] (a fine popular treatment of the ministry of Jesus).

DJG articles: 'Clean and Unclean', 'Destruction of Jerusalem', 'Divorce', 'Eschatology', 'Ethics of Jesus', 'Forgiveness of Sins', 'Kingdom of God/Kingdom of Heaven', 'Last supper', 'Law', 'Oaths and Swearing', 'Rich and Poor', 'Sabbath', 'Sermon on the Mount/Plain', 'Servant of Yahweh', 'Sinner', 'Son of David', 'Son of God', 'Son of Man', 'Table Fellowship', 'Temple', 'Temple Cleansing', 'Trial of Jesus', 'Triumphal Entry' (all short, reliable summary articles on key topics).

E. P. Sanders *The Historical Figure of Jesus*. London/New York: Penguin, 1993 (the heart of Sanders' 'new perspective on Judaism' view in an accessible form).

N. T. Wright *The Challenge of Jesus*. London: SPCK, 2000/Downers Grove: IVP, 1999 (a highly accessible outline of Wright's view of Jesus).

INTERMEDIATE

G. R. Beasley-Murray *Jesus and the Kingdom of God*. Grand Rapids: Eerdmans/Exeter: Paternoster, 1986 (a careful discussion of key passages in Jesus' teaching).

J. D. Crossan *The Historical Jesus: The Life of a Mediterranean Jewish Peasant*. New York: HarperSanFrancisco/Edinburgh: T. & T. Clark, 1991 (the fullest treatment by a scholar committed to using the 'apocryphal' Gospels to construct a picture of Jesus, producing a radically different portrayal).

R. T. France *The Gospel According to Matthew: An Introduction and Commentary*. Tyndale NT Commentaries. Leicester: IVP, 1985/Grand Rapids: Eerdmans, 1987, 333-58 (helpful treatment of Matt. 24–25).

R. T. France *Jesus and the Old Testament*. London: Tyndale Press/Downers Grove: IVP, 1971 (careful discussion of Jesus' use of the OT).

A. E. Harvey *Strenuous Commands: The Ethic of Jesus*. London: SCM/Philadelphia: Trinity Press International, 1990 (valuable discussion of Jesus' ethics, placing them in the setting of Jesus' day and culture).

G. E. Ladd *The Presence of the Future: The Eschatology of Biblical Realism*. Grand Rapids: Eerdmans, 1974 (helpful study of Jesus' eschatology from a salvation-historical approach).

G. E. Ladd & D. A. Hagner (ed.) *A Theology of the New Testament*, revised ed. Grand Rapids: Eerdmans, 1993/Cambridge: Lutterworth Press, 1994, chs 3–15 (judicious discussion of Jesus' ministry, focused on the kingdom).

R. N. Longenecker *The Christology of Early Jewish Christianity*. London: SCM/Naperville, Allenson, 1970 (valuable discussion of how Jewish believers understood Jesus' status and nature).

I. H. Marshall *The Origins of New Testament Christology*. 2nd ed. Leicester: Apollos/Downers Grove: IVP, 1990 (a thoughtful discussion of the various titles ascribed to Jesus in the Gospels).

S. McKnight *A New Vision for Israel: The Teachings of Jesus in National Context*. Studying the Historical Jesus. Grand Rapids/Cambridge: Eerdmans, 1999 (a valuable and readable overview of Jesus' teaching against the content of Judaism in the first century).

E. P. Sanders *Jesus and Judaism*. London: SCM, 1984/Philadelphia: Fortress, 1985 (a fuller book from the 'new perspective' on Judaism).

G. Theissen & A. Merz *The Historical Jesus: A Comprehensive Guide*. London: SCM/Philadelphia: Fortress, 1998, chs 8–16 (an accessible guide with helpful activities to try).

G. Vermes *Jesus the Jew: A Historian's Reading of the Gospels*. London: Collins, 1973/Philadelphia: Fortress, 1981 (a seminal interpretation of Jesus' Jewishness, by a Jewish scholar).

N. T. Wright *Jesus and the Victory of God*. London: SPCK/Philadelphia: Fortress, 1996, parts II–IV (very stimulating and readable discussion of Jesus in his historical context, but long).

GETTING INTO
THE FOUR
GOSPELS

Chapter 9

MARK

STRUCTURE

As we saw earlier (pp. 62-4), Mark is likely to be the earliest of the Gospels to be written, and so we are studying it first. Mark shares some features of other genres of ancient literature, particularly the 'lives' or *bioi*, but it is also doing something new, particularly because of its focus on the death of Jesus. We can see the weight which Mark gives to the cross from the proportion of the book given to the last week of the life of Jesus: from 11:1 onwards the action is in Jerusalem – almost half of the book – and Mark leads us through this section with more precise notes of the progress of time (notice 11:12, 20, 27; 14:1, 12; 15:1; 16:1, 2), by contrast with his vaguer time links earlier in the story (e.g. 2:1; 3:1, 19; 4:1; 6:1).

While the death of Jesus is hinted at from early in the Gospel (note 2:19f.; 3:6 particularly), it does not come fully into focus until the series of predictions of the death of Jesus in 8:31; 9:31 and 10:33f. Until 8:31 our attention is drawn again and again to the question of Jesus' identity (see pp. 202f. on Mark's Christology), recognized by Peter at 8:29, 'You are the Messiah', although Peter's response to Jesus' next

words about his forthcoming suffering and death shows that his grasp is still only partial (8:32f.). However, the identification of Jesus is then confirmed by the voice of God on the mountain (9:7), and from this point Mark turns the spotlight onto the cross.

These observations lead to a two-part outline of Mark:

1:1–8:30	Who is this man? The road to Caesarea Philippi
8:31–16:8	Why will Jesus die? The road to Jerusalem

We shall see more as we turn to a journey through Mark passage by passage.

A WALK THROUGH MARK

Mark begins his Gospel with a declaration which ensures that his readers know from the start who Jesus is as Messiah (= 'Christ') and son of God (1:1). Although some ancient manuscripts do not have 'the son of God' in this verse, it seems most likely that it was in Mark's original text, not least because of the counterpart 'son of God' at the end of the Gospel (15:39, the centurion's recognition of Jesus at the cross). The rest of the book will fill out this brief summary, which is perhaps

Digging deeper:
GETTING AN OVERVIEW OF MARK

Read through the whole of Mark's Gospel (preferably at one sitting, so that you get the big picture of the book) noting (with references) what Mark says about Jesus under four headings: (1) his identity (2) his actions (3) his teaching (4) the reactions of others to him. Note also any questions which reading Mark right through has raised for you. This should take a couple of hours.

If you meet with others to discuss this, you might then:

● spend five minutes individually writing down: (a) something which surprised you about Mark; (b) something which was a new insight; (c) a particular question which was raised for you; (d) a point you want to find out more about.
● in pairs share your notes on these four points with your partner, and then get each pair to tell the group something from (a) or (b) which they found.
● divide into four groups, and each group take one of the four topics you thought about as you read Mark (Jesus' identity, actions, teaching, and others' reactions to him) and spend 15 minutes producing a short summary of your findings (as a one-paragraph statement or a series of bullet points).
● share the summaries in turn with the whole group, and give the other three groups time to ask questions of the group who wrote each summary, to clarify or explain points more fully.

meant as a title to the whole book. Mark's choice of 'beginning' may suggest 'origin' or 'source' – in other words, Mark is narrating the events which are the basis of *the* good news about Jesus (see pp. 51f. on 'gospel').

1:2-13 then sets the scene, first by introducing John the Baptist (vv. 4-8), a figure fulfilling OT prophecy (1:2f. combines Isa. 40:3 and Mal. 3:1) whose role is to prepare the way for Jesus, and then by introducing Jesus (vv. 9-13). Here we see Jesus baptized by John, hearing God's voice identify him as God's servant from Isa. 42:1 and as the royal 'son' of Ps. 2:7, a psalm for a king (v. 11), and empowered by the Spirit (v. 10). Jesus' baptism leads to Mark's brief report of his temptation in the desert by Satan (vv. 12f.; cf. Matt. 4:1-11; Luke 4:1-11) – led there by the Spirit.

1:14–3:6 then shows us Jesus at work and introduces many of the major themes which Mark will develop in his book, particularly focusing on the authority of Jesus.

First, Jesus announces his message (1:14f.), which Mark identifies as 'the good news of God', a message with three key elements: 'the time is fulfilled', 'the kingdom of God has come near' and 'repent and believe in the good news'. The first indicates that the decisive moment of history has arrived – God's promises through the prophets are now going to be fulfilled; the second that God is about to arrive to rule (cf. the use of the same Greek word here translated 'has

---

MARK: A WRITER IN A HURRY!

Mark's story always seems to rush along: things happen 'immediately' (or equivalent phrases in English, such as 'as soon as') over 40 times (e.g. 1:20, 29; 3:6; 5:2). He connects sentences together in strings with 'and', rather than using shorter sentences. And his is the shortest of our four Gospels. That said, when Mark shares a story with Matthew and/or Luke, his version of the story is usually the longest.

SECRECY

In the early chapters of Mark Jesus regularly commands people and demons to say nothing about what has happened, or who he truly is (e.g. 1:25, 34, 44; 3:12; 5:43; 7:36). There are times when Jesus withdraws, sometimes to pray (1:35; 3:7, 13; 7:24). He also gives some teaching privately to the disciples (e.g. 4:33f.; 7:17; 9:28f., 30-32) and tells them not to tell others about it (8:30; 9:9). Further, he appears to tell parables in order to prevent people outside the disciple group understanding him (4:10-12, 33f.).

This leads some, particularly William Wrede, to argue that the secrecy theme was an attempt by Mark to explain how the Jesus whom the early Christians worshipped as son of God and Messiah (titles which Wrede thought really meant the same thing, a divine figure) had not been recognized as such during his lifetime. Three key factors argue against this view and clarify the kind of secrecy that may have been behind these reports.

- As well as the commands to secrecy there are also examples of Jesus healing or exorcizing in public (e.g. 1:12; 3:3-5; 5:30). And Mark records that people didn't always keep quiet (e.g. 1:45).
- Mark highlights the disciples' lack of understanding at key points, not least when Jesus teaches about his forthcoming suffering (e.g. 8:32; 9:32). This is entirely consonant with the frequent claim in the speeches of Acts and the NT letters that the resurrection of Jesus was the event which clarified who Jesus was (e.g. Rom. 1:3f.; Acts 2:32-36).
- Wrede was mistaken in thinking that the miracles would have been interpreted as pointing to Jesus' divinity: some OT prophets raised the dead (e.g. Elijah and Elisha) and were not regarded as divine (cf. Luke 7:16).

Overall, then, Wrede highlights a key theme, but draws mistaken conclusions from it. It is entirely possible that Jesus himself did use parables to avoid being understood publicly too quickly. To use enigmatic stories and sayings was a way of raising the issues he was concerned about without saying things so blatantly that the crisis came too early for Jesus' understanding of the purposes of God through his life (Wright 1996, 179f., 181f., 236f.). Such stories and sayings also allowed people time to discover Jesus' identity for themselves.

---

come near' [ēngiken] in 14:42, where it is translated 'is at hand'); and the third that a response is required of wholeheartedly turning back to Yahweh and trusting entirely in the message Jesus brings.

Jesus next calls his first followers (1:16-20), who respond without hesitation to his summons to go and 'fish for people' (v. 17). Mark then shows us what Jesus can do (1:21-33), by giving us a Sabbath day in the life of Jesus, during which he teaches with authority (v. 22), casts out a demon (vv. 23-26), heals Simon's mother-in-law (vv. 30f.), and then further defeats both disease and demons in the city of Capernaum (vv. 32-34). No wonder that the people are amazed and tell others (vv. 22, 27f.) – although Jesus himself forbids the demons to say who he is (v. 34). This 'typical day' is followed by a tour of the region with the same features, preaching and power (1:35-39). The healing of a man with leprosy (1:40-45) adds to our growing sense of Jesus' authority, for Jesus, by healing the man, restores him to the community – a community from which the Jewish law had excluded him (cf. Lev. 13:45f.). Jesus carefully ensures that the man will have his healing verified by the priest, the public health official of the day (cf. Lev. 14:1-32), thus showing that Jesus is not against the law. As with the demons, Jesus tells the man not to tell others (v. 44) – although without success (v. 45).

On completing his travels, Jesus returns to Capernaum (2:1) and is in demand (2:2). In healing the paralysed man (2:3-12) Jesus then encounters the first of a series of challenges to his authority. At this stage of the story, however, the challenges are indirect: they come by Jesus knowing people's thoughts (2:6-8; 3:2), by people asking Jesus' disciples questions (2:16), or by others asking Jesus about his disciples (2:18, 23). There is no direct confrontation with Jesus about himself yet. As we read these conflict stories we learn more about Jesus: he can forgive sins as well as heal (2:5-12); he calls sinful people to follow him, including mixing with the hated tax collectors (2:13-17); he brings something new which means that fasting is inappropriate, thus undermining the Jewish law (2:18-22); he is greater than the institution of the Sabbath, one of the pillars of Judaism, so that his disciples can pluck and grind grain on that day (2:23-28), and he himself can heal on the Sabbath (3:1-6).

Looking back from 3:6, we have met the personal authority of Jesus as healer, exorcist and teacher, an authority which is critical of Jewish tradition and practice, particularly in the area of purity – this is a man who mixes with sinful people, who touches lepers and who violates the Sabbath! So it is no surprise that opposition against Jesus is beginning to stir, opposition which displays 'hardness of heart' (3:5), a characteristic of Pharaoh in opposing what Yahweh was doing in saving the people through Moses from slavery in Egypt (Exod. 7:13f., etc.). This opposition begins to organize itself as the uneasy alliance of the political élite (the Herodians) and the purists (the Pharisees) confer how to get rid of Jesus (3:6).

3:7–6:6 begins with a Markan summary (3:7-12) which shows that Jesus' ministry is spreading wider than Galilee (v. 8). Jesus then selects his key core group, the twelve apostles (3:13-19a) who will be with him to be trained and then sent out by him (cf. 6:7). During the remainder of this section we shall see how Jesus acts while the disciples are with him, before they go out *for* him.

Up to this point we know nothing about Jesus' background and family. Now we find Jesus opposed by his relatives: first, they hear stories that he is crazy and so they go to stop him (3:19b-30), leading Jesus to warn about the danger of saying that the work of the Holy Spirit is actually the work of evil (vv. 28-30); second, his mother and brothers are put in their place, for blood relationships are now to be superseded by a community based on obedience to the new revelation of God's will (vv. 33-35).

Although Mark regularly says that Jesus teaches (e.g. 1:21; 2:13; 6:2, 6, 34), he gives us rather less of the *content* of Jesus' teaching than the other evangelists. But here (4:1-34) we encounter Jesus' characteristic teaching style – in parables – and theme – the kingdom of God (note 4:11, 26, 30) (see pp. 100–4). In Mark's presentation the parable of the soils (4:3-9) offers an explanation of differing reactions to Jesus' preaching (4:13-20 – note that Jesus speaks 'the word' in 4:34, which the sower sows in 4:14). Sandwiched between the parable and its explanation is more general teaching about the nature of parables (4:10-13). The following three parables then speak of the need for the light of the kingdom to be seen (4:21-25), the secret growth of the kingdom (4:26-29), and the all-encompassing nature of the kingdom (4:30-32) – the latter perhaps hinting at the inclusion of Gentiles in the people of God. The section is rounded off by a Markan summary (4:33f.).

Four acts of power follow, each demonstrating Jesus' authority: having seen Jesus teach, we now see him act. First he stills the storm on the Sea of Galilee (4:35-41), recalling OT teaching that Yahweh alone has power to control the elements (e.g. Pss 89:8f.; 93:3f.; 106:8f.; 107:23-20; Isa. 51:9f.) – and addressing the waves with the same rebuke he has spoken to the demons, 'Be silent!' (4:39; 1:25). This climax of the story is the disciples' reaction of awe, focusing their (and Mark's readers') attention on the identity of this man (4:41).

Second, Jesus heals a demonized man in the Decapolis, a Gentile area where pigs were kept (5:1-20). Again the demons recognize him and again Jesus delivers the man. However, this time there is no command to silence, but rather the reverse: the man is told to tell what the Lord has done for him (5:19). The previous story parallels this one: Jesus calms aberrant nature, in the storm, and calms aberrant human nature, in the demonized man.

Third we meet another Markan 'sandwich', with the raising of Jairus' daughter (5:21-24, 35-43) wrapped around the healing of the woman with a haemorrhage (5:25-34). In both stories Jesus is in contact with impurity – the girl is dead and the woman is unclean because of the blood. By contrast with Jewish law, which treated impurity as contagious, Jesus' purity flows into the impure, so that the woman is healed by touching Jesus (vv. 27-30) and the girl is raised as Jesus takes her hand (v. 41). In one case Jesus commands silence (v. 43) and in the other forces the public confession of what has happened (vv. 30-34).

In 6:1-6 we again see Jesus in contact with his roots in his home town and, as with the earlier encounter with his family (3:31-35), Jesus is rejected – the unbelief of his own people contrasts starkly with the faith of the woman who was healed (6:6; 5:34).

6:7–8:26 has as a theme the disciples' continuing lack of faith and understanding: throughout they seem to take two steps forward and then three steps back!

Immediately Mark's sandwiching technique reappears, but this time he wraps a story in present time – the mission of the twelve (6:7-13, 30-32) – around a flashback to the death of John the Baptist (6:14-29). During their mission the disciples move forward, reproducing and extending the ministry of Jesus (6:12f.; cf. 1:15, 32-34, 39), which leads to Herod's curiosity (6:14-16) and the account of John's death. John's death foreshadows Jesus' own death, for Jesus too is righteous

What do you think?
MARKAN SANDWICHES

Mark frequently uses a sandwiching technique (known technically as 'intercalation') with stories, wrapping one story around another. Possibly the best-known example is the combination of Jesus' cursing of the fig tree and his demonstration in the temple (11:12-21). When Mark does this readers should ask how Mark is using the interaction between the two stories: for example, do they help to interpret each other, or is there a contrast implied by this juxtaposition? Often the central part of the sandwich is highlighted by this arrangement.

Consider the Markan sandwiches in 5:21-43 and 14:1-11. What literary and theological effect(s) has Mark created by using this technique in each passage? How far does recognizing this technique help in understanding the point(s) Mark is making in each case?

What do you think?
INCIDENTAL DETAILS IN MARK

Mark is a vivid writer, painting scenes with touches which help readers to visualize them. He includes details unimportant to the meaning of the story, and these may be signs of the use of eyewitness testimony by Mark: for example, the 'green grass' (6:39), suggesting that this event took place in the early spring, before the heat made it brown; or the very precise description of actions of Jesus (7:33; 9:36; 10:16). Mark 9:14-29 and 10:17-22 contain large amounts of such incidental detail (contrast the much briefer versions in Matt. 17:14-21; Luke 9:37-43 and Matt. 19:23-20; Luke 18:24-30).

Consider the examples above, using a Gospels synopsis to see the parallels in Matthew and Luke, if possible. What other explanations could be offered for Mark's use of detail? Which explanation(s) do you find most persuasive and why?

(v. 20) and will be put to death because of political manoeuvring (vv. 19, 22-28).

The next two stories occur together in three of the four Gospels (the exception is Luke, who lacks the second): feeding five thousand people and walking on water (6:30-52). Both show Jesus' great power and authority, now over nature and not simply disease and demons, as well as the disciples' dullness, for they cannot see how the crowd can be fed (v. 37) and panic when they see Jesus walking on the lake (vv. 49f.). There are OT overtones from the stories of Elijah and Elisha in the feeding story (cf. 1 Kgs 17:10-24; 2 Kgs 4:32-44), hinting that Jesus is greater than these prophets. Then, in the midst of the storm, Jesus takes to himself the name of

God, 'I am' (v. 50), usually translated, 'It is I' – and this takes the disciples' understanding on from the previous stilling of the storm (4:35-41). Mark's readers are being led to see Jesus' true nature.

MARK'S LINGUISTIC BACKGROUND

Mark writes Greek as his second language. There are a number of places where he uses semitic turns of phrase which show that he thinks in Aramaic – rather like someone today whose mother tongue is English having to write in German. Examples include the unnecessary duplication of verbs of speech, such as 'he answered and said' (e.g. 6:37; 7:28 – often seen more clearly in older, more word-for-word English translations such as the AV/KJV) or 'X began to ...' (e.g. 1:45; 4:1; 6:2, 7) (see further Cranfield 1959, 20f.).

A Markan summary follows (6:53-56), describing Jesus' continuing ministry in the villages of Galilee, before another controversy, about ritual purity (7:1-23). As with the previous controversies (2:1–3:6), the accusation is not directly against Jesus (v. 5), and the outcome undermines the place of tradition (vv. 9-13), and even of the law itself (v. 19, although this looks like Mark's editorial comment from a later perspective: it would be hard to understand why there were such controversies about food in the early church if Jesus had settled the matter clearly). More than that, Jesus brings in a new, messianic age, where the torah is superseded, and this again identifies him as Messiah.

After meeting the hostility of Jewish teachers, Mark presents a Gentile woman who has faith in Jesus (7:24-30), a contrast which would have been welcome to Gentile readers of the book. Again Jesus' power is seen, for here he exorcises at a distance (vv. 29f.). As normally during his ministry, Jesus does not seek the woman out, but helps Gentiles who come to him for help. Jesus, still in Gentile territory (v. 31), then heals a deaf and dumb man (7:31-37), and Mark reports the Aramaic word used, 'Ephphatha' (v. 34) and translates it, 'Be opened', suggesting that his readers do not know Aramaic. Mark's second feeding miracle (8:1-10) is located within this same Gentile region, and thus need not be seen as merely a 'doublet' of the earlier feeding (6:30-44) for the second story shows Jesus as the bread of life for Gentiles as well as Jews. This group of stories set in a Gentile context shows Jesus as one who cares for Gentiles as well as Jews, and thus shows Mark's (mainly) Gentile readers that they too are included in God's purposes because of Jesus.

After all that Jesus has done, readers might then be surprised at the lack of understanding and opposition in the three following paragraphs, all of which are set in Jewish territory. First, the Pharisees come and ask for a sign (8:11-13) – after Jesus has done so many! Then the disciples do not understand Jesus' comments about being cautious of the yeast of the Pharisees and Herod, for they are still thinking too literally (8:14-21). Mark then tells the story of the healing of the blind man at Bethsaida (8.22-26), which offers a commentary on the disciples' lack of understanding: just as they see what Jesus is saying only in part (vv. 17f.), so the blind man comes to see partially and then fully. What follows, both immediately and in the rest of the book, will be the gradual dawning of full sight on the disciples.

8:27–9:8 is a key series of stories for the disciples' understanding of Jesus and his mission, and bridges the two halves of the book. First Jesus asks them who others are saying that he is (8:27-30), and the answers echo those Herod heard (6:14-16). Jesus then presses the point, and asks who the disciples themselves think he is. Peter's response shows how far the disciples' understanding has grown, calling Jesus directly 'Messiah'. But Jesus goes on to speak (for the first time in this Gospel) concerning both his own forthcoming suffering (8:31) and the accompanying suffering of his followers (8:34-38). The first of these is too much for Peter, who rebukes Jesus and is in turn rebuked by Jesus, who calls Peter 'Satan' – a startling title (8:32f.). The partial sight theme is still with us, for although Peter has seen that Jesus is Messiah, he has not yet seen that this will involve suffering and death – and glory to follow, for Jesus will come 'in the glory of his Father with the holy angels' (8:38). Mark 9:1 closes this scene enigmatically: what does Jesus mean by seeing 'that the kingdom of God has come with power' and when will it happen? It may refer back to 8:38, which seems to hint of the 'coming' seen in Dan. 7:13 and echoed in Mark 13:26, or it may refer forward to 9:2-8, the transfiguration of Jesus six days later, or to the resurrection of Jesus (which the transfiguration foreshadows).

That appearance of Jesus in glory develops the understanding of the three disciples present further, for they experience the voice from heaven (v. 7), echoing the voice at Jesus' baptism (1:11) – but this time it is addressed to the disciples rather than to Jesus. The scene echoes the experiences of meeting God on a mountain of Moses (Exod. 19, 24) and Elijah (1 Kgs 19:8-18), who both appear and speak with Jesus – but it also shows Jesus as greater than either of these great men of the past as the beloved son of God, the one who is to be listened to with care.

9:9–10:52 picks up themes which have already been mentioned, but with a focus on what it means to follow Jesus. The section from 8:27 to 10:52 can be seen as a painting in three panels, each beginning with a prediction of Jesus' suffering and each containing teaching on discipleship. It looks like Mark is gathering teaching material on this topic together thematically (Best 1983, 84-9). Thus, in the first panel (8:27–9:29), 8:27-33 is the passion prediction, underlined in 9:12. Mark then presents Jesus teaching that discipleship will involve suffering (8:34-38) and listening to Jesus (9:7). Indeed, Jesus is the one who succeeds where his faithless disciples fail to exorcise the epileptic boy (9:14-29) – they fail because they have not prayed (9:29) or trusted God sufficiently (9:23).

The second panel (9:30–10:31) begins with a passion prediction (9:30-32) which, again, the disciples fail to understand, and then focuses on the relationships among the disciple group. To their argument about greatness Jesus responds by teaching about how to treat the weakest (9:33-37). To their argument about who should be included in the group, Jesus responds inclusively and warns against putting stumbling blocks in the way of others, or oneself (9:38-48). A call to peaceful relationships sums this up (9:49f.), and is then spelled out in two ways. First, Jesus is opposed to divorce (10:1-12) because he believes in the importance of the marriage relationship on the basis of Gen. 2:24; and second, Jesus sees children as within the family of God (10:13-16), rather than as unworthy of his attention. The challenge of discipleship is hammered home by the rich man who goes away sad when told by Jesus that he must give up everything to follow him (10:17-31).

The third panel (10:32-52) again begins with a passion prediction (10:32-34) and is followed by another argument among the disciples about greatness, precipitated by James and John asking for the best seats in Jesus' kingdom (10:35-45). Jesus teaches in response that true greatness is about following him in the way of suffering, imaged by a cup and a baptism (v. 38), and that service is the way to be great in his kingdom (vv. 43f.) – service which Jesus himself models by giving his own life as a ransom (v. 45). The disciples will be servants because their master has first served them in his death. The panel then closes with the suggestive story of Bartimaeus' healing (10:46-52), echoing the healing of the blind man in 8:22-26, just prior to this 'discipleship' section of the Gospel. In Bartimaeus' case the discipleship motif is seen in that he moves from sitting 'by the way' (v. 46) to following Jesus 'in the way' (v. 52) after he is able to see – the way which leads to the cross. This vividly illustrates the journey the disciples must take as they are able to see who Jesus is and what he does more and more clearly. Mark's irony comes out in showing that blind Bartimaeus' sight is clearer than the disciples', for he acclaims Jesus as 'son of David', a messianic title, twice (vv. 47f.) and thus shows that he sees who Jesus truly is.

11:1–13:37 From 11:1 we move to Jerusalem, and Mark now focuses on the events leading to the death of Jesus. A key theme of Jesus' kingship comes into greater focus as Jesus enters the city as king, but riding a donkey, which symbolizes an arrival in peace rather than war (11:1-10). Thus, after again demonstrating his power over nature in riding an unbroken donkey (v. 2), he is welcomed as bringing the kingdom of David (v. 10, echoing 'son of David', 10:47f.), his arrival alludes to Zion's king arriving on a donkey (Zech. 9:9), and there may be an echo of Solomon's arrival (1 Kgs 1:38-40). (See more fully p. 156.)

After his arrival Jesus inspects the temple (11:11) as he will inspect the fig tree the following morning (11:12-14). To curse the fig tree as Jesus does looks irrational to modern Western eyes, but notice how Mark has sandwiched this story with the demonstration in the temple (11:15-17; the fig tree's demise is noted in 11:20-25). This sandwiching suggests that the cursing is an acted parable of the coming destruction of the temple, symbolically acted out in Jesus turning over tables and throwing out the traders – and about which ch. 13 will warn more explicitly.

Mark then leads us through a series of controversy stories (11:27–12:37) and now, as the plot against Jesus accelerates, the controversies are directly about him and addressed to him. First all three major groups of Jewish leaders – chief priests, scribes and elders – ask about his authority to act as he does, not least in the light of the demonstration in the temple (11:27-33). Jesus responds brilliantly by linking his own authority with that of John the Baptist, leaving the authorities in an impossible position (vv. 31f.), which demonstrates their duplicity. Jesus goes on to tell the story of the tenants in the vineyard (12:1-12), saying as clearly as he can that the Jewish leadership will lose their power (v. 12), and the vineyard – a symbol for Israel (Isa. 5:1-7) – will be handed over to the leadership of others. The leaders' fear of the crowd (v. 12, cf. 11:32) means that they withdraw and send others to take Jesus on (v. 13). The alliance of Pharisees and Herodians (cf. 3:6) ask about the legality of paying taxes to Caesar and receive Jesus' ingenious response which exposes their hypocrisy in asking and

prioritizes the service of God (12:13-17). The Sadducees characteristically ask about resurrection (12:18-27) and Jesus argues that resurrection is there in the Scriptures they recognize, citing Exod. 3:6, 15 to show that the patriarchs are still alive. A question from a more friendly scribe follows (12:28-34) about the greatest commandment, to which Jesus responds with a combination of Deut. 6:4f. and Lev. 19:18. The scribe recognizes Jesus' wisdom, and Jesus responds further with warmth (v. 34) – the only occasion in Mark when a scribe is portrayed positively in relation to Jesus.

Now that Jesus has silenced the questions of all the major groupings who oppose him (v. 34b), he can ask his own question, based on Ps. 110:1, again picking up the theme of Jesus' kingship. Jesus' question suggests that the Messiah, who is expected to be a Davidic descendant or 'son', is also greater than David. Having interpreted the law well in his answers to the Sadducees and the scribe, Jesus now interprets the prophets with wisdom – demonstrating him to be the supreme interpreter of Scripture, rather than the official teachers of Judaism. Not only that, but these teachers are dangerous and hypocritical (12:38-40), even causing the poor widow to suffer (12:41-44).

This teaching has taken place in the temple, and we now learn Jesus' view of the temple in ch. 13. This chapter's meaning is hotly debated, as to whether Jesus is speaking about the destruction of the temple in AD 70, about his future 'second coming', or about both (see p. 163). The destruction of the temple is clearly in view, at least some of the time (vv. 1f., 14-18), and the chapter is using vivid language of cosmic destruction (e.g. vv. 24f.) to convey the importance and power of the events being spoken about.

14:1–16:8 form Mark's passion narrative proper, and spotlight the cross. Now the threefold prediction (8:31; 9:31; 10:33) will come to fulfilment as the son of God, Israel's king, dies for the nation and the world. Mark 14:1-11 sets the scene by highlighting the plot against Jesus (vv. 1f.), the anointing of Jesus for burial (vv. 3-9), and Judas' agreement to betray Jesus (vv. 10f., cf. vv. 18-21). Mark then shows us the meaning of the cross in the new Passover which Jesus initiates (14:12-25), focused in the words over the bread and cup. Jesus is accomplishing a new exodus, greater than that which Moses led; instead of the blood of animals it will be his blood – his life laid down in death – which will seal this covenant (v. 24).

The Passover theme continues as the group sing the Passover psalms (from Pss 113–118) and go to what seems to have been a regular place of prayer for Jesus (14:26, 32). As they walk there Jesus tells them that they will all abandon him, even Peter, who protests his faithfulness (14:27-31). Almost at once they fail Jesus by sleeping when he has asked them to wait for him (14:32-42), and Mark portrays Jesus struggling with the cup of suffering to come (cf. 10:38f.) – a scene with only Jesus present to see it. As Jesus is still rebuking the disciples for sleeping Judas arrives with an armed gang from the Jewish leaders. They take Jesus away and, as he has prophesied, the disciples all abandon him (14:43-52).

Jesus then faces two trials, first before a Jewish Sanhedrin (14:53-65; 15:1a) and then before Pilate, the representative of Roman power (15:1b-15). In between Mark places the trial of Peter (14:66-72), as Peter fails to stand up for his master. Ironically, Peter is fulfilling Jesus' prophecy as Jesus is on trial as a false prophet (note v. 65)!

IRONY

Mark tells his story in a way which often brings out irony. We have already noticed this in his paralleling of the claim that Jesus is a false prophet with the fulfilment of Jesus' prophecy that Peter will deny him three times (14:30, 65-72), and there are numerous other examples (Camery-Hoggatt 1992, esp. ch. 5).

The Jewish trial centres on failed attempts to find agreed testimony about Jesus (vv. 55-59), and hinges on the high priest's direct challenge (v. 61). Finally, when there is no escaping the question, Jesus agrees that he is Messiah and son of God, but goes on to explain this in terms of the 'son of man' figure from Dan. 7:13f., a figure who represents the people of God (Dan. 7:18). In responding this way Jesus blasphemes (v. 64), for he was claiming to speak and act in the name of Yahweh – whereas those who tried him were clear that he was undermining their faith and way of life.

The Jewish law forbade passing a sentence of death at night and so early the following morning, probably at 6.00 a.m., the Jewish leaders passed the formal sentence (15:1a) and then took Jesus to the Roman procurator (15:1b). The hour of day makes it likely that the crowd who called for Jesus' death were a 'rent-a-mob' under the control of the priests (note v. 11), for what Passover pilgrim would be wandering around near the procurator's palace at that hour during the festival?

Throughout the Roman trial and execution Jesus is portrayed as king (15:2, 9, 12, 18, 26, 32), the one who represents Israel in his own person, the messianic son of David and son of God (15:39 – ironically, recognized by a

Gentile soldier). Mark's choice of language shows us that this man is supremely qualified to die on behalf of the people, for as king he represents them. But kingly language suited the Sanhedrin's purpose too, for to Roman ears it would sound political and revolutionary. Mark also weaves in the story of the replacement of the guilty criminal Barabbas by Jesus (15:6f., 11, 15), suggesting more about the meaning of Jesus' death, for here Jesus, who has done no evil (v. 14), stands in the place of one who is guilty (v. 7).

Mark tells the story of the crucifixion itself very economically and without gory detail (15:21-41). In spite of the mockery of the watchers Jesus does not respond: his words are saved for prayer, praying the words of Ps. 22:1 (v. 34), a psalm of innocent suffering, which shows the depth of his alienation from God at this point – he does not address God with the characteristic 'Abba, Father' (cf. 14:36). The darkness (v. 33) underlines the sense of abandonment by God. Only the women stay with Jesus in his suffering (vv. 40f.).

But in the suffering of Jesus the world is changed: as he dies the temple curtain is torn, perhaps demonstrating the absence of God from the Holy of Holies – the temple truly has been abandoned by Yahweh and will ultimately be destroyed, as Jesus has prophesied (13:1f.; cf. 14:58, ironically!). Access to God is no longer through this building and its sacrificial system, but through the broken body of Jesus. And this is universal, illustrated by the presence of a Gentile soldier at the foot of the cross who recognizes who Jesus truly is (15:39). The scene closes as Jesus is buried by Joseph of Arimathea (15:42-47), underlining that he really was dead, in spite of Pilate's astonishment that he should die so quickly (v. 44).

THE ENDING OF MARK

There is very wide agreement that the two 'endings' of Mark found in some manuscripts are not from Mark's own hand. The 'shorter ending' (16:8b), found in just one manuscript, consists only of a brief summary, and the 'longer ending' (16:9-20) is clearly a patchwork of passages from the other Gospels' resurrection stories, sometimes using their precise words:

> vv. 9-10 = John 20:10-18
> v. 11 = Luke 24:11
> vv. 12-13 = Luke 24:13-32
> v. 14 = Luke 24:36-49
> vv. 15-19 = Matt. 28:16-20

Further, the transition from v. 8a to v. 9 is awkward, the language of vv. 9-20 is not typical of Mark, and our oldest manuscripts end at v. 8a.

This leaves us with the somewhat puzzling ending at v. 8a. It is not easy to decide why this would happen; some possibilities are:

- Mark never finished his Gospel; but even so the break is at an odd place – to finish a Greek sentence with 'for' (*gar*) is poor Greek, even for Mark!
- Mark's original conclusion was lost or destroyed, deliberately or accidentally; but he could have rewritten it unless this happened after his death – but by then there would likely be multiple copies already.
- Mark meant to finish at v. 8a, in parallel with the 'suspended' ending of Acts 28:30f., which leaves the fate of Paul open.

Mark's account of the resurrection is the briefest of our Gospels, for it is likely that it ends at 16:8a (see above for the status of the various 'endings' of Mark found in ancient manuscripts). Nevertheless this ending still accentuates the emptiness of the tomb (vv. 4f.). But to close 'for they were afraid' (v. 8) appears surprising, especially when Mark records that the women said nothing to anyone. However, 'fear' can be a positive thing elsewhere in Mark (e.g. 4:41, where NRSV translates 'great awe'), as is 'amazement' earlier in the verse (cf. 5:42) and so this may be a statement of holy awe rather than abject terror.

SOME KEY THEMES

CHRISTOLOGY

Central to Mark's purpose is enabling his readers to see Jesus as Mark sees him. Notably, Mark uses a number of key descriptions of Jesus to help readers grasp Jesus' identity.

Jesus is the *son of God*. This is the first description of him (1:1) and is given a central place throughout the Gospel. Jesus is recognized as such by demons (1:23-27; 3:11; 5:7), by the divine voice at the baptism and transfiguration (1:11; 9:7) and finally by the centurion who has watched him die (15:39). Only when compelled to do so by oath does Jesus himself accept this description (14:61f.) – and it leads to his death (14:63f.).

With this language go a number of places where the figure of Jesus functions in the same way as Yahweh himself functions in OT passages: he forgives apart from the Jewish priesthood (2:7, 10); he walks on the sea (6:48; cf. Pss 89:9f.; 93:3f.; Job 9:8); he uses the divine title 'I am' (6:50; cf. Exod. 3:14; 6:6; Isa. 48: 12); he identifies John the Baptist as Elijah, who prepares the way for Yahweh himself to come to his temple (1:12f.; 9:12f.; cf. Mal. 3:1; 4:5f.); and Jesus' words will not pass away (13:31; cf. Isa. 40:8). Mark's Jesus shares the power and attributes of God himself.

Jesus is also *Messiah, king and son of David* – all related descriptions. 'Messiah' is sometimes translated 'Christ' in English Bibles, reflecting the different Hebrew and Greek words used. Apart from 1:1, Jesus is described this way predominantly in the latter part of the Gospel, beginning with Peter's recognition of him as Messiah (8:29; 9:41; 12:35; 13:21), and it is notable that the high priest's question (14:61) coincides with Peter's confession except for the presence of the question mark. The Messiah was expected to be a descendant of David, so the use of 'son of David' fits with this evidence also – again, all in the later part of Mark's presentation and including, famously, a blind man who sees better than the sighted disciples and crowds (10:47f.; cf. 12:35-37; 11:10). Jesus is also portrayed as king, entering Jerusalem in kingly fashion (11:1-11; cf. Zech. 9:9) and charged with being king of the Jews in his passion (15:2, 9, 12, 18, 26, 32). Thus Mark paints a picture of a Jesus who fulfils the Scriptures and Jewish hopes.

Jesus is also the *son of man*, in Mark Jesus' favourite self-designation. Until the interview with the high priest the other phrases are not found on Jesus' lips, but 'the son of man' is regularly used this way. In Jewish thought it is not a way of speaking of Jesus' humanity (although Mark is convinced of the reality of that, e.g. he speaks of Jesus' emotional life in 1:41; 3:5; 8:12; 10:14), but alludes to the figure of Dan. 7:13f. who represents the people of God (Dan. 7:18) and is presented to God to receive power, honour and authority (esp. 13:26; 14:62) (see pp. 175 and 183f.). This description is used particularly when Jesus speaks of his suffering and death (8:31; 9:9, 12, 31; 10:33, 45; 14:21, 41), but also of his present ministry (2:10, 28) and his future exaltation and glorification (8:38; 13:26; 14:62). It identifies Jesus as a representative figure who uses a description which is not politically sensitive in the way that 'the son of God' and 'Messiah/king/son of David' would be, but one whose overtones readers with ears to hear would pick up.

Jesus also fulfils the OT image of the *servant of God* found principally in the later chapters of Isaiah. He brings good news (1:14f.; cf. Isa. 52:7), following in the steps of the baptiser who prepares for this news (1:2f., quoting Isa. 40:3f.). At his baptism the Spirit comes on him as upon the servant (1:10; Isa. 61:1). He is treated with contempt (9:12; cf. Isa. 53:3). In 10:45 a cluster of allusions to the suffering servant of Isa. 52:13–53:12 occur: he 'serves' (52:13); he 'gives his life' (53:10, 12); his life is a 'ransom' (53:10, 'offering'); and it is 'for many' (53:11f.). At the Last Supper Jesus initiates a new covenant, again 'for many' (14:24; cf. Isa. 42:6; 49:8; 53:2, 11f.). Here is a description which points to the centrality of the suffering and death of Jesus for Mark's theology.

DISCIPLESHIP

Following Jesus is central to Mark's story, from the disciples whom Jesus calls to follow him at the beginning; they leave everything to go with him (1:16-18; 2:14). Two key favourite Markan words highlight this theme: 'the way' (Greek *hodos*) and 'follow' (Greek *akolouthe̅o*). John prepares 'the way of the Lord' (1:2f.) and Jesus teaches 'the way of God' (12:14). In that light other references to 'the way' are suggestive of discipleship. Mark uses the verb 'follow' frequently, almost always in relation to following Jesus, both the wider group who follow him (e.g. 2:15; 3:7; 8:34) and the select group of disciples (e.g. 6:1).

We noticed when we read through Mark that 8:27–10:52 contains key teaching on discipleship as Jesus is 'on the way' to

WHY DOES MARK PRESENT JESUS LIKE THIS?

Some scholars attempt to reconstruct the background to the Gospel on the assumption that Mark is arguing against a particular view in presenting Jesus this way.

For some, Jesus is being presented in the same colours as the 'divine men' of Græco-Roman thinking, and 'son of God' is Mark's equivalent to 'divine man'. It is argued that there are parallels between Jesus' miracles and those of these figures, and that Mark is writing in order to show that Jesus is superior to such people. However, there was great diversity among the descriptions of Græco-Roman miracle-workers, and the terms 'divine man' and 'son of God' are both very rare in Hellenistic writers. Further, there is a strong Jewish tradition of miracles being done without the miracle-workers being supposed to be divine, such as Elijah, Elisha and Moses from the OT.

Weeden's view (in Weeden 1971) is that Mark is correcting what he sees as a mistaken Christology focused on power and authority, and the debate about Jesus' identity in the Gospel is a dramatized version of this conflict. The disciples hold to a 'divine man' Christology focused on power and authority, which Mark sets up in order to knock it down. So 1:16–8:26 presents the disciples failing to understand Jesus, 8:27–14:9 has the disciples wanting Jesus to be a 'divine man', and 14:10-72 has the disciples rejecting Jesus, since he does not fulfil their desires. Weeden believes that Mark is promoting a servant Christology in preference to this mistaken view.

However, outside Weeden's reconstruction of the circumstances of Mark we have no evidence of such a debate in the earliest churches, and it perhaps reflects modern scepticism about miracles rather too much to be a credible explanation of *Mark's* purpose, as well as being based on the same errors about 'divine man' ideas found above.

Jerusalem. In this section, as more widely, Mark draws his readers into the story by using 'whoever' (Greek *hos an* or *tis*) to show that they, too, are invited to be followers of Jesus. Notice particularly the uses in 3:35; 8:34f.; 9:35, 37, 41, 42; 10:11, 15, 43, 44; 11:23 (some are 'hidden' in English translations as 'you' or 'any of you').

Digging deeper:
MORE ON DISCIPLESHIP

With the aid of a Bible concordance find the uses of 'the way' and 'follow' in Mark. Use them to outline Mark's teaching on discipleship, both what it meant for the first followers of Jesus and what Mark is communicating to his readers about what it will mean for them to follow Jesus.

Then read carefully through 8:27–10:52 and note the teaching Jesus offers on discipleship here, and use it to fill out the picture you already have. What might this picture suggest for Christians today about their discipleship?

(Further reading: Best 1983, ch. XIV or Hurtado 1996.)

The portrait of the disciples contributes to Mark's teaching on this topic too, and Peter is shown as one who fails by denying that he knows Jesus (14:66-72) – he even curses Jesus (14:71, using the same root word which Paul warns about in 1 Cor. 12:3). But there is the hint of restoration in 16:7, for the angel names Peter specifically. Hurtado wisely observes the relevance of Jesus' words in 14:27-31 to Mark's first readers:

Jesus' promise of the restoration of the Twelve – even after their desertion and denial – is the message that Mark holds out to readers who, like Peter, may have failed under threats but may still experience forgiveness and restoration. In a first-century setting, where opposition from relatives and neighbors or intimidation from Jewish and Roman authorities might have led some Christians to compromise their witness, this hope would have been very meaningful. (Hurtado 1996, 25)

BACKGROUND AND PURPOSE

A careful reading suggests a number of features of the typical readers whom Mark has in mind.

- They do not know Aramaic and lack understanding of some Jewish customs, for Mark explains both in Greek (5:41; 7:1-4, 11, 34; 10:46; 14:36; 15:22, 34, 42), which suggests they are predominantly Gentile.
- However, they know some Jewish customs and religious language, for these are unexplained (e.g. Satan 1:13; 3:23; Gehenna 9:43, 45, 47; Hosanna 11:10).
- They are likely to know Latin or speak a kind of Greek influenced by Latin, for Mark uses a number of Latin loanwords or phrases, e.g. 'bowl' (*modius* 4:21), 'executioner' (*speculator* 6:27), 'poll tax' (*census* 12:14), 'flog' (*flagellare* 15:15). Notably, the *quadrans* coin, which Mark says was the value of the widow's two coins (12:42), only circulated in the west of the Roman empire, not in Palestine.
- They may be suffering persecution for their faith, during which some may have denied their faith, for Mark has teaching which fits such a situation (e.g. 8:34-38; 10:30; 13:9-13; 14:27-31).

The second-century writer Clement of Alexandria says that Mark wrote in Rome.

There is an early tradition that Peter, with whom the early writers say Mark worked, was martyred there. It is certainly possible that Mark wrote in Rome, although the Latin words in his book do not point decisively to that view, since they would be in wide use in many parts of the Roman empire.

Later tradition reported by Jerome in the fourth century links Mark with Alexandria, although if Mark were linked with that city it is surprising that Clement does not report this. Some scholars link Mark with Syria or northern Transjordan or even Galilee. The reality is that we cannot be sure of the location of Mark as he wrote – and the outline of his readers above fits with Bauckham's proposal that he and the other Evangelists wrote for a wide audience in the Roman empire, rather than targeting a particular church community in one location (see pp. 78f.).

AUTHORSHIP AND DATE

The book itself is anonymous: the title 'according to Mark' was probably attached to the book in the first half of the second century. But there is no dispute in the ancient manuscripts concerning the name attached – it is always 'Mark'. The earliest testimony about Mark's identity comes from Bishop Papias of Hierapolis early in the second century, recorded by the church historian Eusebius:

Mark became Peter's interpreter and wrote accurately all that he remembered, not, indeed, in order, of the things said or done by the Lord. For he had not heard the Lord, nor had he followed him, but later on, as I said, followed Peter, who used to give teaching as necessity demanded but

not making, as it were, an arrangement of the Lord's oracles, so that Mark did nothing wrong in thus writing down single points as he remembered them. For to one thing he gave attention, to leave out nothing of what he had heard and to make no false statements in them. (Eusebius, *Hist. eccl.* 3.39.15, LCL translation)

This testimony is repeated by later writers, and led to Mark being identified as John Mark, the cousin of Joseph Barnabas mentioned a number of times in Acts and the NT letters (see Acts 12:12, 25; 13:5, 13; 15:37, 39; Col. 4:10; 2 Tim. 4:11; Phlm 24), although there he is mainly linked with Paul rather than Peter – the exception being 1 Pet. 5:13. This remains a widely held view in scholarship (e.g. Hengel, Cranfield, Lane and – with reservations – Hooker). If correct, it links at least some of the stories in Mark to an eyewitness, and offers a plausible explanation for many incidental details in the Gospel. It also fits well with Mark's reports of occasions when only Peter and a few others were present (e.g. 1:16-20, 29-31; 9:2-8; 14:27-31), and the frequent mentions of Peter's failures and mistakes (e.g. 8:32f.; 9:5f.; 10:28-31; 14:29-31, 66-72).

Others are more doubtful of Papias' words, suggesting that he may have constructed his theory on the basis of the references to John Mark in the NT, and noting that Mark is sometimes vague about Palestinian geography (e.g. 5:1, where it has proved difficult to identify the location, to the extent that there are at least three possibilities in ancient manuscripts). A further view is that we can only construct a portrait of the 'implied author' of the Gospel, but cannot easily access the historical author, for we lack sufficient data to do so. Either of these views would leave us with an anonymous author.

Those who accept the Papias tradition draw the conclusion that Mark wrote shortly after the death of Peter, in the mid to late sixties AD. This date fits well with the teaching on persecution, for that was the period of the Emperor Nero's attacks on Christians, with Mark 13's description of the fall of Jerusalem, which does not seem influenced by actual knowledge of the events of AD 70, and with the use of Mark by Matthew and Luke (assuming Markan priority) – for that requires allowing time for Mark to be circulated before the later writers composed their Gospels. In fact, a date in the mid to late sixties is very widely accepted, whoever Mark is thought to be, with some suggesting the early seventies.

SOME ISSUES FOR TODAY

● Christians throughout history have swung between the two extremes of seeing the Christian life as about power, glory and victory on one hand, and involving suffering, pain and discipline on the other. Mark presents a portrait of Jesus who holds these two together, for he exercises power as son of God, but at the same time follows the way to the cross. Mark offers resources in reflecting on both ends of this tension in the Christian life.

● Mark focuses on what he sees as the central, crucial things about Jesus – his identity and his death – perhaps because he is filling out a 'gospel message outline' such as Acts 10:34-43 (see pp. 51f.). The tendency of Christian scholarship has sometimes been to get so wrapped up in peripheral questions that those which are Mark's focus get lost. Mark offers a corrective to this tendency.

● Mark's Jesus is thoroughly human, showing his emotions, entertaining doubts about going to die in the Garden of Gethsemane, lacking knowledge at times and needing human support and relationships. Sometimes Christians have so emphasized Mark's (and the NT's) portrayal of Jesus as divine that they have missed his identification with ordinary people – something stressed by Jesus accepting John's baptism, a baptism for sinful people. It is worth reflecting on the way that Mark's Jesus stands where people stand, for it is by this means that he enables people to stand where he stands, in relationship with God.

● Mark is called 'Gospel', which means that it is seen as preaching the gospel message about Jesus – and yet it is done by telling a story. This is suggestive for communication of the Christian message in modern western society, where stories have become central to how people define themselves. It implies that Christians today can also share their faith with others by telling stories about Jesus – although there will naturally be a job of cultural transposition to be done in the way the stories are told today.

ESSAY TOPICS

INTRODUCTORY

● How far do you agree with the description of Mark as 'a passion narrative with a circumstantial introduction' (Martin Kähler)? In other words, how far is the rest of the Gospel just preparation for the story of the cross?

● What is the message of Mark's miracle stories? Consider how he presents them and the contribution they make to his overall message.

INTERMEDIATE

- What, according to Mark, is the meaning of the death of Jesus? Consider both Mark's description of the event and the way the cross is presented throughout the book.

- What portrait of the disciples emerges from Mark? What message(s) is Mark conveying through this portrait about what it means to follow Jesus?

FURTHER READING

* denotes books assuming knowledge of Greek; most can be used by all students.

INTRODUCTORY

E. Best *Mark: The Gospel as Story*. Edinburgh: T. & T. Clark, 1983 (very good overview from redaction-critical perspective).

M. D. Hooker *The Message of Mark*. London: Epworth, 1983 (helpful short book of essays).

R. P. Martin *Mark: Evangelist and Theologian*. Exeter: Paternoster/Grand Rapids: Zondervan, 1972 (worthwhile overview).

W. R. Telford *Mark*. NT Guides. Sheffield: Sheffield Academic Press, 1995 (good recent study of the Gospel and Markan scholarship).

INTERMEDIATE

*J. Camery-Hoggatt *Irony in Mark's Gospel: Text and Subtext*. SNTS Monograph Series 72. Cambridge: Cambridge University Press, 1992 (a major study of this theme).

R. T. France *Divine Government: God's Kingship in the Gospel of Mark*. London: SPCK, 1990 (excellent study of the kingdom of God in Mark).

L. W. Hurtado "Following Jesus in the Gospel of Mark – and Beyond" in *Patterns of Discipleship in the New Testament*, ed. R. N. Longenecker. Grand Rapids/ Cambridge: Eerdmans, 1996, 9-29 (excellent brief study of discipleship in Mark).

W. R. Telford, ed. *The Interpretation of Mark*. Studies in NT Interpretation. 2nd ed.

Edinburgh: T. & T. Clark, 1995 (variety of useful articles from 1964 to 1989).

T. J. Weeden, Sr. *Mark: Traditions in Conflict*. Philadelphia: Fortress, 1971 (proposes that Mark is attempting to correct a mistaken Christology).

N. T. Wright *Jesus and the Victory of God*. London: SPCK/Philadelphia: Fortress, 1996, 174-82, 236f. (excellent discussion of parables and the secrecy theme in the ministry of Jesus).

COMMENTARIES

*C. E. B. Cranfield *The Gospel according to St Mark*. Cambridge: Cambridge University Press, 1959 (good older commentary, helpful on Markan style and theology).

*R. A. Guelich *Mark 1:1–8:26*. Word Biblical Commentary 34A. Waco: Word, 1989 (full commentary with lots of good things to offer).

M. D. Hooker *A Commentary on the Gospel according to St Mark*. London: A. & C. Black/Peabody, MA: Hendrickson, 1992 (good recent mid-level commentary).

L. W. Hurtado *Mark*. New International Biblical Commentary 2. Peabody, MA: Hendrickson, 1989 (helpful mid-level commentary).

W. Lane *Commentary on the Gospel of Mark*. New International Commentary on the NT. Grand Rapids: Eerdmans/London: Marshall Morgan & Scott, 1974 (careful and reasonably detailed commentary).

C. S. Mann *Mark*. Anchor Bible 27. Garden City, NY: Doubleday, 1986 (based on the Griesbach view that Mark is 'editing' Matthew and Luke into a shorter Gospel).

D. E. Nineham *Saint Mark*. Harmondsworth/ New York: Penguin, 1963 (classic form- and redaction-critical commentary).

D. Rhoads, J. Dewey & D. Michie *Mark as Story: An Introduction to the Narrative of a Gospel*. 2nd ed. Philadelphia: Fortress, 1999 (second edition of a pioneering 'narrative' reading of Mark).

Chapter 10

MATTHEW

Matthew's Gospel comes first in our NT, and there is an appropriateness in that, since Matthew so explicitly connects the story of Jesus to the OT. His Gospel has been influential in all sorts of ways: the sermon on the mount, for example, has given ethical inspiration and challenge to countless Christians and non-Christians; the great commission of 28:16-20 is perhaps the most important 'mission statement' of the Christian church.

A LOOK INTO THE GOSPEL

Chs 1–2 After his opening words: 'The book of the "genesis" of Jesus Christ son of David son of Abraham', Matthew presents a family tree of Jesus, in three sections, each of 14 generations long (according to Matthew's calculation):

> Abraham-David
> David-the exile of Israel in Babylon
> Exile-Jesus

A striking feature of the genealogy is the appearance in it of four unusual women: Tamar, Rahab, Ruth and Bathsheba (vv. 3, 5, 6).

Jesus' miraculous birth is then described, and its immediate aftermath (1:18-23).

Digging deeper

What is special about Matthew? Go through a copy of Matthew's Gospel with cross-references, and:

- mark in blue stories and sayings of Jesus that are also found in Mark;
- mark in red those that are also found in Luke;
- list all that is left and that is unique to Matthew.

Do you notice any particular themes that are especially important for Matthew?

Striking in the narrative is:

- the prominence of Joseph, Jesus' legal father;
- angelic appearances to Joseph;
- dreams as divine communication;
- the names given to Jesus, i.e. 'Jesus' = saviour and 'Immanuel' = God with us;
- the OT quotations, including the first of Matthew's distinctive quotations: 'All this took place to fulfil what the Lord had said through the prophet, "The virgin shall conceive and bear a son, and they will call him Immanuel, which means 'God with us'"' (1: 22, 23);

- the appearance of Gentile astrologers to worship Jesus;
- the fury of King Herod over the birth of a new 'king of the Jews';
- the move of Jesus from Bethlehem, city of David, to Egypt, and finally back to Nazareth.

Chs 3–4 The camera swings forward next to the prophetic figure John the Baptist, baptizing people at the river Jordan. Jesus is baptized there, and the Holy Spirit descends on him. He is then led into the wilderness to be tempted by the devil.

Distinctive to Matthew's portrayal of John is:

- his message – he announces 'the kingdom of heaven has come near' (as Jesus will later);
- his reluctance to baptize Jesus, and Jesus' reply, 'Thus it is necessary for us to fulfil all righteousness'.

After these important preliminaries Jesus' ministry begins in Galilee, where he teaches, preaches, heals and calls his first disciples. Matthew organizes this material into alternating blocks of teaching and narrative.

Chs 5–7 The first major section is the so-called sermon on the mount. This has a partial parallel in Luke 6, but notable about Matthew's sermon are:

- it is the first of five major sermons which punctuate Matthew's Gospel;
- the theme of the sermon is discipleship and the kingdom of God;
- a particular focus is on Jesus as the one who fulfils the law and the prophets of the OT (5:17; 7:12);
- the sermon contrasts the 'righteousness' of Jesus with that of the scribes and Pharisees – the so-called antitheses contrast OT teaching as understood by the Jewish

teachers with 'But I say to you' (5:21-48); then Jesus calls for piety done before God as Father not for human glory (6:1-18);

- a concluding series of warnings against sham religion and the challenge to obey Jesus' teaching, thus building on rock not sand (7:13-27).

Chs 8–9 This astonishing teaching is followed by astonishing action on Jesus' part, as Matthew goes on to describe a sample of Jesus' miracles, and calls people to follow him.

Ch. 10 The next teaching block is Jesus' instruction of twelve special disciples, whom he sends out to continue his work. The focus in Matthew is distinctively on mission within the boundaries of Israel (10:5, 23).

Chs 11–12 People ask questions – first John the Baptist (who is now in prison), then Jesus' Jewish critics, notably the Pharisees, who question his Sabbath observance and accuse him of working by the power of the 'Beelzebul, the prince of demons'. Jesus responds by speaking of the coming of the kingdom of God.

Ch. 13 The next teaching block is a selection of eight parables about 'the kingdom of heaven'. Unique to Matthew are:

- the wheat and the tares;
- the treasure;
- the pearl;
- the net;
- the trained scribe.

Chs 14–17 Two miraculous feedings are described – one at the beginning, of over 5,000 people, one at the end, of over 4,000 people. In between there is the climactic moment when Peter hails Jesus as 'the Messiah, the son of God' and Jesus speaks of

Peter as the rock on which he will build his church. Then Jesus begins to speak of coming suffering, to his disciples' dismay. His ministry also seems to begin to look outward to the Gentiles, as he questions Jewish rituals, meets a Gentile woman with outstanding faith, heals in Gentile areas and feeds the 4,000.

Ch. 18 The focus shifts now to the church, with the next block of teaching speaking of how the disciples should relate to each other, humbly, reaching out to 'brothers' who go astray, dealing carefully with problems and forgiving one another.

Chs 19–23 The scene now switches from Galilee to Judea, with Jesus teaching about discipleship, and in due course entering the city of Jerusalem and the temple. Controversy with the Jewish authorities leads to a fierce denunciation of the 'hypocritical' practices of the 'scribes and Pharisees', and to a solemn warning of coming judgement (ch. 23).

Chs 24–25 Jesus' view of the future is explained here. This teaching includes distinctive material, notably the parables of the wise and foolish virgins, and of the sheep and the goats.

Chs 26–28 The final scene is the passion of Jesus – his Last Supper, arrest, trials, crucifixion and resurrection. Matthew's account is distinctive in various ways:

- he describes Judas being hit by remorse for betraying innocent blood, and hanging himself (27:3-5);
- the wife of the Roman governor Pilate has a dream and tells Pilate to have nothing to do with 'this righteous man'. He finds Jesus innocent and washes his hands symbolically (27:19-26);

- the Jews accept responsibility – 'his blood be on us and on our children' (27:25);
- when Jesus dies and the temple veil is torn in two, the earth quakes, with tombs being broken open and dead saints being raised to life, appearing in Jerusalem (27:51-53);
- the Jewish authorities have the tomb sealed and a guard set (27:62-66);
- on the first day of the week there is an earthquake, the tomb of Jesus is opened by an angel, the guards are terrified but are bribed by the Jews to say that the disciples of Jesus stole the body (28:2-15);
- Jesus appears to the women on their way back from the tomb (28:9, 10), and then in Galilee, where he meets his followers (28:16-20).

In this climactic scene:

- Jesus appears on a mountain;
- his followers worship him;
- he speaks of 'all authority that has been given' to him;
- he instructs the disciples to go and make disciples of all nations, by baptizing them in the name of Father, Son and Holy Spirit, and teaching them to keep 'all that I have commanded you';
- he promises them that 'I am with you to the very end of the age.'

HOW THE GOSPEL IS STRUCTURED

Matthew's Gospel is not a casual collection of stories and sayings of Jesus, but a carefully constructed narrative. It is significant, first, that the Gospel opens with 'The book of the genesis...' (1:1) and ends with 'until the end of the age' (28:20) – the story of Jesus is set in a wide framework, going back to the beginning of God's purposes for Israel and reaching forward to the 'end of the age', and by implication to the coming of the new age.

The Gospel starts firmly rooted in the OT story of Israel, with a genealogy linking Jesus to Abraham, father of Israel, and David, the great king, and ends with Jesus being revealed in great authority and with the church being sent to all 'nations' (the Greek word *ethnē* could be translated 'Gentiles'). Jesus is seen as the destination of the OT history, but also as the content and purpose of the church's mission with the disciples sent to bring others under the authority of the risen Jesus. Matthew's division of OT history into three lots of 14 generations may be intended to mean that Jesus' coming marks the beginning of the seventh seven, with seven being symbolically the number of perfection, and Jesus being the one who brings God's purposes for the world into effect.

The story of Jesus that is set in this theological framework falls into two main sections:

● Jesus' life and ministry in Galilee;
● from Galilee to the cross and resurrection.

The turning point comes in ch. 16, where Peter confesses Jesus and Jesus speaks of the building of his church. Matthew then continues: '*From that time on* Jesus began to explain to his disciples that he must go to Jerusalem and suffer many things ... and be raised to life ...'(16:23).

Matthew has a rather similar phrase in 4:17: '*From that time on* Jesus began to preach, "Repent, for the kingdom of heaven is near".' And it is possible that we should think of Matthew's story of Jesus as falling into three parts (so J. D. Kingsbury 1975):

● the preparation, including Jesus' birth, baptism and temptation (1:1–4:16);
● 'the kingdom proclaimed in word and deed' (4:17–16:20);

● the way to the cross, resurrection and the end of the age (16:21–28:20).

Among the most striking features of Matthew's Gospel are five big teaching blocks, each of which has a distinctive characteristic or theme:

● chs 5–7   the manifesto of the kingdom of God;
● ch 10   mission;
● ch 13   parables;
● ch 18   life in the church;
● chs 24–25 the future.

Each is followed by a phrase such as 'When Jesus had finished these sayings...' (7:28; 11:1; 13:53; 19:1; 26:1).

Some have argued that the Gospel is modelled on the Pentateuch, the first five books of the OT, which were traditionally ascribed to Moses (notably B. W. Bacon in *The Expositor* 1918). However, although Matthew does see Jesus as the new and greater Moses, it is not easy to divide the whole Gospel neatly into five books, or to see this as its main organizing principle.

It is possible that there is a chiastic structure through the five blocks (28:20):

Matt. 5–7 – the kingdom manifesto;
    Matt. 10 – the mission of the church;
        Matt.13 – the kingdom ministry of Jesus and the church;
    Matt. 18 – the community life of the church;
Matt. 24–25 – the future kingdom.

This analysis has its attractions, but it would suggest that the centre of the Gospel is in Matt. 13, whereas other considerations suggest ch. 16, with Peter's confession as the centre.

Chiasm is an x-shaped pattern (the Greek letter chi looks like an x). Two sayings A and B might then be followed by two similar sayings B and A, thus giving the shape

A		B
	X	
B		A

The arrangement of Matthew's Gospel is no doubt partly determined by the traditions of Jesus that he received, and the stories of the Gospel are not all in some highly systematized or logical arrangement. But still there is definite movement, from the OT to Jesus, from Galilee to Jerusalem, from Israel to the world. A general outline may be proposed as follows:

- **1:1–4:11** Jesus' origins: from the OT, to his birth, to his baptism and temptation.
- **4:12–16:20** God's kingdom revealed in Jesus' present word and action, including:

5–7	Teaching 1: The kingdom manifesto: Jesus' word
8–9	The power of the kingdom: Jesus' miracles
10	Teaching 2: The mission of the kingdom: Jesus' disciples sent to Israel
11–12	Questions and opposition to the kingdom
13	Teaching 3: The parables of the kingdom
14:1–16:12	Jesus feeds Jews and moves out to Gentiles
16:13-20	Peter confesses Jesus and is commissioned as the rock.

- **16:21–28:16** Jesus and his disciples move towards the future, through suffering to glory:
  16:21–17:27 Jesus talks of suffering

18	Teaching 4: Life in the church
19–23	Jesus journeys to Jerusalem and into conflict with the Jews
24–25	Teaching 5: The future explained until the end of the age
26:1–28:15	Jesus' death and resurrection
28:16-20	Jesus in authority sends the church to the world.

STYLE

Matthew's Greek is more literary and less disjointed than that of a writer like Mark (cf. 12:46 and 13:1 with Mark 3:31 and 4:1); he also writes more concisely (e.g. cf. Matt. 8:28-34 and Mark 5:1-20). His material is systematically, though not rigidly, arranged, e.g.:

- his structured genealogy in ch. 1;
- his five teaching blocks, each with its own theme, and a following transitional phrase 'When Jesus had finished all these sayings...';
- a section like the sermon on the mount has a coherent shape.

A similarly systematic arrangement is found elsewhere in the Gospel, for example in the chapter of parables (in Matt. 13).

There are sometimes things that seem to interrupt the pattern in Matthew (e.g. the Lord's prayer in 6:7-15), and it is not possible to be certain how much of the arranging is Matthew's own handiwork, and how much may derive from his sources. But Matthew's own systematic bent is suggested by his repeated use of formulae such as 'All this took place to fulfil what was spoken by the prophet(s)...' when introducing OT

213

SERMON ON THE MOUNT (Matt. 5–7)

Opening beatitudes and sayings (5:1-16)

Introductory saying about Jesus fulfilling the law and prophets (5:17),

leading into a major discussion of Jesus, the law and his righteousness and then of other subjects (5:17–7:12).

Within the section on the law (5:17-30) there is definite order:

it begins with a *general statement* ('Think not that I have come to destroy the law and the prophets ...'); and it continues with a sample of Jesus' ethics – the so-called '*antitheses*'.

The antitheses themselves are orderly, with the formula: 'You have heard that it was said ... but I say to you' coming repeatedly. The first antithesis urges reconciliation with one's brother, the last speaks of loving one's enemies.

concluding saying about the law and prophets, the so-called 'Golden Rule' of 7:12.

End challenges and warnings (7:13-end).

---

prophecy, and 'there will be weeping and gnashing of teeth' in concluding sayings of judgement (8:12; 13:42, 50; 22:13; 24:51; 25:30).

What do you think?
MATTHEW 13

What do you notice about the arrangement of Matt. 13? How many parables or pairs of parables are there? (Some people see Matt. 13:52 as a mini parable.) What themes are brought out in the parables?

THEOLOGICAL THEMES

The Gospel is, patently, all about Jesus; it is, as scholars say, thoroughly 'christological'. This is clear from 1:1, 'Jesus Christ, son of David son of Abraham', right through to 28:20, 'I am with you always'. But how does Matthew present Jesus?

JESUS FULFILS THE OT STORY

No one can miss Matthew's interest in linking Jesus with the OT.

THE FORMULA QUOTATIONS

The formula quotations (1:22-23; 2:15, 17-18, 23; 4:14-16; 8:17; 12:17-21; 13:35; 21:4-5; 27:9-10, also perhaps 2:5-6):

- are unique to Matthew;
- are introduced by Matthew's typical formula 'this took place to fulfil what was spoken...';
- often use a translation from the original Hebrew that is different from the well-known Greek 'Septuagint' text;
- sometimes use the OT in a strange way (by modern standards), as in 2:15 where the words of Hosea about Israel being rescued from Egypt, 'out of Egypt I have called my son', are applied to Jesus;
- sometimes seem to correspond hardly at all with the OT, thus in 2:23 'he shall be called a Nazarene' is said by Matthew to be in 'the prophets', but is not found in so many words anywhere in the OT.

Matthew's rather creative use of the OT has been compared to what we find in the Dead Sea Scrolls: in so-called 'pesher' interpretation the scribes from Qumran interpreted OT texts to refer to themselves, sometimes very curiously.

(See further K. Stendahl *The School of Matthew.* Philadelphia: Fortress, 1968.)

The family tree (1:1-17) explicitly links Jesus with Abraham and David.

Matthew's Gospel is punctuated with OT quotations. Particularly notable are his so-called 'formula' quotations (see p. 214).

Jesus re-enacts and so fulfils the OT. When Matthew applies an OT text like 'out of Egypt shall I call my son' to Jesus, he is presumably reinterpreting the text quite deliberately. He understands that the original reference was to the Exodus of Israel from Pharaoh's Egypt, but he sees the OT story as pointing to Jesus and Jesus as bringing that story to its divinely intended goal and completion. Jesus may be seen as somehow embodying Israel, and fulfilling God's purpose for Israel in himself. Scholars speak of 'typological' fulfilment, with the OT reality seen to be a type (as in our English 'prototype') anticipating Jesus, who far surpasses the anticipation. (See further France 1989.)

Matthew compares Jesus to:

- Israel, God's 'son', coming out of Egypt (2:15);
- Israel, God's 'son', tempted in the wilderness (4:1-11); cf. Ex. 4:19;
- Moses in Egypt, persecuted by a wicked king (e.g. Matt. 2:20);
- Moses the great teacher (5:21f., cf. 17:3);
- David the king, and also the priests (12:3-5);
- Jonah the dying and rising preacher (12:40-41);
- Solomon the wise son of David (12:42);
- the sacred temple itself (12:6).

JESUS FULFILS THE LAW AND BRINGS THE HIGHER RIGHTEOUSNESS

Not just the OT story, but also the OT revelation of God's will, is fulfilled and surpassed by Jesus.

Righteousness is a key term for Matthew (but completely absent from Mark).

- Jesus must 'fulfil all righteousness', as he explains to John the Baptist when undergoing his baptism and thus associating with his 'return to righteousness' movement (3:15).
- His followers should 'hunger and thirst for righteousness', seeking first 'God's kingdom and his/its righteousness' (5:6; 6:33).
- Righteousness is the characteristic of the kingdom and of people who will enter it, e.g. 'Blessed are those who are persecuted for righteousness' sake, for theirs is the kingdom of heaven' (5:10).
- This righteousness is devastatingly demanding: 'Unless your righteousness exceeds that of the scribes and Pharisees, you will not enter the kingdom of heaven' (5:20).
- It involves high standards of ethics and genuine piety (5:21-48; 6:1f.).
- It is illustrated by a man like Joseph (1:19), but supremely by Jesus himself (27:4, 19).

In Jewish thinking righteousness and the God-given law of the OT went very closely together. In Matthew the law is important.

- Matt. 5:17 is a key verse: 'Think not that I have come to destroy the law and the prophets; truly I say to you, I have not come to destroy them, but to fulfil them.'
- Jesus affirms even the details of the law (5:18, 19; 23:1, 2).
- The word 'lawlessness' (*anomia*) sums up what is wrong and brings the judgement of God on people (7:23; 13:41; 24:12).

And yet:

- Jesus demands a level of righteousness that goes beyond the letter of the OT law and that surpasses the high achievements of the expertly law-abiding scribes and Pharisees (5:20f.).

- He criticizes them because although they are outwardly pious and law-abiding, they are inwardly compromised. Jesus sets before his disciples a standard of purity of heart (5:8, 27-28; 6:1f.).
- He also criticizes them because they are good on the minutiae of the law (like tithing herbs) and weak on the big principles (like justice, mercy and faith). Jesus emphasizes the priority of love and of doing to others what you would have done to you (7:12; 23:23).
- Jesus' standard is that of the perfect heavenly Father (5:48).

PRACTICAL OBEDIENCE AND JUDGEMENT

What is clear about righteousness and law in Matthew is that practical ethical obedience is central to Christian discipleship. Saying

---

MATTHEW AND THE LAW

Did Matthew expect every Christian, including Gentiles, to keep every OT law including, for example, the food laws?

Some scholars say yes (e.g. D. C. Sim The Gospel of Matthew and Christian Judaism. Edinburgh: Clark, 1998), and think that he rejected Paul's view of Christians being 'free of the law'. In favour of this are:

- The strong statements about the continuing validity of even details in the law, e.g. 5:19; 23:2, 3; 23:23
- The absence in the discussion of hand-washing and uncleanness in Matt. 15 of the Markan comment that Jesus 'declared all foods clean' (7:19).

However, several things deserve to be said about this.

- Matthew is describing Jesus teaching in a Jewish environment in the context of mission to Jews. We cannot be certain that he would have regarded the law as binding on Gentile Christians in the same way.
- Jesus in Matthew clearly gives priority to the 'moral' aspects of the law, as opposed to the 'ritual', twice citing the words of Hosea 'I desire mercy not sacrifice' (9:12; 12:7; cf. 15:1-20).
- In the uniquely Matthean story of the coin in the fish's mouth, Jesus refers to his disciples as 'sons of the kingdom' who are 'free' of temple taxation (17:24-27).
- Matthew sees some of the requirements of the OT law as superseded by the higher standard of the kingdom of heaven, e.g. the OT laws about perjury (5:33-37).

- Jesus himself, as the son of God who brings the kingdom, has a greater authority than the OT law. So that 'you have heard that it was said to the people of old times...' is now superseded by Jesus' authoritative 'but I say to you...' (5:18-48). It is Jesus' commands that are to be taught to all nations (28:20; cf. 7:24-29).
- Jesus himself acts with great, indeed divine, authority, e.g. as lord of the Sabbath (12:12) and of the temple (20:12-17, 23-27, 41-45; cf. 12:6).
- Jesus speaks of judgement on the temple, and of a covenant in his blood, bringing forgiveness of sins and leading to the kingdom (20:12-17; 24:2; 26:60, 27-29). Jesus dies to bring new access to God and, we may infer, the 'new covenant' of Jer. 31, written in people's hearts.
- Jesus can thus contrast his 'easy' and 'light' yoke with the heavy yoke of Pharisaism (11:28, 29, 23:4). The way to the righteousness of the kingdom is by 'coming' to Jesus as the 'poor in spirit' (5:3; 11:28).

A possible conclusion is that Matthew (a) wants to assert the continuity of Jesus with the OT and to show that the coming of the kingdom of God means higher not lower moral standards and (b) sees the law of Moses and its demands as giving way to Jesus and his perfect teaching.

(For Matthew's view of the law see Senior 1996.)

'Lord, Lord' to Jesus and even doing wonderful things in his name is not enough without obedience (7:22). Judgement depends on practically obeying the teaching of Jesus (7:24-27; 25:31-46).

What do you think?
WHAT IS THE SERMON ON THE MOUNT ALL ABOUT?

People sometimes applaud the teaching of the sermon on the mount and claim to agree with it, without knowing what it is all about. Look through the sermon (Matt. 5–7) and consider what the main emphases of Jesus' teaching are. Do you think it is possible to keep the demands of the sermon without the relationship with God and Jesus of which it speaks?

The demands made in the sermon have understandably seemed very daunting to Christians over the ages: does Jesus really expect perfection (e.g. 5:48)? Or is the sermon deliberately setting an impossible standard in order to show us our need of divine mercy and grace (as the Reformer Martin Luther suggested)? What seems likely is that we have in the sermon kingdom-of-God ethics. In reply to the criticism that he and his followers are lowering the standards of the OT (5:17), Jesus explains that on the contrary the coming of God's kingdom means the end of moral compromise and the breaking in of perfect divine love and righteousness. The disciples are called to live in that love as children of God, depending on God's grace and asking for forgiveness when they fail (5:3; 6:12).

That still leaves the question as to how literally the teaching of the sermon should be taken. Should Christians, for example, always refuse to take oaths or to defend themselves and their families? Or is the teaching of Jesus a personal ethic for individuals, not directly applicable to state and society as well? Is Jesus painting vivid pictures of what kingdom ethics look like (as 5:29 would suggest), rather than giving hard and fast rules? Whatever the answer given to these questions, there is no doubt that Matthew sees practical behaviour as of vital importance for the Christian disciple.

Matthew has a strong stress on judgement, notably through parables such as:

- the wise and foolish builders (7:24-27);
- the wheat and the tares (13:24-30, 36-43);
- the net (13:47-50);
- the wise and foolish virgins (25:1-13);
- the sheep and the goats (25:31-46).

Matthew emphasizes the joy that there will be for the 'sons of the kingdom' and the misery for those who are condemned. The criterion of judgement is discipleship of Jesus expressed in practical righteousness and faithful preparing for the coming of the Lord.

JESUS BRINGS GOOD NEWS TO THE WORLD: JEWS, GENTILES AND THE CHURCH

Matthew's Gospel is in many respects a highly Jewish document:

- he interprets Jesus in thoroughly Jewish categories, notably in relationship to the OT;
- he uses typically Jewish terminology, e.g. preferring 'kingdom of heaven' to 'kingdom of God' (in line with Jewish sensitivities about the use of God's name), and speaking of God as 'heavenly Father' or 'Father in heaven';
- he reflects Jewish attitudes, e.g. negative ones towards Gentiles (18:17 'Let him be

to you as a Gentile or a tax collector'; also 6:7, 32);

- Jesus and his disciples' ministry (in the first instance) is to 'the lost sheep of the house of Israel' (10:5; 15:24).

At the same time Matthew seems in some ways anti-Jewish:

- there is very sharp polemic against the scribes and Pharisees, who are 'hypocrites' (e.g. ch. 23);
- the Jewish leaders engineer Jesus' death, and say to Pilate, who has washed his hands, 'His blood be on us and on our children' (27:25);
- Jesus speaks of judgement coming on the Jewish nation within a generation, and of the 'kingdom' being taken from them and given 'to another nation' (21:43);
- Matthew can speak of 'the Jews' and 'their synagogues', implying a split between Jews and Christians (e.g. 4:23; 9:35; 10:17; 28:15).

Matthew also has a definite interest in Gentiles:

- in the climactic 28:19, Jesus sends his followers to make disciples of all 'nations'. This could be translated 'all the Gentiles', with the Jews now excluded, but it probably has the wider connotation, with no one excluded;
- in the story of Jesus' birth the magi are evidently Gentiles; so possibly are the women in the genealogy (1:3, 4, 6);
- in 4:12-16 Jesus' ministry in Galilee is introduced with a quotation from Isa. 9, which speaks of 'Galilee of the Gentiles';
- Jesus' second recorded miracle is the healing of a Gentile centurion's servant (7:5-13);
- in 15:21-28 Jesus at first rebuffs the Canaanite woman who asks for help, but

then heals her daughter, and goes on in that chapter to minister (apparently) to Gentiles.

The mixture of Jewishness and anti-Jewishness, and of apparent antipathy to Gentiles and favour towards Gentiles, could prove that:

- Matthew is confused;
- there are different layers of tradition in Matthew's Gospel, with, for example, a final pro-Gentile layer having been super-imposed on a strongly pro-Jewish layer;
- Matthew sees Jesus as having come to the people of Israel as their promised king ('pro-Jewish'), but their rejection of him leads to judgement on them ('anti-Jewish') and to the giving of the kingdom to the whole world.

Digging deeper

Matt. 23 is the most sustained piece of polemic against the Jewish religious leaders anywhere in the NT. List the criticisms made of the scribes and Pharisees. To what extent might these criticisms have been relevant also to the church of Matthew's day? For a detailed study of Matt. 23, see D. E. Garland *The Intention of Matthew 23*. Leiden: Brill, 1979.

Some see Matthew's hostility to the Jews as so great as to count it as antisemitism. But, although some of Matthew's language is very strong (e.g. 27:5) and has been used anti-semitically by Christians in later centuries, we should appreciate that Matthew was writing at a time (a) when different Jewish groups were typically forthright in their condemnation of those with whom they disagreed and (b) when Christians were the minority who were on the receiving end of Jewish persecution, rather than the persecuting majority.

THE CHURCH

How does the church fit in? Matthew is the only synoptic evangelist to use the word 'church' (16:18; 18:17), and to speak directly of the community of Jesus' followers.

The word 'church' (*ekklēsia*) is used in Greek versions of the OT to refer to the people of Israel when gathered together. Significantly, Matthew links Jesus' twelve apostles with the twelve tribes of Israel (19:28). The story and people of Israel in one sense continue in the story of Jesus and the church, and yet at the same time Israel comes under judgement for its rejection of the Messiah, and the church is the other 'nation' to which the kingdom of heaven is now given (21:23).

The point of continuity and discontinuity is Jesus himself. He is Israel's Messiah born in Israel and sent to Israel, and the Jewish nation in rejecting him cut themselves off from God's Israel, whereas the followers of Jesus in accepting him as Messiah are his family of 'little ones' (10:40-42; 12:50; 18:1-13), who are the Israel of God who now have the task of taking the good news to the nations of the world.
\
In this new people the twelve are foundational. They are:

- called by Jesus (4:18-22);
- sent out to Israel to proclaim and bring the kingdom (10:1-15);
- given understanding of the mysteries (13:11-17).

Peter is the first to be called, and he features in various special ways in Matthew (e.g. in walking on the water with Jesus in 14:29-30,

What do you think?
WHAT SORT OF CHURCH LIFE?

Matt. 18 has a particular focus on church life. What does it suggest are the problems that will affect church life and that may have been affecting Matthew's church? What are the solutions it recommends?

and as the rock on which the church will be built in 16:16-20).

Whereas in Mark the disciples seem to fail repeatedly to understand Jesus or do what he wants, in Matthew the focus is also on what they do understand (e.g. 13:16, 17, 18, 23, 52, etc.). Mark wants to help his readers understand Jesus and his death, and so brings out the disciples' struggles in understanding Jesus; Matthew wants to emphasize discipleship as obeying the teaching of Jesus, as taught by his followers, and so brings out their growing, albeit imperfect, understanding of Jesus.

KINGDOM AND CHRISTOLOGY

If we had to isolate one overarching theme for Matthew, 'fulfilment' (which we have looked at already), kingdom and Christology would all be strong contenders.

In Matthew it is John the Baptist who first announces the coming of the 'kingdom of heaven', but Jesus takes the theme up in his preaching, in the sermon on the mount, in parables and elsewhere. The kingdom is the treasure beyond price, the pearl surpassing all others (13:44-46). It is what prophets and righteous men have been longing for: the day of salvation, the time when God's promises are fulfilled (13:16, 17). It is a time when moral compromises will no longer be appropriate (Matt. 5). It is thus in a real sense 'eschatological', when 'this age' will come to an end and God will rule perfectly.

For Matthew this time has come with Jesus: he is fulfilling the promises and is casting out Satan (11:4, 5; 12:28). And yet in another sense the time has not yet come, and Jesus teaches his disciples to pray 'Your kingdom come' and speaks of the future coming of the son of man to 'gather the elect' and to judge the nations (6:10; 24:30).

Matthew holds the present and future of the kingdom together in parables, such as that of the wheat and the tares, which are to be left growing together 'till harvest' (13:30). The present is a time when the kingdom is growing, but there is ambiguity: the perfection lies ahead, beyond Jesus' epoch-changing death when finally the son of man will return (13:37-43).

But, if the kingdom is important in Matthew, Christology is even more so. It is Jesus who brings the kingdom and fulfilment of God's promised salvation (11:2f.); it is he whose death triggers the opening of the graves and the beginning of the final resurrection of the dead (27:51-53). He is the Messiah, son of David and king of the Jews, more than that he is the unique son of the Father (11:27; 28:20), and indeed 'God with us' (1:23; 18:20; 28:20). All of this is reflected in his massive authority. Greater than Moses, he teaches with the authority of God, forgives people's sins, acts as lord of the Sabbath and of God's temple. He is the authoritative son of man now, and will come in the future on the clouds, to be judge of all nations and all people (25:3). He is one who is appropriately worshipped (2:11; 14:33; 28:17,18) and also obeyed.

SOURCES OF MATTHEW'S GOSPEL

Matthew's Gospel has a great deal in common with Mark and Luke.

- Some 90% of the content of Mark is paralleled in Matthew.
- The shape of Matthew is similar to Mark.

Matthew, however, has a significant amount of extra material, some of which is in common with Luke, notably teaching material, some which is unique to his Gospel (e.g. his stories of Jesus' infancy).

THE TWO SOURCE THEORY
The most widely accepted scholarly explanation of this is the so-called two source theory, according to which Matthew and Luke both used Mark and a collection of Jesus' sayings that scholars have labelled Q. The arguments for and against this theory are discussed in ch. 4 (pp. 64–6).

Matthew according to this view used Mark as his narrative framework, using Q and his other own sources of information to supplement Mark. Thus in Matt. 13 we have:

Markan parables	Q parables	Matthew's own
Sower and interpretation	Mustard seed and leaven	Tares and net
Mustard seed		Treasure and pearl
		Scribe

Matthew on this view is a skilful theological editor of his sources.

- He writes economically, particularly in narrative, where he is usually briefer – but also less colourful – than Mark when describing the same event (e.g. in 8:28-34; cf. Mark 5:1-20).

- He integrates his source materials into an impressive whole, e.g. in the sermon on the mount and in the chapter of parables he is thought to have welded together material from diverse sources.
- He brings out particular theological concerns.

For example, in 5:17-20 Matthew is thought to have had one Q saying (i.e. 5:18), but to have built it into a section where much of the wording and thought is his own, notably in v. 17 with its emphasis on the law and the prophets, and in v. 20 with its call for righteousness.

Questions about the two source theory

There are features of Matthew that at least raise questions for the two source theory.

- Some material that is only found in Matthew (M material) looks very ancient. For example, the sayings about Jesus and the disciples going only to the lost sheep of the house of Israel (10:5; 15:24) do not appear to reflect Matthew's own priorities for the church in his day (see 28:16-20), and probably go back to the Palestinian context of Jesus. There is evidence that Paul was aware of the Jewish focus of the ministry of Jesus and the first apostles (Rom. 15:8; Gal. 2:7, 8).
- Some material which has been seen as Matthean redaction, i.e. as deriving from Matthew himself and not from his sources, may well go back behind Matthew. In this category are the sayings about Peter and the church in 16:16-20, which may have been familiar to Paul (compare Gal. 1–2, where Paul compares himself to Peter, and note especially 1:15; 2:7). Also Matt. 5:17, with its important statement about Jesus as the fulfilment of the law and the prophets, has some sort of parallel in Luke 24:44

(cf. 16:16 on 'the law and the prophets'). It is true that much of this M material reflects Matthew's own particular interests (in judgement, righteousness, scribes and Pharisees, the church, etc.), but that would be expected as much if Matthew was supplementing his main sources from other sources as if he were adding material of his own.

- There is no consensus among scholars about Matthew's sources (apart from Mark). Scholars are unclear whether Q, if it existed at all, was written or oral, whether M existed as a source, whether and how Mark, Q and M overlapped with each other. It seems likely that there will have been considerable overlap. This means that in contexts where Matthew is usually thought to be following Mark, there is often reason to suspect the influence of other sources or traditions. Thus there are intriguing agreements between Matthew and Luke, e.g. in the parables chapter the hard saying about parables is significantly different in Matthew and Luke from in Mark.

What do you think?

Compare Mark 4:11 ('To you the mystery has been given of the kingdom') with Matt. 13:11 and Luke 8:10 ('To you it has been given to know the mysteries of the kingdom').

There are a number of places where Matthew seems more original than Mark. For example, in the discussion about the washing of hands in Matt. 15, Mark's interpretative comment 'cleansing all foods' looks like an addition, and Matthew's words about Jesus being 'sent only to the lost sheep of the house of Israel' look like words of Jesus that Mark could well have omitted (Mark 7:19; Matt. 15:24).

Given such evidence, it is not surprising that some scholars have questioned the two source theory, some actually postulating that Matthew's Gospel was used by Mark, not vice versa, others abandoning the Q hypothesis. What emerges anyway is that it is a mistake to think of Matthew writing his Gospel by stitching together extracts from different sources one after the other. It is much more probable that he drew on a fund of traditions (including perhaps Mark), choosing from his sources and expressing his own theological concerns and interests through the story as he retold it.

BACKGROUND AND PURPOSE

The Jewishness of Matthew's Gospel and its stress on fulfilment strongly suggest that the author was writing in a Jewish Christian context. The sharply polemical attitude towards 'the Jews' and especially to the 'scribes and Pharisees' in 'their synagogues' is not necessarily in tension with this, and may indeed partly reflect Matthew's closeness to those he criticises (compare the bitterness of the Qumran community to the Jerusalem authorities). It is widely agreed that Matthew was written in a situation of conflict between Jewish Christians and non-Christian Jews, between 'church' and 'synagogue'.

The Gospel has often been linked to the so-called Council of Jamnia, which took place in about AD 90 (e.g. W. D. Davies *The Setting of the Sermon on the Mount*. Cambridge: CUP, 1963). It is argued that the Jews started to regroup and reorganize in Jamnia (in

Galilee), following the catastrophic destruction of Jerusalem and the temple in AD 70. The Pharisees were now the controlling group, and others such as the Sadducees did not get a look in. As for the Christians, a new clause invoking a curse against them was supposedly introduced to the synagogue liturgy, which made for a final split between church and synagogue. Jewish Christians had been able to see themselves as part of the broad church of Judaism up to this point, but now they were excluded.

Features of Matthew's Gospel thought to reflect that situation include:

- the strong claim in the Gospel that Jesus is the fulfilment of Judaism;
- the bitter polemic against the Pharisees in particular and 'their/your synagogues', also the rejection of the title 'rabbi' (4:23; 9:35; 10:17; 23:8, 24);
- the references in the Gospel to Jewish persecution of Christians (10:17; 23:34).

Against this, some have argued that certain features of the Gospel (e.g. the injunction to obey the teaching of the scribes and Pharisees in 23:2-3; the reference to paying the temple tax in 17:24-27; also 10:5) point to the Christians still being 'within' Judaism and perhaps to the temple of Jerusalem still standing. It is clear that tensions between church and synagogue were acute from a very early date, as when Saul the Pharisee spearheaded persecution of the early Christians. It is therefore possible to see Matthew as reflecting not the Jamnian situation, but more that of earlier Palestinian Christianity, such as Acts describes in Jerusalem, where Jewish issues (about Jesus, the law and righteousness) dominate, and the Gentile mission is not the most pressing concern. (The idea that 5:19 is anti-Pauline is not very plausible, but it is quite thinkable that Matthew's Gospel as a whole was written in the context of debate between Christians and Jews about the Jewishness of Christianity and the law.)

Although Matthew's broad context may have been one of conflict between church and synagogue, his purpose was not just polemical. He was concerned with problems and probably divisions within the church (as is suggested by ch. 18 and by the emphasis in the Gospel on Christians forgiving each other, e.g. 6:14, 15). And, although Matthew's emphasis on righteousness, law and obedience may have partly been in response to Jewish opponents of Christianity who were criticizing Christians for their 'lawlessness', it was also probably because of Matthew's own concern about antinomian tendencies in the church (such as Paul experienced in the charismatic Corinthian church, cf. Matt. 7:21-23).

AUTHORSHIP AND DATE

Within the text of the Gospel, the author's name is not given, but the name of Matthew was attached to it from a very early date. Papias, bishop of Hierapolis in Turkey, said (early second century): 'Matthew compiled the oracles in the Hebrew dialect and each interpreted them as best he could' (Eusebius *Hist. eccl* 3.39.16). We know of no challenge being offered to this view in the first Christian centuries.

Modern scholars, however, see difficulties with the traditional view.

- Markan priority is generally accepted, and people see it as unlikely that Matthew the apostle would have used Mark as his source.
- Papias's reference to Matthew writing in the Hebrew dialect – perhaps meaning the

Aramaic language – does not seem to be reflected in the style of Matthew's Gospel as we have it, and in any case seems to contradict the view that Matthew used Mark as his source. Scholars have accordingly wondered if Matthew's 'oracles', as referred to by Papias, are Matthew's Gospel at all, or perhaps some of the source material used by Matthew, even perhaps the hypothetical Q. Others have suggested that Papias's reference to 'the Hebrew dialect' might refer not to the Hebrew language, but to the Hebraic and distinctively Jewish idiom of Matthew's Gospel. Or, even if the reference is to the Hebrew/Aramaic language, it could be that Papias assumed that the apostle Matthew, writing in so Jewish an idiom and in a Jewish context, must have written originally in Hebrew/Aramaic. Quite how he understood the relationship of our Matthew to the supposed original is hardly clarified by the statement that 'each interpreted them as best he could'.

The internal evidence of the Gospel does not settle the question of authorship. But:

- it seems likely that the author was a Jewish Christian, writing in a Jewish environment;
- he has a particular interest in scribes and Pharisees, which might be described as a love-hate relationship at least so far as scribes are concerned, since he can speak disparagingly of Jewish scribes but positively of Christian scribes (e.g. 23:34);
- in particular, 13:52 is a mini-parable about the 'scribe who is trained/discipled for the kingdom of heaven', and who is like a 'householder who brings out of his treasure things old and things new'. Scholars have noted that this very much describes the perspective of the writer of

Matthew's Gospel, who could see himself precisely as such a kingdom disciple-scribe.

What about the references to the apostle Matthew within the Gospel? These give very little away, so far as the authorship question is concerned. Mark and Luke describe Jesus calling *Levi* the tax collector ('son of Alphaeus', according to Mark) but then go on to refer to Matthew as one of the twelve apostles (and to James as 'son of Alphaeus'). Matthew's Gospel refers to the tax collector and the apostle both as 'Matthew' (Mark 2:14; 3:18; Matt. 9:9; 10:3). The most probable explanation of this remains the traditional one, i.e. that Levi and Matthew are the same person. It is not clear why Mark and Luke call him Levi at his call and Matthew later, whereas Matthew loses the name Levi altogether. But it could conceivably have something to do with the authorship of the Gospel.

IS THERE ANY PLAY ON NAMES?

The apostle's name in Greek is *Matthaios*.

- Matt. 13:52 speaks of the scribe discipled (=*mathēteutheis*) for the kingdom of heaven.
- Matt. 28:19 has Jesus send his followers out to disciple (=*mathēteuein*) all nations.

The arguments for and against Matthew as the author are inconclusive. It would be surprising if Matthew the apostle based his Gospel on Mark's in the sense that he copied Mark word for word, adding nothing of his own; but it is not impossible that he decided to use Mark as a framework for his own account. We saw evidence of Matthew's Gospel having non-Markan traditions, which would make sense if Matthew was the author. As for Papias's comments, it is

perfectly possible that the first Christian Gospel was in Hebrew/Aramaic, and that our Matthew is in some way the Greek successor of that primitive account of Jesus.

MATTHEW AND LUKE'S PARABLE OF THE VINEYARD

Luke 14:15-24 is a parable in which a rich man makes a banquet, and the invited guests make excuses (buying a field or oxen, or marrying a wife), infuriating the host, who then sends his servants out to bring the poor and needy into the banquet instead.

Matthew 22:1-14 has a king making a banquet, guests making excuses and attacking the servants of the king. The king therefore 'sent his army and destroyed those murderers and burned their city', and then sent the servants to gather in guests from the streets.

Some scholars think that Matthew has adapted the parable in the light of Jewish persecution of Christians and the destruction of Jerusalem in AD 70; others think that we have similar, but different, parables.

Most scholars date Matthew after Mark, and often relate it to the Jamnian council of c. AD 90. But some argue that things such as the story of the temple tax in 17:24-27 and references to mission within Palestine (e.g. 10:23) could point to an earlier date.

SOME ISSUES FOR TODAY

- In a world where we tend to individualism in religion and spirituality, we may be challenged by Matthew, who sees Jesus in the context of God's purpose for the people of Israel and for the world, and who has a high view of the church as the community founded by Jesus to fulfil God's purpose.

● A major issue for the church and the world today is that of Judaism and anti-semitism, especially after the holocaust. Matthew writes in a different context, when the Jews were the majority and Christians the persecuted minority. But it is worth reflecting on (a) how affirmative he is of the OT and Jewish heritage, (b) how critical he is of empty and hypocritical religion and (c) how strongly he believes in Jesus and his teaching as the only way to life. Rejection of Jesus is seen as a sure road to judgement.

● Matthew's critique of religion includes bogus Christian discipleship. For him discipleship is not just profession of faith or even religious experience, but obedience to the teaching of Jesus. Ethics are not an optional extra, but an essential part of the 'righteousness' that Jesus came to bring.

● In a pluralist world where most things seem to be believed and practised, Matthew's serious emphasis on divine judgement deserves pondering. Matthew believes that there is a clear difference between true and false religion, and that the good news of life in Jesus is to be set against the bad news that some will be cast into outer darkness.

ESSAY TOPICS

INTRODUCTORY
● Book endings are often important in the NT. What do we learn about Matthew's purpose from the first six verses and the last five verses of his Gospel?

● What is the good news of Matthew's Gospel?

INTERMEDIATE
● What sort of people are in focus in the solemn words of 7:21-23? (Note that 'evil-doers' is literally 'workers of lawlessness'.) Is this a clue to the purpose of the sermon on the mount? (cf. 1 Cor. 5:1–6:20)?

● Why has Matt. 13:52 been seen as a clue to the purpose of Matthew's whole Gospel?

FURTHER READING

* denotes books assuming knowledge of Greek; most can be used by all students.

INTRODUCTORY
DJG article 'Matthew, Gospel of '.

J. P. Meier 'Matthew, Gospel of ', Anchor Bible Dictionary, vol. 4, ed. D.N. Freedman. New York: Doubleday, 1992, 622-641.

J. Riches *Matthew*. Sheffield: Sheffield Academic Press, 1996.

D. Senior *What are They Saying About Matthew?* Mahwah, NJ: Paulist, 1996.

INTERMEDIATE
*G. Barth, G.Bornkamm & H. J. Held *Tradition and Interpretation in Matthew*. London: SCM/Philadelphia:Westminster Press, 1963 (influential collection of essays from a redactional critical point of view).

R. T. France *Matthew Evangelist and Teacher*. Exeter: Paternoster Downers Grove: IVP, 1989 (a particularly useful exploration of Matthew's themes).

J. D. Kingsbury *Matthew as Story*. Philadelphia: Fortress, 1986 (one of the most influential of recent writers on Matthew).

U. Luz *The Theology of the Gospel of Matthew*. Cambridge: Cambridge University Press, 1995 (Luz has written a huge three-volume commentary on Matthew; this short book brings together some of his ideas about Matthew's theology).

G. N. Stanton *A Gospel for a New People*. Edinburgh: T. & T. Clark, 1992/Louisville: Westminster/John Knox Press, 1993 (a significant collection of slightly technical articles on the Gospel of Matthew).

COMMENTARIES (INTRODUCTORY)
C. Blomberg *The New American Commentary, vol. 22, Matthew*. Nashville: Broadman, 1992.

D. A. Carson 'Matthew'. In The Expositor's Bible Commentary, vol. 8, ed. F. E. Gaebelein. Grand Rapids: Zondervan, 1984, 3–599.

R. T. France *The Gospel according to Matthew*. Leicester: IVP, 1985/Grand Rapids: Eerdmans, 1987.

D. E. Garland *Reading Matthew*. London: SPCK/New York: Crossroad, 1993.

H. B. Green *The Gospel according to Matthew*. Oxford: Clarendon, 1975.

D. Senior *The Gospel of Matthew*. Nashville: Abingdon, 1997.

COMMENTARIES (INTERMEDIATE)
*D. A. Hagner *Matthew*, 2 vols. Dallas: Word, 1993, 1995.

*W. D. Davies and D. C. Allison *The Gospel According to Saint Matthew*, 3 vols., International Critical Commentary. Edinburgh: Clark, 1988.

Chapter 11

LUKE

LUKE-ACTS: A TWO-VOLUME WORK

Luke is unique among the Gospels in having a 'part two' in the shape of Acts, continuing the story of Jesus into the life of the church. Luke leaves hints that he conceived the books as a two-volume work in the introductions to the two books (Luke 1:1-4; Acts 1:1-5). The books share a dedication to Theophilus (Luke 1:3; Acts 1:1), who may be Luke's literary patron, arranging for the publication of his books. The books also share a common theme, for Acts 1:1 says that the previous book (Luke) was about 'everything … which Jesus *began* to do and teach', implying that Acts will describe what he continued to do and teach, but now through his followers.

Therefore, in reading Luke, we need to have half an eye on Acts, and there are key moments where knowledge of Acts will shine light on the pages of Luke, as a theme reappears, a prophecy is fulfilled or a character mirrors another in the other volume. I shall comment on a few of these, but there are lots of others to look out for.

STRUCTURE

Like Matthew, Luke begins his story with the birth of Jesus, although from a different angle, and ends with quite a full description of Jesus' resurrection appearances. He has several blocks of stories which follow essentially the same sequence of events as Mark. However, unlike either, he has a long 'journey' section (9:51–19:27) during which Jesus travels to Jerusalem. Much of this section contains stories unique to Luke, and this Gospel is to some degree organized around it, falling into five major sections:

1:1–2:25	The births of John and Jesus
3:1–4:13	Preparations for Jesus' ministry
4:14–9:50	Jesus in Galilee
9:51–19:27	Jesus' journey to Jerusalem
19:28–24:43	Jesus in Jerusalem: his death and resurrection

It is worth noticing that, while the movement of Luke is towards Jerusalem, Acts moves broadly in the opposite direction, away from the city (where Acts 1–7 are located) to 'the ends of the earth' (Acts 1:8), finishing with Paul preaching in Rome (Acts 28:17-31). More than that, it may be that Luke is beginning from a context of Roman rule (notice Luke 1:5; 2:1; 3:1) and ending his two volumes at the heart of the Roman empire. At the heart of his two books, then, sit the death and resurrection of Jesus, which form the basis of the Christian proclamation in Acts (see C. L. Blomberg *Jesus and The Gospels*, Leicester: Apollos/ Nashville: Broadman & Holman, 1997, 140-2 for this view).

JOURNEYING WITH JESUS IN LUKE'S GOSPEL

1:1-4 Luke begins his book with a statement of his purpose (see pp. 57f.), paralleled only by John 20:31. Luke writes in order to instruct Theophilus about Jesus. We know nothing more of this man, but Luke clearly expects him to know something of the Christian faith already (v. 4) and writes in order to provide him assurance about its truth.

LUKE AS A HISTORIAN

Luke presents his writing in the style of ancient technical writers and claims to have researched his material carefully, thus placing himself among the ancient historians. His editing of Mark is generally conservative, not radically altering his source, and where we can check his information about settings, local customs and rulers (especially in Acts), he gets his information right (see more fully, Marshall 1970, ch. III).

Hans Conzelmann , a key figure in Lukan studies and a pioneer of redaction criticism, argued (Conzelmann 1960) that Luke was the first to tell the story of Jesus as part of the history of God's actions for his people (*Heilsgeschichte* or 'salvation history'). Conzelmann believed that Luke saw time in three parts – the period of Israel, the period of Jesus and the period of the church – by contrast with the more usual Jewish division into this age and the age to come. Thus the period of Jesus was the middle of time, a period free of Satan's activity (based on 4:13 and 22:3).

THE DELAY OF THE RETURN OF JESUS

Behind Luke's 'salvation history' interpretation, Conzelmann believed, was a church struggling to come to terms with the 'delay of the parousia', the fact that Jesus had not yet returned, and becoming institutionalized (the latter particularly seen in Acts' picture of leaders in the early church, which Conzelmann saw as largely fictional). Thus Luke played down teaching of Jesus focused on his imminent return.

Critics of Conzelmann have argued that he underplays or ignores evidence of an imminent expectation in Luke (e.g. 3:9; 9:27; 10:9, 11; 12:39f., 42-46; 17:23-27; 21:32) and the presence of the kingdom in Jesus' ministry (e.g. 11:20f.). These emphases show that Luke has not moved the parousia to an indefinite future time. Further, Conzelmann fails to notice evidence for an interval before the parousia in the teaching of Paul, an acknowledged early writer who can identify himself with those who live or those who have died at the parousia (e.g. 1 Thess. 4:15; 5:10; Rom. 14:8f.; 1 Cor. 6:14; Phil. 1:20-26).

Luke's stress appears to be on the certainty of Jesus' return (Acts 1:11) rather than its timing. Nevertheless, Conzelmann has identified key issues in interpreting Luke, and his work has been highly influential on subsequent scholarly debate (see more fully, Marshall 1970, ch. IV).

1:5–2:52 Luke then jumps into the story of the births of John the Baptist and Jesus, overlapping the stories and highlighting similarities and differences of the two. Both have a miraculous birth following a message from an angel; both accounts contain songs of praise to God (1:46-52, 67-79; 2:29-32); both are filled with the Spirit (1:15, 35; cf. 4:1); their development is similar (1:80; 2:52). But John is the messenger who prepares the way for Jesus, as chs 3–4 will make clear; he is a prophet, but Jesus is the son of God, the Messiah who brings salvation (1:16f., 31-33, 35; 2:10f., 26-32). (See further Green 1995, 51-5.)

What do you think?
ZECHARIAH AND MARY

Luke seems to parallel and contrast these two characters in his account in Luke 1–2. Divide a piece of paper into two columns, heading one 'Zechariah' and one 'Mary', and then note in each column the points Luke makes about them, particularly in their response to what God says to them by the angel messages. What portrait of these two characters emerges? How are they similar and how are they different? What might Luke be saying to his readers by this paralleling of the two?

The Greek language and style of this section of Luke is strongly influenced by Hebrew and Aramaic forms of expression, and much of it reads like Greek which has been translated from one of those languages, rather like the Septuagint. The combination with strongly Jewish themes gives these chapters a feel rather like the OT, emphasizing that Jesus fulfils Scripture.

This section closes with the only story about Jesus' youth in the canonical Gospels (2:41-51), highlighting the theme of Jesus' birth by the Spirit – which means that God is his true Father (v. 49).

3:1–4:13 jumps forward to the adulthood of John and Jesus and sets the scene for Jesus' public ministry. As he has done before, Luke locates events in the context of world history (3:1f.; cf. 2:1f.), hinting that Jesus is to be saviour of the world and not just Israel.

Digging deeper:
THE HYMNS OF LUKE 1–2

There are three major songs in Luke's infancy stories (1:46-55, 68-79; 2:28-32). Read them aloud as if you were a Jewish revolutionary who wanted to throw the Roman occupiers out violently. What are the major themes which come out? As a revolutionary, would you agree with these songs or have problems with them? How would these songs sound to Theophilus, as a Roman official? What hints are there that God's purposes include Gentiles? Why do you think Luke includes them – what do they contribute to his message?

If you can, read Green 1995, 7-9, 29-31 or the *DJG* articles 'Mary's Song', 'Simeon's Song' and 'Zechariah's Song'. Now re-read the songs in the light of these articles: how would you now answer the questions above? What picture emerges of what Jesus comes to do?

LUKE'S PORTRAYAL OF TIME

Time moves at differing speeds in Luke's story, sometimes very fast, such as 2:40 (covering 12 years), 52 (covering some 18 years). In other places he slows down 'narrative time', the speed at which the story moves, so as to focus attention on something, such as the arrest, trial and death of Jesus (22:1–23:56, covering no more than 48 hours).

Luke gives us more detail on John's ministry, especially his preaching, than the other evangelists (3:10-14), although like Matthew and Mark, Luke sees John's ministry as fulfilling Isa. 40:3-5 (quoted in 3:4-6). John underlines that his role is to prepare for another (3:15-17). After Jesus' baptism, reported in similar language to Mark (3:21;

Digging deeper:
JESUS AND THE SPIRIT IN LUKE

Luke mentions the role of the Spirit much more in relation to Jesus than the other evangelists. Here, he adds further references to the coming of the Spirit at Jesus' baptism (4:1 [twice], 14). Read Luke 1–4 and note the various activities of the Spirit there.

Two theories about this portrait are: (a) the Spirit is the 'Spirit of prophecy', in line with OT and Jewish teaching that the Spirit principally inspires speech, and the Spirit does not have 'ethical' influence or produce miracles (so Robert Menzies); and (b) at his baptism, the Spirit brings Jesus a new experience of God's kingdom and his own divine sonship (so James Dunn). How far do you think the evidence supports these views?

(Further reading: Turner 1996, ch. 2.)

cf. Mark 1:9-11), Luke inserts his genealogy (3:23-38), which traces Jesus' roots through Joseph, back to Adam and God (again hinting at the universal salvation Jesus comes to bring), by contrast with Matthew, who follows the line through Mary and stops at Abraham (Matt. 1:1, 16).

4:14–9:50 takes us into Jesus' ministry in Galilee. Blocks of Markan material (4:31–44; 5:12–6:19; 8:4–9:50) alternate with blocks of Q and L material mixed together (4:14-30; 5:1-11; 6:20–8:3). Where Luke uses Markan stories here, he also uses Mark's sequence of these stories, although he frequently rewrites the stories in his own words and brings out his own emphases.

Luke 4:14-30 offers a story of Jesus' rejection in the synagogue at Nazareth that is both much fuller than the other synoptic

Gospels (cf. Mark 6:1-6; Matt. 13:53-58), and which is located much earlier in Jesus' ministry than in Matthew and Mark. Luke alone says that Jesus read from Isa. 61:1f. (plus a phrase from Isa. 58:6), and we read much more of the events which follow (vv. 20-30). The Isaiah reading acts as a 'manifesto' for Jesus' ministry in Luke and highlights the key Lukan theme of reversal: captives will be released, blind people will see and the oppressed will be free (perhaps echoing OT Jubilee legislation, see Lev. 25). The mention of two Gentiles whom God blessed (vv. 25-27) is again a hint of God's purpose to bless the world through Jesus.

Digging deeper:
JESUS AND THE POOR

Who does Luke see as the 'poor' to whom Jesus brings good news (4:18)? Two possibilities are the literally (economically) poor and the 'religiously' poor (cf. Pss 34:6; 40:17; 70:5; 74:19). Trace the use of 'poor' through Luke: it comes in 4:18; 6:20; 7:22; 14:13; 14:21; 16:20; 16:22; 18:22; 19:8; 21:3. Who are the poor for Luke and what is Jesus' good news for them?

The remainder of the chapter outlines a day of ministry in Capernaum (vv. 31-41) and Jesus' departure to other places (vv. 42f.), with only small variations from Mark's wording.

Luke alone tells the story of the call of the disciples in detail (5:1-11; cf. Mark 1:16-20; Matt. 4:18-22), including the miraculous catch of fish, Luke's first example of Jesus' power over nature. Next (returning to Markan material) is Jesus' first healing, which brings an outcast sufferer with leprosy back into the community (5:12-14). Jesus heals a paralytic let down through the roof (5:17-26), a story which Luke contextualizes into a setting where roofs have tiles (v. 19; cf. Mark 2:4 – a more traditional wood and earth roof through which the man's friends dig).

The call of Levi the tax collector (5:27f.) leads to a party at Levi's house for his associates (vv. 29-32) during which the Pharisees and their scribes criticize Jesus to his disciples for mixing with such people. Having received a firm response from Jesus which makes clear that he calls sinners (vv. 31f.), his opponents then criticize Jesus' disciples because they do not fast properly (v. 33). Jesus' answer (vv. 34-39) hinges on Jesus' identity and role, for he is the bridegroom of his story and the one who brings new wine which will require fresh ways of living, 'new wineskins'. Further controversy follows, on the Sabbath (6:1-11), highlighting the newness which Jesus brings as Lord of the Sabbath.

The choice of the twelve (6:12-16) leads into Luke's sermon on the plain (6:17-49), a rather briefer equivalent of Matthew's sermon on the mount (Matt. 5–7) and based on Q material. Jesus' blessings are each paired with corresponding woes found in Luke alone (6:20-26), echoing themes from the Nazareth sermon (4:14-30) and further showing Luke's interest in reversal of human ideas by Jesus. This theme develops through teaching which expounds Jesus' values: loving enemies (6:27-36), not judging others (6:37-42), and the link between the kind of fruit produced and the tree on which it grows (6:43-45). The two builders' story closes the sermon (6:46-39; cf. Matt. 7:21-27, a story in a more Palestinian setting).

Luke's healing of the centurion's servant is a much fuller story than Matthew's equivalent (7:1-10; cf. Matt. 8:5-13), and portrays the centurion remarkably similarly to Cornelius, the godly centurion of Acts 10–11 (compare Luke 7:4f. and Acts 10:2) – something that would be congenial to Roman officials reading the two books. Luke's Jesus not only assists Gentiles, but also touches the dead and brings them to life (7:11-17, unique to Luke), showing that the old view that uncleanness spread (e.g. Lev. 5:2f.; Num. 5:2) was now reversed, for Jesus' holiness now even restores a ritually unclean dead body to life.

Luke then clarifies Jesus' relationship to John the Baptist (7:18-35). During this story Jesus again echoes the words of Isa. 61 read in the Nazareth synagogue (v. 22; cf. 4:18f.) and praises John's ministry. Luke highlights the division brought about by John and Jesus (vv. 29f., unique to Luke). The welcome Jesus offers to 'sinners' (and the judgement he brings to the self-righteous) is further underlined by the forgiveness of the weeping woman and the telling parable of the unforgiving servant (7:36-50; see the superb discussion in Bailey 1983). Not only that, but Jesus is financially supported by women who have been made clean by contact with him (8:1-3).

Mark's sequence and material then return, and 8:4–9:50 parallel sections of Mark 4–6 and 8–9. Luke is not simply copying Mark, however: he continues to shape the material himself. Thus, Luke's portrait of the visit of Jesus' mother and brothers (8:19-21; cf. Mark 3:19-21, 31-35) is not openly critical of them, but uses them to illustrate the good soil of the parable of the soils (8:8, 15).

Four miracles (8:22-56, all found in Mark) show Jesus' awesome power over the wind and waves, demons, illness and death (notice

vv. 25, 37, 47, 56). In the light of Jesus' power, he sends his disciples to extend his ministry (9:1-6, 10f., not found in Mark). The focus on Jesus' identity continues with Herod's question (9:7-9), a further nature miracle, feeding 5,000 people (9:12-17), and Jesus himself asking about his identity (9:18-20), which leads to the first occasion he teaches about his coming suffering and death, and the concomitant suffering of his followers (9:21-27). Further revelation about Jesus follows in the transfiguration (9:28-36), during which Jesus speaks with Moses and Elijah about his 'exodus' (v. 31, a word unique to Luke) in Jerusalem. On coming down from the mountain of transfiguration Jesus encounters the demonized boy whom his disciples cannot help and further shows his power in exorcizing the demon (9:37-43, note v. 43).

Digging deeper:
LITERARY PROPHECY IN LUKE-ACTS

Luke uses a technique of including a prophecy of an event to come and later reporting the fulfilment of the prophecy. This can happen where both come within Luke's Gospel, where one comes from the OT and the other is found in Luke, where one is found in Luke and the other in Acts, or where both are in Acts. Examine the examples below and think about what Luke is achieving by using this device.

Luke 9:21f., 44; 18:31-33 and 24:6-8, 44
Luke 7:20f. and Isa. 29:18f.; 35:5f.; 61:1f.
Luke 7:27 and Mal. 3:1
Luke 21:12-15 and Acts 4:3-5, 14; 5:17-42
Luke 9:5; 10:11 and Acts 13:51
Luke 22:30 and Acts 5:1-11
Acts 21:10-14 and Acts 21:30-35

Now that his identity is clearer Jesus speaks again about his death (9:44f.) and then resolves an argument among the disciples, who squabble like children over greatness, by using a child to show that the apparently unimportant are the ones who truly matter – another example of reversal (9:46-48).

9:51–19:27 form Jesus' journey to Jerusalem, and Luke marks out the new section in 9:51 (unique to Luke, as is 9:52-56) showing his readers again where the journey is leading (cf. 9:22, 44). Luke 9:51 is the first of a series of notes by Luke focusing on Jesus' travelling to Jerusalem: others come at 9:53, 56, 57; 10:1; 13:22, 31, 33; 14:25; 17:11; 18:31, 35f.; 19:1, 11, 28. A good deal of the contents of this section is unique to Luke (over 40%), and there is a particular focus on teaching and parables. As Jesus journeys, so we read what it means to travel with him as his disciples learn this. In particular, following Jesus involves:

● prioritizing discipleship above all other demands (9:57-62);
● going out to proclaim the kingdom in preaching and healing (10:1-12);
● rejoicing at belonging to Jesus (10:17-20);
● wholehearted love for God and neighbour (10:25-37);
● devotion to Jesus which listens at his feet (10:38-42);
● learning to pray from Jesus (11:1-13).

After this extended section addressed to his disciples, we now hear Jesus speaking with the crowds (11:14, 27, 29; 12:1, 13) and handling controversy (11:14-54). Jesus refutes the claim that he uses evil powers to exorcize (11:14-23); he warns of judgement on those who seek signs rather than obey his word (11:27-32); and he criticizes the Pharisees and scribes for their misinterpretation of the torah, both to their faces and to his disciples (11:37–12:3).

We then return to the theme of discipleship, and Luke brings together a variety of material found spread around in Mark and Matthew (12:1–13:9; in more detail, see Walton 2000, 118-27). Jesus warns of the cost of discipleship and the need for alertness in the face of various pressures:

- the threat of being killed for following Jesus (12:4-7);
- the need to own up to being a disciple, especially when on trial (12:8-12);
- the dangers of covetousness (12:13-21), reinforced by assurance that God will care for Jesus' followers (12:22-32), so that wealth can be given to the needy (12:33f.);
- a group of parables on readiness (12:36-48) and a call to read the signs of the times (12:54-56);
- a warning about the division Jesus brings (12:49-53);
- a warning of the consequences of not repenting and bearing fruit by following Jesus (13:1-9).

As he travels to Jerusalem, Jesus is re-forming the people of God, but now centred around himself. So who can be a disciple? Luke 13:10–17:19 keeps returning to this question, providing a range of answers. Here the disciples mostly fade into the background and Jesus' main conversation partners are the Pharisees (13:31; 14:1, 3; 15:2; 16:14). Three characteristics are vital in disciples.

Welcome Disciples see restoring people to the people of God as more important than rigid adherence to Sabbath traditions (13:10-17; 14:1-6), and they are humble people who welcome the weak, the poor and needy, and children, and are ready to be servants, and true disciples (14:7-14; 17:1-10).

Openness to others, for the kingdom is open to all. The 'birds of the air' symbolize the nations (13:18f.). People will come from the four points of the compass (13:22-30). Sinners are welcome (15:1-31; note the setting in vv. 1f.). Outcasts (sufferers with leprosy) are welcome, not least foreigners (Samaritans) (17:10-19).

Response to God's invitation (14:15-24). Sadly, Jerusalem will reject Jesus and lose its place in God's purposes (13:31-35). Response to Jesus is costly and needs to be weighed carefully, for the kingdom takes priority over wealth (14:25-33; 16:1-15). But Jesus' invitation is not new – it repeats the invitation found in Scripture (16:16-31; note vv. 29-31).

The pace of narrative time picks up from 17:11 onwards, and there are more frequent references to Jesus' movement to Jerusalem. As the city looms larger, questions of discipleship continue to appear (18:18-30), but are now interspersed with more teaching about Jesus' destiny in the city. Two central themes recur.

First, Jesus' arrival in Jerusalem will not precipitate the kingdom coming visibly (17:20-37; 19:11-27). Hence, his disciples must be faithful in the interval before the visible appearing of the kingdom (18:1-8; 19:11-27). Such faithfulness includes humble dependence on God in the interval, like that of a child (18:1-8, 9-17).

Second, Jesus will suffer, die and rise again (18:31-34), for he is Israel's Messiah, recognized by a blind man whom he heals (18:35-43). Indeed, he has come for the lost, to reincorporate them into God's people (19:1-10, note v. 9).

As we leave the journey section and Jesus arrives in the city, Luke has painted a clear picture of who Jesus is, what he is to accomplish, and what it means to be his followers.

19:28–24:43 Luke tells the story of Jesus' time in Jerusalem in broadly similar sequence to the other synoptics, although throughout his own interests are evident. The greatest differences come in Luke's account of the death of Jesus (ch. 23), although also Luke's time notices are vaguer than Mark's (19:29, 45; 20:1; 21:5; 22:1, 7; cf. Mark 11:12, 20, 27; 14:1, 12), and give the impression of Jesus spending a substantial period in Jerusalem before the crisis leading to his death (note also the summaries in 19:47; 21:37f.).

Luke 19:28-48 recounts Jesus' arrival in the city on a donkey (vv. 29-40) followed by a story unique to Luke in which Jesus weeps over the city (vv. 41-44; cf. 13:31-35), and the demonstration in the temple (vv. 45-48). Then Luke reports, in the same sequence as Mark and Matthew, a series of controversy stories (20:1-44) and Jesus' denunciation of the scribes and the wealthy (20:45–21:4).

Luke 21:5-36 is Luke's version of Jesus' teaching on the future (cf. Mark 13; Matt. 24), and shows a number of touches which suggest his expected readership need Jewish customs and ideas explaining (compare vv. 20-24 with Mark 13:14-20 and Matt. 24:15-22) (see pp. 163–6). C. H. Dodd saw vv. 20-24 as heavily influenced by OT prophecies of the fall of the city in 587 BC, and therefore argued that it did not necessarily display knowledge of the actual events of AD 66-70 – and thus did not compel a date for the composition of Luke after AD 70.

A Lukan summary (21:37f.) leads into the unveiling of the plot to kill Jesus (22:1-6).

Luke omits the anointing of Jesus at Bethany (Mark 14:3-9; Matt. 2:6-13), perhaps because he has a similar story at 7:36-50, and cuts to the action of the Last Supper (22:7-38; see Walton 2000, 100-17). Jesus explains his forthcoming death by reinterpreting the Passover meal (vv. 8, 11, 13, 14). Luke's version of the words over the bread and wine is rather different from that in Mark and Matthew (22:15-20; cf. Mark 14:22-25; Matt. 26:26-29), and follows the sequence cup-bread-cup (assuming vv. 19b-20 to be part of Luke's original: see Nolland 1993, 1041 or Fitzmyer 1985, 1387-9). Luke uniquely includes the disciples' dispute about greatness (vv. 24-30), phrased very differently from a debate on the same topic elsewhere in Mark and Matthew (Mark 10:41-45; Matt. 20:24-28). Those who think Luke is rewriting and relocating this story usually appear not to realize how endemic arguments about who is most important can be to a human group! After reporting Jesus' prophecy of Peter's denial and restoration (vv. 31-34), Luke uniquely reports a saying which reverses the mission instructions given earlier (vv. 35-38; cf. 10:3f.), highlighting that something new is happening.

From there Jesus goes to the garden to pray. He is failed by his disciples who cannot stay awake to pray with him (22:39-46), and then arrested (22:47-53). Luke's report of the trials of Jesus (22:63–23:25) contains material unique to this Gospel, especially:

- he omits the night-time hearing before Caiaphas (Mark 14:53-65; Matt. 26:57-68);
- he gives a fuller account of the morning hearing (22:66-71; cf. Mark 15:1; Matt. 27:1f.);
- he tells of Jesus' meeting with Herod (23:6-13).

Digging deeper:
THE CHARGES AGAINST JESUS

Read the charges brought against Jesus (23:2) and then consider what in Luke's record of his teaching might have led to these charges being brought, looking from the point of view of a member of the Jewish establishment (high priests, Sadducees, etc.).

● In what ways could Jesus have been seen by the Jewish establishment as 'perverting the nation'?
● How could Jesus' answer in 20:21-26 have been seen as urging non-payment of Roman taxes?
● In what ways could Luke's Jesus be thought to claim political power as a king?

After you have thought about this yourself, consult commentaries (see further reading at the end of the chapter) to add to your understanding.

Luke's crucifixion narrative (23:1-56) presents the meaning of Jesus' death rather differently from Mark, focusing on the theme of Jesus' innocence, declared eight times (vv. 4, 14, 15, 22, 41, 47, 48, 51). Luke's innocent Jesus therefore dies in place of both the guilty Barabbas (vv. 13-25) and the guilty nation who have rejected Jesus and will face God's judgement (vv. 27-31, 48). The darkness shows this innocent one bearing the evil of others, and therefore facing God's absence (vv. 44f.). Jesus dies tranquilly and in control: he speaks with the women (vv. 28-31); he speaks with the two criminals (vv. 39-43); he uses words of trust in God at his death (v. 46); and he prays to God as 'Father' (vv. 34, 46) – all points unique to Luke's version of the story, highlighting the willingness of Jesus to go this way for the sake of others. Finally, Joseph's action (vv. 50-53) contrasts with the verdict of the Jewish leaders and Pilate.

Luke's resurrection account (24:1-53) centres on appearances in Jerusalem (whereas Matthew focuses on Galilee), so that the Gospel begins and ends there. Four major events happen:

● the women find the empty tomb and Peter visits it (vv. 1-12);
● two people meet Jesus in a 'hidden' form on the road to Emmaus, and after walking with them he is revealed as he breaks the bread (vv. 13-35);
● Jesus appears to the disciples and eats fish with them (vv. 36-49);
● Jesus departs and the disciples return to Jerusalem rejoicing (vv. 50-53). (See also p. 267.)

Two themes recur in these stories. First and foremost, God acted in raising Jesus from the dead in fulfilment of Scripture (vv. 5-7, 25-27, 44-47; note 'it is necessary' vv. 7, 26, 44). Second, questions of the reality of the resurrection are addressed. The women see clearly which tomb Jesus is buried in (23:55f.), so there can be no doubt that that tomb is empty (24:2f., 12). But witness to the resurrection of Jesus is met by perplexity and unbelief (vv. 4, 11, 22-25, 37-40, 41-43). However, crucially, the risen Jesus eats (vv. 41-43), demonstrating that he is no mere ghost.

SOME KEY THEMES

SALVATION

If Luke has one major theme, it is salvation (see Marshall 1970, chs IV-VIII). Luke uses the language of salvation more than other evangelists: the noun 'salvation' (Greek *sōteria/ sōterion*) is found seven times (never in Mark or Matthew); God and Jesus are 'saviour' (Greek *sōter*, 1:47; 2:11 – never in Mark or

Matthew); and the verb 'save' (Greek *sōzō*) is used 17 times (Mark 13; Matt. 14), sometimes in the sense 'heal' (e.g. 8:48, 50), but often in a spiritual sense (e.g. 7:50; 8:12; 13:23; 19:10 – all unique to Luke) and there are a further 27 uses of this word group in Acts. Within this framework are to be placed Jesus' declaration of freedom to captives (4:14-30), his healing ministry, his offer of 'forgiveness of sins', a Lukan phrase (Luke 1:77; 3:3; 24:47; cf. Acts 2:38; 5:31; 10:43; 13:38; 26:18; it is found only once each in Mark and Matthew), and Luke's view of Jesus' death and resurrection.

SALVATION FOR ALL

Luke particularly emphasizes that salvation is for all, notably through his focus on Gentiles, Samaritans and marginalized people within Israel:

- the hymns of the infancy narrative highlight that Jesus comes for all, including Gentiles (2:14, 32; unique to Luke);
- Jesus' genealogy is traced to Adam (and God), thus including all humankind in his care (3:38; contrast Matt. 1:2, focusing on Abraham, the founder of the Jewish people);
- Jesus speaks positively of the widow of Zarephath and Naaman, both Gentiles (4:25-27; unique to Luke);
- Jesus responds to a Gentile centurion seeking healing (7:2-10);
- Jesus' teaching hints at the inclusion of Gentiles in God's purposes 13:28f (cf. Matt. 8:11f.); 14:23f. (unique to Luke);
- the disciples are sent to 'all nations' (24:46f.), a story which Acts tells much more fully;
- Jesus goes to a Samaritan village (9:52; although they do not welcome him, v. 53);
- Jesus makes a Samaritan the hero in a parable (10:30-37);

- the one person with leprosy who thanks Jesus is a Samaritan (17:15-19);
- women have a prominent place (see box below);

Digging deeper:
JESUS AND WOMEN

What evidence is there that Luke presents women particularly prominently? Consider the passages below, comparing them with Mark and Matthew in a synopsis, if you can, to see where material is unique to Luke or shows signs of Lukan emphasis or editing. It is worth noticing how Luke 'pairs' a man and a woman (as in chs 1–2, with Mary and Zechariah, and Anna and Simeon), sometimes showing them as equal, and sometimes presenting the woman as a positive model by contrast with the man. Is Luke's view of women more positive than the other evangelists?

chs 1–2
8:1-3; 10:38-42
7:11-15, 37-50; 8:43-48; 13:11-13
15:8-10; 18:1-8; 21:1-4; 23:27-31, 49, 55 (cf. 22:54-62)
24:1-12 (compare the reactions of the men and women)

(Further reading: Knight 1998, 154-160 or *DJG* article 'Women'.)

- Jesus comes with 'good news to the poor' (4:18; see box opposite);
- the standard criticism of Jesus is that he associates with 'tax collectors and sinners' (5:30; 7:34; 15:1f.; 19:7);
- Jesus mixes with people with leprosy, who were social outcasts (5:12f.; 7:22; 17:11-9);
- Jesus is crucified with two convicted criminals (23:39-43);

LUKE, POVERTY AND RICHES

Luke is often said to have a particular emphasis on the poor, from the opening of his Gospel, when Jesus is born to a poor family (hence the sacrifice they offer is two pigeons, 2:24; cf. Lev. 12:8), to the end, when he is buried in a borrowed tomb (23:50-53). Jesus' mission is for the poor, as Mary's song makes clear (1:52f.) and Jesus' 'Nazareth manifesto' (4:18, quoting Isa. 61:1f.; cf. 7:22) states firmly. Luke's Jesus encourages care for the poor: they are to be invited to banquets (14:12-14), and his poor disciples are blessed (note 'you poor', 6:20, spoken while Jesus looks at his disciples).

By contrast, the rich are the bad guys in Jesus' parables. They build huge barns to keep extra-large harvests and do not prepare to meet God (12:13-21). They cannot follow Jesus because they will not give up their riches (18:18-30) – it is easier for a camel to get through a needle's eye than for a rich person to enter the kingdom (18:25). Luke follows this story, which would be deeply shocking (for riches were widely seen as a mark of God's blessing) with the healing of a blind beggar (18:35-43) and the amazing change of Zacchaeus, a rich man who gives

up his riches (19:1-10). By contrast, those who stay rich receive woe (6:24).

This is a startling reversal of the usual way things are. Although possessions are not in themselves evil for Luke or Jesus, they are best used for the benefit of the poor – the rich man should have cared for poor Lazarus sitting at his gate, a location which meant that the rich man therefore knew and walked past Lazarus regularly (16:19-31). Selling possession and giving to the poor shows that a person's heart is in heaven (12:32-34). This radical form of discipleship demonstrates real trust in God, for he will give the kingdom to such people (12:32f.).

Luke is not advocating that all Christians should sell everything, for he will go on to tell in Acts of the disciples meeting in homes, which means that not everyone sold them (e.g. Acts 2:46; 12:12). But he is warning of great dangers in wealth, which can easily lead to self-trust, rather than reliance upon God (again note the rich fool, Luke 12:13-21).

(Further reading: *DJG* article 'Rich and poor'; Green 1995, 9-12, 13-18, 76-84; Tuckett 1996, ch. 5.)

● Luke uniquely draws attention to Jesus healing an only son or daughter, illustrating the value Jesus places on children, by contrast with the culture of his day (7:12; 8:42; 9:38).

This material needs to be read in the context of Luke's emphatic placing of Jesus' ministry in Israel, and Jesus' focus on a calling to serve the Jewish people – thus Luke is not antisemitic, for he also believes Jesus brings 'glory to your people Israel' (2:32). (See also pp. 292f.)

THE HOLY SPIRIT
The work of the Spirit is clearly prominent in Acts (see pp. 291f.) but Luke prepares for Acts by highlighting the ministry of the Spirit in Jesus' time. Thus, John the Baptist and

his parents are filled with the Spirit (1:15, 41, 67), and Simeon is a man of the Spirit (note the threefold reference in 2:25-27). But supremely Jesus is the man of the Spirit, conceived by the Spirit (1:35), empowered by the Spirit (3:22; 4:1, 14, 18) and the baptiser of others with the Spirit (3:16). He teaches that the Father gives the Spirit (11:13; cf. Matt. 7:11), he warns against blasphemy against the Spirit (12:10), he promises that the Spirit will instruct the disciples (12:12; cf. Acts 4:8; 6:10; 7:2, 55), and after his resurrection Jesus promises that the Spirit will come to clothe the disciples (24:49).

PRAYER AND PRAISE
'Luke's is a singing Gospel', writes Leon Morris (1988, 50), summing up well. From

Digging deeper:
PRAYER

Luke highlights the prayer life of Jesus far more than the other evangelists (3:21; 5:16; 6:12; 9:18, 28f.; 10:21f.; 11:1; 22:31f., 41-44; 23:46 – almost all unique to Luke). Not only that, but Jesus frequently teaches about prayer (6:28; 11:1-13; 18:1-8; 20:46f.; 22:40, 46).

Read these passages carefully and note: (i) what picture of God's character and nature comes across; (ii) what different types of prayer are seen; and (iii) what is said about how to pray, in both technique and attitude.

(Further reading: P. T. O'Brien, 'Prayer in Luke-Acts', *Tyndale Bulletin* 24 (1973), 111-27 or A. A. Trites, 'The Prayer Motif in Luke-Acts' in Talbert 1978, 168-86 or Fitzmyer 1985, 244-7.)

the hymns of the infancy narratives (1:46-55, 68-79; 2:30-32) onwards, there is a strong note of joy and rejoicing. Jesus comes to replace mourning by laughter (6:21), and angelic rejoicing accompanies his ministry (2:13f.; 15:10, both unique to Luke). Indeed, repentance brings joy (15:7, 10, 23, 32; 19:6). The book closes with the disciples experiencing 'great joy' and 'continually … blessing God' (24:52f.). Luke's vision of Jesus is that he brings joy.

LUKE'S SOURCES

Luke acknowledges that he has used sources in composing his book by referring to his literary predecessors (1:1), but also claims to have used eyewitness testimony (1:2) and his own research (1:3). But working out precisely what Luke got from where is not straight-

forward, for Luke shares a good deal of material with Mark and Matthew, but also has his own distinctive perspective and contents.

The large majority of Mark's book is parall-eled in Luke in more or less the same sequence, although Luke sometimes rewrites it in his own style and draws out his particular theological emphases and interests. Generally Luke is more conservative in his editing of the words of Jesus from Mark than with the surrounding narrative. Here we seem to be seeing him using a written source.

Luke also shares stories with Matthew which are not found in Mark (the so-called Q material), some phrased almost word for word the same (e.g. Luke 3:7-9; Matt. 3:7-10) and some much more loosely parallel (e.g. Luke spreads the material in Matthew's sermon on the mount all over his Gospel in a different sequence: see table on p. 65). This makes it difficult to accept that Q was a unified written source – for Luke's use of Mark, which was a written source, is very different from his apparent use of the Q stories. The majority view in scholarship remains that Luke made use of Mark and a source shared with Matthew in composing his book, but there are a wide variety of views of the nature of the Q source(s). Here we may be seeing Luke working with some written sources and some oral tradition.

Luke tells quite a number of his own, unique stories, totalling some 33-40% of his book, including his infancy narratives (chs 1–2), his version of Jesus' rejection in Nazareth (4:14-30), some parables (e.g. 15:1–16:9; 16:19-31; 17:7-10; 18:1-14), some healing stories (e.g. 7:11-17; 17:11-19), the encounter with Zacchaeus (19:1-10), elements of his crucifixion scene (23:1-16, 24f., 27-31, 39-43, 48, 51), and his resurrection narrative (ch. 24). These L stories (as they are sometimes called) cluster mainly at the beginning and end of the book and in the journey section (9:51–19:27). These parts may stem from Luke's own research and the use of eyewitness material.

Because Luke seems to alternate between blocks of material which are from Q or L or a combination of the two, and Mark (see the box below), a few scholars have suggested that Luke did a first draft of his book (known as 'proto-Luke') which was based on Q and L alone, and then added in other stories from Mark when he discovered it – an idea that goes back at least to B. H. Streeter (1924) – although this idea has not commanded general support.

LUKE AND HIS SOURCES

1–2	L
3:1–5:11	Mark's framework (Mark 1:1-39) with Q and L stories added
5:12–6:19	Mark
6:20–8:3	Q and L
8:4–9:10	Almost entirely Mark
9:51–18:14	Almost entirely Q and L
18:15–24:12	Mostly Mark with some L and a little Q

To some extent our view of Luke's sources is tied up with our view of who Luke is, and that is an issue which we shall address later, after studying his second volume, Acts. But we need to remind ourselves that Luke is no mere collector of traditions, as though he has merely glued them into a scrapbook; rather, he is a creative writer who brings stories together – and rewrites them – in his own way in order to communicate with his readers.

LUKE'S READERS, PURPOSE AND AUTHORSHIP

Because Luke needs to be considered with Acts, we shall look at questions of readership, purpose and authorship at the end of the chapter on Acts (pp. 293–6).

SOME ISSUES FOR TODAY

● Luke 1:26-38 is a major NT witness to the virginal conception of Jesus; outside Luke and Matthew there are few explicit references to this topic. This theme shows Luke's supernatural understanding of Christianity, for it is quite different from Greco-Roman stories of sexual intercourse with the gods producing miraculous children. It shows that Luke sees Jesus as fully human, sharing our experience of life, and as a divine gift to humankind, bringing God to us. In him, therefore, we see human life as it is meant to be, as well as God's generous giving of himself to us.

● Luke stresses concern for the poor, the marginalized, Samaritans and Gentiles, and underlines the inclusiveness of the community of Jesus. In many modern societies social and economic divisions exist which are just as sharp as those in first-century Palestine. In such situations Luke presents a challenge to the Christian churches to cut across such social boundaries and to find ways of including those whom that society regards as 'outsiders'. Similarly, Luke challenges Christians worldwide to ensure, as far as they are able, that poorer Christians and their homelands are not disempowered by the actions of rich countries and wealthier Christians.

● Luke's Jesus is positive towards women, more so than the cultural contexts of

Palestine and the Greco-Roman world into which he writes. Historically, Christians have sometimes been in the vanguard of the encouragement of women to fulfil their potential, encouraging education (cf. 10:39) and greater opportunities for women. But some periods of history have seen the church as oppressive to women, often simply following the cultural mores of the day in doing so. Luke's portrait of Jesus challenges male Christians to include the female half of the human race and give them appropriate opportunities. It also calls female Christians to be ready to take risks in serving God, including challenging the consensus where it is harming women's expression of their humanity and gifts.

● Luke's stress on the work of the Spirit, highlighting that John and Jesus are empowered by the Spirit and calling his disciples to wait for the Spirit to come, invites reflection on how far Christians today depend on the Spirit, and how far they have evolved systems of thought and ways of living which mean that they do not need to depend on God the Spirit to act. This is not limited to any tradition of Christianity, for any and all major Christian traditions can become rigid and inflexible – showing the uniformity of a graveyard rather than the riotous life of a field of flowers through which the Spirit can blow.

ESSAY TOPICS

INTRODUCTORY

● Compare and contrast Mark's and Luke's presentations of the Pharisees: in what ways are they the same and in what ways are their emphases different?

● How far do you agree that 4:14-30 sets the agenda for Jesus' ministry in Luke?

● A contemporary Christian hymn/song writer (you may choose who it is!) has asked you to outline the key ideas in Luke's understanding of salvation in order to help him/her write some new songs/hymns on that theme. Write a letter to this person in response to this request.

INTERMEDIATE

● Why, according to Luke, was Jesus crucified? In responding, pay attention both to the political/religious/historical reasons and to what Luke sees as God's purposes in the death of Jesus.

● What does Luke mean by his declaration of purpose in 1:1-4, and how do the various elements of his book contribute to this aim?

FURTHER READING

* denotes books assuming knowledge of Greek; most can be used by all students.

INTRODUCTORY

DJG article 'Luke, Gospel of '.

J. B. Green *The Theology of the Gospel of Luke*. NT Theology. Cambridge: Cambridge University Press, 1995 (fine study of Lukan theology).

J. Knight *Luke's Gospel*. NT Readings. London/New York: Routledge, 1998 (helpful narrative introduction to Luke and his major themes).

C. M. Tuckett *Luke*. NT Guides. Sheffield: Sheffield Academic Press, 1996 (good survey, grouped under major Lukan themes).

INTERMEDIATE

(covering Luke and Luke-Acts: see also pp. 298f.)

K. E. Bailey *Poet and Peasant and Through Peasant Eyes*. Grand Rapids: Eerdmans, 1983 (superb studies of Luke's parables with good attention to the cultural setting – originally published as two separate books).

F. Bovon *Luke the Theologian: Thirty-three Years of Research (1950-1983)*. Allison Park, PA: Pickwick, 1987 (helpful survey of Lukan scholarship grouped by major themes).

H. Conzelmann *The Theology of St Luke*. London: Faber & Faber, 1960/New York: Harper & Row, 1957 (classic redaction-critical study of Luke as a theologian).

P. F. Esler *Community and Gospel in Luke-Acts*. SNTS Monograph Series 57. Cambridge: Cambridge University Press, 1987 (key work from a sociological perspective).

L. E. Keck & J. L. Martyn, eds. *Studies in Luke-Acts*. London: SPCK, 1968/Nashville: Abingdon, 1966 (classic collection of key essays).

I. H. Marshall *Luke: Historian and Theologian*. Exeter: Paternoster/Grand Rapids: Zondervan, 1970 (key study, arguing that Luke is both historian and theologian).

C. H. Talbert, ed. *Perspectives on Luke-Acts*. Edinburgh: T. & T. Clark/Danville, VA: Assn. of Baptist Professors of Religion, 1978 (valuable collection of articles).

R. C. Tannehill *The Narrative Unity of Luke-Acts: A Literary Interpretation, vol. 1: The Gospel according to Luke*. Philadelphia: Fortress, 1986 (pioneering 'narrative' approach focused on characters and major themes; very thoughtful).

M. Turner *The Holy Spirit and Spiritual Gifts Then and Now*. Carlisle: Paternoster Press/Peabody: Hendrickson, 1996 [new ed. 1998], ch. 2 (on Jesus and the Spirit in Luke).

*S. Walton *Leadership and Lifestyle: The Portrait of Paul in the Miletus Speech and 1 Thessalonians*. SNTS Monograph Series 108. Cambridge: Cambridge University Press, 2000 (a detailed study of Acts 20:18-35 against the backcloth of Luke and 1 Thessalonians).

COMMENTARIES

D. L. Bock *Luke*. IVP NT Commentary. Downers Grove/Leicester: IVP, 1994 (helpful mid-level commentary with an eye on preaching Luke).

*J. A. Fitzmyer *Luke*. 2 vols. Anchor Bible 28A & 28B. Garden City, NY: Doubleday, 1981, 1985 (standard work with a good survey of Lukan theology in vol. 1, 143-258).

J. B. Green *The Gospel of Luke*. New International Commentary on the NT. Grand Rapids/Cambridge: Eerdmans, 1997 (very fine 'narrative' commentary).

L. T. Johnson *The Gospel of Luke*. Sacra Pagina 3. Collegeville: Liturgical Press, 1992 (commentary with good sensitivity to Luke's literary artistry).

*I. H. Marshall *The Gospel of Luke*. New International Greek Testament Commentary. Exeter: Paternoster/Grand Rapids: Eerdmans, 1978 (especially valuable on grammar, style and historicity).

*J. Nolland *Luke*. 3 vols. Word Biblical Commentary 35A, B & C. Dallas: Word, 1989-93 (very comprehensive).

L. L. Morris *Luke: An Introduction and Commentary*. Tyndale NT Commentaries, revised ed. Leicester: IVP/Grand Rapids: Eerdmans, 1988 (good, brief introductory commentary).

R. H. Stein *Luke*. New American Commentary, vol. 24. Nashville: Broadman, 1992 (good redaction-critical approach).

R. C. Tannehill *Luke*. Abingdon NT Commentaries. Nashville: Abingdon, 1996 (complements his study above by going through Luke in order).

Chapter 12

JOHN

John's Gospel contains some of the most beautiful and powerful stories we know about Jesus, some of his best known sayings, and some of the most profound and mystical teaching that we find in the Christian Scriptures. It offers a strikingly different picture of Jesus from the one found in the three synoptic Gospels, Matthew, Mark and Luke, the very name 'syn-optic' reflecting the perception that Matthew, Mark and Luke see Jesus in one way, whereas John is different.

A WALK THROUGH THE GOSPEL

John's Gospel has a clear focus on Jesus the Messiah the Son of God (20:31); this is the recurring theme, especially in chs 1–12. It also has a definite sense of movement – towards the 'hour' of Jesus' death and glorification – notably in chs 13–21.

CHS 1–12 FOCUS ON JESUS' IDENTITY

The Gospel starts with a distinctive, poetic prologue which speaks of the eternal 'word' of God that was 'in the beginning' and which then became flesh in Jesus (1:1-18). The first human figure to come on stage is John the Baptist: he testifies to Jesus, as the lamb and

Spirit-filled son of God. John's disciples and others come to Jesus, and also confess him, right at the start of the Gospel, as Messiah, king and son of God (1:6-8, 19-51).

Jesus' miracles in John's Gospel are 'signs' of his divinity, and significantly his ministry opens in Cana of Galilee with his turning of the water to wine in 2:1-11. Jesus then goes up to Jerusalem (as he does frequently in John); it is Passover time and he drives the traders from the temple, speaking of the destruction and raising up of the temple (2:12-25).

The first of many theological dialogues with Jewish religious leaders follows, as Jesus tells the Pharisee Nicodemus that he must be born again (or 'from above'), and speaks of the son of man being 'lifted up', as Moses lifted the snake in the wilderness (3:1-22). Jesus is then described as having a period of ministry in Judea, baptizing (with his disciples), almost in tandem with John, who again affirms the greatness of Jesus (3:22–4:3).

Jesus moves from Judea to Samaria, where he offers living water to the Samaritan woman (4:1-42), then to Galilee where he heals the nobleman's son (4:43-54). Then back in Jerusalem he heals the lame man at the pool of Bethesda, which leads into a discussion of Jesus' authority with 'the Jews' who are hostile to him (ch. 5). In ch. 6, 5,000 are miraculously fed in Galilee, which leads into a discussion of Jesus as the bread come down from heaven (including the first of the great 'I am' sayings in 6:35) and as the one who gives his flesh for the life of the world. Ch. 7 has Jesus back in Jerusalem for the feast of tabernacles, and the people argue fiercely over whether Jesus is the Christ. In ch. 8 Jesus speaks of himself as the light of the world, and claims controversially that 'before Abraham was, I am' (v. 58). Ch. 9 has Jesus heal the man born blind, with the Pharisees threatening to expel from the synagogue anyone who confesses Jesus as the Christ. In ch. 10 Jesus speaks of himself as the good shepherd, and in ch. 11 Jesus astonishingly calls his dead friend Lazarus out of the tomb, thus provoking the authorities to determine to eliminate Jesus, because of his dangerous popularity. Ch. 12 may be seen as a sort of transitional chapter as we begin to head towards Jesus' death at Passover time: he is anointed by Mary, but plotted against by others.

CHS 13–21: THE ROAD TO GLORY

Jesus prepares his followers for his death, washing their feet in ch. 13 and warning of his betrayal. In chs 14–16 he speaks openly of his coming departure, of the sufferings the disciples will face, and of his return to them through the Holy Spirit (Paraclete or Advocate) to strengthen them in their witness. In the great prayer of ch. 17 Jesus dedicates himself for what lies ahead and prays for his disciples, present and future. Chs 18–19 describe his arrest, trials and death. Jesus is seen as the king with full authority, who allows himself to be crucified and who conquers

through his death, saying 'It is finished' when he dies. Ch. 20 describes his resurrection, with the tomb being found by Mary Magdalene, and with the risen Jesus appearing to her, to the twelve and to unbelieving Thomas, who now proclaims Jesus to be 'My Lord and my God'. The story of Thomas is a climax to the Gospel, with Thomas's confession 'my Lord and my God' expressing precisely the faith that the author wishes for all his readers (cf. 20:29-31). Ch. 21 seems almost an afterthought, with the story of a miraculous catch of fish leading into Jesus challenging Peter about his love three times and calling him to feed his sheep, and then with a discussion about what Jesus had said about the deaths respectively of Peter and of the 'disciple whom Jesus loved'.

STYLE

The Greek of John's Gospel is simple (and a good place for beginners in the language to begin!). But the style is varied – from the semi-poetic prologue, to the long prayer of ch. 17, to the relatively straightforward narrative of chs 18–20.

Perhaps most characteristic of John are the vivid dialogue/discussion scenes, such as ch. 3 where Jesus challenges the teacher Nicodemus, or ch. 4 where he engages brilliantly with the Samaritan woman, or ch. 9 where there is almost humorous debate between the blind man, the Jewish authorities, the man's parents and finally Jesus himself. Scholars have spoken of the dramatic quality of John's Gospel.

One of the characteristic features in the dialogue is the way people misunderstand Jesus (whether Nicodemus misunderstanding being 'born again' or the Samaritan woman mistakenly thinking that Jesus was offering literal water to drink, 3:4 and 4:11); the misunderstanding then opens up the way for further teaching.

John often sees double meanings in what people say: thus Jesus can speak of being 'lifted up', literally referring to crucifixion, but at a deeper level referring to his vindication and glorification (12:32). Not far removed from this is the irony that comes out when, for example, Caiaphas speaks of the necessity for Jesus to die for the people, which the evangelist takes in a very different sense from that intended by the high priest (11:49-52).

John does not have the short parable stories that are characteristic of Jesus in the synoptics; but he does have powerful figurative discourses, notably the good shepherd discourse in ch. 10, and the vine in ch. 15.

THEOLOGICAL THEMES

The authors of the Gospels all had their own agendas. John specifies his in 20:31: 'These were written that you may believe that Jesus is the Christ, the Son of God, and that believing you may have life in his name.' This looks like the end of the main part of the Gospel, and sums up what the Gospel writer is seeking to achieve in chapter after chapter, story after story.

John's primary focus is on the identity of Jesus. Matthew, Mark and Luke are interested in this too. But they give a more general picture of Jesus' teaching and work, and are answering questions particularly about Jesus' suffering and death (Mark) and about the relationship of Christianity and Judaism (Matthew and Luke). John has a much narrower focus, and is absorbed particularly with the question of who Jesus is, i.e. with Christology.

JESUS AS JEWISH MESSIAH

Jesus is, first, 'the Christ' (Hebrew 'Messiah', i.e. anointed one). By this John means that Jesus is the king from the family of David, whose coming to save God's people was predicted in various OT passages (e.g. Isa. 9:1-7; 11:1-3).

John's Gospel was at one time seen by scholars as a Greek reinterpretation of Jesus and much less 'Jewish' than the synoptic Gospels. But all sorts of things have persuaded scholars that John is actually a very Jewish Gospel, including the finding of the Dead Sea Scrolls, since they contain what may be seen as Johannine emphases (e.g. on light and darkness). These similarities have impressed some scholars so much that they have suggested that the author of the Gospel may have been an Essene, like the authors of the Scrolls (e.g. Ashton 1991, 205).

But it is evidence within the Gospel that makes John's Jewishness most clear: in the synoptics the emphasis on Jesus as Messiah is definitely muted, though Peter's confession of Jesus at Caesarea Philippi marks a turning point in Jesus' ministry (Mark 8:29). In John, however, Jesus' messiahship is freely discussed by people from ch. 1 onwards (1:41, 49; 7:25-31, 41-44). Some scholars translate 20:31: 'These things are written that you may believe that the Christ, the Son of God, is Jesus', which brings the question of Jesus as the Jewish Messiah even more into prominence (see p. 53).

John is interested in the Jewish pilgrimage festivals, with Jesus going up regularly to

Jerusalem. He refers not just to the final Passover when Jesus died (as in the synoptics), but to three Passovers, to the feast of tabernacles and the feast of dedication (i.e. Hanukkah) (1:13; 5:1; 6:4; 7:2, 10; 10:22; 12:1). John sees Jesus as somehow fulfilling the symbolism of the festivals: thus John 6 has Jesus at Passover time comparing himself to the manna that the Israelites ate at the time of the Exodus, and John 7–8 have Jesus speaking about water for the thirsty and light for the world in the context of the feast of tabernacles, which involved water-pouring and torch-carrying rituals (7:37; 8:12).

John frequently portrays Jesus in conflict with 'the Jews' in a way that suggests that Jewish issues are still very much alive for the author (e.g. in ch. 9). Scholars have debated the precise force of John's 'the Jews', and some have suggested that John comes close to antisemitism (so Casey 1996). But, despite the terminology, John writes, as we have seen, from a Jewish perspective himself, and believes that 'salvation is from the Jews' (4:22), Jesus being the Jewish Messiah.

Digging deeper:
JOHN AND THE OT

Work through John's Gospel, noting references to OT stories, people and verses, and reflecting on how John understands the relationship of Jesus and the OT story and Scriptures.

JESUS AS DIVINE SON

Jesus is not just Jewish Messiah, but also 'son of God'. John emphasizes this more than the synoptics, and makes it clear that Jesus is 'son of God' in a very strong sense. John uniquely has Jesus speak of himself as one who 'descended from heaven', who was with the Father in the beginning before the world began (3:13; 17:24). Jesus in John can say 'Before Abraham was, I am....', and be rewarded by his opponents seeking to kill him for blasphemy (8:58, 59). Jesus in John's Gospel is 'pre-existent', something not explicit in the synoptic Gospels, and divine.

One important category that John uses in the prologue to the Gospel is that of 'the word' (Greek *logos*). This has been seen as a thoroughly Greek idea, since Stoic philosophers, among others, spoke of a logical principle of order behind the world – *logos* can mean 'word' or 'reason'. But it is also a thoroughly Jewish concept, since the OT speaks of God creating the world by 'his word' and of his word powerfully accomplishing his will (Isa. 55:11; Ps. 33:6). A Jewish background is suggested by the opening words of the prologue 'in the beginning' and by the subsequent reference to 'light in darkness', both reminding us of Gen. 1, where God's creative word is so powerful. Furthermore, the whole idea of God creating through the agency of his word is reminiscent of various Jewish texts which speak of divine wisdom as God's creative agent (e.g. Prov. 8; Wis. 8); such Jewish thinking about God's wisdom is important background to various NT texts, including John 1.

John quite probably chose a term which spoke evocatively to both Greeks and Jews. It is interesting that the first-century Alexandrian philopher Philo, who tried to synthesize Jewish and Greek thought, spoke of the divine logos as God's instrument in creation (though without identifying that *logos* with a person) (*Her.* 205f.).

246

More important than the background is the function of the term *'logos'* in the Gospel. For John Jesus is the word, because he is God's way of communicating with us. Like the cartoonist's speech bubble, the word comes out from the speaker, in this case from God, and reveals God to us. Jesus is God made audible and made visible. The Jews had a ban on making any image of God. But Jesus could say 'He who has seen me has seen the Father' (14:9). John 1:18 sums the point up: 'No one has ever seen God. It is … the only Son, who … has made him known.'

A person's word may in one way be seen as part of that person, and yet, when it comes out, it takes on a life of its own (capable of being captured in a tape recorder!). One of the questions that has most engaged readers of John, from earliest times, is: how does John understand the relationship of Father and Son – is Jesus Son of God in the sort of way the creeds would later speak of him? Or is he simply a human agent through whom the divine life shines, one with the Father in purpose and love ('functionally'), but not in his being and nature ('ontologically')? Jewish thought could speak in very strong terms about the authority of someone's agent and representative, and in John's Gospel Jesus is 'sent' by the Father, and is dependent on and obedient to him (e.g. 5:19, 36f.; 7:29, 57). He can also speak of the Father as 'greater than I' (14:28).

And yet Jesus in John seems much more than God's agent. When he says in 8:58 'Before Abraham was, I am', he both asserts his pre-existence, but also speaks of himself in a way that recalls the OT's way of speaking about God. (See the 'I am' of Exod. 3:14, also the 'I am he' of Isa. 40–55, e.g. 41:4, translated in the Greek Septuagint as 'I am'.) The implication, which his opponents recognize, is that Jesus is claiming something that would be blasphemous for any human being. Human beings, who receive Jesus, are 'children of God' (1:12), but Jesus is uniquely the son, not by rebirth but from the beginning; so he can work on the Sabbath, as God does, but as no human being should (5:17). So Thomas at the end of ch. 20 can worship the risen Jesus as 'My Lord and my God', which is an appropriate climax to John's Gospel, but would be quite inappropriate in a Jewish monotheistic context for one who was not really divine in a strong sense.

REASONS FOR BELIEVING: SIGNS AND WITNESSES

But why should anyone believe that Jesus was divine? The answer for John comes in 20:30, 31: 'Jesus did many other signs in the presence of his disciples … these are written that you may believe that Jesus'. The miracles of Jesus for John are signs – signposts, we might say – of his divinity. He has seven (or eight) miracle stories:

- water to wine (ch. 2);
- healing of the nobleman's son (ch. 4);
- healing of the lame man (ch. 5);
- feeding of 5,000 and walking on water (ch. 6);
- healing of man born blind (ch. 9);
- raising Lazarus (ch. 11);
- the resurrection (chs. 20, 21);

John's selection of miracles is distinctive (only the feeding and walking on the water being closely similar to the synoptics), but so also is his interpretation of them. In the synoptics the miracles are related to the coming of the longed-for kingdom of God. The miracle at Cana may be similarly understood with weddings and wine being associated in Judaism with God's day of salvation (e.g. Isa. 25:6; 62:4-5), but John sees the miracles primarily as revealing who Jesus is and as evidence for believing in Jesus. So 2:11: 'He thus revealed his glory, and his disciples believed in him'. The glory is the divine glory of the only son of God (1:14); the miracles are works of God, which should lead to a response of faith (10:25).

Digging deeper:
GLORY

Trace the theme of glory through John's Gospel (1:14; 2:11; 5:41, 44; 7:18; 8:50, 54; 9:24; 11:4, 40; 12:41, 43; 17:5, 22, 24). How does John understand the glory of Jesus?

Believing is also appropriate in response to various witnesses to Jesus. The miracles are witnesses, but so are John the Baptist, Moses, the Scriptures and supremely God himself (5:31-47). Jesus' followers are also to be his witnesses through the Holy Spirit (15:26, 27). And John sees his own Gospel as such a witness: it derives from the 'disciple whom Jesus loved', is true and is designed to lead to belief – belief in Jesus as Son of God (e.g. 19:35). People may refuse to believe, but that is because of culpable blindness, not because of deficient evidence.

IS JESUS HUMAN IN JOHN?
John's portrayal of Jesus as divine is so strong, that some scholars have doubted whether his Jesus is really human. They have spoken of John as tending to 'docetism' – docetism being the second century heresy which asserted that Jesus only appeared (Greek *dokei*) to be human (e.g. E. Käsemann *The Testament of Jesus*. London: SCM, 1968/ Philadelphia: Fortress, 1978).

Most striking of all is John's account of the death of Jesus (see below).

In Mark's Gospel	In John's Gospel
Jesus suffers intensely: in Gethsemane he is in agony (14:33f.)	Jesus seems in total control: when soldiers come to arrest him, he asks who they are looking for. They reply 'Jesus of Nazareth'. Jesus then replies 'I am' (literally in the Greek), and the arresting party then fall to the ground – as one might when confronted with the divine 'I am' (18:1–16).
His disciples run away (14:34-52)	Then Jesus continues to control the situation, telling the guards to let the disciples go (18:7-8).
Eventually he dies in apparent despair, crying: 'My God, my God, why have you forsaken me?' (15:34).	At his trial Jesus is seen to be the king with even more authority than the Roman governor, Pilate, and, when he dies, his cry is of victory: 'It is finished.' (18:33–19:30)

What do you think?

Read through John's passion narrative (chs 18–19) and note down all the evidence of Jesus being in control of the situation.

In favour of the real humanity of Jesus are the following.

- The key statement in 1:14, where John specifically says that 'the word became *flesh*'. The emphasis on flesh and blood (used also in 6:51-59) sounds distinctly un-docetic.
- The Jesus of John has what seems to be normal human attributes – getting tired (4:6), shedding tears (11:35), being thirsty (19:28; cf. 4:7).
- Although there is less sense of struggle in John than in the synoptics, still Jesus is troubled at the prospect of his death (12:27); and the laying down of his life is seen as a hugely costly sacrifice (10:11; 15:13).
- Although Jesus is victor not vanquished at the cross, it is a real crucifixion that is described. It is doubtful if ancient readers, familiar with crucifixion, would see John's story as deficient in suffering. What will have impressed them is how Jesus conquers in and through terrible suffering. John's purpose may have been precisely that: to demonstrate the glory of the horrible event for people tending to deny its importance.

THE DEATH OF JESUS: HOW DOES IT WORK?
Scholars have not only claimed that John portrays a suffering-free crucifixion, but also that John does not see Jesus' death as an atoning sacrifice for sin (e.g. R. Bultmann, *Theology of the NT*. London: SCM/New York: Scribner, 1955, 2. 54).

It is true that John does portray the cross mainly as a victory over Satan, who is called 'the ruler of this world' (14:30). The picture is of Satan having hijacked God's world, and of Jesus on the cross confronting Satan and

---

THE CRUCIFIXION AND THE PASSOVER IN JOHN

The Jewish day began at dusk (not at midnight), and the Passover meal was held in the month of Nisan on the 15th day in the evening, the lambs having been killed just before in the afternoon (= Nisan 14th). The synoptic Gospels suggest that Jesus' Last Supper with his disciples was a Passover meal, thus presumably on Nisan 15th evening; but John suggests that Jesus died before the Passover meal (18:28; 19:31). This notorious Gospel discrepancy has been explained in various ways:

- John altered the correct synoptic identification of the Last Supper with Passover in order to have Jesus die at the same time as the Passover lambs were killed (i.e. on Nisan 14th afternoon). This would fit with John's interest in the Passover theme, but is it likely that he changed known chronology for that reason?
- Jesus actually held a Passover-type meal ahead of the official Passover, because he anticipated his arrest. John refers correctly to the official timing of Passover.
- Different Jewish groups had different religious calendars, so that people will have celebrated the feast on different days. John and the synoptics are both correct.
- Jesus celebrated Passover on the official day. When John speaks of the Jews preparing to 'eat the Passover' after the crucifixion, he is referring not to the first night of the week-long festival when the Passover lamb was eaten, but to other festival meals in that week.

(The standard discussion of this is J. Jeremias *The Eucharistic Words of Jesus*. London: SCM/New York: Scribner, 1966; see also commentaries.)

Satan confronting Jesus. The confrontation is a dark moment, but the outcome is 'the judgement of this world' (i.e. of Satan's kingdom) and the 'casting out of Satan' (12:32). The Gospel which fails to describe any of Jesus' individual exorcisms still has the idea of Jesus casting out the evil cosmic ruler through his death.

But how does Jesus cast out Satan through the cross? John gives a host of clues.

- He sees Jesus as the new Passover lamb. That is probably implied in the references to Jesus as 'the lamb of God' in 1:29, 36,

and even more probably in the crucifixion story, which is set so clearly in a Passover context and where John cites the OT law about not breaking the bones of the Passover lamb (19:36; cf. Exod. 12:46).

- John compares Jesus' death with the bronze snake lifted up by Moses in the wilderness, to save the Israelites from their sins (3:14; cf. Num. 21:9).
- Jesus gives 'his flesh for the life of the world' (6:51, 54).
- He is the good shepherd giving his life sacrificially for 'the sheep', to gather people into the one flock (ch.10).

JESUS' DEATH, THE LAST SUPPER AND THE EUCHARIST

John 6 is one of the most fascinating passages in John. It starts with Jesus feeding the 5,000. Then there is a typically Johannine discussion of Jesus as the bread come down from heaven, surpassing the old manna. 'I am the bread of life,' Jesus says, 'he who comes to me shall not hunger, and he who believes in me shall never thirst' (v. 35).

The chapter takes a new turn at v. 51, where Jesus speaks of 'giving his flesh for the world' and then of the necessity of eating his flesh and drinking his blood. The focus seems to shift here from a general portrayal of Jesus as the living bread from heaven, in whom we should have faith, to a specific emphasis on his death as what brings life, and on the need to have faith in his sacrifice. (We move from an emphasis on incarnation to an emphasis on atonement.)

How do the verses that speak of the flesh and blood of Jesus relate to the synoptic Last Supper, where Jesus invites his disciples to eat 'my body' and to drink 'my blood'?

- Has John transplanted the words from their synoptic context into his chapter 6, with its thematic focus on bread?

- Did Jesus say much the same thing on more than one occasion?

The scholarly argument about the relationship of the Johannine and synoptic sayings has often been interwined with wider discussion about John and the sacraments, and about whether 6:51-59 was meant by John to refer to the eucharist (or Lord's Supper).

Some scholars have suggested that John has the discussion of Jesus' flesh and blood here, not at the Last Supper, in order to counteract excessive sacramental emphasis on the part of some Christians (see C. K. Barrett *The Gospel according to St John,* 2nd ed. London: SPCK/Philadelphia: Westminster Press, 1978, 297). But would John then have retained 6:53 in his Gospel? John does overwhelmingly emphasize faith as the way to salvation, and it is unlikely that he intends to introduce sacramental participation as an additional condition of salvation in 6:51-59. However, it is possible that for the writer and the readers of the Gospel the obvious way to express faith in the Lord's death will have been through receiving the eucharistic bread and wine, and that John (with his love of double meanings) will at least have intended an allusion to the eucharist.

- Caiaphas unwittingly gets it right when he says of Jesus 'that it is better for you that one man die for the people than that the whole nation perish'. John takes this to mean that Jesus will die so that people may not perish, but be gathered into God's saved people (11:50-52; cf. 12:32).

ETERNAL LIFE

John says that he has written his Gospel 'that you may ... have life in his name' (20:31). Whereas the synoptic Jesus announces the kingdom of God, John only uses the phrase 'kingdom of God' twice (in 3:3, 5), whereas he continually talks about life and eternal life. (In the synoptics 'eternal life' is the subsidiary theme, e.g. Mark 10:30.)

For John eternal life is all to do with Jesus. One of the most striking features of the Gospel is the unique 'I am' sayings: Jesus says: 'I am…

- the bread of life' (6:35);
- the light of the world' (8:12);
- the door' (10:9);
- the good shepherd ... who gives his life for the sheep' (10:11);
- the resurrection and the life' (11:25);
- the way, the truth and the life' (14:6);
- the true vine' (15:1).

All of the sayings in one way or another make it clear that Jesus is the way to life.

But what is life? For John it is the opposite of 'perishing' or being destroyed (e.g. 3:16). John believed in divine judgement – it is an important theme in his Gospel (A. E. Harvey *Jesus on Trial*. London: SPCK, 1976/Atlanta: John Knox, 1977, sees the whole of the Gospel as a sort of trial narrative, with Jesus being put on trial but actually putting the world on trial) and for him the importance of believing in Jesus is because everyone will

What do you think?
THE 'I AM' SAYINGS

What force would Jesus' 'I am' sayings have had in his first-century Palestinian context? For example, 'bread of life' would have been a very powerful picture of spiritual sustenance in a poor country where bread was the staple diet.

(For a discussion of the important OT background to the sayings, see D. Ball *'I Am' in John's Gospel*. Sheffield: JSOT, 1996.)

appear before God, with believers being saved and others dying 'in their sins', remaining in spiritual darkness, and experiencing the judgement of God (like the Israelites in the desert, 8:24; 3:14; 13:30).

Eternal life is pictured positively in many of the sayings and stories of the Gospel, e.g. as wedding wine (2:1-12), thirst-quenching water (4:14), resurrection from the dead (ch. 11). But most importantly 17:3 defines it: 'This is eternal life, that they know you the only true God, and Jesus Christ whom you have sent.'

'Knowing' here is to be understood not as theoretical knowledge, but in personal terms. In the OT and NT 'knowing' can mean sexual intercourse (Gen. 4:1; see also Matt. 1:25). In John 17:3 there is no sexual connotation, but the knowledge of God referred to is a strong, even intimate relationship – like that of the shepherd knowing his sheep by name and loving them sacrificially (10:3, 15). In 14:23 Jesus says: 'If a person loves me, he will keep my word, and my Father will love him, and we will come to him, and make our home with him.'

A NOTE ON WATER AND BAPTISM

In John 3:5 Jesus challenges Nicodemus about the need to be born again (or 'from above', as it may be translated) of 'water and the Spirit'. What is the 'water' here? The background is probably in Ezek. 36, where God promises: 'I will gather you from all the countries and bring you back into your own land. I will sprinkle clean water on you, and you will be clean; I will cleanse you from all your impurities ... I will give you a new heart and put a new spirit in you; I will remove from you your heart of stone and give you a heart of flesh. And I will put my spirit in you, and move you to follow my decrees and be careful to keep my laws ... you will be my people, and I will be your God.' (vv. 24-28) Jesus is telling Nicodemus that this day has come, and that he needs to get in on the new situation – to be cleansed and given a new heart by the Spirit of God.

But is there any reference to baptism? Is baptism the way for Nicodemus and others to be 'sprinkled with clean water ... and cleansed from impurities'? Some argue that John could not mean that baptism is essential to being born again, since this would contradict John's unambiguous emphasis on saving faith, and they suggest that the 'water' may be a reference to natural birth (e.g. to the waters of the mother's womb; or to male semen which was sometimes described as 'water'), or just to spiritual cleansing or to the work of the Holy Spirit (cf. 7:38, 39). (For such a position see Carson 1991, 191-6.) However, in John chs 1–4 there is a lot of discussion of John's baptism and of Jesus' baptizing people (from 1:33 onwards). Most strikingly in 4:1, 2 Jesus and his disciples are said to 'make disciples' by baptizing people. So there is a good contextual case for the 'water' in 3:5 being baptism.

Baptism in the early church seems to have taken place at the time of conversion: it was the way people expressed their faith, and was associated with the gift of the Holy Spirit (e.g. Acts 2:34-41). So John's readers, many of whom will have experienced such baptism, will surely have understood Jesus' words to Nicodemus baptismally, and seen no contradiction between this and the priority of faith.

The word translated 'home' in 14:23 is literally 'abiding or dwelling place', and is related to the word used in the passage about the vine in ch. 15, where Jesus encourages his disciples to 'abide in me'. Eternal life for John is being brought into the divine family: Jesus 'abides' in the Father in love and unity, and his mission and prayer in ch. 17 is that his followers also may be one 'as you Father are in me, and I in you ... may they also be in us' (v. 21). It is in keeping with this that John emphasizes so strongly the importance of his followers 'loving one another' (15:12, 17; 13:34, 35).

John's Gospel has sometimes been seen as emphasizing individual salvation. But eternal life in John is not the Greek idea of the immortality of the individual soul; it is life shared – with God and with the people of God. It is being part of one flock under one shepherd, or a branch in the true vine (chs 10, 15); the pictures of the vine and the shepherd are OT ideas associated with Israel (e.g. Ps. 80; Isa. 5; Ezek. 34). The OT looked forward to God gathering his divided and scattered people (e.g. Ezek. 36:24), and John sees Jesus' death precisely as 'for the Jewish nation, and not only for that nation, but also for the scattered children of God, to bring them together and make them one' (11:52; cf. 12:32). This is eternal life.

The OT also looks forward to the day when God's restored people will 'know' God in a new way within a new covenant and when

God by his Spirit will do a new work of cleansing and renewal in people's hearts (thus Jer. 31:31-34 and Ezek. 36:24-36, where the ideas of release from exile and spiritual change are both found). Jesus in John has come to bring that day, and when he says to Nicodemus that he must be 'born again' (ch. 3) and to the Samaritan woman that the time is coming 'when you will worship the Father neither on this mountain, nor in Jerusalem ... but ... when the true worshippers will worship the Father in spirit and in truth' (4:21-23), he is not making generalized statements about the inwardness of true religion, but announcing the coming of the day promised by the prophets. This is eternal life.

If this is the correct understanding of 'eternal life' in John, it turns out to be a Jewish rather than a Greek understanding, and much closer than sometimes recognized to the synoptic teaching about the new age of the kingdom of God. Significantly the Greek word for 'eternal', *aiōnios*, can mean 'everlasting'; but the Hebrew/Aramaic for 'eternal life' which Jesus probably used was, literally translated, 'life of the age', meaning 'life of the coming age'. In synoptic language this is 'life of the kingdom of God'.

THE HOLY SPIRIT

In the OT the 'wind' or 'breath' of God comes mightily on many of the leaders of God's people, and in John Jesus is a new Spirit-endowed leader (1:3; cf. Isa. 11:1, 2). But he is also the one who brings the universal experience of the Spirit to God's people of which the prophets spoke (e.g. Ezek. 36). This experience is closely connected with eternal life, since it is precisely through the Holy Spirit that the Father and the Son come to dwell with the believer. This is clear from the closely

parallel phrases in John 14, where Jesus speaks at one moment of himself coming to the believer with the Father and at the next of the Holy Spirit coming (vv. 15-17, 23).

If eternal life in John starts during Jesus' ministry because of Jesus' presence with the disciples, it is still his death that brings cleansing, eternal life and the experience of the Holy Spirit (7:38, 39). Paradoxically it is Jesus' going away that enables him to come back through the Holy Spirit, and this is eternal life. So it is after his death in John 20:22 that the risen Jesus 'breathes on/in' the disciples and says 'receive the Holy Spirit'. The description is reminiscent of Gen. 2:7 where God breathes his creative life into Adam.

HOW DOES THE GIFT OF THE SPIRIT IN JOHN 20 RELATE TO PENTECOST IN ACTS 2?

Views:

- Luke and John are describing the same mysterious experience differently (and in ways that are historically contradictory).
- The disciples have two separate experiences of the giving of the Spirit.
- The incident in John is to be seen as an acted parable or sign of what the disciples were to experience at Pentecost, just as the last supper was an acted parable of the Lord's death.

(Further reading: Max Turner, *The Holy Spirit and Spiritual Gifts Then and Now*. Carlisle: Paternoster Press/Peabody: Hendrickson, 1996 [new ed. 1998], ch. 6.)

For John the Holy Spirit is closely associated with Jesus: he comes on Jesus, but is also his agent, as Jesus is the agent of the Father; he witnesses to Jesus and reveals him; like Jesus he is a 'paraclete' to the disciples (see chs 14–16 especially). The Greek word *paraklētos* could be translated 'encourager', but may well have legal connotations and suggest a legal 'advocate' who stands with his client when under trial.

John's teaching on the Spirit is distinct from that of the synoptics, and much fuller. But there are points in common – with Jesus seen as the Spirit-filled anointed one, bringing a new era and covenant and giving the Spirit to his followers, to help them in times of trial (e.g. Mark 1:8; 14:24; Matt. 10:20; Mark 13:11).

FUTURE HOPE?

In John eternal life has come already for those who have faith (3:18; 5:24), and there is relatively little emphasis on the Lord's future return or on a final judgement day. Scholars speak of John's 'realized eschatology'. It has been argued that John lived at a time when the church was having to adjust to Jesus' failure to return (the so-called 'failure of the parousia'), and that he chose to emphasize Jesus' spiritual presence in the church through the Holy Spirit: for John Jesus did promise to 'come again', but meant by this to refer to the coming of the Spirit. (See C. H. Dodd *The Interpretation of the Fourth Gospel*. Cambridge: Cambridge University Press, 1953, 390-422; R. Bultmann *Theology of the NT*. London: SCM/New York: Scribner, 1955, 2:57-58.)

However,

- the synoptics, as well as John, emphasize salvation in the present (e.g. Matt. 13:16, 17; Luke 4:21);
- there is future hope in John (notably in 21:22, but also in 14:1-3; 5:28, 29);
- in chs 14–17 Jesus looks forward to the time after his departure when his disciples will have to endure suffering – it is clear full eschatological salvation has not yet come.

We could say that eternal life has three phases in John:

- beginning in the ministry of Jesus as the disciples have fellowship with him;
- continuing after his departure through the indwelling of the Spirit;
- being complete in the future when the disciples have come through their troubles and see the divine glory which Jesus had before the foundation of the world.

Digging deeper:
JOHN 14–17

What sort of future does Jesus foresee for his disciples, and how does he expect them to act and behave?

BELIEVING

For John the way to enter into such eternal life is by 'believing' (20:31) – 'believing that' Jesus is the Christ the Son of God, and also 'believing in' him. 'Believing in' means, in

What do you think?
THE IMPORTANCE OF THOMAS

Beginnings and endings of ancient books are often significant. The story of the risen Jesus meeting Thomas in 20:24-29 is unique to John, and is the final story in the Gospel before John's summary of his purpose in 20:30, 31. Consider:

- the point and emphasis of the story as a whole (note that in v. 27 the Greek may be translated 'don't be unbelieving, but believing…');
- the importance of John 20:29;
- the connection of the story to vv. 30-31;
- the connection of the story with the beginning of the Gospel in 1:1f.

other words, 'coming' to Jesus and 'receiving' him (6:35; 1:11-13). It is by receiving Jesus that people enter the family of Jesus (which is what eternal life is all about), and are born again by God's Spirit. (See note above on baptism in John.)

For John this sort of believing and receiving of Jesus is only possible through the work of God's Spirit. People are naturally blinded by the devil, the prince of this 'world', and so 'No one can come to me unless the Father who sent me draws him' (6:44). And yet the way the Spirit of God brings people to new birth is through the witness of the disciples and indeed of the author of the Gospel himself, who wrote 'so that you may believe' (20:31).

THE SOURCES OF THE GOSPEL

Scholars have seen evidence within the Gospel of a variety of sources having been used, and/or of the Gospel having passed through various editions.

JOHN 2.I
Chapter 21 arguably looks like some sort of appendix to the Gospel:

- John 20:30, 31, with the climactic story of Thomas just before, sounds like a conclusion;
- the Gospel up to ch. 20 has had a consistent Christological focus, but ch. 21 is primarily about Peter and 'the disciple whom Jesus loved';
- certain stylistic considerations seem to set the chapter apart, e.g. the unnecessary identification of Thomas in 21:2 (following 20:24), and in the same verse the unprecedented reference to 'the sons of Zebedee';
- the first person plural in 21:24 could be someone other than the main author testifying to the author's reliability: 'we know that his testimony is true'.

THE PROLOGUE
Scholars have argued that the prologue to the Gospel was a poem to the 'logos' (not necessarily Christian originally) which has been taken over and adapted by the author of the Gospel. They have observed that:

- ideas (notably the primary idea of Jesus as the word) found in the prologue do not feature elsewhere in the Gospel;
- the poetic parallelism of, for example, v. 5 is interrupted by the prose description of John the Baptist in vv. 6-7.

On the other hand:

- thematically the prologue has much in common with the Gospel that follows;
- it is hardly surprising that 'the word' does not occur within the narrative itself – the idea of Jesus revealing God certainly does;
- the prose 'insertions' have an entirely intelligible function in their present position, because John is deliberately bringing together the concept of the eternal word with the reality of the contingent world of first-century Palestine – he appropriately moves from the poetic to the prosaic.

DISLOCATIONS IN THE TEXT
John 14:31 has puzzled scholars: Jesus says to the disciples 'Rise, let us go', but then carries on teaching without apparently going anywhere. Scholars have proposed that 14:31 was once followed by the departure of Jesus and his disciples from the upper room, but then further teaching of Jesus was added into the Gospel. Why then did the editor making the addition fail to move or eliminate the 'Rise, let us go'? (see 'What do you think?' at the top of p. 256).

Scholars have also proposed that ch. 5 once belonged between chs 6 and 7, where it fits

What do you think?

What different explanations could be given of the words 'Rise, let us go' 14:31? Which explanation is most persuasive to you, and why?

well, and that 7:19-24 belonged after ch. 5. Again, the difficulty is to explain why an editor 'spoiled' an originally smooth text.

A SIGNS SOURCE

Various scholars, notably Rudolf Bultmann (*The Gospel of John*. Oxford: Blackwells/ Philadelphia: Westminster Press, 1971) and Robert Fortna (*The Gospel of Signs*. New York/Cambridge: CUP, 1970), have postulated that John had a 'signs' source which he has drawn on in chs 1–12. This collection of miracle stories was the source of John's distinctive stories, and evidence of such a collection has been seen in John's numbering of the signs in 2:11 and 4:54.

THEOLOGICAL VARIATION

People have also claimed to see theological variations in John's Gospel that point, if not to sources, to different stages of redaction. Rudolf Bultmann (1971) famously argued that there is evidence of an ecclesiastical redactor who, among other things, modified the strongly realized eschatology of the Gospel (e.g. 5:24) with his own more traditional future eschatology (e.g. 5:25), and who introduced sacramental material (e.g. in 6:51-55). But his analysis of John's thought is arguably oversimplified, and perhaps reflects Bultmann's own unease with eschatology and the sacraments more than John's!

An equally distinguished scholar of John's Gospel was Raymond Brown. He argues that the different ideas found in the Gospel enable one to identify at least five layers of material in John's Gospel, corresponding to developments and controversies in John's church (in Brown, 1971, 1: xxxiv-xxxix). Despite the brilliance of his suggestions, his confidence in analysing the history of John's community and allocating different strands in the Gospel to different stages in the church's life is questionable.

THE SYNOPTIC GOSPELS

Most scholars assume that Matthew, Mark and Luke were written before John. But did he know any of them?

He has things in common with them, for example the story of the feeding of the 5,000, followed by Jesus walking on the water, and including Jesus' words 'I am; don't be afraid' (Matt. 14:13-33; Mark 6:32-52; John 6:1-21; cf. Luke 9:10-17). He also has specific agreements with Luke, e.g. the two men running to Jesus' tomb on Easter day (Luke 24:12, 49; John 20:3-23).

John also seems to presuppose knowledge of things described in the synoptics, without himself describing them, e.g. the arrest of John the Baptist (3:24).

This evidence could reflect John's familiarity with the synoptic Gospels, but John clearly had other sources (whether oral or written) which must inevitably have overlapped with the synoptics.

What do you think?

Look through John, and note down things that John has in common with the synoptic Gospels, e.g. themes, features of Jesus' ministry, etc.

The whole question of sources is especially difficult, since John's own style shines through the entire Gospel, even in the words of Jesus. Whatever sources John has used, he has retold the stories in his own way and idiom, to such an extent that the quest for sources is highly speculative. (Further on the sources of John see D. M. Smith *Johannine Christianity*. Edinburgh: T. & T. Clark, 1987/Columbia: University of South Carolina Press, 1984).

THE BACKGROUND AND PURPOSE OF JOHN'S GOSPEL

John and the synoptics have much in common thematically.

However, the differences between John and the synoptics are still considerable.

Remarkable things in the synoptics but not in John

Jesus' baptism
Temptation
Exorcisms
Pithy parables
Much reference to the kingdom of God
Transfiguration
Institution of the Last Supper

Remarkable things in John and not in the synoptics

The turning of the water to wine
Jesus baptizing in Judea before working in Galilee
Raising Lazarus
The great 'I am' sayings
Explicit affirmations of Jesus' pre-existence

In addition, there are differences in the chronology, geography and presentation of Jesus' ministry:

- in the synoptics Jesus drives traders out of the temple at the end of his ministry, whereas in John it's at the beginning (John 2:12-25; Matt. 21:12, 13; Mark 11:15-17; Luke 19:45, 46);
- in the synoptics he ministers mostly in Galilee and goes up to Jerusalem momentously at the end of his life, whereas in John he seems always to be travelling between Galilee and Judea;
- in the synoptics he is not acclaimed as Messiah by the disciples until Peter's confession at Caesarea Philippi (Mark 8:29) which seems even then to be a secret – whereas in John Jesus' messiahship and divine sonship seems to be a rather open secret from the very start;
- in the synoptics he is a popular storyteller, whereas in John a forceful disputant.

There is also the 'dualism' of John – the way he contrasts light and darkness, Jesus and the world, what is above and what is below – and also his particular vocabulary, e.g. his fondness for words like 'truth' and 'know'.

What do you think?

List in importance the differences that seem to you to be most surprising. How could they be explained? What is your preferred explanation?

POSSIBLE EXPLANATIONS OF THE DIFFERENCES
A free artistic retelling of the story of Jesus
The most widely held scholarly explanation is that John is the story of Jesus told with a lot of artistic licence. People have compared Shakespeare's historical plays, and have spoken of John's Gospel as 'poetic' and/or 'charismatic' history (so Stibbe 1993, 18-19). The phrase 'charismatic history' suggests

John's artistic licence is explicable in terms of the author's prophetic inspiration, such as may indeed be alluded to when John emphasizes the Spirit leading Jesus' followers into all truth (cf. 14:26; 15:13-15).

The view of many scholars would be that John knew sayings and stories of Jesus, which he then elaborated, added to and reformulated. For example, the story of the feeding of the 5,000 may be seen as John's text, and the following 'bread of life' discourse as his sermon on it. More drastically, some scholars have seen the story of the turning of water into wine as John's handiwork based on the synoptic sayings about the new wine and wedding guests (Mark 2:19-22), and the story of Lazarus in John 11 as based on the Lukan parable of Luke 16:19-31 (H. H. Wendt 1902; A. Richardson 1959).

A Greek and gnostic interpretation of Jesus

Although John's creativity is widely admitted, there is less unanimity about the background to the narrative. One widespread view has been that John has written his account under the influence of Greek thought and in order to communicate with Greeks. Thus John's use of the idea of the divine *logos* has been explained in terms of Stoic philosophy.

More specifically, scholars have looked in the direction of Greek gnosticism as a key to the Gospel: John's emphases on 'knowing' and on Jesus as the one who comes down from heaven and reveals God have some parallels in second century gnosticism. Rudolf Bultmann (1971), the famous German scholar, found striking parallels between John's ideas and ideas found in the literature of the Mandaeans; C. H. Dodd, one of the most notable British scholars, found parallels in

the Hermetic literature (*Historical Tradition in the Fourth Gospel*. Cambridge: OUP, 1965).

GNOSTICISM

Gnosticism is a term used to describe a variety of dualistic movements that flourished in the second century AD and later. They believed in a heavenly redeemer, who came into the world to save people from bondage to the material world by giving them 'divine knowledge' ('*gnōsis*').

The gnostic theory is now on the wane, for various reasons.

- The evidence for some of the ideas mentioned, notably for the so-called gnostic redeemer myth, comes mostly from after the NT period: the Hermetic literature dates from the second century, the oldest surviving Mandaean texts from the fourth or fifth century AD. The ideas go back much earlier, but there is a good chance that the gnostics were influenced by John rather than vice versa. Certainly the second-century Valentinus, who was the leader of one gnostic party, was familiar with the Gospel.
- Scholars have in any case become much less confident about calling certain ideas 'Greek' or gnostic and sharply distinguishing these from what is Hebraic and Palestinian. For example, John's 'dualism', e.g. his contrasting of light and darkness, and his emphasis on knowledge and revelation, are all important in the Dead Sea Scrolls, and thus have a good first-century Palestinian pedigree.
- Generally, scholars have become increasingly aware of how very Jewish John's Gospel is (see especially Evans, 1993).

John is addressing a church that has split from Judaism

The common view now is that he was writing in the late first century AD, after the Christians had finally been expelled from the synagogue by the Jewish authorities (see discussion, p. 222 on Matthew).

This context is thought to explain:

- the negative, almost hostile, way John speaks of Jesus' opponents as 'the Jews' (though Jesus himself was a Jew!);
- the references to the Jews putting followers of Jesus 'out of the synagogue' (9:22; 16:2), something not referred to in the synoptics and not known to have occurred during Jesus' ministry;
- the 'dualism' of John's Gospel and negativeness towards the Jews – like many hurt and excluded groups of people, the Christians claimed they had the truth of God and that the Jews, who had pushed them out, were blind and under God's judgement;
- the inward-looking emphasis on 'loving one another' (rather than loving everyone), being characteristic of 'sectarian' groups who feel themselves excluded by others;
- their high Christology – John portrays Jesus as a divine figure come down from heaven in order to show why the Jews and others failed to believe. The heavenly Jesus can only be understood through special divine revelation to people chosen by God, i.e. the church.

Something like this view is very widely held by scholars today (e.g. Martyn 1979), but questions have been raised about it:

(1) there is considerable doubt about exactly what happened at Jamnia and its impact on Jewish Christian relations;

(2) the features of John's Gospel referred to are almost without exception paralleled in parts of the NT that are much earlier than Jamnia.

JOHANNINE FEATURES ELSEWHERE IN THE NT

- For Christians being expelled from the synagogue by 'the Jews', see Paul's very early letter 1 Thess. 2:14-16.
- On Christology, cf. Matt. 11:25-27 and Luke 10:21-22, often seen as early Q tradition. Note the emphases on Father/Son, knowing God, relevation, etc.
- On Jesus' divine pre-existence, cf. Phil. 2:5-11, where Paul also speaks of Jesus being highly exalted/lifted up.
- On the call to 'love one another', see 1 Thess. 4:9 and 'the law of Christ' in Gal. 6:2, which may be connected to the 'new commandment' of Jesus in John (13:34; 15:12).

More historical perspectives

Various scholars, notably the radical bishop-theologian John Robinson, have found John to be much more historical than has been conventionally accepted by scholars (Robinson 1985).

In favour of this:

- names and places in the Gospel have been archaeologically or historically confirmed, e.g. the pool of Bethesda in John 5, excavated in the 1930s, and also Jacob's well in Sychar in 4:5.
- all sorts of things in the Gospel are historically plausible, given what we know of first-century Palestine, e.g. people wanting to make Jesus king (6:15), the authorities' nervousness about Jesus (11:48).

(in ch. 3 it is unclear where Jesus' words end and John's comments begin). He presumably chooses language that would communicate with his readers, rather than using Jesus' actual words (*ipsissima verba*) all the time.

AUTHORSHIP AND DATE OF THE GOSPEL

The Gospel apparently claims to be written by an eyewitness, or based on eyewitness testimony. This is probably implied in 1:14; 19:35; 21:24, where the 'disciple whom Jesus loved' is identified as the witness behind the Gospel.

The 'disciple whom Jesus loved' is referred to in 13:23; 19:26; 21:7, 20, and may also be referred to without being named in 1:35-39; 18:15; 19:35; 20:2-10. This mystery disciple has been identified with John the son of Zebedee (the traditional identification), Lazarus (because of 11:3), John Mark (Acts 13:5), or an otherwise unknown John. Some scholars have argued that he is not an actual historical individual, but is an 'ideal' figure – a model disciple (who, for example, is with Jesus at the cross) – hence the otherwise rather pretentious 'disciple whom Jesus loved'.

IN FAVOUR OF THE TRADITIONAL IDENTIFICATION

- The earliest external evidence that we have comes from the second-century bishop of Lyon in France, Irenaeus, who commented: 'Finally John, the disciple of the Lord, who had also lain on his breast, himself published the Gospel, while he was residing at Ephesus' (*Haer.* III.1.). Irenaeus is said to have got this information from Polycarp, an acquaintance of the apostles (*Hist. eccl.* 5.20). The tradition does not

appear to have been seriously questioned, except by a few groups who did not like some of the teaching in the Gospel.

- It helps to explain why John is not otherwise named in the Gospel, except for one reference in 21:2 to 'the sons of Zebedee'. John, with his brother James and with Peter, were members of the inmost circle of Jesus' followers and then prominent leaders in the earliest Christian church (Acts 3:1; 4:1; 12:2; Gal. 2:9). If John is not the beloved disciple, where has he gone to?

- The beloved disciple is mentioned in association with Peter, thus in 13:23 and especially in chs 20–21, where there is possibly a sense of some friendly rivalry between Peter and the beloved (or other) disciple. No one known to us fits into the role of 'rival' to Peter so obviously as John the apostle.

It thus makes good sense to suppose that the Gospel comes to us from church circles where John was a specially honoured figure – an ideal figure in the sense that his disciples saw him as exemplary in various respects, 'beloved' in the sense that he was close to Jesus.

AGAINST THE TRADITIONAL IDENTIFICATION

- John has been seen as Hellenistic and Greek rather than Palestinian and Jewish. This view is now seen to be mistaken. But even if it were true, that could partly be explained via the tradition that John son of Zebedee resided and wrote in the Greek environment of Ephesus.

- The opinion has been expressed that John the fisherman could not have written as sophisticated a document as John's Gospel. But the Greek of John's Gospel is not particularly sophisticated; ancient fishermen (from families wealthy enough to own fishing boats and have servants, Mark 1:20) will not necessarily have been uneducated; Jesus' disciples will have learned a huge amount from Jesus himself and through their own reflections as they later taught about him.

- John's theology and Christology have been seen to represent a developed stage in the evolution of early Christian doctrine. But John's ideas have parallels in early strands of the NT, and it is unwise to use an evolutionary model for the history of Christian doctrine. Paul is our earliest NT writer, and his thinking is not at all underdeveloped!

- John son of Zebedee seems unlikely to have failed to mention events that he was involved in, like the transfiguration. But it is equally unlikely, perhaps even more so, that anyone else would have omitted, let alone been ignorant of, very 'Johannine' stories such as the baptism and transfiguration (with their portrayal of Jesus as the 'beloved son'). Our Gospel writer was selective, and chose not to describe either the baptism or the transfiguration of Jesus, while conveying the theological truth of the events throughout his Gospel (cf. 1:14; note the words 'lived', literally 'pitched his tent', and 'glory').

IF NOT BY JOHN...

Probably the most popular alternative to the view that the Gospel derives from the apostle John directly or indirectly, is the view that the Gospel went through multiple editings by different people, and scholars have spoken of the Gospel emanating from a Johannine 'school' (which possibly had the apostle as its founder). Most of such theories are overspeculative, but it is conceivable that the Gospel may have been written up by

someone other than the apostle, as could be inferred from 21:24.

As for the date of the Gospel, a latest date is provided by the important papyrus fragment that was found in Egypt (and is now preserved in the John Rylands Library in Manchester). Rylands Papyrus 457 was published in 1935, and contains just a few verses from John 18 (vv. 31-33, 37-38). Experts have dated it to about AD 125.

The little evidence that we have from the early church points to John being the last Gospel being written, with the apostle John living to a good old age. The conventional scholarly dating of about AD 90 is quite possible, but there is nothing decisive to negate a much earlier date.

SOME ISSUES FOR TODAY

- John wrote his Gospel to refute those who saw Jesus as human only and not divine, emphasizing and illustrating his divinity and supremacy. He was convinced that this was the true Jesus who can and should be believed in. The question of the identity of Jesus is as acute today as it was for John.

- For John Christian unity and love are not desirable extras in the Christian life, but are a central part of the eternal life that Jesus came to bring. He came to bring us into the divine family, and we are to live together as his followers in love. In a world where society is fragmented and religion is individualistic and consumerist, John's emphasis on community is important.

- John emphasizes that eternal life is something that has come into the present; it is not just pie in the sky when you die. This is relevant to people today who are looking not just for ideas and promises, but for a relationship with God in the present and for a living spirituality.

● Our modern world values love, tolerance and pluralism. John combines a strong emphasis on love (divine and human) with a moral and spiritual dualism, which distinguishes sharply between truth and falsehood, and between belief and unbelief. For John these are matters of life and death, not just of personal preference.

ESSAY TOPICS

INTRODUCTORY

● Take either the story of Jesus with the Samaritan woman of John 4 or the story of the blind man in John 9, and explain (a) how the 'drama' of the story unfolds, as John describes it, and (b) how the story illustrates ideas and themes that are important to John.

INTERMEDIATE

● History and theology in John: what are the historical issues raised in John's passion narrative in chs 18–20? And what are the theological themes that John brings out?

FURTHER READING

* indicates books assuming knowledge of Greek; most can be used by all students.

INTRODUCTORY

G. M. Burge *Interpreting the Gospel of John*. Guides to NT Exegesis 3. Grand Rapids: Baker Book House, 1992.

G. E. Ladd *A Theology of the New Testament*. Grand Rapids: Eerdmans/Cambridge: Lutterworth, 1993.

B. Lindars *John*. Sheffield: Sheffield Academic Press, 1990.

INTERMEDIATE

J. Ashton, *Understanding the Fourth Gospel*. Oxford: OUP, 1991 (major critical study).

M. Casey, *Is John's Gospel True?* London: Routledge, 1996 (lucid attack on the reliability of John).

J. D. G. Dunn, 'Let John be John' in P. Stuhlmacher (ed.) *The Gospel and the Gospels*. Grand Rapids: Eerdmans, 1991, 293–322.

*C. Evans, *Word and Glory*. Sheffield: JSOT, 1993 (excellent on the background to the prologue and the Gospel).

J. L. Martyn *History and Theology in the Fourth Gospel*, rev. ed. Nashville: Abingdon, 1979 (very influential explanation of the Jamnia view).

J. A. T. Robinson *The Priority of John*. London: SCM, 1985 (readable defence of the historicity of John).

S. S. Smalley *John Evangelist and Interpreter*. 2nd ed. Carlisle: Paternoster/Grand Rapids: Eerdmans, 1998 (excellent account of scholarship and bibliography).

COMMENTARIES

*G. R. Beasley-Murray *John*. Waco: Word, 1987

*R. E. Brown *The Gospel according to John*, 2 vols. London: Chapman, 1971/New York: Doubleday, 1966, 1970.

*R. Bultmann *The Gospel of John*. Oxford: Blackwells/Philadelphia: Westminster Press, 1971.

D. A. Carson *The Gospel According to John*. Leicester: IVP/Grand Rapids: Eerdmans, 1991.

R. Kysar *John*. Minneapolis: Augsbury, 1986.

B. Lindars *The Gospel of John*. London: Oliphants, 1972/Grand Rapids: Eerdmans, 1981.

M. W. G. Stibbe *John*. Readings: A New Biblical Commentary. Sheffield: JSOT Press, 1993

R. A. Whitacre *John*. Downers Grove/Leicester: IVP, 1999.

B. Witherington III *John's Wisdom*. Louisville: Westminster John Knox Press/Cambridge: Lutterworth, 1995.

THE ACTS OF
THE APOSTLES

Chapter 13

ACTS

Acts is a challenging and wide-ranging book, telling the story of the growth and development of the church, as it expands geographically (from Jerusalem to Rome) and ethnically (beginning with Jewish people and gradually including Gentiles). This longest NT book covers a considerable range of ideas and cultures in its pages, but all focused on telling what God did to take the message of Jesus to the then-known world.

ACTS AS LUKE'S VOLUME TWO

Acts needs to be seen not simply as a free-standing book (although it can profitably be read that way), but as 'part two' of Luke's overall project (see p. 227).

ACTS 1–2 AS BRIDGE

Luke retells the story of Jesus' departure (Luke 24:44-53; Acts 1:1-11) in similar manner to a modern TV series, where one programme ends with a preview of 'next week's show' and the next episode opens with a reminder of what happened 'previously' in the series. Luke does not simply repeat the story, however, but highlights key themes which will be important in the rest of Acts. And throughout Acts 1–2 there are echoes of themes and language

from Luke which also anticipate major themes in Acts 3–28:

- **the fulfilment of Scripture or God's promises** is spotlighted (Acts 1:4, 16; 2:16, 30, 33, 39; cf. Luke 24:25, 27, 37, 42, 44, 45, 49), and this prepares for Acts' emphasis on the OT as the source-book for what God is now doing (e.g. 3:24; 7:51f.; 8:30-35; 17:2, 11; 18:28).
- **God's direction of history**, stressed by Luke's use of 'it is necessary' (Greek *dei*) Acts 1:16, 21; cf. Luke 9:22; 13:33; 17:25; 22:37; 24:7, 26, 44.
- **the teaching and example of Jesus**, summed up as 'speaking about the kingdom of God' (Acts 1:3), echoes Luke's frequent use of this term in his Gospel (33 times) and anticipates the key summaries of Acts 8:12; 19:8; 28:23, 31.
- **the resurrection, exaltation and authority of Jesus**, highlighted in the account of Jesus' departure (Acts 1:9-11) and Peter's Pentecost sermon (Acts 2:24, 31-33), and central to the evangelistic speeches of Acts (e.g. 3:15; 5:20; 25:19), are also key themes in Luke (notably Luke 24, but also prophesied by Jesus in 9:22; 18:33).
- **blessings for Israel as a result of Jesus:** they are the 'target audience' of his work

(Acts 1:6; 2:36), and God's purpose is to restore Israel (e.g. Luke 1:16, 54, 68; 2:25, 32, 34); throughout Acts the phrase 'men, brothers' is used only when Jewish people are addressed (1:16; 2:29, 37; 7:2; 13:26, 28; 15:7, 13; 22:1; 23:1, 6; 18:17).

- **forgiveness of sins** as a major blessing resulting from Jesus' death and resurrection, central to the response required to Peter's sermon (Acts 2:38) and resonating with the teaching and actions of Jesus (Luke 5:20f.; 23f.; 7:47-49; 11:4; 23:34).

- **people from other nations will join the community of believers**, for the apostles will go to 'the ends of the earth' (Acts 1:8) – the (Jewish) crowd at Pentecost hints at this, for it includes people from 'every nation under heaven' (2:5). Simeon's hymn (Luke 2:32) together with other hints of Gentile mission in the Gospel (see pp. 236f.) suggests that this is how Acts 2:5, 39 ('all who are far away') are to be understood. The remainder of Acts will tell the story of how Gentiles hear about and respond to Jesus.

- **the promise and coming of the Spirit** is clearly central (esp. Acts 1:4, 8; 2:1-4), as it has been emphasized in Luke (see p. 237). The Spirit's work and empowering will be central to the church's life and growth in Acts (e.g. 4:8, 31; 5:31f.; 6:3f.; 8:29, 39, etc.) – indeed, the pentecostal outpouring of the Spirit is a model for subsequent comings of the Spirit (notice 'just as we did', 15:8f.).

- **prayer is a key** theme of Luke (see pp. 237f.). Here, Jesus' followers pray as they wait (Acts 1:14) and prayer characterizes their common life (Acts 2:42). Acts offers a rich portrait of the prayer life of the earliest Christians.

Digging deeper:
THE DEPARTURE OF JESUS

Read the two accounts of Jesus' departure (Luke 24:44-53; Acts 1:1-11) and compare and contrast the way Luke presents each of them. Which information and emphases are the same in the two accounts, and which points are presented differently? In the light of your study, consider the role of this story in (a) the Gospel; (b) Acts; (c) Luke-Acts, seen as a two-volume work.

(Further reading: see the commentaries on these passages.)

WHAT KIND OF BOOK IS ACTS?

Where does Acts fit among the literature of the ancient world? What expectations would it raise among readers who encountered it for the first time? Luke presents his account in narrative form, but he writes not simply to entertain but also to persuade, as the preface to his Gospel makes clear (Luke 1:3f.). So as we read we seek to hear the points he is making in and through the narrative.

Some argue that Luke is writing a history, noticing the parallel with Josephus' prefaces to his *Against Apion*, Books 1 and 2, in which he re-tells Jewish history:

> I suppose that by my books of the Antiquity of the Jews, most excellent Epaphroditus, I have made it evident to those who peruse them, that our Jewish nation is of very great antiquity … However, since I observe a considerable number of people giving ear to the reproaches that are laid against us by those who bear ill-will to us, and will not believe

what I have written concerning the antiquity of our nation … I therefore have thought myself under an obligation to write somewhat briefly about these subjects, in order to convict those that reproach us of spite and voluntary falsehood, and to correct the ignorance of others, and withal to instruct all those who are desirous of knowing the truth of what great antiquity we really are. *Ag. Ap.* 1.1 (= 1:1-3)

In the former book, most honoured Epaphroditus, I have demonstrated our antiquity, and confirmed the truth of what I have said…I shall now therefore begin a confutation of the remaining authors who have written any thing against us. *Ag. Ap.* 2.1 (= 2:1f.)

The resemblance with Luke's two prefaces is striking. Luke also shows an historian's instinct for cause and effect, writing a linear history which shows how and why developments in his narrative happen (such as the gradual acceptance of Gentiles into the Christian community). Luke is alone among our evangelists in providing chronological references for key events, which tie the story of Jesus and the church into world history (e.g. Luke 2:1f.; 3:1; Acts 18:12). Further, there are resemblances between Acts and OT history writing which suggest that Luke sees himself within a Jewish tradition of historical writing, as well as writing a book for a Graeco-Roman audience.

However, Loveday Alexander (1993) has examined the prefaces of Luke and Acts in considerable detail by comparing them with prefaces in other ancient writers, and she shows that they most closely resemble the introductions of technical works on subjects such as mathematics, astronomy, medicine or engineering. Historians' prefaces tend to

be longer than Luke's two and do not normally address their subject in the second person (Luke 1:3, 4). Alexander's work does not necessarily mean that Luke is writing a technical treatise, but it does suggest that the expected audience of Luke-Acts is not simply the very highly educated, whom the historians normally addressed, but people who, while educated, were more 'ordinary'.

Richard Pervo (1987) proposes that Acts is an ancient historical novel, written to entertain its readers. He notes that Luke writes in an entertaining way, including shipwrecks, adventures, dramatic episodes, humour (e.g. Acts 12:12-16!) and irony. Pervo's comparison with ancient novels, mostly focusing on romantic novels, highlights the parallels with Acts. However, Lucian of Samosata, writing in the second century AD, recommends that the mind of an historian should 'have a touch of poetry … he will have need of a wind of poetry to fill his sails and help carry his ship along' and that he should 'give his audience what will interest and instruct them' (Lucian, *How to Write History*, 45, 53). Thus, it is not really possible to distinguish historical writing and fiction in antiquity by their entertainment value, for both would aim to engage their readers' imaginations. Pervo's conclusion is unwarranted.

On balance, then, it seems likely that Acts is being presented as in a tradition of writing which is not 'high flown', but written for 'ordinary people'. Its structure and content would certainly remind ancient readers of the literary genre of 'acts' which they knew, for it is full of the deeds of its characters – it is a book of action (see p. 49). But Acts also has features in common with the 'lives' of antiquity (see pp. 49f.), such as the focus on particular individuals, notably Peter and

Paul, and with ancient history writing. Perhaps, then, Acts, rather like the Gospels, should be seen as breaking new ground, in that it did not fit straightforwardly into a single ancient literary genre.

STYLE AND PRESENTATION

'Luke is a stylistic chameleon', says Johnson (1992, 408), for the early chapters of both Luke and Acts sound like the Septuagint, echoing both its language and its rhythm, whereas the further events move from Jerusalem, the more Hellenistic and less Jewish Luke's Greek sounds. When Paul speaks in Athens (17:16-31) he sounds like a Greek philosopher, whereas when Peter speaks to the Pentecost crowd, he expounds the OT in rabbinic style (2:14-36).

PARALLELISM
A distinctive feature of Luke's writing is his use of parallelism on both large and small scales. He regularly tells a story of Peter and later tells a similar story of Paul: both are equipped by the Spirit (2:1-4; 13:1-3), arrested in the temple and brought before the Sanhedrin (4:1-3; 5:25-40; 21:27-40; 23:1-10), and involved in a raising from the dead (9:36-41; 20:7-12). (See more fully Walton 2000, 35f.) Often both stories echo a story about Jesus from Luke's Gospel. By writing this way, Luke offers his readers connections between his major characters, and shows how Jesus' model of godly living and leadership is seen in his followers' lives.

Luke can also use parallelism to highlight a contrast. Acts 4:34–5:11 first introduces a principle of the early Christians' life (sharing their possessions so that none were needy, 4:34f.), and follows it by a positive example (Barnabas, who sells a field and give the

money to the apostles, 4:36f.) and a negative example (Ananias and Sapphira, who pretend to be giving the whole amount they received for selling a property and both die, 5:1-11).

PROPHECY AND FULFILMENT
Just as Luke presents God's activities through a pattern of an event being prophesied and later happening in his Gospel (see p. 232), so also in Acts. There are a number of examples of prophecies from the Gospel which are fulfilled in Acts, as well as other prophecies in Acts fulfilled later in the book.

PROPHECY AND FULFILMENT: SOME EXAMPLES

Luke 21:12-15 Jesus predicts tribulation for his followers;
Acts 4:3-5, 14; 5:17-42 Peter and John are tried and flogged.

Luke 9:5; 10:11 Jesus tells his disciples to shake the dust off their feet where they are not welcomed;
Acts 13:51 Paul and Barnabas shake the dust off their feet outside Pisidian Antioch.

Luke 22:30 The Twelve to be judges over Israel;
Acts 5:1-11 Peter acts as 'judge' of Ananias and Sapphira.

Acts 21:10-14 Agabus predicts suffering for Paul;
Acts 21:30-35 Paul is mobbed and then arrested in Jerusalem.

What do you think?
PROPHECY AND FULFILMENT

Read Acts 7:51-60 and 13:40-48. How does the pattern of prophecy and fulfilment work out within each of these two passages?

'THE END OF THE EARTH' (1:8)

When Jesus speaks of his followers being witnesses 'to the end of the earth', where exactly does this mean? Two main possibilities have been entertained by scholars.

- *Rome* is the end of the earth, since it is the greatest city of the world. But for this reason Rome would be seen, rather, as the *centre* of the earth.
- *Spain* is the end of the earth, for it is the furthest point west in the Roman empire – and we know that Paul planned to travel to Rome (Rom. 15:28). There are ancient references to Gades, on the western coasts of Spain, as 'the end of the earth' (Strabo, *Geography*, 3.1.8).

However, 'the end of the earth' is drawn from Isa. 49:6 (as is its echo in Acts 13:47), and Septuagint use suggests that the phrase simply means 'the whole world', without having a particular place in mind as 'the end of the earth' (see Isa. 8:9; 14:22; 48:20; 49:6; 62:11; Jer. 10:13; 28:16 [= 35:16 LXX]; 32:32 [= 39:32 LXX]; 38:8 [= 45:8 LXX]; 1 Macc. 3:9).

ACTS AS FULFILMENT OF 1:8

1:1–5:42	**Witnesses in Jerusalem**
1:1–2:47	The beginning of the church
3:1–5:42	The church in Jerusalem
6:1–11:18	**Witnesses in Judea and Samaria**
6:1–9:31	The church begins to expand
9:32–11:18	The beginning of the Gentile mission
11:19–28:31	**Witnesses to the ends of the earth**
11:19–14:28	The mission from Antioch to Asia Minor
15:1–35	The discussion concerning the Gentiles in the church
5:36–18:17	Paul's mission in Macedonia and Achaia
18:18–20:38	Paul's mission in Asia
21:1–28:31	Paul's arrest and imprisonment

Acts 1:8 is a particularly striking example of this pattern: 'you will be my witnesses in Jerusalem, in all Judea and Samaria, and to the end of the earth'. The whole book can be seen as fulfilling this prophecy (although, as we shall see, there are other ways of analysing the book's structure).

In reading Acts, therefore, we need to look for the narrative connections Luke provides in parallels, contrasts, and prophecy and fulfilment.

STRUCTURE

A strong feature of Acts is Luke's focus on the progress of 'the word of God/the Lord'. This favourite Lukan phrase occurs some ten times in Acts (and four times in Luke), frequently to highlight the growth of the

Acts 6:7	The word of God continued to spread; the number of the disciples increased greatly in Jerusalem, and a great many of the priests became obedient to the faith.
9:31	Meanwhile the church throughout Judea, Galilee, and Samaria had peace and was built up. Living in the fear of the Lord and in the comfort of the Holy Spirit, it increased in numbers.
12:24	But the word of God continued to advance and gain adherents.
16:5	So the churches were strengthened in the faith and increased in numbers daily.
19:20	So the word of the Lord grew mightily and prevailed.
28:30f	[Paul] lived there two whole years at his own expense and welcomed all who came to him, proclaiming the kingdom of God and teaching about the Lord Jesus Christ with all boldness and without hindrance.

church, which Luke expresses as (literally) 'the word of God grew' (6:7). Six times Luke summarizes the growth of the church, sometimes using other phrases (see the box on p. 271).

Some (e.g. Longenecker 1981, 233f. = Longenecker 1995, 29f.) see these as 'markers' of the end of the major sections of Acts. However, 19:20 comes in the middle of Paul's visit to Ephesus, prior to the story of the riot (19:23-41), which suggests that the natural break comes when Paul begins the next phase of his travels at 20:1. Thus the outline of the book is:

1-2	Introduction
3:1–6:7	The mission in Jerusalem
6:8–9:31	Stephen, Philip and Saul
9:32–12:24	The gospel spreads in Syria-Palestine
12:25–16:5	The first 'missionary journey' and the Jerusalem Council
16:6–19:41	The second and third 'missionary journeys'
20:1–28:31	To Jerusalem and then Rome

Each section shows the spread of the Christian message to new territories or among new peoples, with the earlier part of the book focusing on the Jerusalem church, particularly Peter, Stephen and Philip (Acts 1–12), and the latter part focusing particularly on Paul's mission (Acts 13–28).

A READING OF ACTS

SETTING THE SCENE
1–2 After the dedication (1:1-2) and Jesus' departure (1:3-11), the remainder of ch. 1 is about preparation for the coming of the Spirit, promised by Jesus in 1:8. Thus the church is devoted to prayer (1:12-14) and

Peter takes the lead in the choice of a successor for Judas as an apostle (1:15-26).

The church then really takes off with the coming of the Spirit. Acts 2:1-4 describe what happens, and Luke then explains the meaning of these events. We hear the varying reactions of the crowd (2:5-13), and Peter offers an explanation centring on the day's events and the ministry, death and resurrection of Jesus as fulfilment of the OT, citing as evidence Joel 2:28-32 (Acts 2:17-21), Ps. 16:8-11 (Acts 2:25-28) and Ps. 110:1 (Acts 2:34f.). He explains four elements of response, human and divine, which will be repeated often in Acts: repentance, water baptism in the name of Jesus, forgiveness of sins and the gift of the Spirit (2:38f.). We then get a snapshot of the early church's life, with four components: the apostles' teaching, shared life (including sharing possessions, vv. 44f.), shared meals (probably the eucharist, but see the box below) and shared prayer (v. 42). Again, this pattern will be repeated frequently in Acts.

What do you think?
'THE BREAKING OF THE BREAD' IN LUKE-ACTS

Acts 2:46 is the first mention in Acts of 'they broke bread' and similar phrases. Read the passages listed below, and consider in each case whether you think it refers to the Christian eucharist, a (Jewish-style) 'blessing' said over the bread, shared meals or something else. Does Luke use the phrase consistently? After you have thought about this yourself., see what some of the commentaries (see p.299) say on these passages.

Luke 22:19; 24:30; Acts 2:46; 20:7, 11; 27:35

MISSION IN JERUSALEM

3:1–6:7 The healing of the lame man (3:1-10) opens an opportunity to speak about Jesus (3:11-26), but leads to the apostles' arrest and trial (4:1-23, fulfilling Luke 12:11f., 21:12-15). Peter and John refuse to accept the Sanhedrin's attempt to silence them (4:17f., 21), but place God's authority higher than the Sanhedrin's (4:19f., fulfilling Luke 12:11f.; 21:14f.). Luke again notes the group's unity and the sharing of possessions (4:32-35), giving a positive and a negative example (4:36f.; 5:1-11).

Acts 5:12-16 picks up the theme of the church's 'power evangelism' (see 4:33) and adds more, including further pressure from the Jewish authorities (5:17f.) and an angelic rescue (5:19-21a). The apostles are again brought to the Sanhedrin (5:21b-42), and Peter enrages the Sanhedrin by telling them that Jesus, whom they had killed, is now raised up and offers a new way for Israel (5:30-32).

The counsel of Gamaliel the Pharisee prevents their execution (4:33-39 – contrast Stephen, 7:54-60). The apostles are flogged – no small punishment for men who are being freed, but not uncommon in the ancient world (5:40f.). This section closes with practical arrangements being made to care justly for widows, whether Greek- or Aramaic-speaking (6:1-7) – arrangements which avoid tying up the apostles in administration, but keep them free for 'prayer and serving the word' (6:4). These just dealings and the apostles' preaching and prayer mean that the church continues to grow, still within a Jewish framework (6:7).

THREE BIG MEN

6:8–9:31 focuses on three characters, Stephen, Philip and Saul. The first two are among the seven who 'wait on tables' (6:2, 5), and we now meet them as evangelists pushing out the boundaries of the church. Stephen – a Greek name, so likely Greek-speaking – performs powerful deeds (6:8), which leads him into debate with a synagogue of Greek-speaking diaspora Jews (6:9), and to arrest and trial (6:11-15). Stephen's speech – the longest in Acts – surveys Jewish history, arguing that Jesus' followers are the true Jews, not those who reject Jesus. He downgrades the temple (7:48-50, quoting Isa. 66:1f.), and echoes Jesus' warning that they are repeating their ancestors' errors in killing Jesus (7:51-53; cf. Luke 6:22f.; 11:47; 13:34). They kill Stephen, but not before he sees Jesus as 'the son of man' at God's right hand (7:56; cf. Dan. 7:13f. and pp. 175, 183f.).

Stephen's death marks a parting of the ways, for the Jewish authorities now actively persecute the church (8:1-3). Philip travels north to Samaria, to people not seen as 'pure' Jews by the Jews of Judea and Galilee, but whom Jesus had helped on occasion (Luke 17:11-19). Philip's ministry (8:5-7) leads to Peter and John praying that the new believers might receive the Spirit. Simon offers money for such powers (8:9-13, 18f.) and is rebuked for treating Christian faith as magic, something that can be bought and sold (8:26-23). Here is a theme that will return, for Christian faith is opposed to magic, seeking to gain power over the gods in order to get them to do what the magician's client wants (cf. 19:18f.). Rather, following Jesus means doing what *he* wants (cf. 4:19f.; 5:29). Luke leaves a narrative gap here, for we never learn what happens to Simon (8:24), but the inclusion of Samaritans in the church continues (8:25).

Philip goes to the desert road and meets a high-ranking Ethiopian eunuch (8:26-40).

Digging deeper:
THE DAMASCUS ROAD ENCOUNTER

Luke tells this story, including Saul's early days as a believer, three times, in Acts 9:1-22; 22:3-21; 26:2-23. Make notes on the three accounts in three parallel columns, identifying what they have in common and what is different.

Who is the speaker or storyteller in each case, and who is the audience? When do you think Saul learned that he was to be a missionary to Gentiles? What particular emphases come through in each account?

Use your table to try to reconstruct the historical sequence of events of this period of Saul's life. When you have tried to do this yourself, have a look at one or two commentaries on Acts and see how they handle it.

A further issue in modern discussion of this event is whether it should be considered Saul's conversion or his call. Those who think it is a call argue that Saul does not change one 'pattern of religion' for another in becoming a follower of Jesus, but rather that he sees following Jesus as the fulfilment of his Judaism. What do you think about this question?

(Further reading: G. F. Hawthorne, R. P. Martin & D. G. Reid, eds. *Dictionary of Paul and the Letters*. Leicester/Downers Grove: IVP, 1993, article 'Conversion and call of Paul'.)

Again, the gospel's boundaries are spreading, for this man would be forbidden to take a full part in Israel's worship because of his castration (Deut. 23:1). Philip hears him reading Isa. 53 aloud (the normal way of reading in antiquity, even when reading privately), tells the eunuch about Jesus, and baptizes him as a believer. Philip disappears from the narrative as quickly as he leaves the eunuch's sight (8:39), and reappears much later (21:8f.).

Finally, we meet Saul (9:1-30). He appeared as the one who looked after the coats of Stephen's killers (7:58; 8:1) and a persecutor of the church (8:3; 9:1f.). However, the one who thinks he is pursuing others finds that God is pursuing him, for he meets the risen Jesus and his life is turned around. The encounter has elements in common with the calls of OT prophets, particularly hearing a heavenly voice (cf. Isa. 6:8; Jer. 1:4, 9, 11, 14), and includes a startling commission to tell Gentiles about Jesus (given at this stage to Ananias, rather than directly to Saul, 9:15). Saul has to escape from those who had been his supporters (9:23-25). Barnabas reappears and (characteristically) acts generously in introducing Saul to the apostles, when others were fearful.

THE GOSPEL SPREADS IN SYRIA-PALESTINE
We enter a further expansion of the message in Israel and Syria. Peter travels to Lydda (9:32-35), and then to Joppa, a coastal town (9:36-43; cf. Jesus raising the dead in Luke 7:11-17; 8:40-42a, 49-56). Peter stays with a tanner, a ritually unclean trade in Judaism, since he worked with the skins of dead animals – surprising, in view of Peter's stated care over unclean animals (10:14).

Luke tells the story of the uncircumcized Gentile godfearer Cornelius twice (10:1–11:18; he also alludes to it in 15:7-9). As with Saul's call/conversion, repetition highlights this story. With this story the road begins towards admitting Gentiles as believers without requiring them to become Jews. The story operates at two levels, for both Cornelius and Peter undergo a profound change. Luke highlights that God initiated this new move: God acted through an angel (10:3-6), a vision (10:10-16), advance knowledge (10:17-21), and the Spirit's coming as at Pentecost (10:44-47 – note 'just as we have', 10:47; 'the same gift that he gave us' 11:17). This leads even the 'circumcision party' to conclude that God welcomes Gentiles (11:18; cf. 11:12).

Other developments follow: the first Gentile church comes into being (11:19-26). Saul now reappears, fetched by Barnabas (again the encourager in supporting this new congregation and in drawing Saul in) to help with the new church. Agabus' prophecy leads to a new form of sharing possessions (cf. 4:35f.), as this Gentile congregation sends help to the Judean messianic Jewish communities (11:27-30).

The death of James casts a shadow over the growth of the church (12:1f.), and is rapidly followed by Peter's arrest, which leads into one of the most comical scenes in Acts, involving Peter being mistaken for his 'angel' – probably his ghost (12:15; cf. Luke 24:36f.)! Herod, who had James killed, then dies as a result of his pride (12:20-23), and Luke concludes this section with a summary of the church's growth (12:24).

PAUL BEGINS TO TRAVEL; THE JERUSALEM MEETING

12:25–16:5 In 13:1-3 we get a rare glimpse in Acts of the life of an early Christian congregation, as they (or perhaps their leaders) meet for worship. As they pray and fast, the Spirit speaks, probably as a member of the group speaks what they believe God is saying (cf. 21:11). Barnabas and Saul are commissioned and sent. In Cyprus (13:4-12) it seems that Saul takes the lead – he is usually named first from 13:13 onwards – and

he is now known by his Roman name, Paul (13:9). (See map on p. 276.) Sailing from Paphos they arrive in Perga (on the southern coast of modern Turkey), where John Mark leaves them (13:13), something which will be significant later (15:36-41). Barnabas and Saul go on to Pisidian Antioch.

In Antioch a pattern of evangelism emerges: Barnabas and Saul go first to the synagogue and speak about Jesus (13:14-43) and this has the effect of dividing the Jews: some accept their message and others reject it (13:43, 45). The unbelieving Jews then attack the missionaries (13:45), which results in the missionaries taking their message to Gentiles (13:46-49). Eventually, persecution by non-Christian Jews forces the missionaries to leave (13:50f.). Luke shows this is a pattern by 14:1: 'The same thing occurred in Iconium.'

Lystra is different, for it is a pagan town without a synagogue (14:8-20). Here a healing opens the way as Paul preaches (14:9f.), but it leads to a misunderstanding, for the people think that Paul and Barnabas are gods. Luke sketches the rest of this journey briefly, recording a visit to Derbe and return visits to the other towns (14:21-23), before they travel back to Syrian Antioch (14:24-26).

The question of whether Gentile believers need circumcision surfaces again as a group from Judea come to Syrian Antioch, and Paul and Barnabas debate with them (15:1f.; it is likely that Paul writes Galatians in the midst of this crisis). The meeting which follows is a key turning point in Acts, for after much debate it is accepted that Gentile believers do not need to become Jews. A clinching argument is that the experiences reported by Peter, Barnabas and Paul are prophesied in the OT, as James cites Amos 9:11f. (Acts 15:16f.).

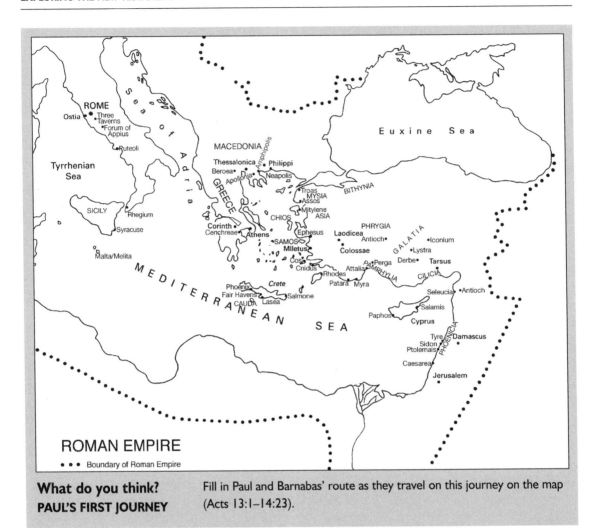

What do you think?
PAUL'S FIRST JOURNEY

Fill in Paul and Barnabas' route as they travel on this journey on the map (Acts 13:1–14:23).

Although Gentile believers need not be circumcized, James proposes restrictions (15:20), echoing requirements from Lev. 17–18 (notice 17:8; 18:26-30, which specify that these regulations apply to 'aliens' living among the Israelites). Historically, this compromise does not hold for long, and the meat requirement is gone by the time of Mark's Gospel (Mark 7:18f.; see p. 196).

Paul initiates a further journey, which precipitates an argument with Barnabas over John Mark (15:36-41). The result is that Barnabas heads for Cyprus with John Mark (the last

we hear of them in Acts), and Paul for Syria and Cilicia, going overland to Derbe, with Silas.

In Derbe Paul meets Timothy, a man recommended by the church, whose mother is Jewish. Deciding to take Timothy, Paul has him circumcized, thus demonstrating that Paul does not oppose circumcision for Jews, but only the requirement that Gentile believers must be circumcized in order to be saved (16:1-3).

PAUL'S SECOND AND THIRD JOURNEYS
16:6–19:41 focuses on Paul's two long journeys, each lasting some years. The first

276

FULFILMENT: A THEME IN ACTS

The language of 'fulfilment' is prominent in Acts, both the verb 'fulfil' (Greek *plēroō*) in various forms (1:16; 3:18; 13:27, 32f.) and language about God's plan (Greek *boulē*; 2:23; 4:28; 5:38f.; 13:36; 20:27) or will (Greek *thelēma*; 21:24; 22:14).

The sermon in Pisidian Antioch (13:16-41) highlights this theme strongly:

- v. 27 speaks of Jesus' condemnation fulfilling (Greek *eplērōsan*) the (OT) prophets;
- v. 29 says that the Jerusalem dwellers and their leaders carried out (Greek *etelesan*) everything written (in Scripture) about Jesus;

- v. 33 sees the raising of Jesus as fulfilling (Greek *ekpeplērōken*; Ps. 2:7);
- with the sermon there is much citation of Scripture in support: vv. 33 (Ps. 2:7), 34 (Isa. 55:3), 35 (Ps. 16:10), 41 (Hab. 1:5).

Luke also stresses that certain events are 'necessary' (Greek *dei* = 'it is necessary', a Lukan favourite), thus claiming that God was behind them (for that was why they had to happen) e.g. 3:21; 5:29; 17:3. He further uses the language of God predetermining events which take place by his choice or purpose (e.g. 10:42; 17:31; 22:14; 26:16).

(Further reading: D. Peterson 'The Motif of Fulfilment and the Purpose of Luke-Acts' in Winter & Clarke 1993, 83-104.)

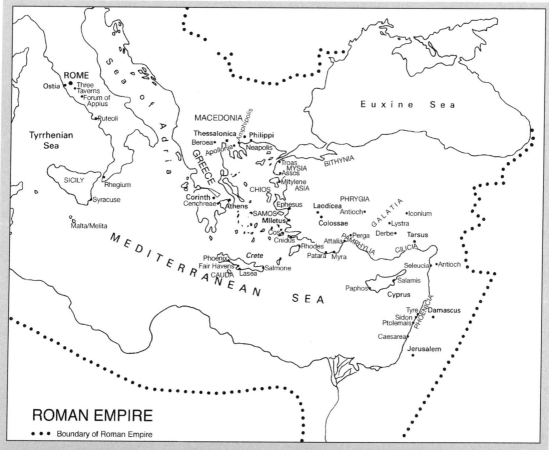

What do you think?
PAUL'S SECOND JOURNEY

Fill in Paul's route as he travel on this journey on the map (Acts 15:36–18:22).

(16:5–18:22) includes at least 18 months in Corinth (18:11, 18), and the second over two years in Ephesus (19:10), both major cities in their regions.

Acts 16:6-10 presents the only significant occasion in Acts where Paul finds it hard to know where to go next, as God prevents him, Silas and Timothy from entering Asia and Bithynia (16:6, 7). God then intervenes in a vision and the group travel to Neapolis, the port of Philippi, bringing the gospel to Macedonia (modern Greece) for the first time. Philippi evidently lacks a synagogue – it is a 'retirement colony' for Roman soldiers – so Paul seeks a prayer place near the river on the Sabbath (16:13). There he meets Lydia: she and her household form the nucleus of a congregation there (16:14f.).

Paul delivers a demonized slave girl who predicts the future (16:16-21), so that her owners bring Paul before the magistrates because of the economic loss they suffer. In this Roman colony Paul and Silas are charged with advocacy of Jewish customs (vv. 20f.), whereas in other cities it is usually fellow Jews claiming that Paul proposes abandoning Jewish customs and beliefs (cf. 13:45; 14:2, 19; 17:13; 18:5f., 12f.). In prison an earthquake offers the chance to go free; instead, they explain the gospel to their jailer, who is baptized with his family (16:28-34), before the magistrates propose to let them go in the morning (16:35). Paul produces his trump card, his Roman citizenship, which means that he should not have been beaten without trial (16:37), and the magistrates come to apologize (16:38f.). Paul does this, presumably, in the hope that the new church would be left alone by the authorities.

In Thessalonica Paul's regular pattern resumes (17:1-9) – he goes first to the synagogue and speaks about Jesus. The Jewish community is divided (v. 4), and some godfearers join the new church. Unbelieving Jews lead a mob to attack the missionaries. Their charge echoes the charge against Jesus, that he is another king to rival the emperor (v. 7; cf. Luke 23:2). Paul and the others flee to Beroea (17:10-15). The shortness of the initial visit to Thessalonica fits well with the evidence of 1 Thessalonians, probably written from Corinth during the visit of Acts 18:1-18 after Timothy rejoined Paul (Acts 18:5; 1 Thess. 3:1-6; see Walton 2000, 144-7).

From Beroea Paul goes to Athens alone; Silas and Timothy go elsewhere (Luke does not give details, although 1 Thess. 3:1-6 strongly suggests that Timothy went to Thessalonica). Although there is a synagogue in Athens (17:17), Paul's focus is debate in the *agora*

Digging deeper:
PAUL'S 'MISSIONARY JOURNEYS' AND HIS STRATEGY

Many books speak of Paul's 'missionary journeys' and provide maps of his travels during these periods. That phrase can suggest that Paul planned a long way ahead, whereas at times (e.g. 16:6-8) he and his companions find it hard to know where to go.

From what you have discovered of Paul's travels so far, what are the elements of Paul's strategy as he seeks to persuade others to follow Jesus? Consider the directions of his travels (consult an atlas to see the Roman roads he travelled along and the status of the cities he visited), and his behaviour in each city he visits.

(Further reading: Green 1970, ch. 10.)

THE 'WE' PASSAGES

Acts 16:10 is the first occasion where 'we' do something: until now the narrator speaks in the third person. There are several 'we' passages in Acts (16:10-17; 20:5-15; 21:1-18; 27:1–28:16), and scholars have long discussed how they should be understood (see Witherington 1998, 480-6). Key options are:

(1) Luke is recording events in which he took part, either from memory or from his diary: 'we' is his indication that he was present;

(2) Luke is using a diary or notes from a travel companion of Paul, and he has incorporated this material into Acts without changing 'we' to 'they';

(3) V. Robbins argues that Luke is using an ancient literary convention, particularly associated with fictional accounts of sea voyages, which allowed an author to write in the first person plural, but which would not lead ancient readers to expect him to have been present.

Option (2) seems unlikely, for Luke has everywhere else concealed his sources by putting Acts into his own style and, apart from using 'we', he has done the same in these passages – they do not have a different literary style. Further, there is no plausible reason why Luke should introduce diary material without explaining what it is.

Option (3) is improbable, for ancient writers do not observe this convention at all consistently. Many of the key examples are from books written *entirely* in the first person: Acts appears unique in its variation between first and third person storytelling. Further, some of the 'we' material in Acts is not directly narrating sea voyages, and there are other sea voyages in Acts told in the third person (e.g. 13:4f.; 14:20-28; 18:18-23).

A difficulty for option (1) is that Luke 1:2f. appears to distance Luke from the eyewitnesses, but those verses are probably referring only to the contents of the Gospel and not to Acts. (See further p. 295f.)

What do you think?
PAUL'S AREOPAGUS SPEECH (17:22-34)

This speech has been claimed as out of tune with Paul's letters, especially Romans 1:18-32, where Paul seems critical of pagan religion. In Athens he seems much more positive. Read the two accounts carefully and list similarities and differences. How far do the different audiences of the passages explain the different presentation?

(See further: G. F. Hawthorne, R. P. Martin & D. G. Reid, eds. *Dictionary of Paul and the Letters*. Leicester/Downers Grove: IVP, 1993, article 'Athens, Paul at'.)

(city square) with the philosophers (17:17f.). Paul is invited to speak at the Areopagus, and Luke presents a 'set piece' speech explaining the gospel to pagans.

In Corinth (18:1-18) Paul meets the Jewish Christian couple Aquila and Priscilla and

PAUL IN CORINTH: THE GALLIO INSCRIPTION

Paul's visit to Corinth is one point in the NT that can be dated with some precision. A man was appointed as proconsul in Achaia (Corinth's province) for a year, from 1 July to 30 June the following year. An inscription has been found at Delphi of a letter from the Emperor Claudius to Gallio which allows us to date his proconsulate with a very high degree of likelihood to 1 July 51 to 30 June 52. This suggests that Paul arrived in Corinth in autumn 50 and left in spring 52.

(For an English translation of the inscription, with commentary, see: C. K. Barrett, ed. *The New Testament Background: Selected Documents*, revised ed. London: SPCK, 1987/New York: HarperSanFrancisco, 1995, 51f.)

works with them as a tentmaker (probably using leather, the common material for that purpose), while speaking in the synagogue on the Sabbath. When Silas and Timothy arrive Paul moves into full-time preaching (18:5), which suggests that they brought gifts from the churches they had visited while absent. The typical division of the synagogue occurs and Paul leaves it (18:6); a mixed Jew-Gentile church is founded in the home of Titius Justus, a godfearer (18:7). Significantly for a Roman audience, Gallio, a noted jurist, declares that Paul has no charge to answer when the Jews attack him.

Acts 18:23–19:41 forms Paul's third major journey from his base at Syrian Antioch. First he travels overland to Galatia (southern Turkey). Luke then takes us to Ephesus, to introduce Apollos (18:24-28), a preacher of Jesus who needs fuller instruction from Priscilla and Aquila, for he has only received John's baptism. Apollos is commended to the churches of Achaia (of which Corinth is the chief, 19:1), and this brief account probably explains some of the issues in 1 Corinthians 1–3 about different visitors to Corinth (esp.1:12).

We return to Ephesus for Paul's visit: he

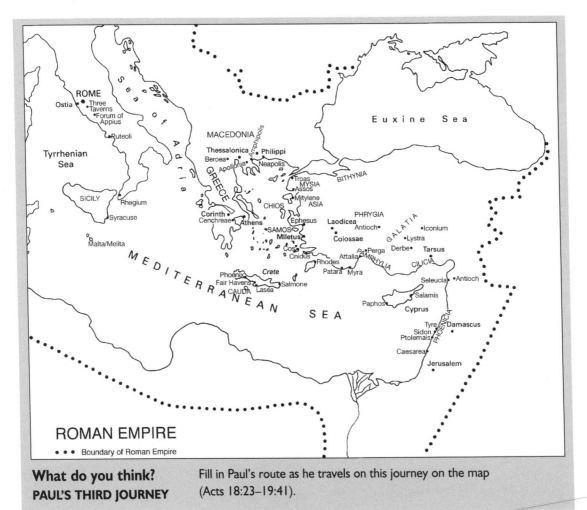

ROMAN EMPIRE

• • • Boundary of Roman Empire

What do you think?
PAUL'S THIRD JOURNEY

Fill in Paul's route as he travels on this journey on the map (Acts 18:23–19:41).

What do you think?
PAUL THE LETTER-WRITER AND ACTS

During Paul's visit to Corinth (Acts 18:1-18) he probably writes 1 and 2 Thessalonians, although it is interesting that Luke never mentions his letter-writing activities. Several possible explanations have been proposed; some are linked to particular views of Luke's identity:

- Luke does not know that Paul wrote letters because he never knew Paul and writes before collections of Paul's letters circulate;
- Luke knows that Paul writes letters, but has not read any of them, for Paul did not write letters at any of the times when Luke was with him;
- Luke knows that Paul writes letters, has read them, and uses them in composing Acts;
- Luke knows that Paul writes letters, but omits this information since it is peripheral to his presentation of Paul primarily as a missionary.

What are the strengths and weaknesses of each of these views? Which evidence from Acts and the Pauline letters do they each find hardest to fit in? Which do you find most persuasive and why?

travels inland to the city, right across modern Turkey, and spends a considerable time there – at least two years (19:10, 22). Luke clearly regards this visit as a time of marked blessing by God on Paul's ministry (19:10). Certainly there is opposition: from the synagogue (19:8f.), from disease and evil spirits (19:11f.), and from the rioting crowd (19:23-41) – but in each case it is overcome. No wonder Luke comments, 'The word of the Lord grew mightily and prevailed' (19:20)!

Luke previews the next major stage of the story (19:21f.), as Paul resolves 'in the Spirit' to go to Jerusalem and then Rome (most likely a reference to the Holy Spirit, since the Greek here contains *dei*, 'it is necessary', which in Luke-Acts normally highlights what must happen because of what God is doing). The journey to Rome, via Jerusalem, will dominate the final section of the book, culminating in Paul's arrival.

Timothy's and Erastus' trip to Macedonia (19:22) is probably to prepare for Paul's visit to gather the churches of that region's contributions to Paul's collection for the needy church in Jerusalem (cf. 2 Cor. 8–9, probably written during this visit to Ephesus), although Luke tells us little of this collection (24:17 is one hint) – an example of his selectivity in writing Acts.

TO JERUSALEM AND THEN ROME
20:1–28:31 The Ephesian riot precipitates Paul's departure, following which he visits the Macedonian churches (20:2; presumably Philippi, Thessalonica and Beroea). Travelling south, he visits the churches of Greece (probably Athens and Corinth), spending some three months there before retracing his steps to the north (20:2f.). By now Paul has quite a group with him (20:4), likely the delegates from the churches who had contributed to the collection. Somewhere along the way (perhaps in Philippi?) Luke rejoins Paul, and 'we' resumes (20:5f.). They cross the Aegean again to Alexandria Troas and wait there for a week, probably for a ship going to Jerusalem.

Having painted a full portrait of Paul the missionary, Luke now sketches Paul the pastor. We know much more of Paul's care for his churches from his letters than from Acts, and that is why the stories in Acts 20, of Paul with a church and a church's leaders, are so interesting. Here we see Paul as preacher to Christians, teaching the Troas congregation all night (20:7, 11). He raises poor Eutychus from the dead – a young man who cannot stay awake during Paul's long sermon (20:9f.)! And he 'breaks bread' with them before leaving – while still talking (20:11)!

The Miletus speech (20:18-35) is the only occasion in Acts where Paul speaks to Christians (his other speeches are evangelistic or judicial), and he packs in advice on how to pastor. There are many echoes of the Pauline letters, particularly 1 Thessalonians (Walton 2000, ch. 5), and of the teaching of Jesus in Luke about leadership (notably Luke 22:24-38; Walton 2000, ch. 4). Luke presents Paul as in the same tradition of leadership as his master, and teaching the leaders of this key church to lay down their lives for the sheep.

In both stories we sense the affection in which Paul is held by his churches: the Troas church will stay up all night talking with him (20:11), and the Ephesian elders weep over the news that they will never see him again (20:25, 37f.).

After slowing narrative time to highlight these incidents, Luke speeds up again as we race across the Mediterranean to Tyre (21:1-3). In Tyre the Christians 'through the Spirit' tell Paul not to go to Jerusalem (21:4: a similar warning follows in Caesarea, 21:10-12).

In the city Paul is warmly welcomed, but the Jerusalem church leaders also want him to demonstrate his Jewish orthodoxy by taking part in a vow and by paying for the hair-dressing expenses of four others (21:20-26). Paul agrees, but Jews from Asia Minor precipitate a riot (21:27-36). Paul is saved from the mob by the Roman garrison (based at the Antonia Fortress, within sight of the

What do you think?
IS AGABUS A FALSE PROPHET?

Compare Agabus' prophecy (21:11) with the detail of the account of Paul's experiences in the temple (21:27–22:30). How accurately does Agabus foretell what happens to Paul in Jerusalem?

What is the best explanation for the differences: (i) Agabus is a false prophet; (ii) Agabus is right in general but wrong in detail and that was acceptable in NT prophets; (iii) Luke is writing the story of Agabus' prophecy in light of what actually happened (something suggested for Luke's account of Jesus' prediction of the fall of Jerusalem, Luke 21:5-36); (iv) something else?

temple). From now on Paul is in captivity, and Paul the prisoner dominates the remainder of Acts.

Paul persuades the tribune to allow him to speak to the people (21:37-40). The speech which follows (22:1-21) contains the second account in Acts of Paul's Damascus road experience, told in the first person, in which he stresses his and other Jewish believers' loyalty to the torah (vv. 3-5, 12, 17) and explains that he is responding to the God of Israel calling him to speak about Jesus to Gentiles (v. 21). The speech gets no further, for the mob cry aloud again and Paul is rescued by the Romans. He invokes his Roman citizenship to avoid a flogging (22:24-29).

A series of formal judicial hearings begin, in which Paul defends himself. The first (22:30–23:10), before the Sanhedrin, has the Jewish charges against him as focus. Paul claims pharisaic credentials, thus dividing the groups within the Sanhedrin against each other.

Nevertheless, the Jewish plot against Paul continues, and 'the Lord' (23:11) encourages Paul that he will testify in Rome. Paul hears about the plot and the tribune sends him to Felix, the Roman governor of Judea, at Caesarea (23:12-35).

The second hearing is before Felix, and involves a formal charge by the Jewish leaders (24:1-9). Luke records the proceedings of this Roman court in line with our knowledge of legal processes of the day. Paul defends himself, arguing that the charges cannot be proven, and that he is a loyal Jew (24:10-21). Felix decides to wait to hear personally from the tribune who arrested Paul, and holds him under an open form of 'house arrest' (24:22f.). After two years he departs, and unjustly leaves Paul imprisoned (24:27).

Thirdly, Festus, the new governor, calls Paul in because of the Jewish leaders' complaints (25:1-3). Again it is Jewish charges that are central (25:7). Paul argues he is a loyal Jew and also a loyal Roman citizen (25:8). Festus wishes to help the Jewish leaders – probably to 'win friends and influence people' as a new governor – and so he offers a trial in Jerusalem. Paul seems to despair of receiving justice, so he appeals to the emperor, a right open to Roman citizens. Paul does not do this lightly: he has attempted on three occasions to be heard fairly, and now exercises this right since Festus intends to act unjustly in sending him to Jerusalem for trial (cf. 28:19, which makes it clear that Paul sees no other way out). Festus accepts Paul's appeal, which stops the trial (25:12).

A fourth opportunity comes when Agrippa, a Jewish client-king, and his wife make a courtesy call on the new governor. Festus seeks Agrippa's advice on Paul's case (25:13-22). Paul's defence is similar to that before the mob, focusing on his loyalty to his Jewish heritage and the changes which resulted from meeting Jesus on the Damascus road (26:1-23). But Paul's real aim is to invite Agrippa to become a follower of Jesus too (26:25-29). Agrippa concludes that Paul has committed no crime worthy of death or imprisonment, and could have been freed had he not appealed to the emperor (26:30f.). The final chapters narrate Paul's journey to Rome (27–28). (See map on p. 284.) Sea travel in the ancient world was dangerous, particularly in the rough seas of winter, and shipwrecks were not uncommon (27:7-12; cf. 2 Cor. 11:25). During the journey Paul is treated well by Julius, the Roman centurion in charge of him (27:1). Julius allows him to visit friends in Sidon (27:3), accepts his advice during the storm (27:30f.) and prevents Paul from being killed (27:42f.).

Luke's account is one of the fullest ancient accounts of a storm at sea. It shows how God's promise that Paul would see Rome (23:11) is fulfilled in spite of great forces against it, and thus would encourage Christian readers who felt under pressure for their faith in Jesus: if God could deliver Paul, then surely he could deliver them.

After two weeks in the storm the ship approaches land, and they are shipwrecked on Malta (27:33–28:1). Luke is highly selective in his account of this visit, covering three months (28:11) in ten verses, evidently choosing the incidents he sees as important.

The final journey to Rome crosses the Mediterranean to Syracuse (on Sicily), Rhegium (at the tip of southern Italy) and Puteoli (western coast of Italy, about 200 km/130 miles south of Rome) (28:11-13).

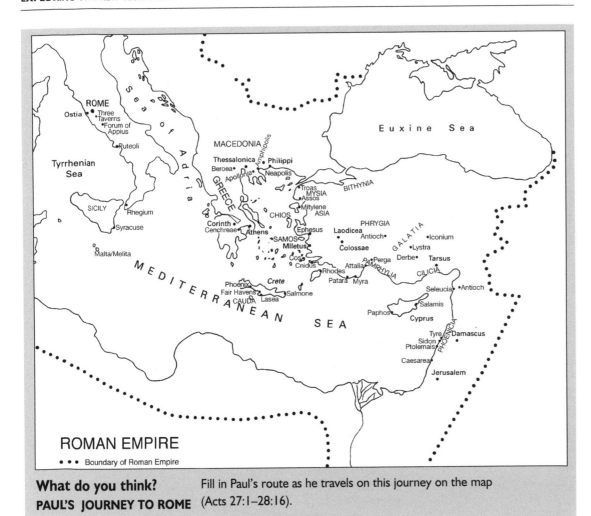

What do you think?
PAUL'S JOURNEY TO ROME

Fill in Paul's route as he travels on this journey on the map (Acts 27:1–28:16).

Setting off to Rome along the Appian Way, Paul's group is met by two groups of Christians (v. 15). These contacts show that Paul is not the first missionary to Rome, for there is already a church there.

Luke's account of Paul's time in Rome focuses not on the church there, but on his relationship with the Jewish community. He speaks with the leaders of that community while under house arrest (v. 16), and they are willing to hear him (vv. 21f.). On a separate occasion they talk with Paul for a whole day (v. 23), and the usual result follows: the Jewish community is divided (vv. 24f.). Thus Luke's closing scene is one of some Jews responding to the gospel, rather than (as is sometimes asserted on the basis of v. 28) a final rejection of the Jewish people in favour of the Gentiles.

Luke's final verses offer an interesting picture of Paul preaching to all who come to see him, and 'without hindrance' (v. 31), a legal phrase which suggests that he was regarded as innocent. Luke leaves his readers with several key themes: the fulfilment of God's promises that Paul would

WHY DOES ACTS END HERE?

Scholars have long puzzled over why Luke ended his book here. Acts 28:30 suggests that Luke may know what happened after two years to change the situation, and there have been a number of suggestions:

- Luke is bringing his readers up to date, and he has no more information. This requires a date for Acts in the early 60s, which is not impossible, but has not persuaded most scholars.
- Luke intends to write a 'volume 3' in which he will tell the next stages of the story. But if this is his intention, there are no hints of it.
- Luke implies that Paul was released, for Roman legislation allowed that if a prisoner's accusers did not appear after two years, the prisoner was released. However, the earliest evidence for this provision is from the sixth century AD, and 23:11; 27:24 state that Paul will appear before the emperor. Further, if Luke knew that Paul was released as innocent, its propaganda value to Luke would have been considerable, which makes it the more surprising that he does not mention it.
- Paul was tried and executed and Luke deliberately does not report this, since he has hinted that it will happen (esp. 20:25), for he wishes his readers to be left with the picture of Paul preaching freely. However, 20:25 and related texts do not actually say that Paul is martyred: they simply state that Paul expects never to see a particular group of Christians again. Equally, if Luke knew that Paul was executed by Nero (as early church tradition records in 1 Clement 5), it is surprising that he presents a picture of the Roman authorities which seems so positive.

None of these views is without difficulties, although it is clear that Luke's focus is not on Paul's fate but the progress of the gospel. It may be that Luke is content to end his story at the point of that message being preached at the heart of the empire by his hero, Paul.

arrive safely in Rome; the fact that nothing can stop the gospel; the gospel being for all, Jew and Gentile; a picture of Paul preaching about Jesus and (in continuity with his master) proclaiming the kingdom of God.

ACTS AND HISTORY

Acts is a book which relates frequently to 'secular' history. There are many points of contact between Luke's story and the ancient world – hardly surprising in an author who writes for a reader whom he seeks to persuade of the truth of the gospel (Luke 1:1-4).

TITLES AND GEOGRAPHY

Generally, Luke gets his description of the ancient world right: places are where he says they are and his descriptions of geography are accurate. For example, travelling overland from the Cilician Gates (16:1), Derbe would be the first city reached, followed by Lystra.

Similarly, Luke's data fits with what we know of the titles of local officials for this period: Cyprus is a proconsular province with a proconsul resident at Paphos (13:7); Ananias is the high priest for the ostensible date of Paul's trial (23:2); inscriptions attest the title 'first man' for the Roman governor of Malta at the date of Paul's visit (28:7). Indeed, sometimes Luke is accurate for the period he describes and we know that a title has changed: the province of Achaia had a proconsul, resident in Corinth, only during 27 BC to AD 15 and from AD 44 onwards, and it is as proconsul that Gallio is introduced (18:12) for a visit during AD 50-52 – exactly right for that date.

TIME AND DATES

The time covered in the various sections of the book is striking, for it varies a great deal.

A CHRONOLOGICAL OUTLINE OF ACTS

Assuming Luke's account to be generally dependable, we have the following rough chronology of the book.

Date	Event	Acts
30	Death and resurrection of Jesus	1:1-11
30	**Pentecost**	2
33/4	**Conversion of Saul**	9:1-22
36/7	Paul's first visit to Jerusalem (Gal. 1:18)	9:23-29
36/7	Paul goes to Tarsus (in Cilicia, Gal. 1:21)	9:30
?43/4	Barnabas fetches Paul from Tarsus to Antioch	11:25
44	Peter's miraculous escape from prison	12:1-7
44	Death of Herod Agrippa I	12:19b-24
46	Famine relief visit to Jerusalem (Gal. 2:1-10)	11:30; 12:25
47-48	**First 'missionary journey'**	13:1–14:28
48/9	Disturbance by Judaizers	15:1-3
49	**Apostolic Council at Jerusalem**	15:4-29
49	Return of Paul and others to Antioch	15:30-35
49-52	**Second 'missionary journey'**	14:36–18:22
early 50	Paul arrives in Corinth	18:1-18
52	Paul leaves Corinth	
52	Brief visit by Paul to Ephesus	18:19-21
summer 52	Paul visits Jerusalem	18:22
52-57	**Third 'missionary journey'**	19:1–21:17
late 52	Trip through interior to Ephesus	19:1
52-55	Ephesian ministry of Paul	19:2–20:1
55-57	Through Macedonia to Greece	20:1-3a
57	Corinth (?for three months)	20:2-3
57	Return through Macedonia	20:3b-6
57	Troas and Miletus	20:6b–21:1
May 57	To Caesarea and Jerusalem	21:2-17
57	Paul's arrest in Jerusalem	21:27–23:22
57-59	**Caesarean imprisonment**	23:23–26:32
59	Trial before Festus	25:1-12
59	Hearing before Agrippa II	25:13–26:32
Sep 59-Feb 60	**Journey to Rome**	27:1–28:16
60-62	House arrest in Rome	28:17-31

Roughly, chs 1–2 cover 50 days or so; 3:1–9:31 some 3–4 years; 9:32–12:24 perhaps 10 years; 12:25–16:5 about 5 years; 16:6–19:41 about 6 years; and 20:1–28:31 about 7 years. In places Luke passes over long periods with little information, notably in 9:32–12:24.

Synchronizing Acts with ancient events is not straightforward. There are five events which can, with some confidence, be fixed. We have considered Gallio's period as proconsul of Achaia (p. 279). Herod Agrippa I's death (12:23) can be fixed by comparison with Josephus' accounts (*Ant.* 19:352 = 19.8.2; 20:10-14 = 20.1.2) in the early part of AD 44. The famine during Claudius' reign (11:28) is also described by Josephus (*Ant.* 20:101f. = 20.5.2), and probably took place early in his reign, in AD 46. Claudius' edict expelling the Jews from Rome (18:2) is mentioned by Orosius as during his ninth year as emperor, AD 49. Finally, Festus' procuratorship (24:27) can be dated by reference to a combination of Roman coinage, Josephus and Eusebius (see Witherington 1998, 716) as beginning in AD 59.

ACTS AND GALATIANS
A major issue in dating Paul's early visits to Jerusalem is the relationship between the visits to the city in Gal. 1:18-24 and 2:1-10, and those in Acts 9:26-30; 11:29f. and 15:1-30. While there is general agreement that the Gal. 1 visit is that found in Acts 9, the identification of the Gal. 2 visit is not straightforward. The two major options are:

Gal. 2 = Acts 15 Strengths of this view are:

- the same people seem to be involved – Paul, Barnabas and Titus on one side, and James and Peter on the other;
- the same issue is debated – the circumcision of Gentile converts;
- the same agreement results – Gentile believers need not be under the Jewish law.

However:

- it is surprising that Galatians never mentions the ruling of the Jerusalem meeting, which would have settled the question of Gentile circumcision which Paul tackles in the letter;
- the people involved are not the same – Gal. 2 records a private meeting with the 'pillars' of the church; Acts 15 records a public meeting of the Jerusalem leadership;
- the issues are not the same – Gal. 2 is about the validity of Paul's apostleship; Acts 15 is about the circumcision of Gentile believers;
- the results are not the same – Gal. 2 concludes with agreement about Paul's ministry and the Gentile churches' obligation to the poorer Christians in Jerusalem; Acts 15 ends with the meeting's decision about Gentile admission to the church without circumcision, which is sent to the churches;
- 'next' (Gal. 2:1) implies that Paul has not missed out any of his contacts with the Jerusalem leadership in his account in the letter, and he firmly states that he is telling the full truth (Gal. 1:20) – whereas this view means that he has omitted the visit in Acts 11:29f.

Gal. 2 = Acts 11 Strengths of this view are:

- the same cause of the visit – 'by revelation' (Gal. 2:1) refers to the prophetic word of Agabus (Acts 11:28);
- it means that the two visits in Galatians are the first two visits recorded in Acts, which fits with Paul's use of 'next' (Gal. 2:1);
- it explains why Paul does not mention the Jerusalem meeting's ruling, for at the time of writing Galatians that meeting was yet to happen;

- it suggests that the 'famine relief' visit (Acts 11:29f.) became the occasion for the consultation of Gal. 2:1-10, which resulted in an agreement about continuing to care for poorer Christians (Gal. 2:10);
- Acts suggests that the visit of 11:29f. happens after the growth of the Gentile church in Antioch (11:19-26), and it would be inevitable that the situation in Antioch would be discussed during the visit.

This view is not without difficulties, for it means that the '14 years' after which Paul visited Jerusalem (Gal. 2:1) includes the 'three years' between the Damascus Road experience and his first visit to Jerusalem (Gal. 1:18) in order to make the dates fit. Nevertheless, its power to explain the nature of Galatians is a very great strength, and the chronology which follows is based on it. (See more fully D. Wenham, "Acts and the Pauline Corpus II. The Evidence of Parallels" in Winter & Clarke 1993, 215-258; R. N. Longenecker *Galatians*. Word Biblical Commentary 41. Dallas: Word, 1990, lxxiii-lxxxiii.)

SPEECHES

About 22% of Acts is made up of speeches, and much of the direct theological teaching of the book is found in them. Most are addressed to those who are not Christian believers, and divide between evangelistic speeches, aiming to persuade the hearers to become followers of Jesus, and judicial speeches, defending Paul in a trial setting.

Scholars ask what kind of record Luke gives of them. Some (e.g. M. Dibelius) argue that they are free inventions, for they claim that Luke has no sources for most of the speeches; others (e.g. F. F. Bruce) believe that Luke was present for many of the Pauline speeches and has access to written or oral sources for others.

Luke is not alone among ancient writers in including speeches in his work, and some conclude that Luke operates rather like the historian Thucydides, who wrote a contemporary account of the war between Athens and Sparta, 431-404 BC:

As to the speeches which were made either before of during the war, it was hard for me, and for others who reported them to me, to recollect the exact words. I have therefore put into the mouth of each speaker the sentiments proper to the occasion, expressed as I thought he would be likely to express them, while at the same time I endeavoured, as nearly as I could, to give the general import of what was actually said. (Thucydides, *History of the Peloponnesian War*, 1.22.1)

Dibelius and Haenchen, in particular, argue that Luke's presentation of the speeches makes the different speakers sound like each other and imposes a common structure upon them, and that their contents do not fit well with the hints we get in the letters of early Christian preaching (e.g. 1 Cor. 15:3-7; 1 Thess. 1:9f.). They identify the language of the speeches as Lukan, and conclude that Luke has composed these speeches using Thucydides' principles. On this view, the speeches reflect Luke's outlook and theology, rather than those of the earliest Christians.

Certainly the speeches are not word-for-word reproductions, for they are too short. Even the longer speeches do not take more than five minutes to read aloud, but we know that Paul could speak at length (20:7!) and that Luke writes of Paul and Peter arguing, testifying and the like (e.g. 2:40; 9:22; 14:1, 3). Thus the speeches can be no more than summaries. Further, there is little or no indication of notes being taken of what was said, or of the early Christians delivering speeches prepared in advance, so that the most Luke would have had, for example, for Paul's speech at Lystra (14:15-17), would be Paul's memory of the speech.

Sometimes Luke reports the same speech in different words: the brief words of the angel to Cornelius are presented differently on the two occasions when they are reported in Acts 10 (vv. 4-6, 31f.), and in any case there are indications in the chapter that the angel said more than Luke has recorded (vv. 22, 33). This story is also an example of an occasion where Luke would only have had access to what was said second-hand, as are the private conversations between Festus and Agrippa (25:13-22; 26:30-32) or the private sessions of the Sanhedrin (4:15-17; 5:34-40). In these cases Luke can be giving only the gist of what was said.

Careful examination of the speeches highlights features of Lukan style, e.g. Paul's speech to the Ephesian elders (20:18-35) echoes the language of Jesus' Last Supper speech (Luke 22:14-38) (see Walton 2000, 100-117 for details). Paul's speech contains a number of words and phrases which are favourites of Luke.

It is unlikely, on the other hand, that Luke is freely inventing speeches. Ancient writers were not gullible or naïve: they thought critically about the material which they used, as the quotation from Thucydides demonstrates. Rather than freely inventing speeches, he attempts to 'give the general import of what was actually said'.

While there are common elements to many of the evangelistic speeches (see pp. 51f.), there is variation too. The elements of preaching to Jews are different from those in preaching to Gentiles. When Paul is on trial, he speaks in the formal rhetorical style required (as does his accuser Tertullus, 24:2-8). These variations suggest either that Luke is using sources for the different speakers, whether written or oral, or that he is a brilliant mimic, able to imitate different types of speech and different speakers' styles in delivering speeches.

In the case of 20:18-35, mentioned above, as well as the Lukan language and style, there are also strong echoes of Pauline language, notably from 1 Thessalonians (see Walton 2000, ch. 5), but also from other Pauline letters. This feature suggests that Luke is using tradition deriving from Paul in writing the speech in the form it is found in Acts 20.

Finally, if we compare Luke's editing of speeches by Jesus from Mark (assuming Luke uses Mark), there is certainly variation and stylistic change, but free invention is very hard to find. Given that this is how Luke behaves when using a source we can identify with a reasonable degree of confidence, it seems likely that he will behave similarly when using sources we cannot identify (since Acts is the only record we possess of these speeches). Thus Luke probably uses and edits his sources conservatively.

In sum, then, the speeches of Acts, while clearly not verbatim reproductions of what was said, should be regarded as Lukan summaries based in many cases on written or oral tradition. Luke is in the best traditions of ancient historiography in this, in providing speeches which are appropriate to their setting in both the literary and historical senses (see further C. H. Gempf "Public Speaking and Published Accounts"

in Winter & Clarke 1993, 259-303;
D. Wenham "From Jesus to Paul – via Luke" in P. Bolt & M. Thompson, eds. *The Gospel to the Nations*. Leicester: Apollos/Downers Grove: IVP, 2000, 83-98).

ACTS AND THEOLOGY: SOME MAJOR THEMES

Luke presents a range of major themes in Acts, but first and foremost it is a book about God and what he is doing. An analysis of the verb subjects of the book shows that a very large number of verbs are the action of God or the Spirit. Not only that, but Luke speaks of divine agents, such as angels, of miracles done by God, of the fulfilment of OT prophecy, and of events being 'necessary', all features focusing attention on what God is about. What kind of God emerges from the pages of Acts?

GOD

At each major stage of the development of the church's life, the activity of God is central. The book begins with the group waiting for the Father to send the Spirit (1:4f.), and the church takes a huge step forward at Pentecost as the Spirit brings new languages to the lips of the believers (2:1-11). Peter's sermon focuses on explaining what God has done in Jesus and what God is now doing by the Spirit.

The lame man at the temple is healed in the name of Jesus the Messiah (3:6), whom Peter explains as being the one glorified by God by reversing the human court's decision in raising him from the dead (3:13-16; 4:10).

Stephen and Philip are both men 'filled with the Spirit' in their service of God. Both perform 'signs and wonders' (7:8; 8:6f.), and

both speak with power – in Stephen's case explicitly said to be by the Spirit (7:9f., 55f.; 8:6). When Philip then goes to the Ethiopian eunuch, he is sent by an angel (8:26), instructed by the Spirit (8:29), finds a man reading a section of OT Scripture prophesying the death of Jesus (8:32-35, quoting Isa. 53:7f.), and is then snatched away by the Spirit (8:39) – altogether an encounter with the fingerprints of God upon it!

Saul's encounter with the risen Jesus on the Damascus Road, which calls him to mission among Gentiles, involves Saul being blinded (9:3-9) and God speaking to Ananias to send him to Saul (9:10-19), in addition to clear activity of God in the appearance of Jesus here.

Peter goes to the godfearing Roman centurion Cornelius in response to multiple activity by God: an angel tells Cornelius to send for Peter, giving his address (10:5); Peter sees a thrice-repeated vision and hears a voice (10:10-16); the Spirit tells him how many men are seeking him and that he should go with them (10:19f.); and God interrupts Peter's sermon by the Spirit falling on the household in a way that was recognizably like the Jewish believers' experience (10:44-48). The conclusion the Jerusalem-based believers come to is that this is God's handiwork (11:18).

The evangelization of Cyprus happens in response to God calling Barnabas and Saul to this work through the congregation in Antioch (13:1-5).

Throughout Acts, when the apostles and others preach, what they preach is the word of God or the word of the Lord, and it is this which advances, not usually the church (see p. 272). Thus Luke's focus is on divine activity, for people alone cannot produce such events. The evangelistic sermons of Acts are peppered with references to what God has done in raising Jesus from the dead, e.g. 13:30. Perhaps one reason that Acts is so full of speeches is that Luke regards the word preached as a powerful agent of God's activity.

Digging deeper:
GOD'S ACTION IN PAUL'S MISSION

Look through the accounts of Paul's travels in 14:1-23 and 15:40–16:40, the accounts of Paul's ministry in various places in Asia and Macedonia, and identify places where Luke speaks of God acting, whether directly or through divine agents, miracles, the fulfilment of prophecy or events being 'necessary'. In what ways does God act, and how well do Paul and his team see what God is doing?

JESUS

Jesus is certainly prominent in Acts, although not in the same way as in Luke's Gospel, for here the focus is on his resurrection. The death of Jesus is not the focus which it is in Luke, for there the story leads up to it; only at Acts 20:28 does an explicit 'atonement theology' surface in Acts. An explanation may well be that Luke has told the story of the death of Jesus so fully in his Gospel that it does not need repetition in Acts.

As in Luke's Gospel, a variety of descriptions of Jesus are used: he is Messiah (or Christ) often (25 times in Acts, especially in Jewish settings), and particularly he is Lord (Greek *kurios*), Luke's favourite description of Jesus in Acts. It is noticeable that this term is used for both Jesus (60 times, e.g. 1:6, 21; 2:34

What do you think?
THE RESURRECTION OF JESUS IN ACTS

Read the passages listed below, all speaking about Jesus' resurrection. What implications and conclusions do the speakers draw from the resurrection? What results does it have in terms of Jesus' present status and power? What can the hearers experience because of Jesus' resurrection? What does Luke communicate by making Jesus' resurrection much more prominent than his death?

Acts 2:24-32; 4:1f., 10, 33; 10:40-43; 13:30-39; 17:18, 30f.; 23:6; 26:6-8, 23

[second use], 36, 47) and God (a further 40 times, e.g. 1:24; 2:20, 25, 34 [first use], 39). The use of the same term for each may indicate an early stage of christological thinking, in which the precise relationship of Jesus to God had not been 'theologized'; however, to the ears of Luke's readers, some years later, it would be likely to suggest that Jesus stood in the same position of authority as the God of Israel.

Luke has a striking emphasis on the *name* of Jesus: forgiveness (2:38), healing (3:6; 4:10, 30), preaching (4:17f.; 5:40; 8:12; 9:27), baptism (10:48; 19:5), suffering (15:26; 21:13) and exorcism (16:18) all happen 'in the name of Jesus'. In places this phrase can stand for Jesus himself (19:17; 26:9), and it seems to represent his power and authority, in similar manner to modern ambassadors, who speak in the name of the government they represent, that is, with the authority and power of that government behind them and their words.

Other descriptions of Jesus are unusual, and

may reflect an early stage in Christological development: he is 'servant' or 'child' (Greek *pais*, 3:13, 26; 4:27, 30), hinting at the Isaianic servant explicitly mentioned in 8:32f.; he is the prophet like Moses (3:22f.; 7:37); and he is 'author of life' or 'leader' (Greek *archēgos*, 3:15; 5:31; found elsewhere in the NT only at Heb. 2:10; 12:2). The fact that these descriptions occur only in the earlier chapters of Acts (and rarely outside Acts in the NT) speaks for the likelihood that they were used in the earliest days of the church, but later became much less prominent.

THE HOLY SPIRIT

It goes without saying that the Spirit is central to Acts, for from first to last he directs the mission of the church. There are five accounts of the Spirit's outpouring (2:1-4; 4:28-31; 8:15-17; 10:44-46; 19:6), each accompanied by signs, whether speaking in other languages, wind, fire or a shaken building. The regularity of such phenomena suggests that the coming of the Spirit can be recognized by these kinds of activities. The phrase 'just as we have' (10:47) identifies the pentecostal gift of the Spirit with the experience of Cornelius' household. Similarly, the fact that Simon the magician could see that the Spirit was given when Peter and John laid hands on people (8:17f.) shows that there must be observable phenomena taking place when the Spirit comes upon people. It is not always speaking in other languages which is prominent, but in three cases that is the feature picked out by Luke (2:3f.; 10:46; 19:6).

The new stages of the mission's development are marked by the activity of the Spirit in particular, as well as other references to God acting which we noted earlier (e.g. 8:29, 39; 10:19; 11:15; 13:2; 15:28; 16:6; 20:22; 21:4, 11). It is noticeable how much the Spirit's work is associated with the church's evangelism and expansion, reflecting Luke's focus on these areas: we learn relatively little about the Spirit's role within the Christian community from Acts by comparison with Paul's letters.

What does the Spirit do as typical signs of his activity? Max Turner summarizes helpfully (Turner 1996, ch. 3), observing that in Acts the Spirit produces the same characteristic results which Jewish sources associate with the Spirit as the 'Spirit of prophecy', namely:

- visions and dreams which reveal God's mind and will 2:17; 7:55f. (plus 9:10-18; 10:10-20; 16:9f.; 18:9f.; 22:17f., 21; 23:11);
- words, instructions and guidance from God 1:2; 8:29; 10:19; 11:12, 28; 13:2, 4; 15:28; 16:6f.; 19:21; 20:22f.; 21:4, 11 (also with reference to the OT in 1:16; 4:25; 7:51; 28:25);
- wisdom or discernment from God 5:3; 6:3, 5, 10; 9:31; 13:9; 16:18 (cf. Luke 21:25);
- 'charismatic' praise produced by God entering the people who give it 2:4; 10:46; 19:6;
- preaching, testimony and teaching e.g. 1:4, 8; 4:8, 31; 5:32; 6:10; 9:17, 31; 13:52.

There is a striking – and not much-noticed – connection between being filled with the Spirit and suffering in Acts: it seems that Luke portrays the Spirit as imitating the suffering of Jesus in people. Peter and John state that the Spirit testifies with them and are beaten for their trouble and respond with joy – a strongly Lukan theme (5:32, 40f.; cf. Luke 1:14, 47; 2:10; 10:21). Stephen is filled with the Spirit and sees Jesus exalted, and is then stoned to death (7:55, 59). Ananias is told that Saul will suffer for Jesus, and then is to lay hands on him to be filled with the Spirit (9:16f.). Paul goes to suffer in Jerusalem 'as a captive to the Spirit' (20:22-24; cf. 21:11-14).

MISSION AND THE CHURCH

If there is one thing which God characteristically does in Acts, it is that he reaches out to people to enable them to hear and respond to the gospel of Jesus and to be incorporated into his people. As we saw, it is consistently God who pushes out the boundaries of the community of believers, to the Ethiopian eunuch, to Samaritans, to a godfearing centurion, and to outright Gentiles – often against the church's initial resistance.

The methods by which mission happens are many and varied. 'Signs and wonders' (healing and deliverance from demonic powers are the main examples) occur, such as the healing of the lame man at the temple gate, which leads to an opportunity to explain how the man has been healed, and thus to preach about Jesus (3:1–26; cf. 8:5-7; 14:8-18; 16:16-18). Debate and dialogue at length occur among Jews and Gentiles in public and private (e.g. 17:10-12; 18:4f., 27f.; 19:8-10). 'Set piece' public speeches also happen, whether straightforwardly proclaiming the message about Jesus (e.g. 10:34-43; 13:16-41) or more apologetic, explaining and defending what Christians believe (notably in Athens, 17:22-34).

The church's role is to co-operate with God in this work, particularly in its proclamation and incarnation of 'the word' (see p. 271). The life of the community is to reflect this message. For example, just as the poor and marginalized are central to the message and concerns of Jesus in Luke (see p. 237), so in

---

Digging deeper:
SHARING POSSESSIONS

Read the following passages, and summarize what Luke says about the early church's use of possessions.

Acts 2:44f.; 4:32–5:11; 6:1-7; 9:36; 10:2, 4, 23-33; 11:27-30; 16:14f., 32-34; 18:3; 20:33-35; 28:1f., 7-10

How far do you think that this was a phase of the church's life in Jerusalem which did not spread to the churches around the Mediterranean which Paul founded? Or are there principles of sharing goods which continue to be important throughout Acts?

(Further reading: L. T. Johnson *Sharing Possessions: Mandate and Symbol of Faith*. London: SCM/Philadelphia: Fortress, 1981.)

Acts special provision is made for Greek-speaking widows (6:1-7), and a wealthier Gentile church contributes to the needs of the poorer Jerusalem church (11:27-30).

The nature of the church is to be as inclusive as the purposes of God, which embrace Jerusalem, Judea and Samaria to the end of the earth (1:8), and the inclusion of Gentiles is one of the most significant events which takes place. Alongside the developing mission to Gentiles goes a continuing concern for the Jewish people. When Paul turns from the Jews to the Gentiles (13:46; 18:6), it is not final, for in later cities he visits he goes to the synagogue (14:1; 19:8). Luke regularly stresses the positive response to the gospel found among Jewish people, even while also identifying the way that the proclamation about Jesus divides the Jewish people (see 4:1-3, 4; 5:14, 17f.; 6:7; 13:42f., 45; 14:1f., 5-7; 17:2-5, 11f.; 21:20). Even at the end of the book we find Paul engaged in speaking about Jesus with Jewish people and seeing some positive response (28:17-31, esp. v. 24). The church in Luke's eyes is not a new thing, but the continuation of Israel, the true Israel, and the believing part of ethnic Israel forms the core of the Christian community (see further Jervell 1996, 34-43).

Thus for Jack T. Sanders (in his book *The Jews in Luke-Acts*) to suggest that Luke is anti-semitic goes beyond the evidence, for Sanders can only make this case by ignoring the positive statements about the Jewish people and their response to the gospel throughout Acts. Further, he neglects to notice that responsibility for the death of Jesus is not attached to the Jews as a race, but to the Jews of Jerusalem and their leaders, along with Pilate and the Romans (note particularly 4:27). The only places where 'you' are said to be responsible for the death of Jesus are in the city of Jerusalem (2:23, 36; 3:13f., 17; 4:10; 5:28, 30; 7:52); in other Jewish settings it is 'they' (= the Jerusalem dwellers and their leaders) who are responsible (e.g. 13:27).

LUKE'S READERS AND PURPOSE

In thinking about Luke's intended readership and his purpose(s) in writing we need to consider both Luke and Acts, for both contribute to the picture.

READERS

A careful reading of Luke-Acts suggests a number of features of his readers:

- they may be Gentile, since a prominent place is given to the inclusion of Gentiles;
- they are not very familiar with semitic

language and Jewish customs, for Luke frequently omits these, whereas Mark includes them with an explanation, and Matthew includes them without an explanation (e.g. compare Luke 21:20f. and Mark 13:14; Matt. 24:15f.);
- they know the OT Scriptures in Greek, for Luke's frequent quotations from or allusions to the OT are usually from the Septuagint;
- a crux is Luke 1:4 – this may imply that 'Theophilus' is already a Christian, or could mean that he is an interested outsider (see the commentaries);
- the preface to Luke (1:1-4) is written in a style which fits with the 'technical' treatises of the ancient world, which suggests that Luke's readers, although educated, are not necessarily highly educated, upper-class people.

This combination leads Nolland (1989-93, vol. 1, xxxiif: see p. 241) to argue that the 'ideal reader' for Luke would be a godfearer, Gentile by birth but drawn into the group around the edge of a synagogue, attracted to the Jewish belief in one true God. There are prominent godfearers who become believers (e.g. Cornelius, Acts 10), which would encourage such people that they, too, could be followers of Jesus.

On the other hand, Luke's account would also be accessible to a wide range of others. For example, diaspora Jews (who frequently used the Septuagint in their worship, rather than the Hebrew Scriptures) would respond to the positive pictures of Jews becoming believers we noticed (p.293). Similarly, Gentile Christians with no synagogue background, but who had become familiar with the Septuagint through it being read in Christian worship, would find Acts accessible, and would welcome Luke's emphasis on the inclusion of Gentiles in the people of God. On balance it is hard to pin down Luke's intended audience: it may be that he aimed at a wide range of people in the Greek-speaking world (see pp. 78f.).

WHY DID LUKE WRITE?

There have been numerous proposals for why Luke wrote his two volumes, many of which contradict each other. Some major theories are as follows (for full discussion see Maddox 1982 or, more briefly, Marshall 1980, chs 2–3; Liefeld 1995, ch. 1):

- to provide a defence brief for Paul at his trial or to defend Christianity more generally from the charge that it was politically subversive (F. F. Bruce, H. J. Cadbury). Paul's positive relations with Roman officials and his never being found guilty by a Roman court would favour this view.
- to present the Christian gospel to outsiders in order to persuade them to become believers (J. C. O'Neill). Luke goes beyond the other evangelists in seeing the story of the church's growth as part of the gospel proclamation; the evangelistic speeches of Acts would be particularly pertinent to this view.
- to explain how a Jewish Messiah gave rise to a (predominantly) Gentile church which should be seen as the true Israel, now heirs to the promises of the OT (R. Maddox). This view sees Luke-Acts as aimed at a Christian readership, providing 'legitimation' for their faith in a later time when there were relatively few Jewish Christians. It combines the positive view of Judaism found in Luke-Acts with the emphasis on judgement for Jews who reject Jesus as Messiah.
- to deal with the problem of the apparent delay in Jesus' return to earth by offering a theology of 'salvation history' focused on the church (H. Conzelmann). On this view, Luke has edited Mark (especially Mark 13) to reduce the emphasis on an imminent End, and shows that the story of the church will carry on potentially for a long time yet.
- to defend Paul – and the church more widely – from attacks by later opponents, whether Jewish (J. Jervell) or gnostic (C. H. Talbert). The effectiveness of Paul's evangelism and his endorsement by the Jerusalem leaders (Acts 15) would both be important for this view. Similarly, Paul and Peter both explain that following Jesus is the natural fulfilment of Judaism, and Paul is found innocent of the Jewish charges against him.

What do you think?
THE PURPOSE(S) OF LUKE-ACTS

Consider what evidence or section(s) in Luke-Acts most strongly supports each of the proposed purposes above, and what evidence or section(s) is the greatest problem for each. Do you think one purpose can adequately explain the whole of the two books, or are multiple purposes required to do this? Which purpose(s) do you find most plausible and why?

AUTHORSHIP AND DATE

In the case of Luke-Acts, views of authorship and date are intertwined, at least to some extent.

WHO IS LUKE?

The traditional view is that Luke is the Luke of Col. 4:14; Phlm 24; 2 Tim. 4:11. There are two main arguments in favour of this view. First, the 'we' passages in Acts (see p. 278) suggest that the book is written by a travelling companion of Paul. When we eliminate those who travel with Paul and are named in Acts (e.g. Timothy, 16:1; 17:14, etc.), and then consider who else is named in the Pauline letters as a fellow traveller of Paul, Luke fits the bill (see more fully Bruce 1990, 3-7).

Secondly, early Christian writers agree in identifying Luke as the author of the two volumes. The earliest clear statement on authorship comes from the Muratorian Canon (late second century), and from the third century onwards all agree:

> The third book of the gospel, according to Luke, Luke the physician composed in his own name on the basis of respect after the ascension of Christ, when Paul had taken him with him as a travelling companion. Neither did he himself see the Lord in the flesh and so wrote as he could find out (what happened). And so he began to write from the birth of John … The Acts of all the apostles were written in one book. Luke compiled for his 'most excellent Theophilus' the several things that were done in his presence, and he plainly shows by the omission of the passion of Peter and the departure of Paul from the city [i.e. Rome] when he set out for Spain. (Muratorian Canon, 2-8, 34-39, as translated in C. K. Barrett *A Critical and Exegetical Commentary on the Acts of the Apostles*, vol. I. Edinburgh: T. & T. Clark, 1994, 44)

If this were simply an educated guess, based on the internal evidence from Acts and the Pauline letters mentioned above, we should expect there to be others named as possible authors, but the earliest writers are unanimous in naming Luke.

The main criticism of this view is that Luke's portrait of Paul appears out of tune with that derived from the Pauline letters, and this is very surprising if Luke is Paul's travel companion. In particular, on four theological points Luke is claimed to have a different perspective from Paul: how far God may be known through nature (Acts 17:22-34 is contrasted with Rom. 1:18-32); the attitude to the Jewish law (Paul himself regarding the law as past, Gal. 5:2-6; Luke's Paul is positive about the continuing role of the law – he can even circumcise Timothy, Acts 16:3); Christology (Paul's beliefs about Jesus are more developed; Luke simply reports the earliest, primitive beliefs about Jesus); and eschatology (Paul expects an imminent return of the Lord, 1 Cor. 7:29-31; Luke does not). (In full, see P. Vielhauer "On the Paulinism of Acts" in *Studies in Luke-Acts*. ed. L. E. Keck & J. L. Martyn.Nashville: Abingdon, 1966/London: SPCK, 1968, 33-50.)

However, these claims are based on a comparison of the Pauline letters – written to Christians – and the speeches in Acts – almost all addressed to people who are not Christians (the only exception is Acts 20:18-35). Further, there are a very considerable number of points of agreement between the portraits of Paul drawn from the letters and from Acts. For example, in both Paul has Jewish opponents (e.g. Gal. 6:12-15; Acts 17:5, 13). The differences that exist seem to be consistent with the difference of perspective between an author writing in person and someone else writing about the author. Acts is focused on mission, on the story of God reaching out to save people; the letters are responses to particular needs of particular churches.

In sum, there is no conclusive evidence against the traditional identification of Luke, and a considerable amount of support for it.

WHEN DID LUKE WRITE?

Three main dates have been canvassed for the writing of Luke and Acts: the early to mid-sixties, shortly after 70, and the late seventies/early eighties. Assuming that Luke has access to Mark, the earliest date when Luke can write is shortly after Mark's publication which, as we saw, is probably in the mid to late sixties (p. 206).

If Luke writes shortly after the events described in Acts 28 (which take place about AD 62), then Acts appears prior to the execution of Paul (most probably in AD 65), and Luke's Gospel is likely to be at least a little earlier, very shortly after Mark. The positive elements in the portrait of Roman authorities would fit well with a date prior to Nero's persecution of Christians in AD 65.

It is possible that Luke writes after the fall of Jerusalem in AD 70. Some argue that Luke's version of Jesus' prophecy of the fall of the city (Luke 21) is written up in the light of knowledge of the actual events. For example, Luke omits Matthew's and Mark's verses inviting the disciples to pray that the siege of the city will not be in winter (Matt. 24:20; Mark 13:18) – and the siege happened during April to September AD 70. However, Luke 21:21 reports the same saying as Mark 13:14, that the disciples should flee to the mountains, and while we know that the early Christians did flee Jerusalem at this stage, they went to Pella, which is several hundred feet lower than Jerusalem – hardly 'the mountains' at all! Further, much of the imagery of Luke 21 reflects the OT accounts of earlier sieges of the city, which could have been done at any time prior to AD 70, and so this part of the case for a post-70 date is not compelling.

It seems likely that Luke writes before the publication of a collection of Paul's letters late in the first century, for otherwise it would be even harder than it is to explain the lack of mention of Paul's letter-writing. Can we bring the latest date earlier? If Luke is Paul's travel companion, a date in the late seventies or early eighties is possible. On such a view Luke closes Acts where he does because he has said all he wishes to say and regards his work as complete.

READING ACTS TODAY

In the case of Acts, Christian readers meet in an acute form the question of how far what the NT authors say is 'universal' and relevant for all Christians everywhere at all times, and how far Luke is simply describing what happened, without necessarily implying that he wants his readers to do the same. For example, it is debated whether the early church were right or wrong to appoint Matthias (1:15-26).

What do you think?
THE APPOINTMENT OF MATTHIAS (1:15-26)

What arguments support the view that the early church were wrong to appoint Matthias to replace Judas? What arguments support the contrary view, that they were right to do so? Which do you find most persuasive and why?

This issue is evident in thinking about forms of church government, since congregationalist, presbyterian and episcopal forms of church structure all point to models in Acts which look something like their view. The entire group chooses the seven who help with care for widows (6:1-6, congregational). The leaders of the Antioch church send Barnabas and Saul out (13:1-3, presbyterian). Paul acts like a bishop in sending for the leaders of the Ephesian church (20:17-38, episcopal).

Some argue that Acts should only be seen as normative when it describes beliefs or practices supported by the teaching material in the NT, particularly the letters. However, the letters were written to particular groups of Christians with particular issues in mind, so the same issue occurs in interpreting them, and our problem is pushed on into that area – this does not help a great deal.

A helpful clue comes from considering whether Acts consistently presents one pattern on a particular point. For example, when people are filled with the Holy Spirit they either proclaim the word of God or do mighty works in Jesus' name (2:4; 5:8, 31; 9:17; 13:9), which suggests that Luke presents this as a pattern which he sees as normal. On the other hand, when Paul in

Ephesus meets magical practices, he does not use the 'Gamaliel principle', that if something is of God then it will grow whatever happens (5:38f.). Rather, the new believers burn their magical books (19:17-20). This strongly suggests that Luke is describing what Gamaliel says, rather than advocating that his readers should adopt it as their practice.

SOME ISSUES FOR TODAY

- Acts treats mission as the heartbeat of the church and therefore challenges forms of church life in which looking beyond the boundaries of the congregation either does not happen or is peripheral to the life of a church. The centrality of proclaiming 'the word of God/the Lord' in Acts highlights the need for Christians to work at communicating the gospel.

- The variety of forms of gospel communication in Acts (e.g. different with Jews and Gentiles) highlights the need to contextualize the message so that it will be heard by people from differing backgrounds and cultures. In the light of the differences between, for example, Paul preaching in Antioch (13:16-43) and Athens (17:22-34), it is important to reflect on how the gospel message may be contextualized into the cultures familiar to you.

- The frequency with which God does something new and the church has then to catch up – notably with the expansion of the church into Gentile territories and peoples – is a sobering warning against being so locked into our particular way of doing things that we miss something fresh which God is doing. It also highlights the need to be looking for what God is doing

---

Digging deeper:
PATTERNS IN ACTS

Consider *either* Acts 2:38 (the four elements in becoming a member of the Christian community) *or* 2:42 (the four elements of early church life).

- For 2:38, analyse the accounts of people becoming believers later in the book and see how far the pattern of 2:38 is reproduced. Do you think Luke presents 2:38 as 'programmatic', that is, setting a normative pattern?
- For 2:42, consider the accounts of early church life in Acts. How far do they describe the four elements found in 2:42? Do you think Luke is advocating these elements as necessary for church life?

and seeking to cooperate with him – the need to be a listening church (cf. 13:1-3).

● The life of the earliest Christians presents a challenge to much modern western church life, where relationships can be superficial. The commitment to shared decision-making (notice the phrase 'with one accord' describing the church, 1:14; 2:46; 4:24; 5:12) shows how important the early church found it to work together to reach a common mind on God's purposes for them. The commitment to shared possessions is perhaps even more challenging in a western context where society encourages holding on to what you have, and getting more if you can.

ESSAY TOPICS

INTRODUCTORY
● How far is it accurate to summarize Acts as 'the Acts of the Holy Spirit'?

● In what ways does Acts 1:1-11 link this book with Luke's Gospel?

INTERMEDIATE
● What is the content of the gospel message which Luke wishes the readers of Luke-Acts to believe and proclaim?

● What principles can Christians use in applying Acts to today's issues?

FURTHER READING

* denotes books assuming knowledge of Greek; most can be used by all students.

INTRODUCTORY
J. Jervell *The Theology of the Acts of the Apostles*. NT Theology. Cambridge: Cambridge University Press, 1996 (stimulating introduction to the theology of the book).

L. T. Johnson "Luke-Acts, Book of" in *Anchor Bible Dictionary*, vol. IV. ed. D. N. Freedman. New York: Doubleday, 1992, 403-420 (very fine overview).

H. C. Kee *Good News to the Ends of the Earth: The Theology of Acts*. London: SCM, 1990 (helpful overview of the theology of Acts).

W. L. Liefeld *Interpreting the Book of Acts*. Guides to NT Exegesis 4. Grand Rapids: Baker Book House, 1995 (useful introductory survey with some helpful material on how to study Acts).

I. H. Marshall *The Acts of the Apostles*. NT Guides. Sheffield: JSOT Press, 1992 (very helpful overview, including good survey of scholarship).

INTERMEDIATE
(see also pp. 240f.)

*L. Alexander *The Preface to Luke's Gospel: Literary Convention and Social Context in Luke 1.1-4 and Acts 1.1*. SNTS Monograph Series 78. Cambridge: Cambridge University Press, 1993 (thorough study of ancient prefaces in parallel with those of Luke and Acts).

M. Green *Evangelism in the Early Church*. Grand Rapids: Eerdmans/London: Hodder & Stoughton, 1970 [new UK ed. Guildford: Eagle, 1995] (good study of the early Christians' evangelistic methods and approaches).

R. Maddox *The Purpose of Luke-Acts*. Edinburgh: T. & T. Clark, 1982 (good study of the variety of purposes proposed for Luke-Acts).

I. H. Marshall & D. Peterson, eds. *Witness to the Gospel: The Theology of Acts*. Grand Rapids/Cambridge: Eerdmans, 1998 (valuable collection of essays on particular topics).

M. C. Parsons & R. I. Pervo *Rethinking the Unity of Luke and Acts*. Minneapolis: Fortress Press, 1993 (important challenge to the consensus view that Luke-Acts is a literary and theological unity).

R. I. Pervo *Profit with Delight*. Philadelphia: Fortress Press, 1987 (demonstrates the 'entertainment value' of Acts in the ancient world, concluding that Acts is fiction).

M. Turner *The Holy Spirit and Spiritual Gifts Then and Now*. Carlisle: Paternoster Press/ Peabody: Hendrickson, 1996 [new ed. 1998], ch. 3 (good discussion of the Spirit in Acts).

J. B. Tyson, ed. *Luke-Acts and the Jewish People: Eight Critical Perspectives*. Minneapolis: Augsburg, 1988 (collection of differing views on Luke's view of Judaism).

*S. Walton *Leadership and Lifestyle: The Portrait of Paul in the Miletus Speech and 1 Thessalonians*. SNTS Monograph Series 108. Cambridge: Cambridge University Press, 2000 (a detailed study of Acts 20:18-35 against the backcloth of Luke and 1 Thessalonians).

*B. W. Winter & A. D. Clarke, eds. *The Book of Acts in its Ancient Literary Setting*. The Book of Acts in its First Century Setting, vol. 1. Carlisle: Paternoster Press/Grand Rapids: Eerdmans, 1993 (valuable collection of articles focusing on Acts against its ancient literary context).

B. Witherington, III, ed. *History, Literature, and Society in the Book of Acts*. Cambridge: Cambridge University Press, 1996 (useful collection of articles covering a wide range of issues).

COMMENTARIES

*F. F. Bruce *The Acts of the Apostles*. 3rd ed. Leicester: Apollos/Grand Rapids: Eerdmans, 1990 (helpful and careful study).

F. F. Bruce *The Book of Acts*. New International Commentary on the NT, revised ed. Grand Rapids: Eerdmans, 1988 (less technical commentary, based on English text).

J. D. G. Dunn *The Acts of the Apostles*. London: Epworth Press/Valley Forge: Trinity Press International, 1996 (excellent shorter commentary).

*E. Haenchen *The Acts of the Apostles*. Oxford: Blackwell/Philadelphia: Westminster Press, 1971 (a key older German commentary; fairly sceptical on historical questions).

L. T. Johnson *The Acts of the Apostles*. Sacra Pagina 5. Collegeville: Liturgical Press, 1992 (fine modern narrative commentary with good links to ancient literature too).

R. N. Longenecker "The Acts of the Apostles" in *The Expositor's Bible Commentary*, vol. 9. ed. F. E. Gaebelein. Grand Rapids: Zondervan, 1981, 207-573 [published separately as *Acts*. Expositor's Bible Commentary. Grand Rapids: Zondervan, 1995] (very helpful).

I. H. Marshall *The Acts of the Apostles: An Introduction and Commentary*. Tyndale NT Commentaries. Leicester: IVP/Grand Rapids: Eerdmans, 1980 (thoughtful shorter commentary which responds well to Haenchen).

R. C. Tannehill *The Narrative Unity of Luke-Acts: A Literary Interpretation, vol. 2: The Acts of the Apostles*. Minneapolis: Fortress Press, 1990 (section by section discussion, sensitive to narrative structure).

*B. Witherington, III *The Acts of the Apostles*. Carlisle: Paternoster Press/Grand Rapids: Eerdmans, 1998 (recent work which is good on seeing the bigger picture of Acts).

GLOSSARY

This gives brief definitions of terms used in the book and a reference in square brackets to the main discussion(s) of this topic in the book.

Antinomian Someone who by conviction and/or lifestyle is anti-nomos, i.e. anti-the-law and its moral demands. [223]

Apocalyptic Literature or ideas associated with God revealing unknown things or events, often in the form of a dream or a visit by an angel. Sometimes used of the belief that God will act to destroy the present universe and replace it. [108–11]

Chiasm The Greek letter chi has an X shape, and chiasm is when sayings or stories are arranged in a pattern, A/B/B/A. [212f.]

Christology Beliefs about who Jesus was and is.

Cynic A Greek philosophical movement originating in the fourth century BC focused on enabling people to live virtuously, particularly by providing good personal examples of a simple and virtuous life. Cynic teachers could be travellers, especially in smaller towns and the country. [132]

Diaspora The 'dispersed' Jews who did not live in the land of Israel/Palestine; sometimes the area inhabited by Jews outside the land is called 'the diaspora'. [34f.]

Docetic Docetism was the second-century heresy, according to which Jesus was a divine figure who only seemed (Greek *dokei*) to be human, but wasn't really. [248]

Double tradition Passages in the synoptic Gospels where only two share a story; can be used particularly of stories found in Matthew and Luke only. [60]

Eschatology Beliefs about the future, particularly to do with how God will act in the near or distant future. [37, 164–6]

Exegesis The art and science of explaining what a text meant for its intended readers. [94–9]

Form criticism The study of the literary forms of the Jesus stories, and their transmission during the 'oral period'. [70–4]

Genre The literary type or category of a book or piece of writing. [47]

Gnosticism A term used to describe a variety of dualistic movements that flourished in the second century AD and later. They believed in a heavenly redeemer, who came into the world to save people from bondage to the material world by giving them divine knowledge (Greek *gnōsis*). [258]

Godfearer A Gentile who attended the Jewish synagogue regularly, kept many of the Jewish laws, including the food laws and the Sabbath, but had not become a full Jew (if a man, he had not been circumcised). Most synagogues in the diaspora had a 'fringe' of such people. [293]

Griesbach hypothesis The belief that Matthew wrote first, Luke used Matthew in composing his Gospel, and Mark used both Matthew and Luke in writing his book. [66–9]

Hermetic literature A body of gnostic-like literature from Egypt dating from the second century AD, having some similarities with John's Gospel. [258]

Herodians A politically influential group of Jews who supported the Herodian family as rulers of Israel (Mark 3:6).

Implied author What we can reconstruct of the knowledge and beliefs of the kind of person who would write a particular text. [84]

Implied reader The kind of reader who would be able to understand and respond to a particular text fully (sometimes called the 'ideal reader'). [84]

Jamnia A place in West Palestine (*Yavneh* in Hebrew), where there is supposed to have been a council of leading Jews about AD 90 which introduced a curse against the Christians into the synagogue worship and so led to the final separation of Jews and Christians. [222, 259]

L The parts of Luke which this Gospel alone has.

Logos A Greek word used by John to speak of Jesus (John 1:1-14). Its background is highly debated, some proposing that it comes from a Jewish thought world, and others a Greek philosophical setting. [246f.]

M The parts of Matthew which this Gospel alone has.

Mandaeans A religious group (still existing today in Iraq) with a literature dating back to the fourth or fifth centuries AD that refers to John the Baptist and has some similarities with gnosticism.[258]

Midrash A Hebrew word, meaning something like 'searching', used to describe the Jewish traditions that grew up interpreting and commenting on the OT. [144]

Minor agreements Places where Matthew and Luke agree in their wording of a story and Mark has a different wording. [67]

Pantheon A collection of gods. [27]

Parousia The 'coming' of Jesus again to earth, expected by the early Christians in line with Acts 1:11. [228]

Pentateuch The first five books of the OT, Genesis to Deuteronomy.

Proto-Luke A suggested 'first draft' of Luke, made up from Q and L. Luke then added material from Mark to make his finished Gospel. [239]

Q Material shared by Matthew and Luke, but not found in Mark. Some scholars regard Q as a source, written and/or oral. [64–6]

Redaction criticism The study of the contribution made to the evangelists by their editing (or redaction) of the Jesus stories. [74–9]

Sanhedrin The Jewish ruling council which handled disputes over Jewish law in the land. [39]

Septuagint The Greek translation of the OT used in Jesus' day (and still today by scholars). [5]

Source criticism The study of the written sources thought to have been used by the evangelists in writing the Gospels. [58–70]

Syncretism The attempt to combine the beliefs of two different systems or religions. [26]

Synopsis A book which lays out the Gospel stories in parallel columns so that similarities and differences can easily be seen. [58f.]

Synoptic Gospels Term used for Matthew, Mark and Luke, since they share a 'common view' and can be 'seen together' (the meaning of 'synoptic'). [58]

Torah The Jewish law; sometimes specifically the Pentateuch (see above). [9–34]

Triple tradition Passages in the synoptic Gospels where all three share a story. [60]

Yahweh The name of God given to Moses (Exod. 3:14), but never actually spoken by Jews of Jesus' day, because it was seen as too sacred to be said. [25f.]